ENGLISH PLACE-NAME SOCIETY.   VOLUME X

GENERAL EDITORS
A. MAWER *and* F. M. STENTON

THE PLACE-NAMES OF NORTHAMPTONSHIRE

LONDON
Cambridge University Press
FETTER LANE

NEW YORK · TORONTO
BOMBAY · CALCUTTA · MADRAS
Macmillan

TOKYO
Maruzen Company Ltd

ENGLISH PLACE-NAME SOCIETY. VOLUME X

THE PLACE-NAMES OF NORTHAMPTONSHIRE

By
J. E. B. GOVER, A. MAWER *and*
F. M. STENTON

CAMBRIDGE
AT THE UNIVERSITY PRESS
1933

The collection from unpublished documents of material for this volume has been made possible by a grant received from the British Academy.

PREFACE

THE publication of the Place-Names of Northamptonshire marks the completion of ten years' work of the English Place-name Survey, during which the place-names of eight counties have been surveyed. The choice of Northamptonshire as the county for treatment in the year 1932–3 was largely determined by the lively possibilities of local help which offered themselves through the inauguration of the Record Rooms of the Northamptonshire Record Society. Those possibilities have been more than vindicated in the course of the two or three years during which we have been actively engaged upon work for this volume. The formal basis of the work had been laid some years since, when the late Major J. de C. Laffan constructed gazetteers of the place-names of the county, and transcribed and identified forms from a large number of published documents with all that thoroughness and care which we associated with his work. The staff of the Survey carried that work still further by completing the work upon published documents, and by working upon masses of unpublished documents at the Record Office, the British Museum, and other libraries.

The great value of the Northamptonshire Record Rooms to us was, in the first place, that it placed at our disposal the many collections of deeds, maps, estate books and the like, once the property of Northamptonshire landowners, and now deposited either on gift or loan in the Record Rooms. Detailed reference is made to most of these documents in the bibliography printed on pp. xxxv–xli. Our indebtedness to those documents was greatly enhanced by the work of Miss Joan Wake and her assistant, Miss Scroggs, upon them. They did much themselves, and were able to do much in directing the labours of Mr Gover when he himself visited the Record Rooms. In addition to this, Miss Wake herself secured lists of place-names from the Enclosure Awards for most of the parishes in the county, and copies of numerous estate maps still in local possession, and herself answered or obtained answers to innumerable questions, historical, topographical, and the like, which we put to her.

Extensive and valuable as has been the help which we have received locally in the most recent volumes, namely those dealing with Sussex and Devon, one's experience in Northamptonshire makes one realise the great possibilities of a central place of deposit for records such as that now in existence in Northampton, and makes one wish all success to the work of the present Master of the Rolls in encouraging the formation of such centres.

The authors of the volume have also profited very greatly by the co-operation of the Northamptonshire Education Committee. Through the kindness of Miss Wake, we were brought into touch with that Committee and its Secretary, Mr J. L. Holland, and with his aid it was possible to secure organised help from some 200 of the elementary and secondary schools in the county in the collecting and recording of field-names as they exist at the present day, together with copies of early maps and other documents and local information which were useful in illustrating the history of those names. The task of collecting the field-names of any county is one which is beyond the resources of the Survey, unless co-operation of this kind is secured. We are deeply indebted to Mr Holland and the Northamptonshire Education Committee for enabling us, at least in this county, to secure as full a record as was possible of the names of its fields. The possibility of the interpretation of that field-name material was governed by very much the same conditions as those prevailing for the interpretation of place-names generally, namely that one can seldom do very much with them unless one has early forms for the names. Here, the ordinary medieval field-name material at our command, supplemented extensively by the masses of field-name material to be found at the Northamptonshire Record Rooms, enabled us to go much further in the direction of interpreting them than had hitherto proved possible. The results of that field-name investigation are set forth on pp. 259–292 of this volume. The results may not be as extensive or as striking as some persons might hope, but it will be seen that they do contribute very definitely to a further and more detailed knowledge of the past history of the county. The results have necessarily been limited by the conditions which will undoubtedly hamper us whenever the task is attempted, namely that there will always be parishes for which the medieval material is very scanty, and there will always be some parishes where for one cause or another it is difficult to secure a full record of the present-day field-names. It is especially to be regretted in this connection that the Education Committee of the Soke of Peterborough found itself unable to co-operate with us in supplying the modern field-names for the Soke of Peterborough where, as it happened, we had a great wealth of medieval material derived from Peterborough documents of every kind. Our experience in this county shows that work upon field-names is well worth doing, if one can secure the kind of co-operation which the schoolmasters and schoolmistresses of Northamptonshire have so readily afforded us. We stand most deeply indebted to them. In thanking Mr Holland for his work, we would desire also to thank Mr F. W. Bentham of the Education Department who, under Mr Holland, laboured untiringly in securing the success of the appeal to the schools.

In a large number of parishes not covered by the schools, the field-names were collected through the Record Society by volunteers too numerous to mention individually, to whom we are deeply indebted.

In the Soke of Peterborough we were very fortunate in having the full co-operation of Mr W. T. Mellows, late Town Clerk of Peterborough. He placed at our disposal his unrivalled collection of photostats and transcripts of Peterborough documents, and helped us with many comments upon points historical and topographical.

Of those who assisted Miss Wake in that part of the work which was carried out in the Northamptonshire Record Rooms, we desire especially to thank Miss Scroggs, Mrs Crick, Miss Prior and Miss Dover. In the work of transcribing names from the Enclosure Awards, our thanks are due to Mr Davidge, who did the bulk of the work, and to others who assisted him, namely Captain Benson, Miss Bridget Benson, Mr Charlesworth, Miss Hennings, Miss Layman, Miss Millburn and Miss Margaret Stockdale. Mr T. P. Dorman and the masters and boys of the Town and County School contributed much useful help by making tracings of both early and modern maps.

Many owners of early estate maps and manuscript collections

made their material accessible to us. In this connection we wish particularly to express our thanks to Mr Brudenell of Deene, the Duke of Buccleuch, the Rev. Sir Henry Knightley, Bart., Mrs Langton, the Marquess of Northampton, and Earl Spencer.

For information with regard to the ancient parish of Oundle we are especially indebted to Mr H. M. King and Mr W. G. Walker, masters at Oundle School, for other details to Mr G. V. Charlton, Mr J. A. Gotch, Miss E. W. Hughes of Harlestone, the Rev. A. Roberts of Harting and Mr Capell Robinson.

To Mr Charles Linnell of Pavenham we are indebted for much help with the place-names of south-west Northamptonshire.

For the use of unprinted material in the collections for the Victoria County History for Northamptonshire we are once again indebted to Dr Page. These collections were especially valuable in saving us from the necessity of going through late Inquisitions post mortem, Patent Rolls, etc.

We desire further to express our thanks to the President and Fellows of Magdalen College for lending the transcripts of their Northamptonshire deeds made by the late Dr Macray, to the Warden and Fellows of All Souls College for allowing us to transcribe names from the valuable series of sixteenth century estate maps in their possession, to the Cambridge University Library for facilities in working upon the Red Book of Thorney, to the Northampton Public Library for similar facilities, and to the Society of Antiquaries for permission to transcribe forms from the two cartularies of the Abbey of Peterborough in their possession. This record would be entirely incomplete were we not also to express our obligation to the officials of the Public Record Office and British Museum for their unfailing willingness to help us in all the work done there.

We are once again indebted to Professor Bruce Dickins, Professor Ekwall and Professor Tait for their kindness in reading through the proofs of the volume and for many useful corrections and suggestions. We are further indebted to Professor Ritter and to Professor Ekwall for comments upon many of our problems at an earlier stage in the writing of the volume. As on many previous occasions we are specially indebted to Professor Ekwall for the time and trouble he has taken in the matter. He is in no sense responsible for the volume as it now stands, but our indebtedness to him is expressly indicated on many pages of it and there are many others which have profited silently by his criticisms or suggestions; for the faults which remain we alone are responsible.

Apart from the preliminary work of Major Laffan, referred to above, the main burden of collection and identification of forms from documents, printed and unprinted alike, has fallen upon the assistant editor, Mr J. E. B. Gover. To him we are also indebted for the first rough draft of a large part of the volume. To Miss Armstrong we are indebted for the Indexes and for untiring work upon the difficult task of securing uniformity of detail in the volume as a whole. To the Cambridge University Press we owe our usual debt of gratitude for the skill and care with which they have passed the volume through the press.

In conclusion, attention may be called to a fresh attempt to deal with the problem of satisfactory accompanying maps. Realising that it is impossible to supply maps containing anything but a small portion of the names with which we deal, we have decided to abandon the attempt to give a large scale map of the county, and in place of it have given a map of the county on the scale 4 miles to the inch, showing the parish and hundred boundaries, the rivers, and the one feature of man's making that is essential for the understanding of the history of the county, namely Watling Street. This county map has been supplemented by a series of small maps on the scale of 10 miles to the inch, showing the distribution of those elements which have a bearing on the history of the settlement of the county from the time of the Anglian invasion onwards.

A. M.
F. M. S.

New Year's Eve, 1932

CONTENTS

INTRODUCTION

THE recorded history of the district which is now North-amptonshire begins with the passage in the *Historia Eccle-siastica* of Bede relating that Saxwulf, whom archbishop Theodore ordained bishop of the Mercians, was founder and abbot of the monastery called *Medeshamstedi, in regione Gyru-iorum*[1]. Later in this work, Bede records that bishop Wilfrid died in the monastery which he had *in provincia Undalum*[2]. The existence of two very ancient monasteries in the Nene valley would have provided an unusual supply of early documents for the illustration of its place-names had it not been for the devasta-tion of this region by the Danes in the ninth century. As it is, Wilfrid's monastery of Oundle has left no records of any kind, and none of the few genuine documents which have survived from pre-Danish *Medeshamstede* relates to land in North-amptonshire. The monks of the restored Peterborough had only a faint tradition of the earlier history of their house, and although it is interesting to have their statement that Brixworth, the greatest seventh century church in England, arose as a colony from *Medeshamstede* in the time of Cuthbald, Saxwulf's successor[3], there is no contemporary evidence to support their assertion.

There is no doubt that Northamptonshire in pre-Danish times lay within the territory of the Middle Angles, whose lands seem to have covered the whole region between the Mercians of the Trent valley and its tributaries and the West Saxons at the foot of the Chiltern escarpment. In historic times, the Middle Angles had no dynasty of their own. They were divided into numerous 'folks,' each with its own name, some at least of which were ruled by separate under-kings. Tondberct, *princeps* of the South Gyrwe, is mentioned by Bede[4]. The South and North Gyrwe appear, each with an estimated population of six hundred

---

[1] *Hist. Eccl.* IV, 6.
[2] *Ibid.* V, 19. The earlier life of Wilfrid by Eddi, his chanter, states that Wilfrid died *in Undolum*, without describing the place as a 'provincia.'
[3] Hugo Candidus, *ed.* Sparke, *Historiæ Anglicanæ Scriptores*, 8, 9.
[4] *Hist. Eccl.* IV, 19.

tribute-paying households, in the archaic list of 'folks' which is commonly called the Tribal Hidage[1]. The boundary between the two divisions of this people cannot now be drawn, but they were clearly the men of the northern fen country, their territory reaching at least as far as Croyland towards the north and Conington in Huntingdonshire towards the south[2]. Even without the express statement of Bede, it would have been safe to infer that Peterborough belonged to them.

The Tribal Hidage, as a whole, represents the local divisions of central England at a date before this region was divided into the shires of later history. It is not surprising that many of the names contained in this record are now obscure. Two of them have sometimes been identified with surviving names of Northamptonshire villages. One of them, which appears in the oldest text of the Hidage as *Bilmiga*, has often been regarded as identical with the name of Billing near Northampton. This identification can no longer be maintained in view of *Bethlinges*, the twelfth century form of the name Billing (*infra* 132). There is still, however, something to be said for identifying the *Widerigga* which follows *Bilmiga* in the Hidage with the modern Wittering. The names, at least, seem to be identical. The one serious objection which might be made to this identification is the situation of Werrington, whose name is apparently derived from that of Wittering, immediately to the north of Peterborough, in the territory, not of the *Witheringas*, but of the *Gyrwe*. If the *Wideriggas* of the Hidage were really settled around Wittering, the boundary between them and the Gyrwe must have run somewhere between Wittering and Werrington. Naturally, there is no record of such a boundary, but the map suggests that one of the Roman roads which diverge at Castor may have served this purpose. In any case, it is virtually certain that Werrington arose as a settlement from an earlier Wittering, and there is no reason why a portion of a folk migrating into adjacent territory should not have kept its ancient name in its new surroundings.

More definite evidence of early settlement than is supplied

---

[1] BCS 297.
[2] The tradition at Ely in the twelfth century was that the Isle of Ely had belonged to the territory of the Gyrwe.

even by the survival of ancient folk-names comes from the discovery of heathen burials and burial-grounds. The Anglian burial-grounds of Northamptonshire are numerous, and point to an intensive settlement of the centre and even of the west of the county before the conversion of the Middle Angles to Christianity. Their distribution is remarkable. Apart from discoveries at Peterborough itself, opposite the early cemetery at Woodstone in Huntingdonshire, little has been recorded from the Nene valley below Thrapston. But at Great Addington, the discovery of a very remarkable urn with marked North German and Scandinavian affinities points to an Anglian settlement of a date not later than the early part of the sixth century. From this point, burial sites extend up the Ise towards Desborough, and up the Nene beyond Northampton to Newnham and Badby, with outlying discoveries at Holdenby to the north and Marston St Lawrence to the south[1]. In all this area, cremation burials are frequent, and the early penetration of the broken country around Kettering and Daventry suggests that the Anglian occupation of the main Nene valley belongs to the earliest wave of Germanic invasion of the midlands, probably in the late fifth century.

It is, at any rate, along the valleys of the Nene and its tributaries that the more ancient place-names of Northamptonshire occur. Along the Nene come Fotheringhay, Oundle, Thrapston, Irthlingborough, Hamfordshoe, and Billing. Up the Ise is Kettering, and above the upper Nene is Daventry. Naseby, on one of the highest points of the Northamptonshire uplands, contains a personal name otherwise found only in heroic poetry and in a local name in the region of early settlement in Hampshire. Of the three names in the county which definitely relate to places of heathen Anglian worship, the Harrowdens are adjacent to the Ise valley and Weedon Beck is by the upper Nene. Weedon Lois in the south of the county, like the heathen cemetery at Marston St Lawrence, five miles away, shows that even this region, remote from the main channel of invasion and in great part wooded, was settled before, at latest, the middle of the seventh century.

[1] See the maps in Baldwin Brown, *The Arts in Early England*, vol. IV and VCH Northants, vol. I. For the Addington urn see Leeds, *Archæology of the Anglo-Saxon Settlements* 97 and Baldwin Brown *op. cit.* IV, 507.

This impression of an early and intensive settlement along the Nene valley and its tributaries agrees very closely with what would be inferred from the physical conditions of the shire. On the west, the valley of the middle Nene is bordered by a wide stretch of country which in early times must have been heavily wooded, and formed the ancient forest of Rockingham. Within this tract, Benefield, the ancient *Beringafeld*, is the only village name which gives an impression of high antiquity. It is only when the forest has been crossed that names of ancient type occur once more in Cottingham and in Rockingham itself, and these names certainly result from an independent settlement of the Welland valley. To the east, the Nene basin is bordered by an expanse of Oxford Clay which was certainly unattractive to early settlers. There are few traces of heathen Anglian occupation between the middle Nene and the Ouse, and Gidding in western Huntingdonshire is almost the only place-name of archaic character. Although the modern appearance of this country would not suggest that it had ever been heavily wooded, the story of Hereward's retreat into *Bruneswald*[1] shows that the district which bore that name could give good cover to outlaws in the eleventh century, and that district must have extended at least as far as from Newton Bromswold to Lutton. It is even probable that a stretch of more or less continuous woodland extended south of Newton Bromswold to join Yardley Chase and the forests of Salcey and Whittlewood. If so, the eastern boundary of Northamptonshire, which runs across this stretch of country, may well represent a natural frontier between two distinct bodies of Anglian settlers.

In their tendency to congregate along the Nene valley and to avoid the central and eastern woodlands adjoining it, the Anglian settlers were unconsciously following the example of their Romano-British predecessors. In Roman times, there was a thick cluster of habitations around Castor on the Nene, a fairly continuous succession of dwellings along the river, and another though less pronounced cluster between Northampton and Daventry on the north and Towcester on the south[2]. Floore

---

[1] See the references given below under Newton Bromswold, pp. 193, 194.
[2] See the map of Romano-British Northamptonshire, VCH Northants, vol. I.

(*infra* 82) near Weedon preserves the memory of a Romano-British dwelling in this region not yet proved by excavation. When all allowance has been made for the accidental nature of archaeological discoveries, the distribution of Romano-British settlements and Anglian burial grounds is undoubtedly significant. The evidence of archaic English place-names is no less suggestive, but cannot easily be expressed in the form of a map. It is, for example, highly probable that Wellingborough, Orlingbury and Kislingbury, to mention only three names, are as ancient as any which have been quoted above. It is hard to imagine any of them arising later than at latest the sixth century. But there is nothing approaching proof that these names might not have come into being at any period within the first century after the settlement of modern Northamptonshire began. All that can be done from place-name evidence towards reconstructing the settlement of a midland county is to note the names resembling those found in regions known from written and archaeological evidence to have been the scenes of the first English settlements. The results can never, by themselves, be conclusive. But when, as in the case of Northamptonshire, the distribution of place-names of ancient type agrees in all essential respects with the evidence of English heathen interments and Romano-British settlements, the coincidence should not be ignored. The whole Nene valley, from the source of the river to its emergence into the fens, must have undergone as early an Anglian settlement as any part of central England.

Whether the site of the present Northampton was occupied during this early settlement remains uncertain. The name tells us nothing as to the date at which the place came into being, nor is its meaning as clear as could be wished. It is on the whole probable that the Old English *hamtun* generally carried something of the sense of the modern 'home farm,' or, in more general terms, of a central residence as contrasted with outlying and dependent holdings. Such a name is hardly likely to have arisen in the earliest period. It suggests a time when something anticipatory of later manorial development had begun to appear— the eighth rather than the sixth century. Where all must be conjecture, it may be surmised that the original Northampton was a royal residence and estate, at which were rendered the dues payable by the men of the folk—the *provincia* or *regio*—settled around it. That it was an administrative centre in any wider sense than this is altogether unlikely. Its mere existence before the Danish period is unproved, and indeed the best argument for its earlier life is the fact that the Danes, under whom it quickly became important, seem generally to have chosen early centres of habitation for their fortified positions[1]. To this it may be added that the country immediately adjacent to Northampton had proved attractive to settlers in times which were ancient even before the Anglian migration began. The Late Celtic settlement on Hunsbury Hill and the Roman settlement, whatever its precise nature, at Duston, show that the lie of the land at this point invited settlement, and its advantages may well have attracted traders to the site of Northampton so that, while it was not among the places earliest settled, it may have been occupied a century or more before the Danish invasion of the midlands.

Nevertheless it is with this occupation that the history of Northampton as an administrative centre begins. By the early part of the tenth century the eastern midlands had been divided out among a number of Danish armies, each, apparently, under its own jarl, and each looking to some fortified town as its centre. The army of Northampton is mentioned more than once in the contemporary narrative of the wars of Edward the Elder contained in the Anglo-Saxon chronicle. It is more surprising to find that as late as the reign of Edgar land was being transferred from one person to another in the assembly of all the *here* (i.e. army) at *Hamtun*[2]. It is evident that the Danes retained some form of military organisation long after they had become fully possessed of the midland regions they had conquered[3]. There is every reason to believe that the origin of Northamptonshire lies here, and that the county of medieval and modern times represents the district occupied by a particular Danish *here* late in the ninth century. The district did not, indeed, coincide precisely with the shire of the present day. The original Northamptonshire certainly

[1] As at Lincoln, Leicester, and Reading.
[2] BCS 1130.
[3] Stenton, *The Danes in England*, 6, 7.

included Rutland[1], and on the other hand, there are facts which suggest that Watling Street may have been its first boundary towards the west[2]. In any case, however, Northampton was the fortified centre of the tenth century army, and its continuous history begins at this point.

Thenceforward until the mid-eleventh century there were two administrative units in England each called *Hamtunscir*. Southampton had risen to importance and given its name to a county before the middle of the eighth century. Early forms of the name Southampton, such as *Omtun*[3] and the variant *Homwic* derived by Simeon of Durham (ii, 42) from the ancient Northumbrian annals, show that the first element of this name was the OE *hamm*, river-bend, not the OE *hām*, 'home,' contained in Northampton. But by the tenth century the two names must have become indistinguishable, and it is somewhat remarkable that the distinguishing prefixes *South* and *North* were so long in coming into general use. *South*ampton was already so distinguished by the year 980[4], while the full form *North*ampton first appears on the eve of the Norman Conquest[5]. These prefixes doubtless arose spontaneously in common speech. Northampton and Southampton were connected by one of the best recorded lines of early medieval travel, the road through Brackley, Oxford, Abingdon, Newbury, Whitchurch and Winchester. It is suggestive that the full form Southampton first appears in the Old English Chronicle in a version written at Abingdon.

Regarded as a whole, the English element in the place-names of Northamptonshire has few distinctive features. It contains a certain number of ancient words rarely found in local nomenclature, such as the *tig* of Tiffield and the *etsce* of Bullicks Wood, but the work of the present Survey is now showing that many elements which on their first appearance seemed rare and only of local occurrence are widely distributed, and that the agricultural vocabulary of the first settlers was, more nearly than had been

---

[1] See the article on the Domesday Survey of Rutland in VCH Rutland, vol. 1.

[2] *Infra* xxi.

[3] BCS 389. This charter has been interpolated, but its formulas show that it represents an ancient original.

[4] OE Chron. C. *sub anno*.

[5] OE Chron. C. 1065. The other MSS. of the Chronicle read *Hamtun* in the annal for this year.

previously suspected, common to them all. When the second volume of the *Place-Names of Sussex* was written, the word *etsce* had only been found in that county, and there only in a very small area. It has since appeared in Surrey, and its occurrence in Northamptonshire shows that it must have been current throughout the whole southern midlands. It may be hoped that evidence from other counties will throw light on the difficult OE element *mealo*, so far noted in medieval records only in Mawsley, Wythemail, and the field-name Long Mollow in Yelvertoft. Elements like this are more likely to be found in field-names than in names of villages or hamlets, and an exhaustive survey of the field-names of even a single county would be a task of many years. In Northampton-shire, as noted above (*supra* vi–vii), it has proved possible to form some idea of the results which might be expected to follow from such an undertaking. The collection which is given below (*infra* 275–289) shows a remarkable number of field-names of medieval or pre-medieval origin preserved in local memory. The collec-tion contains few words otherwise unknown within the county, and suggests that the minor names which are recorded on maps form a series fairly representative of the county vocabulary as a whole. But it is clear that whenever, by a fortunate coincidence, medieval documents have survived for a parish where ancient field-names are still remembered, compounds of the kind familiar from Old English land-boundaries may be expected to appear. Worledge in Brackley and Worley in Moulton, each going back to an Old English *hwyrfel dic*, are cases in point. It is surprising that so many names of this type are still preserved orally in Northamptonshire, for enclosure, which has always tended to obliterate such names, went far in the county at an early date.

For the purposes of general history, perhaps the chief interest of the collection lies in its contribution to the evidence illustrat-ing the Scandinavian influence under which the shire passed in the ninth century. That Northamptonshire was once a Danish earldom, and that late in the tenth century many of its leading men still bore Danish names, are well attested historical facts. But the village names of the county, regarded as a whole, do not adequately suggest the volume of the Scandinavian settle-ment which underlies these facts. It is in the minor names of the county that the chief evidence of this settlement is to be found, and field-names, hitherto unrecorded, make a substantial addition to this evidence.

Our knowledge of the Scandinavian settlement of Northamptonshire, so far as it may be derived from the usual historical sources, is scanty. We may presume that the county west of Watling Street was never in effective occupation by the Vikings, for in the peace of Alfred and Guthrum, Watling Street formed the western boundary of Guthrum's kingdom, northward from the point where that road crossed the Ouse at Stony Stratford. It was at Towcester, on Watling Street, that Edward the Elder established one of the *burhs* which were to give him bases for his advance against the Danelaw. Here it was that in the same year the *here* from Northampton and from Leicester suffered one of its first reverses, and it would seem to have been as the direct result of the fortifying of Towcester that Edward received the submission of the whole '*here* which obeyed Northampton, as far north as the Welland.' Whether this *here* had occupied the country beyond Watling Street is doubtful. That Watling Street remained a significant boundary in this respect right on till the early part of the eleventh century is shown by the entry in the Chronicle (*s.a.* 1013) recording the submission to Sweyn of all the *here* north of Watling Street, and from the significant fact that he only began to harry the county after he had crossed Watling Street.

Such in brief outline is the story of the Scandinavian settlement of Northamptonshire as it is found in the chronicles. What further confirmation, elucidation or elaboration of that story can be drawn from a study of its place-names?

The position in relation to the county west of Watling Street is fairly simple and clear. The hundreds west of Watling Street, viz. Fawsley, Chipping Warden, Green's Norton, King's Sutton, Towcester (part), Cleyley (part) are, except for Fawsley, practically entirely free from Scandinavian influence, alike in their major place-names and in their field and minor names. Canons Ashby and Kirby in Woodend are the only two major place-names showing Scandinavian influence, and there would seem to be no field or minor names showing Scandinavian influence. The position in Fawsley Hundred is somewhat different. Here we have Badby, Barby, Ashby St Ledgers, Catesby, Farthingstone, Kilsby (with Nortoft) among major place-names (all of them parish-names), and a few field and minor names such as Biggin and a medieval *Kirkehil* for Church Hill in Catesby, and a Debdale (which may however be Anglian) in Welton (*infra* 275–6). The impression one gets, even in Fawsley Hundred, is that there can never have been any intensive occupation by Viking settlers. All that can ever have taken place must have been the passing of some of the more important centres of population into the hands of Scandinavian or Anglo-Scandinavian overlords.

In coming to this conclusion one has definitely put on one side, for what seem entirely adequate reasons (*infra* 256), certain *thorpe*-names found in this part of the county[1]. Badby, Ashby, and Kilsby, on the other hand, bring us face to face with three problems about which we must say something before we consider further the Scandinavian settlement of Northamptonshire.

Badby (*infra* 10) serves to remind us that there are doubtless many place-names in *by* which are only partially Scandinavian in origin. We know that in the tenth century this was called indifferently *Baddanby* and *Baddanburh*, and that a place once known as 'Badda's *burh*' (*Badda* being a purely English personal name) had come to be called 'Badda's *by*.' (Incidentally it may be noted that *by* in Northamptonshire clearly denoted a village or hamlet rather than a farmstead.) Other Northamptonshire examples of the same change, though the evidence here only goes back to Domesday, are to be found in Naseby[2], Thornby, and Kirby in Gretton (*infra* 73, 74, 167). We have a further possible example of such changing of an English to a Scandinavian second element in Yelvertoft (*infra* 77) in which we have an Old English personal name followed probably in the first instance by English *cote*, but later by Scandinavian *toft*.

Ashby St Ledgers (*infra* 9) raises a second problem, viz. the history of the numerous *Ashbys* here and elsewhere in the Danelaw. There are five of them in Northamptonshire, some

---

[1] See further, *Germanska Namnstudier Tillägnade Evald Liden*, 110–11.

[2] It may be noted further, with reference to the ultimate English origin of the name, that *Hnæf* is a purely West Germanic name, to which there is no parallel in Scandinavian personal names.

four in Leicestershire, some five in Lincolnshire, two in Norfolk, and one in Suffolk. In Lincolnshire we have numerous ME forms in *Ask-* which suggest that the name might be entirely Scandinavian, but it should be noted that there is no evidence in Scandinavia itself for the formation of such compounds[1].

On the other hand we can hardly take *Ashby* to be for early *Ashbury*, for that is a very rare type of name in England, only noted elsewhere in Berkshire and Devon—indeed it is unlikely that it would ever have been frequent, for there is no particular reason for associating tree-names with old *burhs*. Much the most likely explanation of the *Ashby*-names is that they represent earlier *Ashton*-names, a type of name which is very common throughout the county. If we do find numerous *Askebi*-forms in the Lincolnshire Ashbys and occasionally elsewhere, the explanation is, not that they are genuine compounds of Scandinavian *askr* and *by*, but that the English *sh* of *ash* has been Scandinavianised to *sk* under the influence of Scandinavian *askr*.

Kilsby (*infra* 24) is a good example of a somewhat different type of Scandinavianising which needs careful consideration in Northamptonshire and elsewhere. Here we seem to have Scandinavianising of the sounds of an English element, *cild* becoming *kild*, even though no such word exists in the Scandinavian languages themselves. The same is true of Scaldwell (*infra* 131). There is no Scandinavian *skald*, 'shallow,' and yet we have variation in ME between English *S(c)hald* and Scandinavianised *Scald*, the latter ultimately prevailing. This process is not uncommon in Northamptonshire, though the details of it vary from name to name. In Braybrooke (*infra* 110) we have the substitution of OWScand *breiðr* for OE *brād*, and a curious hybrid name as a result. Kislingbury (*infra* 86) is a difficult name, but it may show confusion between English and Scandinavian forms in its first element, and the same is true of Teeton (*infra* 88). Draughton (*infra* 112) is another possible example of such sound-substitution.

[1] For Norway see *Norske Gaardnavne* passim; for Sweden, Hellquist, *De Svenska Ortnamnen på -by*; for Denmark, Steenstrup, *De ældste Danske Stednavnes bygning*, 106–11, and the volumes of *Danmarks Stednavne*, so far as they have appeared; for Iceland, Finnur Jónsson, *Bæjanöfn á Íslandi* (*Safn til sögu Íslands*, IV, 421–3).

Such examples of Scandinavianising as those just set forth were only possible in places where there was a strong admixture of Viking settlers, and where the relations of English and Scandinavians were close and intimate. It is worthy of note that where the history of the name of some larger unit, generally a parish, requires us to postulate a hybrid name, there is, again and again, strong evidence of Scandinavian influence in the minor names and field-names of the parish. This is especially true of Braybrooke and Draughton (*infra* 110–11 and 110 n., 112).

One or two further examples of possible Scandinavianising of earlier English place-name elements remain to be discussed. In a name like Peakirk (*infra* 241) we have clear evidence that an original *church*-name has been Scandinavianised to *kirk*, and there are sporadic examples of the process elsewhere (*infra* xxxiii). More difficult is the name *Kirby*. There is only one example of this name in Northamptonshire[1], but it is common elsewhere. Is this a Scandinavian name pure and simple, corresponding to Icelandic *kirkjubær*, Dan *Kirkeby*, or is it a Scandinavianising of some earlier English name? The Domesday form *Chercheberie* for the one in Northamptonshire might at first suggest that the Kir(k)bys were only further examples of the Scandinavianising of earlier English names. Further examination of the evidence shows, however, that such a view is impossible. There are some thirty examples of this name in the Danelaw. If they are Scandinavianisings of an earlier English name, they must go back to an earlier *Church-bury* or some other compound of *church*. The evidence derived from the whole of the rest of England is however decisive that, except possibly for Chirbury in Shropshire, compounds of *church* and *bury* are unknown, and compounds of *church* with any other element (except possibly *hill*) are equally rare. We must believe therefore that the Kir(k)bys were the result of a process of deliberate naming afresh, and further, that they must belong to a period of the Viking settlements when the Vikings had abandoned their heathenism and were ready to recognise the church as the centre of life of the district. In other words the form *Chercheberie* is a chance Anglicising of a generally prevailing Scandinavian type, and not a survival of a lost Anglian one.

[1] Kirby in Woodend (*infra* 46) does not belong here.

It is difficult to say how far there may in some names have been deliberate replacement of English place-name elements by Scandinavian ones of entirely different etymology, though of kindred or allied meaning. The only clear and unmistakable example is to be found in Debdale (*infra* 119), which, we know, has taken the place of an earlier *deopandene*, 'deep dene,' and in Badby (*supra* xxii, *infra* 10), where similarity of sound may have helped in bringing about the substitution of *by* for *byrig*, when the similarity of meaning, beyond the vague one of human habitation, is by no means obvious[1].

In some names we have a Scandinavian personal name combined with an English second element, but we have no evidence to tell us whether we have simple replacement of the name of the earlier English holder by that of his Viking successor, or whether the whole name has been refashioned and an alteration made in the second element also. The probabilities are against the latter, as it is not very likely that Viking settlers would replace one English element by another. Such personal-name substitution is clearly to be found in Farthingstone (*infra* 22), Faxton (*infra* 124), Laxton (*infra* 168), Maxey (*infra* 237) and Strixton (*infra* 197). In the last-named there is fairly good evidence that the substitution took place as late as the eleventh century. Similarly a Viking named *Nafarr* seems ultimately to have given his name not only to a Scandinavian *lundr*, but to an English *ford* and *brook* (*infra* 216, *s.n.* Navisford), while Geddington (*infra* 165) involves an *ingtun*-formation from the Scandinavian personal name *Geiti*. Rothersthorpe (*infra* 151) presents a curious anomaly. It was at first called Thorpe pure and simple, and the earliest forms with their frequent spelling *thrope*, agreeing with the modern local pronunciation [θrʌp], suggest that this is an example of an English *thorpe* which chanced to fall into the hands of a lord bearing a Scandinavian name.

When we turn to the terms used in the Scandinavian nomenclature of the county, we find that of those denoting human settlement, *by* and *toft* and *biggin* are used with something of the same frequency as elsewhere, but *garth* is practically unknown and *booth* only found in a few names apparently of quite late

[1] For possible interchange of *by* and *tun*, and *cote* and *toft*, *v. supra* xxii, xxiii.

origin. Of terms used specially in agriculture and farming we may note the great frequency of *wang* and *wong*, and the equal rarity of *ing* (or *eng*) and of *deill* (*v.* EPN) and *wandale* or *wandole* (*infra* 274). *thwaite* is used with average frequency, but *mire* is surprisingly rare. Woodland terms are important in this county, and here we may note the exceeding rarity of *scoe* and the like from *skógr* (*infra* 269), and the equally great frequency of *lundr* (*infra* 251, 256, 267). One has been inclined hitherto to think of this term as a somewhat rare one, used especially of a sacred wood or grove, and there are perhaps traces of this usage in one or two hundred-names (cf. *infra* 96, 176–7), but it is clear that in Northamptonshire it was in wide and general use for any piece of woodland. Of common topographical terms *beck* is curiously rare (*infra* 260) and so is *carr* (ME *kerre*), 'swampy ground overgrown with brushwood' (*infra* 265).

Of terms connected with the social and economic structure of the Danelaw, we may note the one example of Carlton (*infra* 162), a settlement of Scandinavian *carls*, a street inhabited by men of *bondi*-status in Peterborough (*infra* 225), and a *haw* or enclosure of *drengs* in Ring Haw in Nassington (*infra* 205), while in Copeland in Desborough (*infra* 283) we have an example of the rare OScand *kaupa-land*, 'purchased land' (EPN *s.v.*). Finedon (*infra* 181) gives us the one trace of Anglo-Scandinavian *thing*, 'assembly,' while the hundred of Nassaborough is the one hundred to which the Scandinavian term *wapentake* is sometimes applied.

We have already dealt with the extent and character of Scandinavian influences to the west of Watling Street (*supra* xxi, xxii); we may now take a survey of the hundreds to the east of that ancient boundary.

Guilsborough Hundred contains three *bys* and two *tofts*, while Ostor Hill in West Haddon (*infra* 71) is a curious isolated example of a completely Scandinavian name.

The hundred of Nobottle Grove contains three Scandinavian *thorpes*, one *by*, Teeton, Rough Moor for *Rough Mire* (*infra* 80), and lost *Cattescalis* and *Brakebec* in the same parish (*infra* 269, 260), and Kislingbury with which we have already dealt. Of field-names we may specially note Cringleholme and the remarkable hybrid Horsemoor (really *Oustmoor*) (*infra* 280–1) and unidentified *Steynklint* (1215) in Teeton.

Comment has already been made upon many features in the hundred of Rothwell (including the names Braybrooke and Draughton, together with certain minor names in those parishes). We may, however, note also Loatland and Wharf in Harrington (*infra* 114), Clipston, Sibbertoft and Sulby (*infra* 111, 121), Gaultney and Storefield in Rushton (*infra* 120), of which the most noteworthy are perhaps Loatland and Gaultney.

The hundred of Orlingbury contains Scaldwell (*supra* xxiii, *infra* 131), Faxton (*infra* 124) which probably takes its name from its Scandinavian lord, and Clint in Hanging Houghton (*infra* 126), together with a Ho(l)beck (*infra* 284) and such field-names as *Floctoftys*, *Ekedale*, *Thorlokeshegh*, *Gonnildescroft* in Hanging Houghton.

In the hundreds of Spelhoe, Hamfordshoe and Wymersley, centring round Northampton, there is nothing in the major or in the minor names which suggests strong Scandinavianisation. In Spelhoe Hundred we have Billing Lings (*infra* 133) and Walbeck (*infra* 284), together with a few unidentified field-names. Hamfordshoe contains two *bys* and two *thorpes*. Wymersley has one *by*, a Loundes in Blisworth (*infra* 143), a probable Scandinavian personal name in Plaxwell's (*infra* 149), Rothersthorpe (*supra* xxv, *infra* 151) and Arksome (*infra* 152).

Turning to the north and north-west of the county, Corby Hundred is only less strongly marked by Scandinavian influence than Rothwell Hundred. It contains Carlton (*supra* xxvi, *infra* 162), Corby itself, Deenethorpe (*infra* 163, 256), Geddington (*supra* xxv, *infra* 166), and Kirby (*supra* xxiv, *infra* 167), while many of the *haw*-names such as Askershaw (*infra* 175), clearly go back to ON *hagi*, 'enclosure.'

It is in Huxloe and the adjacent Navisford hundreds that we find traces of a powerful Scandinavian landholder named *Nafarr* (*supra* xxv, *infra* 216), while Finedon (*supra* xxvi, *infra* 181), Wigsthorpe, Long Lown and Round Lown (*infra* 185, 187, 188) are further evidence of Scandinavian influence, but there is little or nothing of this influence in the field-names.

On the east side of the county (excluding the extreme north-east) Scandinavian influence is not strong, but there are some interesting traces of it in the Nene Valley. In the lower Nene Valley, in the hundred of Willybrook we may note Apethorpe (*infra* 198), the tell-tale Ring Haw (*supra* xxvi, *infra* 205), unidentified field-names in *lundr* and a purely Scandinavian name *Quernewath* in Glapthorn, a compound of *kvern*, 'mill' and *vað*, 'ford.'

The next hundred up the Nene Valley, that of Polebrook, is, except for Biggin (*infra* 212) and one or two possible Scandinavian *thorpes*, free from Scandinavian influence in its major and minor names alike. Navisford hundred shows a Scandinavian personal name in its name (*supra* xxv), a Thorpe (*infra* 219) and a possible Scandinavian personal name in Achurch (*infra* 219), but that is all. Most southerly of all is the hundred of Higham Ferrers. Here we have Knuston and the eleventh century Strixton (*infra* 192, 197, *supra* xxv), possible traces of Scandinavian influence in the history of Stanwick (*infra* 196), and a curious survival of Scandinavian *vrá*, 'corner' in Higham Ferrers itself (*infra* 288).

In the hundred of Nassaborough in the extreme north-east of the county, though the hundred itself is sometimes called a wapentake (*supra* xxvi, *infra* 223), there is little evidence of Scandinavian influence in the names of the more important places (cf. IPN 73–4). Gunthorpe and Maxey (*infra* 236, 237) are important exceptions, but otherwise we have only the *gates* or 'roads' in Peterborough (*infra* 225), one or two *thorpes*, traces of Scandinavian influence in Newark (*infra* 227 and Addenda lii), *Gunwade* (*infra* 232), Cathwaite, Nab, Grimeshaw, Lound (*infra* 240, 241, 245, 247), and extensive unidentified field-name material such as *Scrathawe* (1501), *Toftwong* (1375), *Westeng* and *Heyninge* (c. 1250), *Ormeswayt* and *Franehawe* (1246), *Meylund* (1270), *Greynes* (1247), *Grymmeswro*, *Lundgate* and *le Storth* (c. 1330).

These details amount, in the aggregate, to a considerable body of evidence. They show that Scandinavian influence in Northamptonshire was stronger than there has hitherto been reason to suspect, and far stronger than in any other county of the southern midlands whose nomenclature has so far been examined. In this, the evidence of place-names agrees very well with the inferences to be drawn from the early social organisation of the county. The proportion of sokemen, that is, of independent Anglo-Scandinavian peasants, to the unfree members of rural society, as that society is described in Domesday Book, is low, if the county is regarded as a whole, though much higher than in any county to the south. But the low proportion for the whole county is due to the fact that hardly any members of this class are recorded in the hundreds west of Watling Street. Towards the north, the proportion rises notably, and in the hundred of Nassaborough is higher than in the adjacent part of the highly Scandinavian Lincolnshire. Socially, and, it may be said, racially, Northamptonshire is really a border county, intermediate between Leicestershire, where Danish place-names dominate the modern map and a free population survived in great numbers even after the Norman Conquest, and the southern midlands, where innumerable peasants, once free, had suffered depression by 1086, and Scandinavian place-names are rarities. Whatever the early boundaries of the county may have been, its southern hundreds undoubtedly resemble the adjacent hundreds of Bedfordshire and Buckinghamshire in social structure as in local nomenclature, and its northern hundreds belong to the essential Danelaw in each respect. There is probably no English county where contrasts of this kind are more strongly marked than in Northamptonshire, and they give a distinctive character to its early history.

NOTES ON THE DIALECT OF NORTH-AMPTONSHIRE AS ILLUSTRATED BY ITS PLACE-NAMES

OE *ǽ* becomes *a* [æ] in ModEng. In ME we usually have *a* but occasionally *e* in names compounded with *æsc* and with *hæsel*. Nassington and Nassaborough, from OE *næss*, show variation between *a* and *e*.

OE *ǽ* (whatever its source) appears usually as ME *a*, and is shortened to ModEng *a* [æ] as in *Haddon, Slapton, Stratford*. It appears as *e* in *Glendon*.

OE eald becomes ME old, ald and ModEng old, ald. We have two non-Anglian ME forms *eld* for Old Town in Brackley, one for Old Gore in Towcester and one for Old Sale in Southwick, while DB has a form *Eldewincle* for Aldwinkle.

OE weald becomes ME wald and (more commonly) wold. ModEng always has *o* except in Walgrave and Wappenham **Wild**. The latter has *a* and *o* in its ME forms, but appears as *Weld* in 1550. *Weld* is found once in ME in Southwick (*infra* 207), *wild* is common in the south-west of the county in field-names (*infra* 271) but no early forms have been found, except for Wappenham Wild.

OE *ēa* with shortening before a consonant group gives ME *e* and *a*. Compounds of east have ME forms *Est-* and *Ast-*, yielding *Aston, Astrop, Astwell* and *Astwick* in the south-west of the county. Elsewhere we have *Easton* (bis), *Eastfield* and *Eastwood* with uniform ME *e*. The long *e* has probably been restored under the influence of *east* itself, cf. the earlier form *Esson* for Easton Maudit. *steap* gives ME and ModEng *step-*. *great* (in Gretton) has *e-* and *a-* forms in ME. *bean* in modern field-names nearly always yields *ban*, but note *Bencroft* in Rushden. *hean* gives ME *Hen-, Han-* and ModEng *Handley* in Towcester.

OE *ēo* generally becomes ME *e*. The only exceptions are two early forms in *Hurte-* for *Hartwell* on the Buckinghamshire border, and a few *o*-forms for Charlton in Newbottle also in the west of the county.

OE *ēo* generally becomes ME *e*. This is true of all compounds of **deop** and for **preost**, except for ME *e* and *u* forms for *Purston* and *o* and *e* forms for *Priesthay*, both in the southwest of the county. *Greatworth* (from **greot**) also in the southwest, varies between *e* and *u* till 1529. *Desborough* and *Darsdale* (from *Dēor*) always show *e*. *Spratton* (probably from *sprēot*), shows *e* (to 1235) and *o*. **hreod** seems always to show *o* in its ME forms in whatever part of the county it is found (see *Rodwell* (bis), *Rodmoor* (bis), *Radmoor* and *Redmoor*).

OE *ie* (Anglian *æ*) is illustrated in the history of *Wansford*. This place-name, on the eastern border of the county, shows Anglian *æ* (ME *a*) in all its forms except the earliest, which is probably an official West Saxon form, and two thirteenth century forms. OE **wiell(e)** uniformly appears as ME *welle*.

OE *ȳ* generally becomes ME *i*, frequently *u*, and only occasionally *e*. In ModEng we always have *i*, except in *Hurn*, *Shutlanger* and *Thurning*, though it is doubtful if even in these names we have a genuine survival of ME *u*. OE **hyll** becomes *hil(l)* and *hul(l)* indifferently in ME, though the *hil(l)*-forms are considerably the more numerous, and the *hull*-forms are for the most part found in the west and southwest of the county. OE **myln** yields ME *mylne, milne*, except for one *mulne* in Wicken in the south-west and one in Irthlingborough in the east of the county.

An unrecorded **metathesis of *r*** is found in more than one name deriving from OE **brycg**. It is found in *Burge* Brook in Helmdon, Goodmans *Burge* in Staverton, in a nineteenth century *Burge* for Bridge Hill in Pitsford, and in Dow *Boards* in Lilbourne, all on the west side of the county. All these go back to ME *brugge*. The same form was noted in Honeyburge (PN Bk 116) and has been since noted in Burge Fm in Bishops Lydeard and in Nynehead (So), for which we have the form *Brugge* (1327 SR). This metathesis may have been found already in OE, if we may trust the form *mintbyrge* (BCS 955) for Mimbridge in Chobham (Sr).

There are **hardly any traces of preservation of voiced initial *f*.** We may note *Vellom Field* in Braunston on the Warwickshire border, and an early *Voxle* for *Foxley* (Hundred) and *Bivelde* for Byfield.

Confusion of *f* and *th* is common, as in *Finedon*, *Life* for *Lithe*, *Thrift* and *Thrif* for *Frith*.

OE ceald appears as Cald-, Cold- except in *Challock* in the south-west of the county, and a late form *Chaldecott* for *Caldecott* in the same district.

OE circe, ME chirche has been Scandinavianised in *Pea-kirk*, and sporadically, in *Churchfield*, *Thorpe Achurch*, *Church Hill* in Catesby and *Church Field* in Walton.

The Inflexional *n* of the weak adjective survives in *Newnham*, *Smanhill*, *Stepnell* and the field-name *Smithnell* in the west of the county and appears sporadically in the *Newtons* found in different parts of the county.

ABBREVIATIONS

(NRS) at the end of an authority refers to collections of original MSS in the possession or custody of the North-amptonshire Record Society in the Record Rooms of the Society at the County Hall, Northampton; also to the Society's collections of transcripts and photographs of documents and to original MSS temporarily deposited on loan.

Abbr — *Placitorum Abbreviatio*, 1811.
Abingdon — *Chron. monasterii de Abingdon* (Rolls Series), 2 vols., 1858.
AC — *Ancient Charters* (Pipe Roll Soc.), 1888.
AD — *Catalogue of Ancient Deeds.* (In progress.)
AD — Unpublished Deeds at the PRO.
Add — Additional MSS in the British Museum.
AddCh — Additional Charters in the British Museum.
AFr — Anglo-French.
AN — Anglo-Norman.
AngloScand — Anglo-Scandinavian.
AOMB — Augmentation Office, Miscellaneous Books (PRO), 399, 403, 430.
AS Bede — *The Old English Bede* (EETS), 1890.
ASC — Anglo-Saxon Chronicle.
Ashby — Canons Ashby Cartulary (Egerton 3033).
Ass — *Assize Rolls for 4 and 5 John* (NRS v.).
Ass — Assize Rolls (unpublished) in PRO, Nos. 614–620, 624–628, 632 and 637. Also for divers counties Nos. 1218, 1226, 1239, 1245, 1293, 1316, 1332, 1366, 1400, 1433, 1488 and 1501.
AS Wills — *Anglo-Saxon Wills*, ed. Whitelock, 1930.
B — Bryant, *Map of the County of Northampton*, 1823.
Baker — G. Baker, *History and Antiquities of the County of Northampton*, 2 vols., 1822–41.
BCS — Birch, *Cartularium Saxonicum*, 3 vols., 1885–93.
Bede — Bede's *Historia ecclesiastica*, ed. C. Plummer, 2 vols., 1896.
Beds — Bedfordshire.
Belv — *MSS at Belvoir Castle*, 4 vols. (HMC).
Berks — Berkshire.
Bk — Buckinghamshire.
BM — *Index to the Charters and Rolls in the British Museum*, 2 vols., 1900–12.
B.M. — bench-mark.
Bodl — *Calendar of Charters and Rolls in the Bodleian*, 1878.
Bodl — Northamptonshire Charters and other documents (unpublished) in the Bodleian Library.
BorRec — *Records of the borough of Northampton*, 2 vols., 1898.
Bracton — *Bracton's Note-book*, ed. Maitland, 3 vols., 1887.
Bridges — John Bridges, *History and Antiquities of Northampton-shire*, ed. Whalley, 2 vols., 1791.
Brudenell — MSS *penes* George Brudenell, Esq. of Deene.

BT	Bosworth, *An Anglo-Saxon Dictionary*, ed. Toller, 1898.
BT Supplt	Bosworth, *An Anglo-Saxon Dictionary*, Supplement by T. N. Toller, 1921.
Buccleuch	*Report on the MSS of the Duke of Buccleuch*, 2 vols. in 3 (HMC), 1899–1903.
Buccleuch	Buccleuch MSS (photographs) (NRS).
C	Cambridgeshire.
Cai	*Admissions to Gonville and Caius College*, 1887.
Camden	*Britannia*, tr. P. Holland, 1610.
Camden (Gough)	*Britannia*, ed. Gough, 3 vols., 1789.
CartN	Carte Nativorum, including charters from the Precentor's Registers *penes* the Dean and Chapter of Peterborough. (Photostat in possession of W. T. Mellows, Esq.)
Ch	Cheshire.
Ch	*Calendar of Charter Rolls*. (In progress.)
ChancP	*Chancery Proceedings in the reign of Elizabeth*, 3 vols. (1827–32).
ChDecRoll	Chancery Decree Roll (PRO).
ChronPetro	*Chronicon Petroburgense* (Camden Society, 47), 1849.
ChronRams	*Chronicon Abbatiae Ramesiensis* (Rolls Series), 1886.
Cl	*Calendar of Close Rolls*. (In progress.)
Cl	Close Rolls. (Unpublished.)
Clayton	Clayton MSS. (Mr J. L. Holland's collection.)
ClR	*Rotuli Litterarum Clausarum*, 2 vols., 1833–44.
Coll. Top. et Gen.	*Collectanea topographica et genealogica*, 8 vols., 1834–43.
Compotus	Compotus Rolls of the Abbey of Peterborough. (Transcript in possession of W. T. Mellows, Esq.)
Compton	MSS *penes* Marquess of Northampton.
Cott	Cotton Charters (BM).
Crawf	*The Crawford Charters*, ed. Napier and Stevenson, 1895.
Ct	Court Rolls (PRO etc.).
CtAugm	Court of Augmentations (PRO).
CtRequests	Court of Requests (PRO).
CtWards	Court of Wards (PRO).
Cu	Cumberland.
Cur	*Curia Regis Rolls*. (In progress.)
D	Devon.
Dane	*Documents illustrative of the history of the Danelaw*, ed. Stenton, 1920.
Daventry	Cartulary of the Priory of Daventry (Cott. MS Claud. D xii).
D & C Linc	Dean and Chapter of Lincoln MSS.
Db	Derbyshire.
DB	Domesday Book.
DBE	*The Domesday of Inclosures*, 2 vols., 1897.
Deed	Unpublished deeds, chiefly at NRS.
Deeds Enrolled	Enrolments of Deeds at the PRO.
Depositions	Exchequer Special Commissions and Depositions (PRO).
DKR	*Deputy Keeper's Reports*, vols. 38–42.
Do	Dorset.
Drayton	Michael Drayton, *Polyolbion*, 1612.
Drayton	Drayton MSS, *penes* N. Stopford-Sackville, Esq.
Dugd	Dugdale, *Monasticon*, 6 vols. in 8, 1817–1830.
DuLaMiscBks	Duchy of Lancaster Miscellaneous Books (PRO), 115, 117.

DuLaSpecCom	Duchy of Lancaster Special Commissions (PRO).
DunBev	*Sanct. Dunelm. et Sanct. Beverlacense* (Surtees Soc. 5), 1837.
Dunstable	*Dunstable Cartulary* (Beds. Rec. Soc. 10).
Easton Neston	Fermor-Hesketh MSS (Transcripts) (NRS).
ECP	*Early Chancery Proceedings* (PRO Lists and Indexes Nos. 12, 16, 20, 29, 38, 48, 50).
EDD	*English Dialect Dictionary*, 6 vols., 1898–1905.
Eddius	Eddius, *Life of Bishop Wilfrid*, ed. Colgrave, 1927.
EDG	Wright, *English Dialect Grammar*, 1905.
EETS	Early English Text Society.
Ekwall, *Studies*	Ekwall, *Studies in English Place and Personal Names*, 1931.
EnclA	Enclosure Award.
EPN	*The Chief Elements in English Place-names*, 1923.
ERY	East Riding of Yorkshire.
Ess	Essex.
Ethelweard	*Chronicon Ethelwerdi* (Rerum Anglicarum Scriptores, ed. Savile, 1596).
Eynsham	*Eynsham Cartulary* (Oxford Hist. Soc., 49, 51), 1907–8.
F	*The County of Northampton....engraved by W. Faden*, 1779.
FA	*Feudal Aids*, 6 vols., 1899–1920.
Falk-Torp	*Etymologisk Ordbog*, ed. Falk and Torp, 1903.
Fees	*Book of Fees*, 3 vols., 1922–31.
FF	*Feet of Fines* (Pipe Roll Soc., vols. 17, 20, 23, 24), 1894–1900.
FF	Feet of Fines (unpublished) at the PRO.
Fenland NQ	*Fenland Notes and Queries*, ed. W. H. B. Saunders (Peterborough 1889 etc.).
Finch-Hatton	Finch-Hatton MSS (NRS).
Fine	*Calendar of Fine Rolls.* (In progress.)
FineR	*Excerpta e rotulis finium*, 2 vols., 1835–6.
For	Pleas of the Forest (unpublished) (PRO).
Forssner	Forssner, *Continental Germanic Personal Names in England*, 1916.
Förstemann	Förstemann, *Altdeutsches Namenbuch*, *Personennamen* (PN), *Ortsnamen* (ON), 2 vols. in 3, 1901–16.
France	*Calendar of Documents preserved in France*, 1899.
Fraunc	The Register of George Fraunceys or the Sacrist's Register. (Photostat in the possession of W. T. Mellows, Esq.)
Fuller	*History of the Worthies of England*, 1662.
Furtho	Furtho Charity Deeds (NRS).
G	Greenwood, *Map of the County of Northampton*, 1826.
Geld Roll	*The Northamptonshire Geld Roll a.* 1076. Printed in VCH i, 297.
Gerv	*Gervasius Cantuarensis* (Rolls Series, 2 vols.), 1867–9.
Gl	Gloucestershire.
GP	Rygh, *Gamle Personnavne i Norske Stedsnavne*, 1901.
Ha	Hampshire.
Harl	Harleian MSS (BM).
Hastings	*Report on the MSS of R. R. Hastings, Esq.* Vol. 1 (HMC), 1928.
H de B	*Estate Book of Henry de Bray* (Royal Hist. Soc., 3rd Series, 27), 1916.

He	Herefordshire.
Hellquist	Hellquist, *Svensk Etymologisk Ordbok*, 1925.
Herts	Hertfordshire.
HistHF	*History and Antiquities of Higham Ferrers*, ed. J. Cole, 1838.
HMC	*Historical MSS Commission*.
HMC Var	*HMC Reports on Manuscripts in Various Collections*, 8 vols., 1901–23.
Hu	Huntingdonshire.
Hyde	*Liber monasterii de Hyda* (Rolls Series), 1866.
Indledning	Rygh, *Norsk Gaardnavne*, Forord og Indledning, 1898.
Inq aqd	*Inquisitiones ad quod damnum*, 1803.
Ipm	*Calendar of Inquisitions post mortem.* (In progress.)
Ipm	Inquisitiones post mortem (unpublished) in the PRO.
IpmR	*Inquisitiones post mortem*, 4 vols., 1806–28.
IPN	*Introduction to the Survey of English Place-Names*, 1923.
Isham	Lamport Collection (NRS).
Jellinghaus	Jellinghaus, *Die Westfälischen Ortsnamen* (3rd edition), 1923.
K	Kent.
KCD	Kemble, *Codex Diplomaticus*, 6 vols., 1839–48.
Kelly	Kelly, *Directory of Northamptonshire*, 1930.
Kelmarsh	J. C. Wall, *History of Kelmarsh*, 1927.
Kingsthorpiana	*Kingsthorpiana,...being a calendar of old documents... in the church chest of Kingsthorpe*, ed. J. H. Glover, 1883.
Knightley	Knightley MSS (NRS).
KPN	Wallenberg, *Kentish Place Names*, 1931.
L	Lincolnshire.
Law	Law, *Oundle's Story*, 1922.
Laws	*Die Gesetze der Angelsächsen*, ed. Liebermann, 3 vols., 1903–16.
Lei	Leicestershire.
Leland	Leland, *Itinerary*, ed. L. T. Smith, 5 vols., 1906–10.
LG	Low German.
Lind	Lind, *Norsk-Islandska dopnamn och fingerade namn*, 1903–15.
LindB	Lind, *Norsk-Islandska Personbinamn*, 1920–1.
Lindkvist	Lindkvist, *ME Place-names of Scandinavian Origin*, 1912.
LN	*Liber Niger Scaccarii*, 1774.
LP	*Letters and Papers, Foreign and Domestic.* (In progress.)
LRMB	Miscellaneous Books Land Revenue (PRO), 160, 165, 174, 182, 201, 202, 221, 222.
Lumley	Lumley MSS (Northampton Public Library).
Lundgren-Brate	Lundgren-Brate, *Personnamn från Medeltiden*, 1892 ff.
LVD	*Liber Vitae Dunelmensis* (Sweet, *Oldest English Texts*), 1885.
LVH	*Liber Vitae of Hyde Abbey*, 1892.
Magd	Deeds in the possession of Magdalen College, Oxford, catalogued and transcribed by Dr Macray.
Mansion	Mansion, *Oud-Gentsche Naamkunde*, 1924.
Map	Maps, chiefly in the possession of the NRS.
Mastin	Mastin, *History and Antiquities of Naseby*, 1792.
ME	Middle English.
MertRec	*The Records of Merton Priory*, ed. Heale, 1898.

MHG	Middle High German.
Middendorff	Middendorff, *Altenglisches Flurnamenbuch*, 1902.
Middleton	*Report on the MSS of Lord Middleton* (HMC) 1911.
MinAcct	Ministers' Accounts (PRO).
Minute Bk	Minute Book of the Feoffees, in the possession of Peterborough Corporation. (Transcript *penes* W. T. Mellows, Esq.)
Misc	*Calendar of Inquisitions Miscellaneous.* (In progress.)
MLG	Middle Low German.
MLR	*Modern Language Review.* (In progress.)
ModEng	Modern English.
Morton	Morton, *The natural history of Northamptonshire*, 1712.
Moulton	*Palaeography, Genealogy and Topography*, Selections from the Collections of H. R. Moulton, 1930.
MP	Matthew Paris, *Chronica Majora* (Rolls Series), 7 vols., 1872–83.
Mx	Middlesex.
Nb	Northumberland.
NED	New English Dictionary.
Nf	Norfolk.
NG	*Norske Gaardnavne*, 18 vols., 1897–1919.
Nielsen	Nielsen, *Olddanske Personnavne*, 1883.
NoB	*Namn och Bygd.* (In progress.)
Norw	Norwegian.
NP	Björkman, *Nordische Personennamen*, 1901.
NRS	*Northamptonshire Record Society.* (In progress.)
NRY	North Riding of Yorkshire.
Nt	Nottinghamshire.
Nth	Northamptonshire.
NthStA	Cartulary of St Andrew's, Northampton (Cott. MS Vesp. E. xvii).
NthStJ	Cartulary of St James', Northampton (Cott. MS Tib. E. v).
NthNQ	*Northamptonshire Notes and Queries*, 1886–96 and 1905 ff.
O	Oxfordshire.
OBrit	Old British.
ODan	Old Danish.
OE	Old English.
OFr	Old French.
OFris	Old Frisian.
Ogilby	Ogilby, *Itinerarium Angliae*, 1675.
OGer	Old German.
OHG	Old High German.
ON	Old Norse.
ON	Ortsnamen.
Ord	Ordericus Vitalis, *Historia Ecclesiastica*, 5 vols., 1838–55.
Orig	*Originalia Rolls*, 2 vols., 1805–10.
O.S.	Ordnance Survey.
OScand	Old Scandinavian.
OSw	Old Swedish.
OW	Old Welsh.
OWScand	Old West Scandinavian.
OxonCh	*Facsimiles of early charters in Oxford muniment rooms*, ed. Salter, 1929.

(p)   Place-name form derived from personal name.

P   *Pipe Rolls*, Record Commission, 3 vols., 1833–44. Pipe Roll Soc. (In progress.) Great *Roll of the Pipe* for 26 Hy 3, ed. Cannon, 1918.

Pap   *Calendar of Papal Registers*. (In progress.)

ParlSurv   Parliamentary Surveys (PRO).

ParReg   Parish Registers.

Pat   *Calendar of Patent Rolls*. (In progress.)

Pat   Patent Rolls (unpublished) in PRO.

PatR   *Rotuli Litterarum Patentium*, 1835.

P (CR)   Pipe Roll, Chancellor's copy.

PeterbA   Cartulary of the Abbey of Peterborough (MS Soc. Antiq. 60).

PeterbB   Cartulary of the Abbey of Peterborough (MS Soc. Antiq. 38).

PipewellA   Cartulary of Pipewell Abbey (Cott. MS Calig. A. xii).

PipewellB   Cartulary of Pipewell Abbey (Cott. MS Otho B. xiv).

p.n.   place-name.

PN IOM   Kneen, *The Place-Names of the Isle of Man*, 1925–8.

Poll   *Copies of the polls at several elections for members to represent the county of Northampton*, 1832.

PRO   Public Record Office.

Pytchley   *Henry of Pytchley's Book of Fees*, ed. W. T. Mellows (NRS ii).

Pytchley   Henry of Pytchley's Book of Charters, Peterborough Cathedral Library. (Transcript *penes* W. T. Mellows, Esq.)

QW   *Placita de Quo Warranto*, 1878.

R   Rutland

Ramsey   *Cartularium monasterii de Rameseia* (Rolls Series), 3 vols., 1884.

RBE   *Red Book of the Exchequer*, 3 vols., 1896.

Recov   Recovery Rolls (PRO).

RegAntiquiss   *The Registrum Antiquissimum of the Cathedral Church of Lincoln* (Lincoln Record Soc. 27), 1931.

Rental   Rentals (unpublished) at BM, NRS and PRO.

Renton   *Records of Guilsborough, Nortoft and Hollowell*, ed. Ethel L. and Eleanor L. Renton, 1929.

RH   *Rotuli Hundredorum*, 2 vols., 1812–18.

Ritter   Ritter, *Vermischte Beiträge zur englischen Sprachgeschichte*, 1922.

RN   Ekwall, *English River-Names*, 1928.

RotDom   *Rotuli de Dominabus* (Pipe Roll Soc. 35), 1913.

Sa   Shropshire.

s.a.   *sub anno*.

Saints   *Die Heiligen Englands*, ed. Liebermann, 1889.

Scand   Scandinavian.

Scot   Calendar of Documents preserved in Scotland.

ScotCh   *Early Scottish Charters*, ed. Lawrie, 1905.

Searle   Searle, *Onomasticon Anglo-Saxonicum*, 1897.

Selby   *The Coucher Book of Selby* (Yorks Arch. Soc. Rec. Ser. 10, 13), 1891–3.

Seld   *Selden Society Publications*. (In progress.)

Sf   Suffolk.

SP   *Calendar of State Papers Domestic*. (In progress.)

Sparke	*Hist. Anglicanae scriptores varii*, ed. Sparke, 2 vols., 1723.
Spencer	MSS *penes* Earl Spencer.
Sr	Surrey.
SR	*A subsidy collected in the diocese of Lincoln in* 1526, ed. Salter, 1909.
SR	Lay Subsidy Rolls (unprinted) in PRO.
SrAS	Surrey Archaeological Society.
St	Staffordshire.
Statutes	*Statutes of the Realm*, 9 vols., 1810–22.
StEng	Standard English.
St Frides	*Cartulary of the monastery of St Frideswide* (Oxf. Hist. Soc. 28, 31), 1895–6.
StJ	*Admission to the College of St John the Evangelist*, 2 vols., 1882–1903.
StudNP	*Studia Neophilologica.* (In progress.)
St Werb	*Cartulary of the Abbey of St Werburgh, Chester* (Chetham Soc. New Series, 79, 82), 1920–3.
Survey	*The Northamptonshire Survey* (12th century). Printed in VCH i, 357–89.
Survey	Surveys of Northamptonshire estates in possession of the NRS.
Swaffham	The Register of Robert Swaffham, MS in Peterborough Cathedral Library (Photostat *penes* W. T. Mellows, Esq.).
TA(B)	Tithe Award (Book).
Tax	*Taxatio Ecclesiastica*, 1802.
Terrier	Terriers in possession of NRS.
Thorney	The Red Book of Thorney (Camb. Univ. Library).
Thorpe	*Diplomatarium Anglicum Aevi Saxonici*, ed. Thorpe, 1865.
Thurgarton	Thurgarton Cartulary (MS in Southwell Cathedral).
Torp	Torp, *Nynorsk Etymologisk Ordbok*, 1919.
TRE	Tempore Regis Edwardi.
TRW	Tempore Regis Willelmi.
VCH	*Victoria County History of Northamptonshire* (unfinished), 3 vols. 1902, 1906, 1930.
VE	*Valor Ecclesiasticus*, 6 vols., 1810–34.
Wa	Warwickshire
Wardon	*Cartulary of Wardon Abbey* (Beds Rec. Soc. No. 13).
WellsR	*Rotuli Hugonis de Welles* (Lincoln Record Society, 3 vols.), 1912–14.
Wills	*Northants and Rutland Wills*, 1510–1652 (The Index Library), 1888.
Woods Rept	*Report of Commissioners on Royal Forests, Woods etc.*, 1787.
WRY	West Riding of Yorkshire.
W.T.M.	*ex inf.* Mr W. T. Mellows.
XtCh	*Cartulary of Christ Church* (Oxf. Hist. Rec. Soc. 92), 1931.
Y	Yorkshire.
ZEN	Björkman, *Zur englischen Namenkunde*, 1912.
ZONF	*Zeitschrift für Ortsnamenforschung.* (In progress.)

PHONETIC SYMBOLS USED IN TRANSCRIPTION
OF PRONUNCIATIONS OF PLACE-NAMES

p	*p*ay	ʃ	*sh*one	tʃ	*ch*urch	ei	fl*ay*
b	*b*ay	ʒ	a*z*ure	dʒ	*j*udge	ɛ	Fr. jam*ai*s
t	*t*ea	θ	*th*in	ɑ·	*f*ather	ɛ·	th*ere*
d	*d*ay	ð	*th*en	ɑu	c*ow*	i	p*i*t
k	*k*ey	j	*y*ou	a	Ger. m*a*nn	i·	f*ee*l
g	*g*o	χ	lo*ch*	ai	fl*y*	ou	l*ow*
ʍ	*wh*en	h	*h*is	æ	c*a*b	u	g*oo*d
w	*w*in	m	*m*an	ɔ	p*o*t	u·	r*u*le
f	*f*oe	n	*n*o	ɔ·	s*aw*	ʌ	m*u*ch
v	*v*ote	ŋ	si*ng*	oi	*oi*l	ə	*e*ver
s	*s*ay	r	*r*un	e	r*e*d	ə·	b*i*rd
z	*z*one	l	*l*and				

Examples:

Harwich (hæridʒ), Shrewsbury (ʃrouzbəri, ʃru·zbəri),
Beaulieu (bju·li).

NOTES

(*a*) On the arrangement of the volume:

(1) The names are arranged topographically according to the Hundreds. Within each hundred the parishes are dealt with in alphabetical order, and within each parish the names of major importance are first dealt with in alphabetical order. In many parishes these are followed by a paragraph dealing with names for which we have no very early forms, or names of obvious origin, e.g. the last paragraph on p. 60, under Syresham. The forest-, river- and road-names are dealt with at the beginning of the volume.

(2) After the name of every parish will be found the reference to the sheet and square of the 1-in. O.S. map (Popular Edition) on which it may be found. Thus, CATESBY 83 C 5.

(3) Where a place-name is found only on the 6-in. O.S. map this is indicated by putting 6″ after it in brackets, e.g. BULLICKS WOOD (6″).

(4) Place-names now no longer current are marked as 'Lost.' This does not necessarily mean that the site to which the name was once applied is unknown. We are dealing primarily with names and the names are lost. These names are printed in italics when referred to elsewhere in the volume.

(5) The local pronunciation of the place-name is given, wherever it is of interest, in phonetic script within square brackets, e.g. Raunds [rɑ·ns].

(6) In explaining the various place-names, summary reference is made to the detailed account of such elements as are found in the *Chief Elements in English Place-names* by printing those elements in Clarendon type, e.g. Carlton, *v.* karla-tun.

(7) In the case of all forms for which reference has been made to unprinted authorities, that fact is indicated by printing the reference to the authority in italic instead of ordinary type, e.g. 1272 *Ass* denotes a form derived from a MS authority in contrast to 1316 FA which denotes one taken from a printed text.

(8) Where two dates are given, e.g. 972 (c. 1200), the first is the date at which the document purports to have been composed, the second is that of the copy which has come down to us.

(9) Where a letter in an early place-name form is placed within brackets, forms with and without that letter are found, e.g. *Ringsted(e)* means that forms *Ringsted* and *Ringstede* are alike found.

(10) All OE words are quoted in their West Saxon form unless otherwise stated.

(*b*) On the arrangement of the maps:

(1) The map illustrating the Anglian elements shows the distribution of those names compounded with the more important elements denoting human habitation.

(2) The map illustrating the Scandinavian element shows the distribution of the more important types of Scandinavian names.

(3) The thorp-map shows the racial distribution of these names on the lines indicated on p. 256.

(4) The map of names in feld and leah shows the distribution of names which are particularly characteristic of old forest areas.

(5) The map showing cot(e) names shows the noteworthy distribution of those names discussed on p. 254.

ADDENDA ET CORRIGENDA

For addenda with appended initials we are indebted as follows:

F.T.S.H.	Mr F. T. S. Houghton
M.S.H.	Miss Mary S. Holgate
J.B.J.	The Rev. J. B. Johnston
S.P.V.	Mr S. P. Vivian
A.C.W.	Mr A. C. Wood.

VOL. I, PART II

p. 62, *s.v. varða, varði*. The primary sense of this word is 'look-out place,' then 'beacon,' then 'cairn, etc., marking such.'

p. 131. Add Puxton (So), *Pukereleston* (1212 Fees), representing the holding of Robert Puckerel (1158 P).

VOL. II

p. 4, *s.n.* GAYHURST. For loss of *t* we may compare the same name Goathurst (So), *Gahers* 1086 DB, *Gaherst* 1167 P (p).

pp. 74, 101, *s.n.* WHADDON. One or other of the Whaddons in Bucks must be the *Hwætedun* of KCD 721.

p. 94. HUDNALL should have been identified with Hudnall in the neighbouring parish of Little Gaddesden (Herts).

p. 131, *s.n.* BOTOLPH CLAYDON. Mr A. C. Wood calls attention to an earlier example of the compound in *Boteclaydon* 1432 *Cl.*

p. 232, *s.n.* DILEHURST. Add from Dugd v, 96 *Cippenham in Dilleherst* 1168, *terra vocatur Dilleherst* 1332, quoted from the Bermondsey Abbey Cartulary.

p. 239, *s.n.* OAK END. Add *Ake* 1220 Fees.

VOL. IV

pp. 36–7, *s.n.* SYNTLEY. Cf. also Saintlow in East Dean (Gl), *Seynteleye* 1281 Peramb. of For. of Dean (F.T.S.H.).

p. 92, *s.n.* CUTMILL. Note also *Cuttemill* (1537 *Rental*) in Budbrooke (Wa) and Cut Mill in Dymock (Gl) (F.T.S.H.).

p. 124, *s.n.* ILDEBERG. Cf. further Elm Bridge in Cranleigh (Sr), *Ildenebrig(ge)* 1241, 1294 *Ass*, *Elden Bridge* 1765 Rocque's Map.

p. 140, *s.n.* HOLDFAST. Cf. Hollyfast in Allesley (Wa), *Holynfast* 1410 Coventry Leet Book (F.T.S.H.).

p. 218, *s.n.* CALLANS WOOD. A further example of this name is the wood called *le Chaleng* (1239 Cur) in Barrow on Soar (Lei).

p. 290, *s.n.* WRENS NEST HILL. A further example of OE *wrasn* in p.n.'s is found in *Grimeswrosne* in Harbury (Wa), 1201 FF (F.T.S.H.).

p. 341, *s.n.* GANNOW. A further example of this name is *Gannow* (1628 Ipm) in Little Swell (Gl) (F.T.S.H.).

p. 406, *s.n.* HARVINGTON (Chaddesley). For '237' read '238.'

VOL. V

p. 120, *s.n.* GROSMONT. For this as a place-name cf. Grismonds Tower in Cirencester (Gl), which is on the site of what William of Worcester in 1460 calls *Grosmund*, an old barrow. See further Baddeley *Hist. of Cirencester* 4–6 (F.T.S.H.).

VOL. VI

p. 4, *s.n.* KENT DITCH. Mr S. P. Vivian notes in a 13th cent. charter (Harl Ch 80, 1, 34) a reference to *aqua que separat comitatum Kancie a comitatu Susexie*.

p. 6, *s.n.* OUSE. For such a river-name from ME *wose*, cf. *aqua de wosepulle* (1345 Ipm) in Aylburton (Gl), referring perhaps to the present Fernley Brook (F.T.S.H.).

p. 17, *s.n.* GREVATT'S. Further examples of collective *et*-compounds have been noted as follows in Surrey: *la Okette* (1294 *Ass*) (from **ac**), *Bushett* (1593 Moulton) in Ash (from **bysc**), *Firzetts* (1725 *Rental*) in Alfold, now Furzen Fm (from **fyrs**), *Ripsette* in Chertsey (1369 Chertsey), an *et*-derivative of the dialectal word *risp*, noted under Ripsley PN Sx 45, Stockhurst (*Stoket* 1311 FF) in Oxted (from **stocc**), Stubbetts in Abinger (*Stubbets* c. 1570 SAS) (from **stubb**), *Stubbet* in Merstham (1522 SAS 20, 94), *Telghet* (1381 *Ct*) in Capel (from OE *telg*, 'branch'), *Thevelette* (1312 *AOMB*) in Limpsfield (from OE *þyfel*, 'tuft, clump'), Thurnetts Copse (*Thurnett* 1548 *LRMB*) in Witley (from **þyrne**) (cf. also Thornet Wood in Bookham, for which no early forms have been found), *la Wythiette* (1354 *Ct*) in Capel (from **wiþig**). A fresh *et*-derivative from an adjective is *le Smethatte* in Camberwell (1344 AD ii) from OE *smeðe*, 'smooth.'

p. 29, *s.n.* INHOLMS COPSE. The word *innom* is fairly common in Surrey, cf. Inholme in Dorking (*Innome* 1342 *Ct*), *boscus q.v. Inname* in Headley (1218 FF), *le Innomes* in Wonersh (1350 AD ii), *campus q.v. Innome* in Limpsfield (1342 *AOMB*).

p. 35, *s.n.* BRIDGER'S POND. A further illustration of this type of pers. name is to be found in John *le Bruggere* also called John de *Ponte* (1294 *Ass*), who lived at Bridge End in Ockham (Sr).

p. 42, *s.n.* MIZZARDS. A further reference is *Musardyslonde* 1431 *Cl* (A.C.W.).

p. 45, *s.n.* RIPSLEY. Further examples of the word *risp* are found in Ribsden in Windlesham (Sr) *Ripsedoune* 1446 Chertsey, and in field-names *Ripsette* (1369 ib.) in Chertsey, and *The Rippys* in Bletchingley (1522).

p. 53, *s.n.* SINGLETON. For the dialectal word *sangle, songle*, cf. *Songlefield* (1638 Ipm) in Upleadon (Gl) (F.T.S.H.).

p. 74, *s.n.* CAMIC POND. Cf. *Cammok lond* in Ash (Sr) (1548 *LRMB*).

p. 83, *s.n.* MEDMERRY FM. A further example of the element *medeme* is Meadfield in Haslemere (Sr), *Med(e)mefeld* 1340, 1384 *Ct*, t. Ed 3 *Rental*.

p. 106, *s.n.* OAKHURST. Add (*H)ochurst* 13th Lewes Deeds (p).

p. 107, *s.n.* SLIFEHURST. The place in Ewhurst (Sr) is now Slithehurst. The form in BM should be *Le Slefherst*. Others are *Slefhurst* 1314 *Rental*, 1332 SR (p), *Slehurst* 1511 LP.

p. 107, *s.n.* SLIFEHURST. Add *Slyfhurst* 13th Lewes Deeds (p).

p. 107, *s.n.* STRUDGWICK WOOD. Add *Stro(u)dwyk* 13th *Lewes Deeds*, *Strodewikes wode* 1399 ib.

p. 111, *s.n.* LURGASHALL. For *Lurga(r)sale* 1529 AD i, read *Lurgasale* 1535 VE.

p. 113, *s.n.* VALEWOOD (See also PN D, Part ii, p. ix). A much earlier form is found in *Felwelle* 1340 *Ct* (p).

p. 117, *s.n.* LIMBO FM. Cf. further *Impaghe* in Horne (Sr), 12th *Lewes* 75 d.

p. 124, under Bury parish. Add BURY HILL 1625–6 *Berrehill, Beere Hill* (SAC xl, 9, 17). The hill must have taken its name from one of the numerous earthworks in the neighbourhood, *v.* burh.

p. 132, *s.n.* GUNSHOT COMMON. A further example of the element *scydd* is found in Denshott in Leigh (Sr), 1241 *Ass Dunschede*, 1255 ib. *Donshudde*, 1272 ib. *Duneshide*, 1279 ib. *Dunshud* (all (p)).

p. 135, *s.n.* RUMBEAM. Cf. Rumbeams Fm in Ewhurst (Sr), *Runbym* (sic) 1428, *Rumbemus* 1456, *Rumbeemes* 1524, *Romebemes* 1624 SrRS xxxi, 58.

p. 149, *s.n.* HIGHFURE. *furh, fyrh* is a common element in Surrey field-names, e.g. *Langefure* (1427 *Ct*) in Ash, *Thornyfere, -fure* (1338, c. 1450 *ChertseyB*) in Bookham, *Mershefure, Stokefure* in Cobham (1548 *LRMB*), *Bradvor, Wowever, le Middelfor* in East Clandon (c. 1350 Chertsey), *Middelver, Middelforesende* (ib.), *Medilfure, Langleyfure, Hatchesfure* in Egham (1548 *LRMB*), *Middelffur* in Fetcham (1279 Chertsey), *Thorinfur* in Kingston (1358 AD i), *Holefurh* in Kingston (1206 Cur). These forms, together with the elements compounded with them, such as *Thorny, Marsh, wowe* from OE *woh,* 'crooked,' show that the second element must be *furh*, meaning 'furrow' or 'ditch.'

p. 155, *s.n.* WANFORD BRIDGE. Add *Wanvorde* (water of, bridge of) 13th *Lewes Deeds, Waneford* bridge and water 1318 ib. The persistent *wan(e)*-forms are somewhat against derivation from OE *wæ(g)n*.

p. 180, *s.n.* THREAL'S FM. The difficult *threle* seems to be found again in *Threleland* in Limpsfield (Sr), 1312 *AOMB*.

p. 181, *s.n.* LAYBROOK FM. An earlier form for Lawbrook (Sr) is *Leybroke* (1314 *Rental*).

p. 185, *s.n.* BINES. In connection with this difficult name, Mr S. P. Vivian notes in a will of Simon Festynden (1473) in Hawkhurst, Kent 'lands and tenements...and the *Byngat*,' and in a Lamberhurst deed of 1459 we hear of 'a hall with all the chambers in it and a kitchen, barn and gardens and *les Byngates* in the same tenement.'

p. 190, *s.n.* POLES PITCH. The word *spic* is fairly common in Surrey. Cf. Fastbridge in Alfold, *Farnspiche* 1342 *Ass* (p), in which it is compounded with fearn, 'bracken.' Cf. also *Heyrespeche* in Alfold (1478 IpmR), *le Heth voc. Spytche* in Ash (1548 *LRMB*), *le Spytche* in Egham (ib.), *Berdespich, Burdispichis* in Frimley (1418 Chertsey), *croft voc. Spiche* in Horsell (1548 *LRMB*). As the sites of these places, except the first, cannot be identified, they do not help us in determining what was precisely the meaning of the term.

p. 200, *s.n.* PEN HILL. A further example of this word *pynd* is to be found in Pendell Court (Sr), the home of Gilbert de *la Pende* (1259 *Ass*), with later addition of *hyll*.

p. 201 and vol. ix, p. x, *s.n.* SOMPTING. Mr G. M. Young calls our attention to an interesting piece of evidence as to the meaning of *sunt*. In an extent of the manor of Somerford Keynes (Gl) taken in 1328 we have mention of a meadow called *Pillesmore* (Chan. Misc. Inq. File 108, no. 12), in an extent taken in 1364 of the same manor the same meadow is called *Pyllesunt* (Chan. IPM Ed 3 File 181). It is clear that *sunt* and *mor* are identical in meaning, both alike being used of marshy ground. Note further 'land called *Suntesland* in Salehurst' in a Survey of 1597 (S.P.V.).

p. 208, *s.n.* STUMBLEHOLM. For the word *stumble* in p.n.'s, cf. West Humble in Mickleham (Sr), *Wystumble* 1248 *Ass*.

p. 208, *s.n.* STUMBLEHOLM FM. A further example of this compound is to be found in Stumbleholt in Dorking (Sr), *Stombelhole* 1281 *Ct* (p).

p. 218, *s.n.* SHIPRODS FM. Cf. Shiprods Gill in Ockley (Sr), *Chyprode* 1448 *MinAcct*, *Shiproddes* 1619 SrAS x, 21.

p. 220, under Woodmancote parish. Add EATON THORN (sic) (6″), for which Miss M. S. Holgate gives us forms from the Parish Register (1668–71) *Heathen-thorne*, *Heathen Thorn House*. It is clear that the modern form is corrupt, and it may be that here, as in Heathens' Burial Corner (*infra* 236), we may have a name surviving from Saxon times.

p. 237, *s.n.* HORSEBROOK COTTAGE. The form *Hursbrok* found in the Godstow Register in a 13th century document, makes it clear that the first element is hyrst (M.S.H.).

VOL. VII

p. 258, *s.n.* HOMEWOOD HO. We may note further Home Wood in Lingfield (Sr), 1279 *Ass Homewode*.

p. 258, *s.n.* RICE BRIDGE. A further example of this name is found in Ridgebridge Hill in Wonersh (Sr), which must have been near the home of Gilbert de *la Risbrigge* (1259 *Ass*).

p. 269, *s.n.* TRUBWEEK. For a possible example of the element *trubbe* or *thrubbe*, cf. Thrubwell in Nempnett Thrubwell (So), *Trubewel* 1201 Ass, *Trubewelle* 1238 FF, *Trubwell*, *Trupwell* 1261 Ipm, *Trobbewelle* 1286 Ipm, *Threbwell* 1298 FF, *Trubwell* 1316 FA.

p. 272, *s.n.* PICKERIDGE. Add *Pykerythe* 1474 *Banco* (M.S.H.).

p. 283, *s.n.* TILTWOOD. Cf. Tilt Ho and Cobham Tilt in Cobham (Sr), *la Tilthe* 1492 Chertsey.

p. 286, *s.n.* MUDDLESWOOD. Miss Holgate notes for us that a Norfolk tenant on these lands of William de Warenne is not unlikely. Cf. Richard de *Norfolk* in the same roll (SRS x, 41).

p. 292, *s.n.* OLD STEINE. Cf. further *le Stene* 1605 *LRMB*, *The Steene*, *The Steane* 1624 *Rental* in Chertsey (Sr).

p. 329, *s.n.* PLAWHATCH. Add *play hatch gate*, *ployes zate* 1650 SAC xxiii.

p. 341, *s.n.* COSTELL'S WOOD. A further example of the compound *cotstedele* is found in *Cotstedele* in Dorking (Sr) (t. Hy 3 BM).

p. 363, *s.n.* SEAFORD. Dr H. P. South in her recent edition of the *Proverbs of Alfred*, pp. 25–42, shows that the name of the place of assembly of Alfred and his nobles, mentioned in the opening lines of the Proverbs is, on the uniform authority of MSS, other than the Jesus one, *Sifford(e)* (thrice), *Siforde* (once). This would seem to make impossible the identification of the place with Seaford. More probably it is Shefford in Berkshire. The old identification with Seaford did receive some support from the neighbourhood of Eastdean, which was long supposed to be the *dene* at which Alfred first met his biographer, but as that is now in all probability to be identified with East Dean near Chichester (PN Sx 47), Seaford and Eastdean can no longer be linked together by association with King Alfred.

p. 364, *s.n.* CHYNGTON. Cf. further the lost *Chinsole* or *Chinsale* in Egham (Sr), *Chynteshal*, *-i-* 1337, 1420 Chertsey.

pp. 391, 460, *s.nn.* THE ROCKS, STONEROCK GILL. Cf. Starrock Green in Chipstead (Sr), *Stonrocke* (1265 Misc (p)).

p. 392, *s.n.* VIEWS WOOD. Cf. The Whewes in Capel (Sr), *Weeves* 1576 SAS 33, 85, *Whewes* 1597 Ct.

p. 417, *s.n.* PLONK BARN. Cf. Plonks Hill in Wonersh (Sr), *Plonke* 1524, 1544 SR, *Plankes* 1684 SrRS xi, 352.

p. 460, *s.n.* COLDHARBOUR. Mr S. P. Vivian notes in a rental of 1659 that this is called *Gillreed otherwise Coldharbour*.

p. 460. Add MERRIMENT FM. Mr S. P. Vivian notes that this corresponds to the *pec. trē vocat. Meremannysland* in 1432 (HarlCh 78 E 50). The land is on the county boundary and *mereman* probably records the fact, *v.* (ge)mære. The modern form is corrupt.

p. 460, *s.n.* MARLPIT SHAW. This is by *Le Marlepit feld* (1629 *Ipm*) (S.P.V.).

p. 466, *s.n.* RUNTINGTON FM. Cf. Runtleywood in Woking (Sr), *Rontele* 1294 *Ass*, 1316 FF, *Runtele* 1332 SR (all (p)).

p. 517, *s.n.* HOUNSTER LANE. Mr G. M. Young points out that in the boundaries of Dauntsey (W), as given in BCS 458, the word *torr* must similarly refer to an out-crop of calcareous sandstone. It cannot have reference to a hill.

p. 559, l. 19. Professor Levett (*History*, xvi, 64), suggests that this means rather 'an endowment for purchasing the *panis benedictus*, the "holy bread" distributed after the mass,' than 'an endowment for providing the bread for the mass.'

VOL. VIII

p. xiii, ll. 3–4. It has been pointed out to us that part of the parish of Maker (Co), on the west side of the Tamar, had been included in Devon since 1086 (DB). It was transferred to Cornwall in 1844.

p. xiii, l. 8 from foot. For 'nearly 100 square miles' read 'more than 100 square miles.'

p. xxv, l. 11. Note also Shave Fm in Donyatt (So), the home in 1327 (SR) of John *atte Schaghe* and Shave Fm in Ilminster (So), the home in 1327 (SR) of *John atte Schaghe*.

p. lii, l. 11. For '15' read '18.'

p. 19, *s.n.* LUNDY ISLAND. Professor Bruce Dickins calls attention to the form *Lundeth*, found in two of the 'Four Maps of Great Britain' designed by Matthew Paris c. 1250. The form is an early one, but probably the *th* is an error for *y*.

pp. 23 and 24, *s.nn.* NORTHERNHAY and SOUTHERNHAY. Col. Webber points out to us that these should be described as lying to the north and south respectively of Eastgate, rather than to the north and south of the city walls.

p. 24, *s.n.* SMITH STREET. Col. Webber points out that the form should be SMYTHEN STREET instead of Smith Street.

p. 77, *s.n.* WELSFORD. Cf. Wellisford in Langford Budville (So), *Wilesforde* 1086 DB, *Welesforda* ib. (Exon), *Weleford* 1284 FA, *Welesford* 1303 ib., *Wellesford* 1298 FF, 1316 FA, 1327 SR.

p. 102, *s.n.* BIDNA. A further example of this lost OE element *byden* seems to be found in Beddlestead in Chelsham (Sr), 1241 *Ass Budenested*. Beddlestead lies in a deep hollow.

p. 161, *s.n.* KISMELDON. Cf. further Christmas Hill in Bishop's Itchington (Wa), *Cristemelhul* 1246 (Reg. Alb. Lichfield) (F.T.S.H.).

p. 184, *s.n.* BILLACOMBE. Cf. also *Bilrewell* in Southam (Wa), 1206 FF (F.T.S.H.).

p. 187, *s.n.* GALFORD. Cf. Gawbridge in Kingsbury (So), *Gavilbrig* 1235 FF, *Gavelbrigge* 1309 ib.

p. 241, *s.n.* MORICE TOWN. For 'Sir Charles Wise' read 'Sir Edward Wise.'

p. 249, *s.n.* PLASTER DOWN. Note further Pleystowe Fm in Capel (Sr), which appears in 1596 (SRS x) as *Plestore*.

p. 283, *s.n.* GNATTON. An early form *Gnardigneton* (c. 1200) is found in a charter printed in Coll. Top. et Gen. viii, 35. This is probably for *Cœnheardingtūn*, 'Cenheard's farm,' cf. ingtun. It is clear that the name has no connection with the common *gnat*.

p. 326, *s.n.* ROLSTER. A further example of this compound is *Rostwode* (1312 *AOMB*) in Limpsfield (Sr).

Add MS 15761 at the BM is a rental of various manors in the counties of Devon, Cornwall and Somerset belonging to Thomas Ormonde, subsequently seventh Earl of Ormonde. The date of the MS is 1478. It supplies a certain number of forms for Devon names either not recorded in the volumes on that county or else insufficiently documented. The additional information is set forth below with the page references for the names in question.

VOL. VIII

p. 82. DELLEY and DELWORTHY. *Delegh, Deleworthy.*
p. 82. WARD. *Est-, West-, Southwarde.*
p. 83. CULVERWELL, STEEPHILL. *Culverwill, Stepwyll.*
p. 83. To minor names add: HOARHOUSE BRIDGE, HOLLICK and VERNON WOOD (all 6″), *Horehous, Est-, Westhollok, Fernham, v.* fearn, ham(m).
p. 96. BEARE HO. *Berhouse.*
pp. 96–97. HOLE, LANGDON. *Hoole, Langedon, v.* holh, dun.
p. 97. To minor names add: KNOWLE, NETHERCLEAVE and YEO FM (all 6″), *Knolle, Nydeclif, Estyeo, v.* cnoll. NETHERCLEAVE lies below a steep slope, cf. Nethercleave in Chittlehampton (vol. ix, p. 359). YEO lies east of the river Yeo (vol. viii, p. 17).
p. 101. Add RIDD COPSE and YEOLDON COPSE (both 6″). *Rydd, Rydmore, piscar de Rydd, Yoldon.* The former may possibly be connected with Brit. *rito-,* 'ford,' Welsh *rhyd.* The latter is probably 'old down' (*v.* vol. viii, Addenda lviii).
p. 117. VENN and SOUTH YEO. *Venhouse, Southyeo.*
p. 135. Add HELE. *Hele, Southhele, v.* healh.
p. 153. BUTTERMOOR. *Botirmore.*
p. 162. WEDFIELD and NORTH WORTHEN. *Wydfyld, Northworthyn.*

VOL. IX

p. 371. Add ESSINGTON. *Estynton in Northtauton.*
p. 380. RUCKHAM. *Rokcombe.*
p. 381. Add TITHING HO (6″), cf. *Tethynglande.*
p. 384. KIPSCOTT. *Kippescote.*
p. 385. Add YEO FM. *Yeo.* It is on an undocumented river Yeo (*v.* vol. viii, p. 17).
p. 415. Add PARK. *Parke.*
p. 415. PENHAY. *Pennehay.*
p. 434. BIGPORT. *Bykeport.*
p. 435. Add HOLELAND (6″). *Hole. v.* holh.

VOL. IX

p. ix, l. 28. For '248' read '247.'
p. 335, *s.n.* CHERRICOMBE. The Rev. J. B. Johnston calls attention to the possible parallel of Chirk (Denbighshire) on the R. *Ceiriog.* In his *PN of England and Wales, s.n.,* he suggests that Chirk is a corruption of the Welsh river-name, and Ekwall makes the same suggestion (RN 72).
p. 358, *s.n.* LITTLE SILVER. Cf. Silverton *infra* 569 (J.B.J.).
p. 380, *s.n.* GOGLAND. Cf. Gogmore in Chertsey (Sr), *Goghemereslane* t. Hy 3.

p. 399, *s.n.* CANNINGTON. Mr J. Benson calls our attention to the true history of this name. It is the last relic of the reputed manor of Witheridge-Cannington, being part of the lands of the dissolved Priory of Cannington in Somerset granted to Lewis Stucley by Henry VIII. The name is therefore manorial in origin.

p. 399, *s.n.* PULLEN'S ROW. Mr J. Benson informs us that this name is of 19th century origin, from a family named *Pullen*.

p. 416, under Poughill. Add NORTH YEO (6″) *Northyea* 1431 *Cl* (A. C. W.). North and South Yeo are by the stream called Holly Water. *v.* Yeo, p. 18.

p. 420, *s.n.* PILEMOOR. The Rev. J. B. Johnston notes the Scottish parallels Pilmore near St Andrews (1296 *Pylemore*), and Pillmuir near Coldingham (1296 *Pylmor*).

p. 429, *s.n.* TREABLE. The Rev. J. B. Johnston would take this to contain the significant British word corresponding to OBrit *ebol*, Welsh *ebawl*, 'colt, foal,' rather than the pers. name derivative *Ebell*. Hence 'house of the foal or colt.'

p. 448, *s.n.* CAWSAND. Cf. Coscombe in Stanway (Gl), *Costicumb* 1248, 1287 *Ass*, *Costecumbe* 1287 *Ass* (F.T.S.H.).

p. 457, *s.n.* VOGHAY. The Rev. J. B. Johnston notes the p.n. Fogo in Duns, Berwickshire, c. 1150 *Fogghou*.

p. 464, *s.n.* CHULEY. For '319' read '219' (J.B.J.).

p. 468, *s.n.* SOLDRIDGE. For Solridge (Ha) read 'Soldridge (Ha).'

p. 482, *s.n.* GRIMSPOUND. Cf. also *fossata q.v. Grimesdich* (1248 *Ass*) in Mickleham (Sr).

p. 488, *s.n.* LUTON. For '1292 Ch' read '1292 Ipm' (*ex inf.* Mr R. L. Atkinson).

p. 507, *s.n.* BOOHAY. For '*Lydewicheston* 1276' read '*Lydewicheton* 1276' (*ex inf.* Mr R. L. Atkinson).

p. 515, *s.n.* WHILBOROUGH. Add the OE form *hweogol* (J.B.J.).

p. 541, *s.n.* TIVERTON. Add DB *Tuuertone* as given in Johnston *PN of England and Wales*, *s.n.*

p. 542, *s.n.* COVE. A possible further use of OE *cofa* is to be found in the OE form *Rumcofa*(n) (ASC *s.a.* 915) for Runcorn (J.B.J.).

p. 551, *s.n.* BACKSWOOD. Add *Baddekesworth* 1242 Fees, showing that this is a compound of a pers. name *Beadoc* (cf. the weak *Beadaca*, *Beaduca*) and worþ.

pp. 585–6, *s.n.* MARSH BARTON. Mr A. H. Gibbs points out that Marsh Barton can have no association with *Hunts marshes alias Saltemarshes*, as that is part of Courtbrook Fm on the other side of the hill.

p. 586, *s.n.* WINSLADE HO. Mr A. H. Gibbs points out to us that the original site of Winslade Ho was 400 yards away from the present house, in the parish of Clyst St George.

p. 597, *s.n.* SYNDERBOROUGH. The first element should perhaps be explained as in Sunderleigh *supra* 532 (J.B.J.).

p. 661, *s.v.* dæl. Add 'Dalwood (?).'

p. 674. The list of Celtic names given here does not include the large number of Celtic river-names set forth on pp. 1–18 (Part I). To the Celtic names other than river-names should probably be added Nymet. To hybrid names should be added Blannicombe(?) and Nympton.

VOL. X

p. 7, *s.n.* MAYORHOLD. It is suggested in the Borough Records (ii, 16) that *Marehold* may have been the place where the mares were secured, while the horses were kept in the Horsemarket.

p. 9. The exact site of the meeting-place has been determined by Miss Joan Wake with the aid of maps placed at her disposal by the Rev. Sir Henry Knightley of Fawsley. It is marked by a circle on an estate map of 1865. The Knob is at the end of a high ridge running from the corner of Badby Wood to the junction of the three parishes of Fawsley, Badby and Everdon and is in land still common to Newnham and Badby parishes. The Knob is 150 yds. from that junction, at the highest point of the ridge. There is a shallow depression round the clump. The beech-tree is itself marked on a map of 1741.

p. 20, *s.n.* DRAYTON. Ekwall (*Germanska Namnstudier tillägnade Evald Liden* 46–70) discusses the Drayton names very fully and distinguishes two main uses of *dray*, (i) of a place where there is portage or the like for taking boats by a short passage from one stream to another, (ii) of a place where there is a steep road or the like necessitating a good draw or pull. He points out that this Drayton is on a steep slope on an important road. He interprets Drayton in Lowick in similar fashion, though the topography is not quite so clear.

p. 81, *s.n.* HOPPING HILL. Mr Williamson provides an early parallel from Db in the forms (t. Hy 3) *Hopynges, le Hoping* for a field in Seal (Db).

p. 93, *s.n.* TIFFIELD. Professor Tait notes 'In Soest (c. 1130) there were *Burrichter* who held their court "in *viculis* illis qui dicuntur *tig*" or "in *conventionalibus* suis quod (sic) *thy* dicitur"' (Keutgen, *Ursprung der deutschen Stadtverfassung* 223).

p. 112, *s.n.* DRAUGHTON. Ekwall, in the paper referred to *s.n.* Drayton *supra*, deals with Draughton, and suggests that this may well be a *dræg*-name, the reference being to the steep hill here. See more fully *op. cit.* 54, 64.

p. 224, *s.n.* PETERBOROUGH. Professor Bruce Dickins notes the name *Gildene burh*, 'golden burh,' given to Peterborough from its rich endowments (ASC (E) *s.a.* 1052).

p. 227, *s.n.* NEWARK. Professor Bruce Dickins notes that the first form may be Scandinavian, from OWScand *nývirki*, rather than English *niwe(ge)weorc*.

p. 276, *s.n.* NEWNHAM. Add Scotch Thorn (*Scottesthorn* 1403 XtCh).

p. 277, *s.n.* NADDOCKS. Dr Schram notes fields called *Nattoks, le Nattocks, Nattokks* in 15th century terriers of Gaywood and Wootton (Nf), and still surviving in field-names *Nattocks* in those parishes. Mr Bradfer-Lawrence tells him that they are names given to little patches of higher ground in the marshes, partly of natural, partly of artificial formation.

p. 285. Under Hardingstone parish add: Flex Pool and Thatchmeadow (1752 Terrier) go back to *Flexpoll* and *Tacheholm* (13th NthStA).

NORTHAMPTONSHIRE

The earliest reference to the shire by name is *Hamtunscir* 11th ASC (C) *s.a.* 1011, *Hamtonascira* 11th (13th) *PeterbA*, *Norðhamtunscir* 12th ASC (H) *s.a.* 1114. See further Introd. xviii–xix.

FOREST-NAMES

Cliffe Forest

foresta de Clive 1198 Fees *et passim* to 1382 Cl with variant spellings *Cliva, Clyve, Clyva, forest of Clifbailly* 1378 Cl

This was originally a part of Rockingham Forest, taking its name from King's Cliffe *infra* 199. *Clifbailly* contains the obsolete *baillie*, 'district under the jurisdiction of a *bailiff* or *bailie*,' here a sub-division of the forest. Cf. *bailliva de Wakefeld infra* 105.

Rockingham Forest

foresta de Rochingeham 1157 P, with a similar run of early spellings to Rockingham *infra* 171, from which it takes its name.

Salcey Forest[1]

bosco de Sasceya 1206 ClR
bosco de Salceto 1212 ClR *et passim* to 1301 Cl, *-ta* 1222, 1226, *Saliceto* 1227 ClR, 1231 Cl, *Salseto* 1248 Cl
Saucey 1213 ClR *et passim* to 1391 Cl (with variant spellings *Sauceya, Saucee, Sause(e), Sausse, Sausce, Sausy, Sausey, Saucy), Sawcey* 1541 Statutes
la Sauceia c. 1220 *For, la Saucey* 1231 Cl, *la Sauce* 1244, 1299 Cl, *la Sause* 1322 Cl
(la) Salcey 1229, 1258 Cl, *Salsey* 1275 Cl, *Salce* 1344 Cl
Sacy 1622 Drayton, 1712 Morton

Salcey [sɑ·si] is from OFr *salceie, sauceie*, late Latin **salicētum*, a derivative of *salix*, 'willow.' The original meaning would have been 'willow wood,' 'place abounding in willows.'

[1] Partly in Bucks.

Whittlewood Forest

Whitlewuda t. Hy 1 Dugd iv, 348, *Wytlewod* t. Hy 2 (1383) Pat, *Witlewude* 1196 P, *With(e)lewode, -wude* 1203–18 BM, c. 1220 *For*

For this name cf. Whittlebury *infra* 45.

RIVER-NAMES AND WATERCOURSES

AVON. The only early reference to this river (commonly known as the Warwickshire Avon), noted in a Northamptonshire document is *aqua de Avene* (1261 *Ass*, Welford context). The earliest spellings given by Ekwall (RN 22) are *Afen* 704–9 (12th), *Afene* 780 (11th) BCS 123, 235. The meaning is simply 'river' (OBrit *abonā*, W *afon*).

CAT'S WATER is *Cattewater, Catteswater, le Cateswater* 1504 *Compotus, Cat Water* 1712 Morton. The forms are too late for any suggestion to be worth much. It is the name of a dyke forming the boundary between Northamptonshire and Cambridgeshire. The persistence of the possessive *Cattes-* suggests that the dyke may take its name from its sometime owner.

CHERWELL

Forms found in Northamptonshire documents are:
Ceruelle 681 (c. 1200) BCS 57
(*to*) *Cear wyllun* 944 BCS 792
Charewell(e) 1247, 1253 *Ass*, 1279 Pat, 1326 Ipm
Charwell(e) 1285 *Ass*, 1299 Cl, 1325 Ipm, 1345 Abbr
Charlewell 1615 *Recov*

Other OE spellings given by Ekwall (RN 75) are: *Cearwellan* 864 (11th) BCS 509, 929 (11th) ib. 666, (*to*) *Cearwyllan* 904 (11th) BCS 607, (*on*) *Cearewyllan* 955 (c. 1200) BCS 906, *Cere willam stream* 1004 (13th) St Frides, *Cearwylle, Cyrwylle* 1005 (c. 1200) Eynsham. The origin of the first part of this river-name is entirely uncertain. For a full discussion *v.* Ekwall *loc. cit.* The second part of the name is clearly OE **wielle**, 'stream.'

HARPERS BROOK (Nene)

(*le*) *Harperesbrok* t. Steph *PipewellB*, t. Ed 3 *For*, *-ris-* t. Ed 1 *PeterbB, -broc* c. 1270 Gerv, *Hareperisbroc* c. 1250 *PipewellB* *le Harperbrok* 1294 *Ass*

'Brook of the harper' (OE *hearpere*), or 'of a man named *Harper*.'

Ise (Nene)

(*andlang*) *ysan* 956 (c. 1200) BCS 943
Yse c. 1270 Gerv, 1292 *Compotus*
Ise t. Ed 1 *PeterbB*, 1285, 1330 *Ass*, 1610, 1611 *Depositions*
Use c. 1540 Leland

Ekwall (RN 214) takes the *y* in the OE form to be original, though the evidence is not decisive, and derives it from an original *Usion, a mutated derivative of the river-name Ouse. If the original vowel was *i*, we should probably link this river-name with the numerous river-names in *Is-* recorded by Förstemann (ON i, 1592 ff.). The river is called *aqua de Wicle* in 1247 (*Ass*) from Weekley *infra* 173.

Nene [nen]

Forms found in Northamptonshire documents are as follows:
Nyn 948, c. 960 (c. 1200) BCS 871, 1129
Nen 12th ASC (E) *s.a.* 963, 1228 Cl, 13th *PeterbA*, 1247 *Ass*,
  Nén c. 1000 Saints
Nien 1206 Ch
Nene 1244 Ramsey *et freq* to 1327 Ipm, *Nena* 1247 *Ass*
Neene 1330 QW, 1631 NRS i
Ene 1357 Ipm
Nine 1702 *Recov*

No satisfactory explanation of this name can be offered. For a full discussion *v.* Ekwall, RN 299.

Ouse

Forms found in Northamptonshire documents are:
Ouse t. Ed 1 *PeterbB*, 1287 *For*, 1377 IpmR
(*the*) *Use* 1277, 1278 Ipm

The earliest spellings given by Ekwall (RN 313) are (*on*) *Usan* 880 (c. 1125) Laws, *Wusan* 905 ASC (A), *Wúsan* 905 (c. 1100) ASC (D), *Úsan* c. 1025 Saints, *Usan* 1010 (1121) ASC (E), *Use* 937 (c. 1200) KCD 621.
For a discussion of this name, *v.* Ekwall, RN 315 ff.

TOVE (Ouse) is *Toue* 1219 *FF*, 1220 ClR, *Tove brok* 1437 *Easton Neston*, *Tea* 1622 Drayton, cf. also *Towe lane* 1609 *LRMB* and Towcester *infra* 94. Ekwall (RN 414) takes this to be a river-name of Germanic origin from a lost **tof*, 'dilatory' and to have reference to its winding course. For a possible earlier Celtic name of the river cf. Towcester *infra* 94.

WELLAND

Forms in Northamptonshire documents are as follows:
Uueolod c. 1000 Ethelweard, *Weolud* 921 (10th) ASC (A)
Weiland 1206 *FF*, *Weylaund* t. Ed 1 *PeterbB*, -*launt* 1285 *Ass*,
   -*lond* 1330 *Ass*, *Wailand* 1394 Cl
Welond 1247 *FF*, *Ass*, 1275 RH, 1298 Ipm, *Weland* 1247 *Ass*,
   1352 Ipm
Wyland t. Ed 1 *PeterbB*
Wellond 1352 Ipm
Wolland 1609 *Recov*

For a discussion of this river-name, *v.* Ekwall, RN 445.

WHILTON BROOK (6") is *Wheltonbroc* 13th *NthStJ*, *v.* Whilton *infra* 89.

WILLOW BROOK (Nene) is *The Willowbrook* 1791 Bridges, *Willow Brook* 1826 G. Earlier spellings are provided by Willy-brook Hundred *infra* 198. 'Willow brook.'

ROAD-NAMES

BEDFORD WAY. In a forest perambulation of the county (1228 Cl), the bounds are said to include all the west side of Market Har-borough bridge "according as the road called *Bedeford Weye* goes to Arthingworth bridge and then by the same road to the cross which stands on the bounds of Harrington and Kelmarsh and so by the same road to the watercourse which comes down between Maidwell and Draughton." Half a mile east of Market Harborough bridge an old track runs direct to Arthingworth bridge, three miles to the south. Thence it goes south for a mile along a road and then again continues for a mile as a foot-path to a small stream which still divides Draughton from Maidwell. After that it links on with the main Northampton road through

Lamport. This is doubtless 'Bedford Way,' so called because it ultimately leads to that town.

CAR DIKE is *Karisdik, Karesdik*, 1245 *PeterbB, Carisdick* c. 1340 *CártN, Caresdyke* c. 1500 *Pytchley, Car Dyke* or *Caer Dike* (sic) 1712 Morton. This, as Professor Ekwall points out, is probably a continuation of the Car Dike in South Lincs, visible near Timberland, at Sleaford, and at Bourne. For this we have forms *Karesdik* (12th Dane) and *Karedic* (*Thurgarton* 107 b). These forms point to a Scand. pers. name *Kárr*, the name of a settler who at one time had something to do with this ancient dyke. The early forms with persistent *a* and almost universal genitival *s* forbid our connecting this name with ME *kerre*, 'marsh' (*v*. kjarr).

WATLING STREET

Forms found in Northamptonshire documents are as follows:

Wæclinga stræt 944 BCS 792
Watlingestret(e) 1202 Ass, n.d. AD iii
Watlingstret 1275 RH, *Watlyngstrete* 1285 Ass
Wattelynstrete 1398 AD iv, 1420 AD iii

For further forms and for a discussion of the name *v*. PN BedsHu 5 ff. In the Denshanger charter it would seem to be called *stan-weg, v. infra* 101 n.

We have reference to *the Portwey* in Easton Neston (c. 1226 AD i), *Portweye* in Brixworth (1216 *NthStA*), *le Portewey, le Portestrete* in Welford (1439 HMC iii App x), *Portweie* in Winwick (1225 *FF*), *le Portweie* in Yelvertoft (1416 AD iii), *Portwei* in Eydon (c. 1200 *Ashby*), *Portwey* in Everdon (1240 *FF*) (cf. *portstræt infra* 26 n.), which is probably the Portway from Woodford to Preston Capes of which Bridges speaks (i, 130), and there is still a track called Portway which runs from the north of Aynho through Walton Grounds Fm. This may be the *Portwey* in Evenley (t. Hy 8 *Rental*).

We have mention of salt-roads in *Sealt-stræt* in Everdon (BCS 792), *Salterestrete* in Rothwell (1330 *Ass*), *Saltwei* in Boughton (c. 1250 AD ii), *Saltweie* in Braunston (1294 AD iii), *Saltergate* in Easton on the Hill (1440 AD ii), *Salteresgate* and *Salteresforde* in Oakley (13th *PipewellA*), *Saltwey* in Quinton

(14th *NthStA*), *Saltstrete* in Evenley (c. 1210 *Magd*). See also Salter's Wood *infra* 233–4.

Examples of 'ridge-way' are as follows: *Ryggewey* in Easton Neston (t. Hy 3 AD ii), *Rugwey* in Boughton (c. 1242 AD ii), *Rigweye* in West Haddon (c. 1260), *le Rigweye* in Helmdon (1457 *Magd*), *Rugweye* in Greatworth (1271 *FF*), *Rigeway* in Addington (1232 WellsR), *Rigeway* in Chalcombe (n.d. AD ii), *Ruggewey* in Brackley (1258 *Magd*). These are not necessarily ridge-roads; they are sometimes only ridge-paths between fields. In 1150 we have mention of *le Ferdeweye*, i.e. 'army-road' (from OE *fyrd*), in Wilbarston.

The importance of Northampton in the medieval road-system is illustrated by the numerous examples of *Hamtune-weie* in early documents, by *Hamtunegate*, i.e. Hampton-road, in Bray-brooke (1199 FF), by *Hantuneford* in Welford (c. 1190 *Add*), still more by *regia strata de Norhamtun* in the bounds of Adlestrop in Gloucestershire (KCD 1367), called also *cynges ferdstræte* in the bounds of Daylesford (in Worcestershire) (KCD 623).

We have also a *Fisshewey*[1] in Evenley (t. Hy 8 *Rental*), a *Bere-strete*, i.e. 'corn street' (cf. Barford PN BedsHu 50), and *Berewei* in Boughton (c. 1250 AD iii).

No early references by name to Banbury Lane, Oxford Lane, or Welsh Road, earlier *Welch Way*, have been found.

Northampton

NORTHAMPTON 83 C 12

Hamtun 10th ASC (Ā) *s.a.* 917, 12th ASC (E) *s.a.* 1140
Norðhamtun 12th ASC (C) *s.a.* 1065, *Norhthamtun* ASC (E)
s.a. 1122, *Norhamptoun* c. 1300 *Harl* 2253

The *north* appears in all subsequent records except *Hamtona* 1219 Fees. One might quote forms from the long series of *Hamtun*-coins, but it is still uncertain whether these should be referred to Northampton or to Southampton. For this name *v.* Introd. xix.

---

[1] For an early reference to the carrying of salt and fish across Northamptonshire see the Assize Roll of 1202 (NRS v, 10 and Introd. xxiii).

NORTHAMPTON STREET-NAMES

NOTE. The following are the chief street-names: ABINGTON ST is *Abindonstrete* 14th *NthStʒ*, *Abyndon Strete* 1304 AD i, leading to Abington (*infra* 132). ANGEL LANE takes its name from an inn of that name (1504 BorRec); earlier *Knyghtstrete* 1499 AD v, *v.* cniht. BEARWARD ST is *Berewardstrete* 1281 Ch, 1330 *Ass*, (*le*) 1316 HMC xv, 10, *le Bere-wardes Strete* 1323 H de B, *le Berwardstrete* 1324 AD ii, *le Berewood strete* 1540 *LRMB*, taking its name from the 'bear ward' or 'keeper of performing bears,' a common sight in the Middle Ages. BRIDGE ST is *Bryggestede* (sic) 1323 Pat, *Briggestrete* 1330 *Ass*, 1332 Pat, *Bruggestrete* 1350 Cl, *Brygystrete* 1499 Ipm, so called because it led to the bridge over the Nene. BROAD ST was earlier *vicum Sci Martini* 1274 RH, *strata Sci Martini* 1330 *Ass*, *Seintmartynstrete* 1444 BorRec, from a chapel which formerly stood here, dedicated to St Martin. CASTLE ST is (*in*) *vico Castelli* 14th *NthStʒ*, *Castle Strete* 1545 LP, from the old castle of Northampton, now demolished. COLLEGE ST is *le Collegelane* 1458 AD iv, from the house of the collegiate clergy of All Saints, founded in the 14th century. DERNGATE is *Dernegate* 1274 RH, *Durne-gate* 1330 *Ass*, *Derneyathe* 14th *NthStʒ*, *le Derne yate* 1540 *LRMB*. It was originally the name of one of the town gates, the first element being apparently the OE *dierne*, 'secret, hidden,' but the origin of the epithet is obscure. The earlier name of the *street* was *Swynewellestrete* 1274 RH, *Swinewelstrete* 1393 IpmR, from a spring called *Swinewelle juxta Derneyathe* 13th *NthStA*. DRAPERY is *Draperia* 1330 *Ass*, *Olde Drapery* 1486–93 ECP, *le Draperye* 1540 *LRMB*. *Drapery*, 'a place where cloth is made,' is on record from 1483 (NED). GOLD ST is (*le*) *Goldestrete* 1330 *Ass*, 14th *NthStʒ*, *Golestrete* 1416 Cl, from the goldsmiths who had shops on the east side (BorRec). THE GUT is *le Guttes* (1545 LP) and runs from Conduit St to Drum Lane. HORSE MARKET is *Horsemarkett* 1545 LP. KINGSWELL ST is *Kyngeswellestrete* 1444 BorRec, *Kyngeswelle lane* 1540 *LRMB*. MAYORHOLD is *le Marehole* 1545 LP. MARKET SQUARE is *le Marketplace* 1444 BorRec. MERCERS ROW is *Mercers Rowe* 1486–93 ECP, 1545 LP, from *mercer*, 'a dealer in silks and velvets.' MILL LANE is *Milnelane* 1330 *Ass*. NEWLAND is *the Newlond* 1318 Deeds Enrolled, *le Newlond* 1418 Inq aqd, *le Newlond strete* 1540 *LRMB*, perhaps because the site was built on after the establishment of the neighbouring house of the Grey Friars in 1245 (BorRec). ST GILES ST is *Seint Gilestrete* 1444 BorRec, *Seynt Jyles strete* 1499 AD v, from the dedication of the adjacent church. SCARLETWELL ST is *Scarletstrete* 1458 AD iv. SHEEP ST is *Shepes Markett* 1540 *LRMB*, *le Shepes Markett* 1545 LP. SWAN LANE was earlier *Cowelane* 1414 Cl. TANNER ST is *Tanners strete* 1540 *LRMB*, 1545 LP. WOOLMONGER ST is *Wellemongerestrete* 1330 *Ass*, *Welmongerstrett* 1540 *LRMB*, -*strete* 1545 LP, *Wolmonger streate* 1550 Pat, presumably from the wool-dealers who resided here.

Lost street-names of interest are: *Barkerstrete* 1540 *LRMB*, from the *barkers* or tanners; *le Bocher rowe* 1540 ib., *Bowcher Rowe* 1545 LP, *le Bocherie* 1549 Pat, a part of the Market Square where the butchers congregated; *Bowlane* 1540 *LRMB*, cf. Bow Lane, London; *le Bryd-strett* 1540 ib.; *Buge Rowe* 1545 LP from the makers of budge fur, cf. Budge Row (London), *Bogerowe* 1356, 1372 Cal. of Wills in Hustings Court; *the Checker* 1570 BorRec; *Crakebelle strete* 1266 Pat, *Krakebollestr* (sic) 1274 RH, *Crakebellestrete* 1330 *Ass*, *Crakebolt Strete* 1545 LP, a continuation of the present Fetter Lane; *Dedemanes Twichene* 1247 *Ass* and *Laurencestwichin* 1330 *Ass*, containing the OE *twicene*, 'crossways'; *Derne Lane* 1545 LP, i.e. 'the hidden or secret lane,' cf. Derngate *supra* 7; *Felterstrett* 1540 *LRMB*, where the workers in felt lived; *Flesshemonggerstrete* 1458 AD iv, possibly an alternative name for Butcher Row *supra* 7; *Groppecuntelane* 1274 RH, *Gropecontelane* 1325 AD vi, a common medieval street-name; *Gyselgot* 1274 RH, a way under the wall on the east side of the town, probably containing the word *gote*, 'water channel'; *le Mattrowe* 1337 AD ii; *le Malte Rowe* 1540 *LRMB*; *Musterstrett* 1540 ib.; *Nete Markett* 1540 ib., *Netesmarkett* 1545 LP, where the *neat* or cattle were sold; *le Smerekerneresrowe* 1353, 1367 AD ii, possibly from ON *smjǫr*, 'butter' and *kerner*, a Scandinavian form for 'churner,' cf. Nicholas *le Smerekernere* t. Ed 3 *SR* (Warkworth); *Spicersrowe* 1414 Cl; *le Strawechepyng* 13th *NthStA*, i.e. 'straw market'; *Taynt yarde* 1540 *LRMB*, i.e. (probably) 'dyers' yard'; *le Tenter Yarde* 1540 ib., i.e. 'yard where cloth is stretched on *tenters*.'

COTTON MILLS was earlier known as *Molendinum Meruini de North* 12th *NthStA*, *Merthenesmylnedam* 1275 RH, *Mervenesmelle* 1395 Cl, *Mervylesmylne* 1404 *Ass*, *Marvells Mills al. Marvelous Mills* t. Eliz ChancP. It is uncertain whether *Marlyns Myll* 1540 *LRMB*, *Marlyns Mille* 1545 LP refer to the same place or not. *Mervin* was clearly the one-time owner of the mill but nothing further is known of him. For other refs. *v.* Farrer, *Honors and Knights, Fees* i, 114–15.

KINGSLEY PARK is possibly identical with *Kingeshala* 1175 BM, *pratum de Kyngeshala* t. Hy 2 (1325) Ch, *meadow of Kyngeshale* 1334 Ipm, *Kyngessale* 1349 Ipm, *v.* healh, hence 'king's nook.' It lay within the manor of Kingsthorpe (*infra* 133).

ST JAMES END is *Brodende Sci Jacobi* 1285 *Ass*, *Seyntiamesende* 1381 *Ass*, *Sent Jamysende* 1414 AD iv, from the old monastery of St James.

ST JAMES END MILLS is *Saint Jeames Mills al. Samwell Mills* 1595 DKR xxxviii. The second name is from the Samwell family of Upton.

I. FAWSLEY HUNDRED

This appears first as *Falewelhundredo* in 1193 P, *v.* Fawsley *infra* 23. It was formed by the union of the two earlier hundreds of *Gravesend(e)* a. 1076 Geld Roll, 1086 DB, 1185, 1189 P, *Graveshende Falewesle* 12th Survey, and *Egelweardesle* a. 1076 Geld Roll, *Alwardeslea, Aluratlea* 1086 DB, *Ailwardeslea* 1189, 1191 P, *Aylwoldesle* 12th Survey. Neither of these names has survived. The former means 'at the grove's end,' *v.* grafa, the latter 'leah of *Aeþelweard* or, less probably, of *Ægelweard*,' a pers. name not on record, but of which both elements occur and which has given the later surname *Aylward*. According to Morton (397) the *Hundred*-court was at one time held under a beech called *Mangrave* in Fawsley Park, which may preserve a trace of the old name of *Gravesende* hundred. Cf. *Mangrove* Knob in the Everdon Enclosure Award (1765), which suggests that the meeting-place was near the Fawsley-Everdon boundary, at the highest point of the road which now divides the parishes. Mangrove is probably a compound of OE *(ge)mǣne*, 'common' and graf, hence 'common grove.' For such a hundred meeting-place name cf. Manhood (PN Sx 79), *v.* Addenda lii.

Ashby St Ledgers

ASHBY ST LEDGERS 73 J 6

> *Ascebi* 1086 DB, *Assebi* late Hy 2 BM, *-by* 1268 Ch, *Aissebi* 1189–95 *AD*
>
> *Essebi* 12th Survey *et freq* to 1258–63 Ipm, *Esseby Sancti Leodegarii* c. 1230 WellsR, (*Cranford*) 1242 Fees, *-bi* 1266 FF, 1304 AD iv, (*Liger*) 1298 Ipm, (*Leger*) 1316 AD iv, *Esscheby St Legers* 1322 AD v
>
> *As(s)heby Leger* 1316 FA, 1339 AD iv, *Assheby Liger* 1328 AD iv, *Asschby Legier* 1330 FA, *Ligeresassheby* 1385 *FF*, *Asschebylegger* 1427 AD iv, *Legarsasheby* 1538 AD iii, *Leogiers Asheby* 1543 AD iii, *Ashby Leagers* 1568 AD iii.

'Ash-tree village,' *v.* æsc, by. For the history of the *Ashby*-names in this county *v.* Introd. xxii–xxiii. The dedication of the church is to St Leger (*Leodegar*). John de *Cranford* had a holding here in 1242.

Foxholes is *Foxoles* 1359 AD iv.   Grove Fm is *Ashby Grove* 1823 B.

Badby

Badby[1] 83 C 6

> *baddan byrig, baddan by* 944 BCS 792
> *Badebi* 1020 (14th) KCD 1316, 1086 DB, 1166 P, *-by* 1252, 1314 Cl
> *Baddeby* 12th Survey, 1166 P (CR) *et freq* to 1475 AD iii
> *Badby* 1316 FA, 1393 Cl

[1] BCS 792 is an original charter of date 944, making a grant of 30 hides at Badby, Dodford and Everdon to Bishop Aelfric. The boundaries as set forth are stated to be those of the three places named. They begin to the north-west of Badby at the little cloven hill and go straight north from that hill to the *wearge dun* between the two little hills. The 'cloven' hill is probably the prominent isolated hill known as Studborough Hill just to the west of the Badby-Staverton boundary, with its much broken slopes. From there the present boundary goes straight north in a slightly zig-zag course to Big Hill, the extreme north-west corner of Badby Parish. Big Hill is almost certainly the *wearge dun* or felons' hill (*Warwedon* in a rental t. Ric 2). It is a prominent landmark. Moreover, Bridges (i, 19) mentions four hills in Badby, of which two, named in succession, are *Little-hill* and *Warriton-hill*. The latter is clearly *wearge dun*, and as it was adjacent to a hill once called Little-hill, probably came to be called Big-hill in contrast (cf. *infra* 13). *wearge dun* was probably applied to the whole hill (as Big Hill is to-day), and the two little hills may be the two areas on the summit, marked by the 700 ft. contours, between which the boundary still runs. The boundary is next (? *þæt* for *þa*) said to run north along the little *dic* at the end of the grove to the small thorns, then from the thorns up on to the middle of the little down, and then from the down east to the east of Fox Hill (*infra* 13). There would seem to have been some slight alteration of boundaries at the north-west corner, but the deflection must have been very slight, for it is almost certain that the old bounds, like the present ones, took the line of the crest here, travelling due east, with a few zig-zags, to the point where they join the bounds of Newnham, east of Fox Hill. (The deflection may perhaps be accounted for by the statement at this point that the king granted to Aelfwine and Beorhtulf the *leah* and the *hamm* to the north of the little *dic*.) The next points are, from the north of Fox Hill to the hollow road, thence to hind-leap, from the hind-leap to the spring at the top of the clearing, from the spring to the hart's wallowing-place, from the hart's wallowing-place due north to the hill, from the hill straight to the *leah*, then past the *leah* to the head of the *widig*-stream, and from the stream due north to the thorny hill on a level with the gate of the old *burh* (and then east). We had reached the point north-east of Fox Hill, where the bounds of Badby and Daventry and Newnham meet. The hollow-road is the old Newnham-Daventry road which makes its way over Newnham Hill in a slight hollow; the hind-leap is clearly the very steep slope just west of the road where the hill falls abruptly from its highest point (marked by a ruined windmill). Just over the crest of the hill the boundary leaves the road and travels due east along the ridge, and just on the south side of it is a large spring. This is clearly

the spring at the top of the clearing. The hart's wallowing-place would seem to have been in the slight hollow near the point where the boundary takes a southward turn. It goes downhill and begins to rise just by the Weedon-Daventry road. Here it turns east and runs to the head of a tiny stream. Then it turns again north uphill to Burntwalls Fm which is in a straight line with Borough Hill Camp further up the hill—the camp being the *burh*. Thence we go east to the boundary-*pytt* and from there to the stone by the stream to the north of Mazedale (*infra* 27). The first part of this stretch of boundary is included also in the Newnham Charter (*infra* 26), where the boundary runs from the boundary of Drayton (now incorporated in Daventry) to the heathen burial-place, and thence along a path to hind-leap. Mazedale is the valley which runs east from the high ground just to the east of the point where the Newnham bounds (*v. infra* 26) turn south, so it may be presumed that the boundary *pytt* is the well-marked natural hollow at that point. From the hind-leap along the path to the *wyrtwalu* and from the *wyrtwalu* to the hart's wallowing-place and from the hart's wallowing-place to the smooth-hill and from the hill to the *furh* and along the *furh* to the *wyrtwalu*, and so by the *wyrtwalu* to *wiðig*-stream and from *wiðig*-stream to the *stod-fald*. From the *stod-fald* we go along the grey or boundary path (and along the path) to boundary-thorn and then due south. No trace of the heathen burial-place can now be found. The 'path' must be the 'hollow-road' of the Badby charter, the hind-leap is as before, the second path is that which still runs along the ridge. The second *wyrtwalu* is at the point where the boundary takes its southward turn, followed immediately by the wallowing-place. The smooth-hill is the slope down to the Weedon-Daventry road. The *furh* is probably the northward stretch of the boundary, the *wyrtwalu* is at the angle where it turns east, the *wiðig*-stream is as before. The *stod-fald* is another name for Borough Hill Camp, giving us a further example of that term as applied to an ancient earthwork (cf. Crawford in IPN 150–1). There is still an old track across the hill here and the boundary-thorn must have been in the boundary *pytt* or hollow, just at the point where the Newnham bounds turn south. We left the Badby boundary at the stone by the stream on the north side of the Mazedale valley (lit. 'valley of the boundary'). Thence it went south along Watling Street and thence to the road to the boundary of the men of Weedon, and then west along the road to the little hill on which the stump stood, and then due south. The present boundary (except for one slight variation) still follows Watling Street, till it comes to the Weedon-Daventry road on the bounds of Weedon. It then goes west to the hill where now stands the Queen's Head Inn, where it takes a straight southward turn. In the charter the boundary now goes due south to the old mill-pool where the willows stand, and then west along the *burna* to where the *Bliðe* flows out and then along the *Bliðe* to the stone-bridge. The boundary still goes south to Dodford Mill, where there is still a mill-pool and where there are some very ancient willows. The *burna* is the Nene. The *Bliðe* is the nameless stream which runs into it just west of Dodford Mill. The boundary still goes up that stream till it reaches the bridge by Everdon Manor House, where it makes a right angled turn to the south-east. In the charter the boundary is then said to travel east along the *dic* to the heathen burial-place and so north by the *wyrt-truma* to the end of the hedge on the boundary of the men of Weedon, thence along that boundary, and so straight to the stump on the east side of the *leah* and then due south to the *stræt*. The *dic* is the road along the boundary, which becomes a foot-path and still follows the boundary when the present road diverges to the west in order to take the steep hill better. The heathen burial-place (of which no trace can now be found) must have been on the northern edge of Everdon Stubbs. At this point the boundaries make a

southerly and then immediately a north-westerly turn, forming three sides
of an irregular oblong (which must be the *wyrt-truma*), which lies on the
boundary of Weedon. Thence the boundary travels south, east, and south
to the old Stowe-Preston road, which must be the *stræt*. The boundary now
goes along the *stræt* to the *furh* which goes due south to the great *stræt* at the
head of the stream on the boundary of Snorscombe, and then west along the
stræt to the ash, and from the ash along the *stræt* between the two *leahs* to the
old salt-*stræt*, from that *stræt* to the *steort* or tail of land, and from the tail of
land along the dirty brook to the *Bliðe*. The present boundary travels in a
south-westerly direction along the Stowe-Preston road. There is no *furh*
going due south, and it would take one right away from Snorscombe which
is on the north side of the *stræt*, and one must assume therefore that *south* is
an error for *north*, and that as there is certainly no 'great' *stræt* near here,
apart from the Stowe-Preston road, we should probably read 'due *north from*
the great *stræt*,' when the *furh* would be the steep valley which runs from the
road, almost due north to Snorscombe, with a stream running down it. This
was probably one of the bounds of Snorscombe, which has now been absorbed
in Everdon parish. The *æsc* cannot be identified, but it was probably at the
highest part of the road (B.M. 554). The salt-street is clearly the old road
from Snorscombe to Preston, which crosses the *stræt* at the point where the
stræt has descended to the bottom of the valley formed by a small feeder of
the *Bliðe*. The *steort* or tail of land is the northerly projection which separates
that feeder from the Kingbrook. (There are fields still called *Sturts* by the
Kingbrook.) The boundary still crosses it and goes down Kingbrook (earlier
'dirty brook') to where it joins *Bliðe*. The boundary then goes along *Bliðe*
until the *lacu* falls into *Bliðe* above stone-bridge, then north along *lacu* to the
dic, then along the *dic* to the *weg* which goes to Fawsley in the *slæd*. The
next phrase is '*þæt on fealuwes lea þær ælfric biscop redan het to þære ealdan
dic*.' This is impossible to translate, and there is almost certainly some corruption in the text, especially as just at this point we have in the Newnham
Charter the phrase '*on þa dic þe ælfric biscop let dician*,' which gives sense,
telling us that the *dic* was made on the orders of Bishop Aelfric. After this
the charter says that the boundary goes along the *dic* to the road which shoots
up to the ridge and along the ridge to the road from Fawsley to Badby for a
little while and then from the apple-tree which stands west of the way through
the *leah* to the great hazel-thicket, and then from the hazel-thicket down to
the black rushes, and from the rushes to the little hedges by the road from
Badby to Charwelton. The boundary still goes along *Bliðe* to a bridge on the
Newnham-Preston road. It then follows the road due north. By the side of
the road is a deep ditch with a trickle of water which doubtless once carried the
lacu, now dammed up, thus forming the little lake at the top. Where the boundary
turns west there are signs of an old road in a slight depression, and this leads
up to the top of the ridge to a road from Fawsley to Badby. Immediately
after, the boundary runs across the deep valley or *slæd* in which stands the
Dower House. Thence it goes to the top of Badby Down till it meets another
old path which 'shoots up' from Badby. Then the boundary follows that
road across the ridge and zig-zags on the slopes of the hill, striking another
old path to Fawsley. The hazel-thicket must have been at the acute angle
pointing due north, thence the boundary runs downhill to a tiny stream,
where must have been the black rushes. It goes along that stream and strikes
the Badby-Charwelton road. In the charter the boundary is then said to go
along the road to the brook which makes its way to Fawsley, as far as the way
to Staverton south of the old *burh* at *Baddanbyrig*, and then west along that
way until it is on a level with the great *dic* to the west of the *burh*, along the
dic and by the west of the *burh* north to the broken hill which is there cloven

This name was originally ' *Badda*'s burh ', with early change of the second element owing to Scand. influence, *v*. Introd. xxii. The burh is perhaps that called *þa ealdan burh æt Baddanbyrig* in the Badby Charter, and if so it is to be identified with the prehistoric camp on Arbury Hill.

ARBURY HILL CAMP is *Arbury* or *Arberry Banks* 1712 Morton, *Arberry-hill* 1791 Bridges. Arbury is a common ' camp ' name, cf. Arbury (C, Herts), Arbury Banks *infra* 37, *Erdeburgh* in Welton (1365 AD iv), Harborough Banks in Lapworth (Wa), *waste of Erbury* 1343 AD iii, *Erthbery* 13th AD i (Mx), and Thenford Hill Camp *infra* 13. It clearly goes back to OE *eorð-byrig* (dat), ' earthwork,' frequently found in OE charters (*v.* Middendorff *s.v.*), but early forms of most of these names are difficult to find. Cf. however Arbury (PN La 98).

BADBY WOOD is *bosco de Baddeby* 1247 *Ass*.

BIG HILL is probably the *wearge dun* of BCS 792 (*v. supra* 10 n.). It must have been called later *Big Hill* in distinction from a *Little Hill* mentioned in a Badby Terrier of c. 1650, and also by Bridges.

FOX HILL is (*on*) *foxhylle* 944 BCS 792, *Foxhill(s)* 1591 *DuLaMiscBks*. Self-explanatory.

Barby

BARBY 73 J 5
  Berchebi 1086 DB
  Beruby 12th Survey, 1255 Fees, 1274 Cl, 1314 Ipm, *Berwby* 1268 *Ass*

on the north-west of Badby. The present boundary crosses the Badby-Charwelton road at the brook which goes to Fawsley and follows an old road westwards along that stream until it reaches an old road in the direction of Staverton of which there are traces to the north and south of the *burh* or camp on Arbury Hill, but which is not continuous. The boundary, as stated, continues west until it is level with the west of the camp. It then follows the camp ditch to the west of the *burh*. Immediately after, it goes straight north to the point at which we started.

The bounds of this charter form the subject of a study by Miss Julia Keays-Young in the *Review of English Studies* vi, 271 ff.; the study suffers, however, from a failure to realise the importance of checking one's conclusions as far as possible against the present parish boundaries and from ignorance of the existence of the Newnham Charter.

Bergebi t. John BM, 1219 *FF*, *-by* 1201 Cur, 1220 Fees,
    Bergheby 1219 WellsR, 1242 Fees, *Bereghby* 1314 Ipm
Bereweby 1235, 1242 Fees, 1274 Fine, *-esby* 1252 Pat, *Berweby*
    1247 Fees
Berughby 1314, 1337 Cl, 1406 AD iv, *Berwgby* 1378 Cl,
    -oughby 1419 AD vi
Boreweeby (sic) 1316 FA
Barby 1508 AD i, *Baroughby* 1550 AD v, *Barowbie* 1601 *FF*,
    Barby al. Barroughby 1613 Recov

'by on the hill,' *v.* berg, by. The village stands on a hill.
Cf. Barrowby (Y), DB *Berghebi*.

CHAPEL FM (6″) marks the site of the former chapel attached to
Onley manor (Baker i, 263).

ONLEY [(w)ɔnli]

    Onle(e) 1273 Ipm, 1337 *Ass*, 1345 Cl, *-leye* 1344 *Ass*
    Oneley 1484 AD iii, *Onley al. Wanley* 1577 *Recov, Wanley al.*
      Onley 1613 *Recov*, 1702 Poll, *Onely* 1823 B
    Oulney 1644 SP

This may be identical with Olney *infra* 44 or it may be '*Ona*'s
clearing or wood,' *v.* leah. For initial *w*, cf. the pronunciation
of the common word *one*. This place was formerly a hamlet,
but is now represented by two farms ONLEY FIELDS and
ONLEY GROUNDS, *v. infra* 16, 17.

Braunston

BRAUNSTON[1] [brɔ·nsən] [brɑ·nsən] 83 A 5

    Brantestun 956 BCS 978, *Branteston* 1175 P (p) *et passim* to
    1291 AD v, with variant spellings *Braunt-* and *-ton(e)*,
    Brampteston 1255 Seld 13

---

[1] BCS 978 is an original charter giving the bounds of Braunston. They
start from the east corner of the *stodfald*, i.e. probably near where the bounds
of Braunston and Welton meet, thence they go to the *pytt*, i.e. probably the
depression through which the Grand Junction Canal now goes, thence to the
southern *beorg*, that is the point where the boundary crosses the Daventry-
Coventry road near the highest point, thence to the *þorn-stybb* which was
perhaps at the next right angle in the boundaries, thence to the head of the
cumb—the next right angle is at the head of a valley—thence straight to the
Leam (at Miry Bridge), then down the Leam to Willoughby. (The boundary
leaves the Leam at the present Willoughby Viaduct.) From Willoughby the

Brandeston(e) 1086 DB, 1216 ClR, 1294 AD iii, *Braundeston*
12th Survey, 1265 Ch, 1280 Cl *et freq*
Braunston 1304 AD iv, (*by Daventre*) 1394 Cl, *Brawnston*
1415 AD v, 1457 AD iii, *Braunson* 1612 NRS iii

This is probably '*Brant's* farm,' *v.* tun. The *Brant-* forms
have their parallel in many of the early forms of Brancepeth
(PN NbDu 29), Brauncewell (L), Braunston(e) (L, Lei, R) and
Brancey *infra* 178. So similarly we have *branteswyrð* in BCS 712,
a late copy of an OE charter, which belongs to Northants
(*v. infra* 101 n.), and Branston (St), BCS 771 (copy) *Brontiston*,
DB *Branteston*. These suggest the probability of an independent
personal name *Brant* (cf. OE *brant*, 'steep') which is supported
by the personal name *Branting*, found as that of a moneyer in
late OE times and in DB, and by the personal name *Brenting* in
the Badby Charter and in the list of Peterborough sureties (BCS
1130). In a few of these names the Anglo-Scandinavian name
Brand is also possible, especially where there is a combination
of consonants which might lead to unvoicing, e.g. in Brancepeth,
where *dsp* might become *tsp*.

BERRYFIELDS is *Beryfeld* 1540 LP, and takes its name from the
manor of *Brandestonbury* 1295 AD iii, *Braundeston Bery* 1305
Ipm, *Brauncestonebury* 1311 Ipm, *Brawndestonbury* 1384 Cl,
v. burh, used here in its manorial sense. The remains of the
manorial house can still be traced (Bridges i, 26).

BRAUNSTON CLEVES is *Falghamwode* 1413 AD iv, *Braunston
Cleves* or *Fallon Wood* 1822–30 Baker, cf. also *Fallamgrene* 1431
AD iv, and the present *Vellom Field* next to *Falkley* (*infra* 16).
This name must clearly be taken along with the lost FAWCLIFF,
a hamlet to the north-east of Braunston 'destroyed some ages
since' (Bridges i, 26) of which the early forms are *Faleclive* 1253
Ass, *Falclyve* 1305 Ass (p), 1317 Ass, 1403 FF, *Falclyff* 1415,

boundary goes to the 'little thorn,' i.e. probably the north-west corner of
Braunston parish, thence to the middle of the mere, i.e. perhaps the mere in
Braunston Cleves Wood, straight to the little brook and up the valley to the
sceardan beorg, i.e. the scarred hill. The reference here is to the much broken
high-land by Cleves Fm at the north-east corner of the parish. Thence to the
rough *hlæw* or hill, i.e. perhaps the point marked 575 near Ashby Grange,
and so to *stanbeorh*, i.e. probably at the right angle just east of Bragborough
Lodge Fm, and so back to the *stodfald*.

1550 AD v, 1638 *FF, Falclewe* 1430 AD iv, *Falkelef* 1457 AD iii, *Falkley Closes* 1776 *EnclA* and present-day, *Fawcliff* 1791 Bridges. The clif has clearly left its mark in the present *Cleeves* (cf. Cleeve Hill (Gl)). The preceding element is probably OE fealh and the compound fealh-clif would denote a ploughed hill. Cf. NED *s.v. fallow* sb. In the neighbouring *Falgham* we seem to have a compound of fealh and hamm.

BRAUNSTON FIELDS FM (6″) is *Braunstonfeld* 1540 LP. *Fields* (added to the parish name) is a common form of farm-name in West Northamptonshire and Oxfordshire. The earlier form was generally the singular form *feld* or *field*, the reference being to the open arable field belonging to the village.

LANGDEN HO (Kelly) is *Langdon* t. Eliz *DuLaMiscBks*. 'Long hill,' *v.* dun. NORTHFIELD HO (Kelly) is *Northfeild* (ib.), *v.* feld.

Catesby

CATESBY 83 C 5

> *Catesbi* 1086 DB *et passim* to 1471 AD i, with variant spellings *Kates-* and *-by, Chatesbi* 1189–95 AC, *Overe-catesby* 1389 AD i
> *Cattesbi* 1189–95 AC, *-by* 1208, 1235 Fees
> *Kattebi* 1209–35 WellsR, *-by* 1227, 1235 ib., *Cattebi* n.d. AD i, *-by* 1231 WellsR, 1246 Ch
> *Cateby* 1246 Cl *et freq* to 1330 FA with variant spelling *Kate-*

v. by. There are names *Káti* in ON, *Kate* in ODan and OSw, one of which probably lies behind this place-name. This should have given English *Cateby*. Possibly early confusion with the common word *cat* arose, and led to the use of genitival *s*. We may note, however, even in ON, the place-name form *Kaats-rud* (*v.* Lind). Confusion with the Scand. nickname *Kátr* is also possible—this would regularly have a genitive in *s* as in *Katzrud* (LindB *s.n.*). There were still an Upper and Nether Catesby in 1702 (Poll). The former was probably the higher part of Catesby round the church.

CATWELL BARN (c. 1825 O.S.) corresponds to *Catholehyll* (1471 AD i) and *Cattwell Hill* (17th cent. *Map*). Colloquial 'Cat'le

Hill' was expanded to polite 'Catwell Hill.' cf. Cattlehill *infra* 46.

DANE HOLE is *le Dene* 1371 AD v, *v.* denu. There is a well-marked valley here. As there is no trace in Northamptonshire of the form *dane* for *dene*, the modern name is probably a piece of folk-history.

NEWBOLD GROUNDS FM is *Neubold'* 1203 Ass *et freq* to 1469 AD ii with variant spelling *New(e)-, Nobold* 1702 Poll, *Newbold al. Nobald* 1708 *Recov.* 'New building,' *v.* boðl and cf. New-bottle *infra* 56. This name gives us the first example of the word *ground(s)*, which is very common in West Northamptonshire farm and field-names. The term *ground* is used in this county (*v.* EDD) for a 'large upland grazing field' and the plural is used of an 'outlying grazing farm' (ib.). The earliest example that has been noted is *Grundes* in Eydon (1281 AD ii).

RYTONHILL is *Rudonemers* c. 1150 *Thorney, Ryden* 1471 AD vi, *Reydon* 1823 B, *Righton* 1826 G. 'Rye hill,' *v.* ryge, dun, with later pleonastic addition of *hill*.

STEPPINGTON HILL is *Stependone* t. Hy 3 *Harl* D 56, (*the*) *Stepyngdon* 1537 Dugd iv, 637, c. 1550 *AOMB*. 'At the steep hill,' *v.* dun. The first element is OE *stēap*, 'steep.'

HIGHFIELD FM is *le Highfeld* 1537 LP, *the High Felde* 1537 Dugd iv, 637. For 'field' in this name and in LOWER FM *infra v.* Braunston Fields *supra* 16. LONG FURLONG FM (6″) is so named in 1779 (F). Cf. the same name PN D 74. LOWER FM may be identical in site with *le Netherfeld* 1537 LP.

Charwelton

CHARWELTON [tʃɑ·ltən] 83 D 5

> *Cerweltone* 1086 DB, *-a* 1107–11 NRS iv, *Cerwalton* 1240 Pap
> *Cheruoltona* 1094–1100 NRS iv, *-walton(e)* 1175 P, 1229 WellsR
> *Cealewetona* 1107–11 NRS iv
> *Charwalton* c. 1150 (c. 1350) *Thorney*

Charwelton(e) 1175 P, 12th Survey *et passim*, *-ueltone* late
12th BM, *Charewelton* 1220 Fees, 1275 RH, *-walton* 1242
Fees, *Charweleton* 1330 FA, *Over-*, *Nethercharwelleton* 1294
Ass

Chereweltona, *-e* t. Hy 2 (1314) Ch, 1221 WellsR

Shereweriton c. 1198 Cur

Charulton 1255 Fees, *Chalwreton* 1280 Ch, *Chardewelton*
1336 AD i

Charwelton al. Charlton 1605 *Recov*, *Charleton* t. Jas 1 ECP,
1674 *ChDecRoll*

'Farm on the Cherwell river' (*supra* 2), *v.* tun. *Nethercharwelleton* may be identical with the present *Church Charwelton*
further down stream.

CHARWELTON HILL must be identical with *le Graundone que jacet
inter campos de Charwelton et Bifeld* (t. Hy 3 *Harl* D 56). This
may be a hybrid name containing OFr *graund*, 'big, great,' and
OE dun. For similar hybrid names cf. *Granwurth*, *Petitewurth*
(1201 FF) in Stepney (Mx).

CHERWELL FM is at the source of the Cherwell river. Possibly it
is the *terre in Charwell* held by Ralph and Gilbert in 1198
(Fees 9).

FOX HALL FM (Kelly) is *Foxole* t. Ric 2 *Rental*. 'Fox-hole.'
SHARMANS HILL. The family of Sherman occurs in Norton a few
miles away in 1612 (NRS iii).

Daventry

DAVENTRY [deintri] [dɔˑntri][1] 83 B 6

Daventrei 1086 DB, *Dauentre* 1199 FF, 12th Survey, 1200,
1206 Cur, c. 1220 WellsR, 1262, 1264 Ipm *et passim* to 1537
St Frides

Dauintre c. 1150 BM *et passim* with variant transcription *Dav-*

---

[1] BROOK ST may be identical in origin with *Brockenstreete*, *Brockene streete*
1591 *DuLaMiscBks*. HIGH ST is *the Highe Strete* t. Hy 8 *Rental*. MARKET
PLACE. Cf. *Hogges-Markett* 1399 *Bodl*, *le Swynechepyng* 1418 XtCh, *v.*
cieping, *Cornhulle* 1418 XtCh, *the Market Place* t. Hy 8 *Rental*. Other street-
names found in old records are: *the Churchewey* (perhaps the present CHURCH
WALK), *Doglane*, *Tavern lane* t. Hy 8 *Rental*, *Marvelleslye lane* 1452 *Bodl* and
Payneleslane 1318 ib.

Davintreia 1155 (1329) Ch
Daivintr' 1216 ClR
Dauntre 1205 Cur (p), 1227 *Ass, Daventre al. Dauntrye* 1572
FF
Daventry 1320 AD i, 1328 Ipm, 1346 FA, *Davyntree* 1388 Cl
Daventre al. Deyntre 1564 *Recov, Dantrey* 1610 Camden,
Daintree 1620 *Recov, Daintry* 1623 Shakespeare (Hy vi),
Dauntrye 1639 *FF, Dawntrie al. Dayntrye* 1640 *Recov,
Daintrey, Dayntry, Daintree* 1657 NRS i
Deventrye 1620 *FF*
Danetre 1791 Bridges[1]

The old pronunciation is preserved in Daintry Wood and
Daintree Fm (PN BedsHu 135, 214) which probably take their
names from men coming originally from Daventry.

The etymology of the name is difficult, but Professor Ekwall
and Dr Ritter agree in suggesting that the second element is
treo, 'tree,' and the first an unrecorded pers. name *Dafa*, the
cognate of OGer *Dabo, Tabo, Tabicho* (Förstemann PN 386),
connected with the stem of OE *dafan*, 'to suit.' Hence 'Dafa's
tree.'

It is worth noticing with regard to this name, that its forms
show remarkable resemblance to those of Deventer in Holland,
10th cent. *Davantria, Dauentri, Taventeri* (Förstemann ON i,
692), but the etymology of that name also is obscure.

BOROUGH HILL. This is called 'the old *burh*' in the Badby
Charter (*supra* 11 n.) and *Borow hill* t. Hy 8 Dugd v, 178,
Burrowgh hill, Burowhill 1591 *DuLaMiscBks*. The burh is the
earthwork commonly known as Borough Hill Camp, and sometimes, quite erroneously, as 'Danes Camp.'

BURNTWALLS FM is *les Brendewalles* 1255 *FF, Burnedwalles* 1591
DuLaMiscBks. v. brende. The name is explained, at least in
part, by the following quotation from Bridges, 'Burnt Walls,

[1] The following statement from Bridges (i, 41) is worth recording as an
example of early speculative etymology. 'The common people have a tradition
that it was built by the Danes, and had thence the name Danetre, as it is now
pronounced,...this name is very probably supposed to be a compound of
the British *Dwy Avon Tre*, the town of the two Avons. From this fanciful
conceit, however, hath been taken the device of the town cryer, who bears
upon his badge the effigies of a Dane cutting down a tree.'

where many loads of stone, of ruined walls and foundations have been digged up' (i, 42–3).

DANE HOLME is possibly to be associated with Henry *a le Dane* (t. Ed 3 *SR*), but as there is no valley here and the form *dane* is not found in Nth the name must in that case be manorial in origin.

DRAYTON is *dræghæma gemære* 1021–3 KCD 736, *Draiton* 1203 Cur *et passim* with variant spelling *Dray-, Dreyton* 1261 *Ass* (p). *v.* dræg, tun. It lies on a small stream. For the first form, with OE hæme attached to the first element, cf. *s.n.* Doddenham PN Wo 46. The reference is to the boundary of the people of Drayton, where it marched with that of Newnham. Drayton has now been absorbed in Daventry, *v.* Addenda lii.

FOUSILL WOOD (6"). Cf. *Foweleswellehul* 13th AD iii, *Foules-wellehull* 13th AD iv. 'Bird's spring,' *v.* fugol, wielle.

HACKWOOD FM (6") is *Hackedwod* 1383 *MinAcct*. This would seem to be the 'hacked wood,' i.e. one in which chopping or felling has been done, an earlier use of *hacked* than any recorded in NED.

MIDDLEMORE FM is *Micklemoor* 1774 F, *Middlemoor* 1826 G, and is identical with *Michelmoreslade* 1591 *DuLaMiscBks*, the modern form being corrupt. 'Big marsh,' *v.* micelmor, slæd. MONKSMOOR (6") belonged to the monks of Daventry priory.

STEPNELL SPINNEY (6") is *Stepenhul* 1343 XtCh, *Stepenhul, Stepunhull,* 15th *Daventry*. 'Steep hill,' a compound of hyll and OE *stēap*. This may possibly be one of the two 'little *beorgas*' mentioned in the Badby Charter (*supra* 10).

FALCONERSHILL is so called in 1804 (*EnclA*) and is to be associated with the family of John *Fawckner* (1621–8 Wills). POPE'S WELL is *well called Popewell, Popeswell* t. Hy 8 *LRMB*.

Dodford

DODFORD 83 C 7

   doddanford 944 BCS 792, *doddafordinga land, doddafordung*
      gemære 1043 KCD 736
   Dodeford(e) 1086 DB *et freq* to 1326 Cl

Dudeford 1166 P, 1227 *FF*, 1241 P
Tuteford 1194, 1195 P
Doddeford 1218 WellsR, 1220, 1255 Fees, 1228 Cl, 1282 Ipm,
   Cl, 1377 Cl
Dadford 1702, 1730 Poll

'*Dodda*'s ford.' The same man perhaps gave name to the
undocumented DODMORE in this parish. In the second form we
have reference to the place where the bounds of the 'people of
Dodford' (*v.* ing), march with those of Newnham. According
to Fuller, *Worthies* (290), the place had its name from a water-
weed called *dod*, which grows plentifully here. The early forms
do not confirm this etymology.

DODFORD MILL. This is by the old *mylier* of the Badby Charter
(*supra* 11 n.). Toller (BT Supplt *s.v. mylen-gear*) is doubtless right
in taking this to be a reduction of the word *mylen-gear*, i.e. 'pool
by the mill.' Cf. Yarwell *infra* 209. HILL HO was the home of
Robert *atte Hil de Dodeforde* (1330 *Ass*).

Everdon

EVERDON, GREAT AND LITTLE, 83 D 7

eferdun 944 BCS 792, *eofordunenga gemære* 1021–3 KCD 736
Everdon(e) 1086 DB *et passim*, (*Great, Little*) 1317 Cl,
   Churche Everdon 1323 *Ass*
Eueredon' 1183 P, *Everedon* 1276 Cl

'Wild boar hill,' *v.* eofor, dun. For the second form cf. Dodford *supra* 20–1. *Churche* Everdon is an alternative name for
Great Everdon, from the presence of the church there.

SNORSCOMB

Snocescumb 944 BCS 792, *Snochescumbe* 1086 DB, *Snokes-
combe* 12th Survey *et freq* to 1293 AD iii, with variant
   spelling *-comb(e)*
Snoxcumbe 1240 *FF*, *Snoxecumbe* 1261 *Ass*
Snoteskumbe 1257 *FF*, *-cumb(e)* 1275 Ipm, 1293–1300 Ipm,
   -comb 1428 FA, *Snotecombe* 1325 Cl
Snoscoumbe 1293–1300 Ipm, *Snoscomb(e)* 1426 AD v, 1577
   Recov, 1823 B, *Snoscom* 1730 Poll
Snorscomb 1764 *Recov*

As the land is much broken here, and there are one or two prominent projections into the valley, we may have a compound of OE *snoc, 'point, projection,' and cumb, hence 'valley forming part of some such projection,' though such a genitival compound seems very unlikely. For the word v. snook sb. 1 (NED) and PN BedsHu 296. Snoxhall in Cranleigh (Sr), Snokeshull(e) 1279, 1288 Ass, 1370 AD iii, would seem to contain the same element, but there is no particularly prominent projection there; cf. also Snokeshacche (1448 Rental) in Dorking (Sr). There is also a field called Snoxford in Blakesley (Nth), for which we have no early forms. The persistence of forms with genitival s in all these names favours the likelihood of a pers. name *Snoc, the strong form of the recorded Snocca.

HEN WOOD (6″) is Hennewudd 1353 AD B 8831, -wode 1426 AD iv. 'Hens' wood.' WESTCOMB HO is Westcombe 1826 G. 'West' as opposed to Snorscomb supra at the other end of the parish.

Farthingstone

FARTHINGSTONE [farəkstən] 83 D 7

> Fordineston 1086 DB, Fordingeston 1183 P
> Fardeneston 1166 P
> Fardingestun 1166 P (CR), c. 1235 Magd, -ton 1176 P (p) et freq to 1478 AD iv
> Fardingston(e) 12th Survey, 1296 Ipm, -yng- 1298 Ipm
> Ferdingestone 1231 WellsR
> Farthingeston(e) 1261 Ass, 1330 FA, 1359 Ipm, Farthengeston 1300 Ass, -yng- 1428 FA
> Fardyngton near Everdon 1357 Cl

'The farm of one Færþegn,' v. tun. Cf. Johnston, PN England and Wales s.n. This is an Anglo-Scandinavian name (NP 39) corresponding to ON Farþegn, ODan Farthin. Among the various forms of it found in late OE are Ferðeng, Fardan, Fardein. Ferðeng is found in the list of Peterborough sureties in BCS 1130.

CASTLE DYKES is so named in 1779 (F). It is a high entrenched hill now overgrown with trees. KNIGHTLEY WOOD. The Knightleys of Fawsley have held land in the parish since 1535

(Bridges i, 63). MANTLES HEATH. John *Mauntel* had possession in the parish of a wood called *Mauntell's Wood* t. Hy 8 (Bridges i, 63), but the family must have been here far earlier, cf. *Maunteleswode* 1346 *For*. WOOD FM. This may be identical with *Lemereswode* 1204 *FF*, '*Lēofmǣr*'s wood.' It is *Farthingstone Wood* 1538–44 ECP.

Fawsley

FAWSLEY 83 D 6

> *fealuwes lea* 944 BCS 792, *F(e)aleweslea* 1107–11 NRS iv
> *Falewesle(i)(e), Felewesleie, Falelau* 1086 DB
> *Felesleuue, Felveslea* 1086 DB
> *Falewelea* 1166, 1174, 1194 P, *Falewellea* 1205 ClR
> *Faleslea* 1166 P, 1209–35 WellsR
> *Falewesle* 12th Survey, 1177 P (CR) *et freq* to 1333 Ipm with
>   variant spelling -*lea*, *Faleuwes*- 1209–35 WellsR, *Fallewes*-
>   1322 Cl, *Fallewysley* 1537 St Frides
> *Falegest* 1205 ClR, -*leg* 1215 ClR, *Falghesl'* 1242 Cl
> *Falwesleye* 1255 Ipm, -*le* 1331 Cl, -*lle* 1402 AD iv
> *Fawllesley* 1531 AD v, *Fausley* 1562 Everdon ParReg

Bosworth-Toller, on the basis of this p.n. as recorded in BCS 792, postulates an OE noun *fealu*, denoting fallow land, and takes it to be the common adj. *fealu*, 'lightish red, fallow,' used as a noun to describe ground recently ploughed. The NED (*s.v. fallow* sb.) notes that the common noun *fallow* (-land), going back to OE *fealg*, was early confused with *fealu*, the name of the colour, and that is what may have taken place here. The name would in that case denote 'clearing or woodland belonging to some larger area of *fallow* land,' but such genitival compounds are rare, and no certainty is possible. The Berkshire Fawley shows a curious parallel in the early forms with genitival *s*, DB *Faleslei*, 1177 P *Faleslege*, (CR) *Faleweslega*.

KINGBROOK SPINNEY (6″). Cf. *Kingbrok* 1240 *FF*. The Kingbrook was earlier known as the 'foul brook,' *v. fulan broc* in the Badby Charter (*supra* 12 n.). It was still called *Fulbrok* c. 1200 (*Ashby*). MILL SPINNEY (6″). Cf. *le Milnemede* 1333 Ipm. SEWELL'S POND (6″). Cf. *Sewellmede* 1333 Ipm, *Sewelle Mede* 1353 ib. The name may be identical with Seawell *infra* 40.

Bridges (i, 64) mentions it as *Seywell*, along with a *Bryesland Spring*. The latter must be for 'St Bride's land spring,' cf. *Seyntebridewell* (1330 *Ass*).

Hellidon

HELLIDON　83 C 47

> *Elliden* 1189–95 *AD* B 11398, *Eliden* 12th Survey
> *Helidon* 1193, 1194 P (p), 1242 Fees, *Heleydon* 1424 IpmR
> *Heylidene*, *Heilidene* c. 1210 WellsR[1], *Heylydon* 1549 *SR*
> *Heliden*(e) 1220 Fees *et passim* to 1452 AD vi with variant
> 　　spelling *Hely-*, *Hellyden* 1538 AD iii, *Helledon* 1622 *FF*
> *Haliden*' 1246 Cl, n.d. AD iv, 1537 LP, *Haledon* 1316 FA

This is a difficult name, and any suggestions with regard to it must depend upon the weight we attach to the third series of forms. On the basis of them, Dr Ritter and Dr A. H. Smith would suggest the OE pers. name *Hægla (as found in Hayling Island (Ha), *heglinga eg* BCS 979), with the same phonological development as in OE *snēl* from *snegel*. Cf. the later forms of Hayling, *Halingei* 1086 DB, *Halyngeia* t. Hy 1 (1318) Ch, *Helingei* 1266 Ch. In that case the full form would be OE *Hæglingdenu*, '*Hægla*'s denu,' with connective ing.

Professor Ekwall would take it to be from OE *hælig*, a secondary form of OE halig, which yields ME *hely*, hence 'holy valley' or 'hill.'

Dr A. H. Smith suggests alternatively the rare OE adj. *hælig*, 'unstable, slippery,' only recorded in the metaphorical sense, but doubtless, like its ON cognate *háll*, used originally of something smooth or slippery. For this word *v*. Torp *s.v. hall*.

ATTLEFIELD BARN (6″) is *Atlefeld* 1306, *Middel Attelfeld* 1402 AD v. '*Ætla*'s open land,' *v*. feld. LEAM POOL (6″) is the source of the Warwickshire Leam.

Kilsby

KILSBY　73 H 6

> *Kildesbig* 1043 (17th) KCD 916
> *Chidesbi* 1086 DB

---

[1] Checked from MS through the kindness of Canon C. W. Foster.

Kylesbia c. 1156 RegAntiquiss, 1329 Ch, *Chilesbei* c. 1225
  RegAntiquiss, *Kelysby* 1426 AD iv, *Kildesby al. Kylsby*
  1554 *FF*

Kildesby 1223 WellsR, c. 1225 RegAntiquiss *et freq* to 1459
  AD iii, with variant spelling *Kyld-*

Childebia c. 1225 RegAntiquiss

Kildeby,-i, 1220, 1237 WellsR, c. 1225 RegAntiquiss, 1230 *FF*

Keldesbi c. 1225 RegAntiquiss

This is a difficult name. One can only suggest that it means
'by of a man named *Kild*,' *Kild* being a Scandinavianising of the
rare and late OE pers. name *Cild*. Cf. *Childeswang* in Welford
(c. 1190 *Add*) and Chilson (O), c. 1200 Abingdon *Cildestun*.

ARNILLS GATE is *Harnold Farm* c. 1825 O.S. *Arnills* may be a
corruption of *Arnold's*, since, according to Bridges (i, 25), a
George *Arnold* held one moiety of the manor of Kilsby in the
18th century.

BARBY NORTOFT [nɔ·tət] is *Nortoft* 1247 *Ass*, 1514 *FF*, *Northtoft*
1330 QW. 'The north topt.' Identical with Nortoft *infra* 71. In
1826 (G) this name appears in the curious form *Naughthut*,
clearly put down on oral authority. 'Barby' to distinguish from
Nortoft *infra* 71. It is just on the boundary between Kilsby and
Barby.

Litchborough

LITCHBOROUGH 83 E 8

Liceberge 1086 DB

Lickesberga 1176 P (p)

Lichesberga 1184 P (p) *et freq* to 1366 AD iii with variant
  spellings *Lyches-* and *-berg*, *-bar(e)we*, *-ber(e)we*, *-barue*

Lichebarue 12th Survey *et freq* to 1366 Cl with variant
  spellings *Lyche-*, *Lycche-* and *-berg*, *-ber(e)we*, *-barwe*

Lecchesbarewe 1287 Ipm, *Lechebarwe* 1290 Cl, *Lecchebarewe*
  1356 *Ass*, *Lecheborowe* 1522 LP

Ekwall (*Studies* 59) suggests with some hesitation that this
may be a compound of OE **licc*, 'stream,' and beorg, 'hill,' but
it seems somewhat unlikely that this well-marked hill should
take its name from a tiny stream at its foot. Probably it is *līc-*

beorg or *līca-beorg*, 'body-hill' or 'hill of the bodies,' from some long-forgotten burials here. The forms with -*es*- are probably due to an attempt to make the name conform to a more common type.

RADMORE FM is *Redmor*' 14th *NthStA*, *Redmorbrigg*' 1330 *Ass*, *Lodmore* (sic) 1823 B. 'Red mor' or 'reed mor,' *v.* read, hreod. SUMMERHOUSE FM is *Summer House* 1823 B.

Newnham

NEWNHAM[1] 83 C 6

   æt niwanham 1021–3 KCD 736, *Newæham* 1020 (14th) KCD 1316

[1] KCD 736 is a charter of date 1021–3 whereby Cnut granted to the monk Aefic five hides at Newnham. The boundary begins at the *dic* which Bishop Aelfric had made (*v. supra* 12 n.). From the *dic* it goes to the church path, along the path to the broad way, along the way to Helmstan's *leah*, from the *leah* between the two roads to the *stocc*, from the *stocc* to the *dic*, from the *dic* to the brook, along the brook to the foul sike, from the heads of the sike to the pit, from the pit to the *dic*, from the *dic* to the *wyll*, from the *wyll* to the *pæð*, from the *pæð* to the boundary pit, from the pit along the *furh* to the 'heads,' along the heads to the green path, along the path back to the heads, along the heads north to the stump, from the stump to the *stræt*, along the *stræt* to the boundary *furh*, along the *furh* to the west heads, from the heads due north to the *wyll* and from the *wyll* to the boundary of the men of Drayton. The first part of this boundary is almost impossible to follow, partly because of its extremely tortuous course, but more particularly because the present parish of Newnham includes three detached pieces of Badby, and because there is also a big piece of land undivided between the parishes of Newnham and Badby. All we can be certain of is the point at which the bounds start, then that the *broc* is the Nene, along which the boundary does run for a short way, that the *stræt* is the Banbury-Daventry road, and that the point on the boundary of the men of Drayton is the one already noted in the Badby charter (*supra* 11 n.). We have under the same charter traced the boundary to the *mærðorn* where it turns due south. Thence it goes to the head-*æcer*, from the heads to the *weg*, from the *weg* to the 'buttocks,' from the buttocks to the brook, along the brook to the red cliff, from the cliff to the *furh*, along the *furh* to Leofsunu's head-*æcer*, and thence along the Dodford boundary to the *port-stræt*. The boundary still crosses the old track from Dodford to Daventry, which must be the *weg*, then it passes between two rounded slopes which may be the 'buttocks,' down to a little stream, along the stream to a place where there is a steepish bank of reddish-brown earth, and then up a shallow dry ditch with a double hedge, which must be the *furh*, over a headland, which must be Leofsunu's head-*æcer*, to the Weedon-Daventry road, which must be the *port-stræt*. Thence the boundary goes due south to the mere and from the mere to the brook, and up along the brook to the *sic* by the bracken-hill and along the sike by the bounds of Everdon to the *stræt*, and along the *stræt*, round the *wyrtwala* back to the *dic* at which we began. The boundary still goes due south past a spring (where the pool may have been) to the Nene or

Neuenham 1166 P *et freq* to 1476 AD iii with variant spellings
Newen-, Niwen-

Niweham 1166 P, *Neuham* 1199 FF, *Neweham* 1255 Fees

'At the new ham.'

Norton

NORTON 83 B 7

Norton(e) 1086 DB *et passim* with variant spelling *-tune*,
(*juxta Davintre*) 1242 Ipm

'North farm' (*v.* tun), probably in relation to Dodford, with
which its bounds march.

MAZEDALE SPINNEY (6″) is *mæresdæl* 944 BCS 792 and *Marsdale-furlong* and *-slade* 1395 XtCh. 'Valley of the boundary,' *v.* dæl,
(ge)mære. It is on the Norton-Daventry boundary.

MUSCOTT

Misecote 1086 DB

Musecot(e) 1202 Ass (p) *et freq* to 1330 Cl, *Muscecote* 1227 *FF*,
Musecotis 1235 Fees, *Mussecote* 1313 *Spencer*

Moscot(e) 1209–35 WellsR

Mosecote t. Hy 3 *Spencer*, 1268 *Ass*, 1274 RH, 1318 Cl, *-cothe*
1209–35 WellsR

Muscot(e) c. 1230 *Spencer et freq* to 1366 AD iii

Mousecote 1294 *Ass*

This is probably from OE *mūsa-cote*, 'mice's cottages,' *v.* mus,
cot(e), perhaps a nickname for some humble dwellings.

NOBOROUGH FM is *Norburgh* 1444 *Ct*, i.e. 'north-hill', or 'north
of the hill,' *v.* beorg.

THRUPP GROUNDS

Torp, Westorp 1086 DB, *Torp* 1288 AD iv

Thorp(e) 12th Survey, 1221 Bracton, 1255–8 Ipm, 1330 FA,
Thorp othe Hull near Daventre 1350 Cl, *Thorp al. Thropp*
1556 *FF*

brook, along the Nene to a tiny sike which turns south just before the
Newnham-Preston road, then along the sike, which here forms the boundary
of Everdon, to the road and along that road till we reach a triangular detached
piece of Newnham on the west side of the road. This triangle must be the
wyrtwala. When it has been round that, it goes a little further along the
road, and we get back to the point where we began.

Trop 1215 ClR *et freq* to 1291 Cl, (*juxta Davintre*) 1235
Fees

Throp 1255–8 Ipm *et freq* to 1336 FA, (*Norton cum*) 1316
FA

v. þorp. The reference is here to a hamlet lying away from
the main village. It is *west* of Norton. For *grounds v.* Newbold
Grounds *supra* 17.

Preston Capes

PRESTON CAPES 83 E 7

Prestetone 1086 DB

Preston(a) 1174 P *et passim*, (*juxta Maydeford*) 1285 *Ass*,
(*Capes*) 1300 Ipm, (*othe Hull*) 1421 Pat, (*Magna*) 1428 FA,
(*on Hill*) 1644 SP

Preston Capes al. Magna Preston al. Preston super montem 1595
Recov

'Priests' farm,' *v.* preost, tun. Hugo fil. Nicholai de *Capes*
held the manor in 1234 (Cl). 'Great' to distinguish from Little
Preston *infra*. The village stands on a hill-top.

LITTLE PRESTON is *Prestetone* 1086 DB, *Parva Preston* 1220 Fees,
Wodepreston 1327 Ipm, 1335 Cl, *Preston Parva al. Wode Preston*
1417 IpmR, *Woodepreston al. Little Preston* 1551 Pat.

CLEAVER'S CLUMP is to be associated with the family of Richard
Cleaver (1603–52 Wills). COW PASTURE WOOD is *Cowepasture*
1537 LP. *Cow Pasture* is a very common field-name in Nth.
TUNNINGHAM is *Tullingham* 1791 Bridges, *Tunningham* 1823 B,
1826 G.

Staverton

STAVERTON [stɛˈətən] 83 C 5

stæfertun 944 BCS 792

Staverton(e) 1086 DB *et passim* to 1552 AD v, *Stauereton*
1199 FF, *Staureton* 1273–81 Ipm

Stareton 1460–6 ECP, *Starton* 1524 Recov, *Starton-on-the-
hill* t. Hy 8 *LRMB*, *Staverton al. Stareton* 1587 *Recov*,
Staverton al. Starton 1702 Poll

This name has been dealt with by Ritter (125–6), who rightly associates it with Starton (Wa), Staverton (Gl, W), and a lost *Stauertuna* (Sf), as shown by their early forms. It should not be associated with Staverton (D), as the full forms of that name (PN D 520) show. The first element may also be found in Stears (Gl), DB *Staure*, and in DB *Staurecote* (Sa). Ritter associates it with ODan *stafær*, 'pole,' a derivative of the common word *stav*, 'staff.' The distribution of the term in the English place-names just noted shows that in them it is of native English rather than of Scandinavian origin, and must come from a lost OE *stæfer*. The compound would denote a tun made with, or marked by, a pole or poles. *staver* is found as a dialect word in English (EDD, NED) with senses 'rung of a ladder,' 'stake for a hedge,' but its distribution in that case suggests that it is the Scandinavian loan-word rather than this Old English word. We have the Scandinavian word in Starbottom (WRY), DB *Stamphotne*, 1268 Pat *Staverbotton*.

ELDERSTUBBS FM is *le Elrenestub* 15th *Daventry*, *Elder Stubbs* c. 1825 O.S. Self-explanatory. Cf. the field-names *Eldernestob* 1354 AD iii (Cransley) and *Eldrestubbe* c. 1370 *Harl* (Hardingstone).

HARTWELL SPRING (B) is reputed to be the source of the Nene (cf. Morton 3–4) and is mentioned in the field-name *Hertwelle-gore* (v. gara) in a *Rental* t. Ric 2.

STUDBOROUGH HILL is *Stroteberewe* t. Ric 2 *Rental*, *Struteberue* 15th *Daventry*, *Strutburgh Hylle* 1471 AD i, *Studbury-Hill* 1712 Morton. This is probably from OE *strūt-beorg*, 'hill of strife or contention.' For such an OE word **strūt*, v. NED s.v. *strut*, sb. 1, and cf. *Strowtham* (1548 *LRMB*) on the bounds of Cobham and Byfleet (Sr) and *Strotfurlong* (t. Hy 7 *MinAcct*) in Ewell (Sr). The hill lies on the Staverton-Catesby boundary. For such a name cf. Threapwood (Ch), Threepwood (PN NbDu 196), Threapland (Cu, Y), Fleet Fm and Flitnell Barn *infra* 84, 85 and possibly Tablehurst (PN Sx 329).

Stowe Nine Churches

STOWE[1] 83 D 8

> *æt Stowe* 956 (c. 1200) BCS 986, *Stowe* 1086 DB *et passim*
> *Stowe Nichurche* 1386 Pat, *Stow with the Nyne Churche* 1418,
>   (*Chirches*) 1439 IpmR, (*cum novem ecclesiis*) 1595 *Recov*, (*of
>   nine churches*) 1725 *Recov*
> *Parva Stowe al. with nyne Steples* 1576 *FF*

v. stow. The exact sense here is difficult to determine. 'Nine
Churches,' according to Bridges (i, 87), from nine churches to
which the Lord of the Manor had a right of presentation.' Bridges
also tells us that Little Stowe was also known as *Butter*-Stowe
'from their delivering their butter at a fixed price throughout
the year to the London carriers.'

RAMSDEN CORNER PLANTATION (6"). Ramsden is the *ramboldes-
dene* of BCS 986. It lies on the Stowe-Weedon boundary.
v. denu. The first element is clearly a personal name. Forssner
(209) *s.n. Rainbald*, would take it to be Continental in origin,
but there are genuine OE *Rægen*-names, and it is more likely
from an OE *Rægen-beald*.

STOWE WOOD. Cf. *bosco de Stowa* 1194 P

Weedon Beck

WEEDON BECK 83 C 8

> *weoduninga gemære* 944 BCS 792

[1] BCS 986 is a grant of land at Stowe. The boundary runs from the ford
of the holy spring or stream along Watling Street to *hludan wylles* (*broc*) and
along the brook to the *fyrdstræt*, along that *stræt* to the second *stræt* and along
the street to Ramsden *supra*, down '... *wyl*,' along the stream back to
halgan wylles ford. It is clear that the bounds begin at the extreme north
corner of the parish where Watling Street crosses a nameless feeder of the
Nene. Here must have been the *halgan wylles ford*. The stream has left a
further trace in the *Haliwellebrok* of an inquisition of 1327 (Ipm). It goes
down Watling Street to the present Geese Bridge and then turns west up the
stream which was once called Ludwell (cf. *Luddal-spring* in Stowe, mentioned
by Bridges (i, 88), Luddle Barn (1853 O.S.) and the present-day field-name
Ludhill). The present boundary turns north before it reaches the *fyrd stræt*,
which seems to be the Stowe-Preston road, and does not pass along it, and
does not really touch the second *stræt*, which must be the Preston-Newnham
road (*supra* 26–7 n.). It does go down the Ramsden valley which gives its course
to a stream which joins the Nene at the point indicated at the beginning of the
charter.

Wedon(e) 1086 DB *et freq* to 1401 Cl with variant spellings
-dun, -down, Northwedon 1289 Cl, (*Beke*) 1379 Cl, (*Beek*)
1432 AD iv
Weddona 1166 P, *-dun'* 1182, *-don* 1183 P
Whedon 1252 Ch, *Weydon* 1285 *Ass*
Over, Nether Wedon 1524 *SR*

'Hill with the temple or sacred place,' *v.* dun and cf. Weedon
PN Bk 85 and Harrowden *infra* 125. The manor belonged to the
monks of the abbey of *Bec Hellouin* (Normandy) (1166 P), cf.
Tooting Bec (Sr). *North* in contrast to Weedon Lois *infra* 45.
It was sometimes called *Church* Weedon (Bridges i, 93) to distinguish it from the adjoining hamlet of *Upper* Weedon. It was
also called *Wedon in the Strete* 1440 Pat, *Wedon in Strett* 1498
AD, *Weedon in ye Street* 1657 NRS i, i.e. on Watling Street,
this part of the parish being now called ROAD WEEDON.

Welton

WELTON 83 A 6

Waletone 1086 DB
Weletone 1086 DB, 1166 RBE, 1199 FF *et freq* to 1324 AD iv,
(*juxta Daventre*) 1281 *FF*
Welton 1167 P *et passim, Wellton* 1448 AD iii
Welleton(a) 1174 P *et freq* to 1303 AD iv, (*juxta Daventre*)
1297 *Ass*

'Spring-farm,' *v.* wielle, tun. It is a parish with numerous
springs. Bridges (i, 96) speaks of six. Some of these are mentioned in deeds printed in AD iii and iv, viz. *Mikelwelle, Bones-
well, Redewell, Halliwelle, Thunnewelle*, while in 1330 (*Ass*) we
have mention of a *Sautwelle*, i.e. salt-well.

CHURCHILL Ho is *Chirchehul* n.d. AD iv, t. Ed 3 *Rental, Churke-
hul* n.d. AD iv, *Chirchehil* 1304, *Chyrchehyl* 1313 AD iv. 'Hill
with the church,' *v.* cirice. The name might have been given by
the people of Daventry to the south.

COCKLE FM (G). Cf. *Cockes mede* 1312 XtCh, *Cockelesmede* 1336
Spencer, Cokkells mede 1366 AD iv.

HOBBERILL FM is *Hoberhul* n.d. AD iii, *Hobber Hill* 1838 *Survey*.
This is almost certainly a triple compound of holh, beorg and

hyll, hence, 'hollow-hill hill.' The farm lies in a well-marked hollow in the side of the hill. Cf. a similar pleonastic name in Hoborough Hill *infra* 65.

MICKLE WELL (6″) is *Michelewellehul* 13th AD iv, *Mikelwell in Welton* 1409 AD iv, 'Big spring,' *v.* micel, wielle. Morton (306) describes this spring as coming forth from a 'Perpendicular Fissure, Four Inches in Depth, and 12 in Width.'

II. CHIPPING WARDEN HUNDRED

Werdunes a. 1076 Geld Roll, *Wardune, Wardone, Waradone, Waredon* 1086 DB, *Wardon'* 12th Survey, 1178 P *et passim*.

v. Chipping Warden *infra* 36.

Appletree[1]

APPLETREE (83 F 3) is *Appeltre* 1175 P (p), 1232 *FF et freq, Apeltre* 1199 FF, 12th Survey, *Apiltre* 1256 Ipm, *Appultre* 1484 AD iv, *Apletree al. Apleby* 1667 *Recov.* Self-explanatory.

Aston le Walls

ASTON LE WALLS 83 F 4

   Eston(e) 1086 DB *et freq* to 1224 WellsR

   Aston juxta Wardon c. 1200 Wardon *et freq*, (*juxta Byfeld*) 1309 *FF*

   Assheton in le Walles 1509 *FF, Aston in the Wall* 1530 *Recov, in the Walls* 1768 *Recov*

   Aston super muras (sic) 1621 *FF*

'East farm,' *v.* tun, lies south-east of the Boddingtons. 'The Walls' probably refers to some irregular entrenchments here (cf. VCH ii, 418). These have been the subject of various conjectures. To the south we have Wallow Bank in Chipping Warden, in line with these entrenchments, which Morton (525–6) believed to be part of the same earthwork, and still further south we have Walton in King's Sutton (*infra* 58) which he took to be named from a southward extension of these fortifications.

---

[1] Originally a hamlet of Aston-le-Walls.

Boddington, Upper and Lower

BODDINGTON 83 E 3

Botendon(e) 1086 DB *et freq* to 1235 Fees
Bottendun c. 1190 *Magd, Bottendon* 1209–18 WellsR, 1217
   AD iii, 1220 Fees, 1245 WellsR, *Bottindon* 1227 *FF*
Botindon, -y- 1199 FF *et freq* to 1368 Cl, *Botintun'* 1209 Seld
   13, *Uvrebotindon* 1261 *Ass, Ovre Botingden* 1289 Cl
Bottelendon 12th Survey
Budinton 1244 Cl, *Bodynton* 1309 Ch
Botyngdon 1358 Ipm, *-doun* 1396 Cl, *-ton* 1428 FA

'*Bōta*'s hill,' *v.* dun.

BODDINGTON FIELDS FM, cf. *in campo de Botintun'* 1209 Seld 13.
v. Braunston Fields *supra* 16.

SPELLA HO is *Spelloe* 1759 *EnclA, Spellow* c. 1825 O.S. This
name is probably identical in origin with that of Speller Fm and
Spelhoe Hundred *infra* 78, 131. The house stands on a prominent
hill, near the THREE SHIRE STONES where Northamptonshire,
Warwickshire and Oxfordshire meet. This is so named in
1779 (F).

Byfield

BYFIELD 83 E 4

Bivelde, Bifelde 1086 DB, *Bifeilt* 1121–39 France, *Bifeldia*
   late Hy 2 BM

Further forms are without interest except *Biffeld* 1206 FineR,
Bifled 1243 Cl, *Bifild* 1582 AD v, *Byfeill* 1539 LP. 'By the open
land,' *v.* feld. Cf. such names as Byfleet (Sr), Bygrave (Herts).
For the possibility of a different interpretation of such names
v. PN NRY xliii.

LUDWELL (6″) is *Lodewell* 1247 *Ass*, t. Ed 3 *SR* (p). 'Loud
spring,' *v.* wielle, and cf. the Stowe Charter *supra* 30 n.

WESTHORP [westrəp] is *Westorp* 1086 DB, *Westrop* 1253 *Ass*
(p), *Westhrop* 1330 Cl, *Westrup* 1637 NthNQ i, *Westrop* 1791
Bridges. 'West village,' *v.* þorp. It lies just west of Byfield.

DODD'S BARN (6″) is to be associated with the family of William
Dod (1629 *SR*). PITWELL FM is *Potewell* 1285 *Ass*. Cf. also

Pittalls Furlong 1779 *EnclA* and Potwell in Cosham (Ha), 1248 *Ass Potwell.*

Edgcote

EDGCOTE   83 G 4

> *Hocecote* 1086 DB, *Hochecote* t. Hy 2 *Cott* xv, 20 *et passim* to 1428 FA, *Hochcote* 1297 Cl
> *Ochecot'* 1220 Fees, 1404 *Ass*, *Ochecott*[1] 1223 WellsR, *Ochocote* 1383 AD iv
> *Hechcot* 1284 (17th) FA
> *Hogecote* 1275 RH, t. Ed 3 *SR*, *-kote* 1285 *Ass*
> *Hoggecote* 1323 AD iv, *Oggecote* 1404 *Ass*
> *Hegecote* 15th Hist. Croyland. Continuatio
> *Edgecotte* 1526 SR, *-coote* 1535 VE
> *Ogecott* c. 1530 *CtRequests*

No satisfactory suggestion can be made for this name.

DANES MOOR is *Danysmore* 1467 *Bodl*[2], *Dunsmore* 1779 F, *Dunsmoor* 1826 B. This was the site of a battle in the Wars of the Roses, fought in 1467 at *Hegecote seu Danysmore*. Unfortunately, the origin of the name is entirely obscure. Tradition of course speaks of a battle of Danes and English (cf. *infra*), but the form would then have to be *Denemore* from the gen. pl. *Dena*.

PADDLE COTTAGE. This must take its name from the spring which Morton (542) calls *Pad-well*, and describes as "a noted Flush Spring in *Edgcote* Grounds." The spring is marked on the 6″ map. Morton records the old saying attributed to the Danes when about to engage in fight on the neighbouring *Danesmore*

> "If we can Pad-well overgoe and Horestone we can see;
> Then Lords of England we shall be."

The *Horestone* he tells us was a famous old stone on the borders of Warwickshire (? Oxfordshire) in Wardlinton (sic) Field. The name Padwell repeats itself in *Padwellestreme* in Long Buckby (1458 *Ct*). It is doubtless a compound of OE *pad(e)*, 'toad,' and wielle.

---

[1] This is the correct reading (*ex inf.* Canon C. W. Foster) and not *Echecott*.
[2] Checked from MS Tanner 2, f. 104 b by the kindness of Mr V. H. Galbraith.

Eydon

EYDON [i·dən] 83 F 5

Egedone 1086 DB

Eindune c. 1200 Wardon, *Eindon(a)* t. John BM, 1202 Ass,
Eyndon(a) 1219 Bracton *et freq* to 1253 *Ass*
Aydona 12th Survey, *Ayndona* 1219 Bracton
Heydon 1219 WellsR
Eidon(e) c. 1220 AD i *et passim* with variant spelling *Ey-
Edon* 1549 *SR*, (*al. Eadon*) 1593 *FF, Eydon al. Eden* 1727
Recov

This probably contains the same first element as Aynho *infra*
48 and *Aeganstan* (BCS 226). It would seem to be a pers. name
*Æga. Professor Ekwall notes that this name is cognate with
such OGer names as *Aigo, Eigio, Aigulf, Aigobercht, Aigofred*
given by Förstemann (PN 47–9, s.n. *Aig*). The stem *aig-* is
found in OE in such words as *āglāc, āglǣcan*.

Greatworth

GREATWORTH [gretwə·θ] 83 H 6

Grentevorde 1086 DB

Gretteworth, -wrth, -wurth 12th Survey *et freq* to 1312 Ch

Gretewrth 1200 Cur, 1227 *Ass*, 1250 Fees, *-worthe* 1313
Eynsham, *Gretworth* 1316 FA

Gruttewrth' c. 1200 *Magd* (p), 1241 P, *-worth(e)* 1275 RH,
1287 *Ass*, 1314 Eynsham, 1383 AD iv, *Grutworth* 1330 FA,
1361 Cl, 1526 SR, 1529 AD vi

Gretiswrth 1201 Cur, *Gretesworth* 1241 P, *Gratewurth* 1225
WellsR

Greetworth 1284 FA, 1702 Poll, *Gretewood* 1602 *FF, Greet-
wood* 1744 *FF*

Gretworth al. Gritworth 1651 Moulton, *Gritworth* 1712
Morton, *Grettworth* 1730 Poll, *Gretworth* 1826 B

This is a compound of greot and weorþ, hence 'enclosure on
the greot.' The soil here is sandy, surrounded by deep clay
(Bridges i, 124). DB *Grent-* is clearly an error for *Greut-*.

COCKLEYHILL FM. Cf. *Cockelowefurlong* 15th *Daventry, Cockley-
meade* 1618 *Clayton*. 'Cock-hill,' *v.* hlaw.

Sulgrave

SULGRAVE 83 G 6

> *Sulgrave* 1086 DB, 1306 Ipm *et freq*
> *Solegrave* 12th Survey, 1294 Ipm, -*greue* t. Hy 3 BM, -*grafe* n.d. AD ii, *Sollegrave* 1285 AD i
> *Sulegrave* c. 1150 *Harl*, 1209–18 WellsR *et freq* to 1329 Ch, *Sullegrave* 1329 Ch
> *Culegrave* 1205 Cur
> *Solgrave* 1300 AD vi, 1301, 1304 Cl
> *Sowgrave al. Souldgrave* 1556 *Recov*, *Sowegrave* 1563 *FF*, *Sowgrave* t. Jas 1 ECP, *Sulgrave al. Sowlgrave al. Souldgrave* 1631 *FF*

Sulgrave lies on a low spur in a broad deep-cut valley. One must take it that the first element is OE *sulh*, denoting a channel or passage of some kind, as noted in Souldrop (PN BedsHu 43), and discussed by Stevenson in *Crawford Charters* 47. We seem to have a compound of the same elements in *sulig graf* (BCS 1108). See further BT Supplt *s.v. sulh*. The second element is perhaps græf, 'pit, trench,' rather than graf, 'grove.'

BARROW HILL is so named in 1672 (*LRMB*), and may be referred to as *le Berwes* in a *Rental* of 1344. A tumulus is marked here (6″). CASTLE HILL (6″) is an earthwork just by the church, and must be the *Chercheknabbe* of the Canons Ashby cartulary (78 d). *knabbe* would seem to be a hitherto unrecorded variant of ME *knobbe*, perhaps formed under the influence of cnæpp, which has the same sense.

Chipping Warden

CHIPPING WARDEN 83 F 4

> *Waredon(e)* 1086 DB, 1205 ClR
> *Wardon* 1163 BM *et passim*, *Westwardon* 1205 *FF*, 1242 Fees, 1349 Ipm, *Chepyng Wardoun* 1389 Cl, *Westwardyn al. Chepingwarden* 1483 IpmR

'Watch hill,' *v.* weard, dun and cf. Warden Hill (PN BedsHu 97) and Warden (PN NbDu *s.n.*). The reference is to the prominent 'Warden Hill' to the east of the village. *Chipping*, 'market,' *v.* cieping. *West* in relation to Warden (Beds) the Abbot of which held lands here (Bridges i, 111).

TRAFFORD HO and BRIDGE

> *Trapeford* 1086 DB, *Trapesford* 12th Survey
> *Trafford(ia)* 1219 Bracton *et passim*, *Traford* c. 1220 AD i, *Traffordebrige* n.d. AD i

This is probably 'trap-ford,' a name for a ford where some trap for catching fish was placed.

WALLOW BANK is *the Wallow-bank* 1791 Bridges. For this entrenchment *v.* Aston le Walls *supra* 32. The name may be a compound of *wall* and hoh, 'hill.'

WARDEN HILL is *la D(o)une de Wardon* c. 1200 Wardon. We have also *la Wardelawe* c. 1200 ib. (*v.* hlaw) referring apparently to the same hill, or perhaps to the highest part of it.

ARBURY BANKS is *Arberry Banks* 1779 F. It is the name of a small fortification. Cf. Arbury Hill *supra* 13. BLACKGROUNDS COTTAGE (6″) is *Black Grounds* c. 1825 O.S. *v.* Newbold Grounds *supra* 17.

Woodford cum Membris

WOODFORD HALSE 83 E 5

> *Wodeford* 12th Survey *et passim* with variant spelling *Wude-*, (*juxta Hynton*) 1287 *Ass*

Self-explanatory. *Juxta Hynton* to distinguish from Woodford *infra* 189. The 'members' are Farndon and Hinton. It is called Woodford *Halse* from the manor of Halse (*infra* 49) of which it is a member (Baker i, 332).

WEST FARNDON is *Ferendon(e)* 1086 DB *et freq* to 1269 Ipm, (*juxta Wodeford*) 1394 *Ass*, *Ferendun* c. 1200 Wardon, *Westfarindon* 1275 RH, *Faryndon juxta Hynton* 1294 *Ass*, *Faryndon* 1316 FA, *Farndon* 1284 FA, *Westfarndon* 1300 Ipm, (*juxta Byfeld*) 1330 QW. 'Bracken hill,' *v.* fearn, dun. *West* to distinguish from East Farndon *infra* 113.

HINTON is *Hinton(e)* 1086 DB *et passim* with variant spelling *Hyn-*, (*by Byfeld*) 1279 Pat, (*by Wodeford*) 1380 Cl, *Hyneton*

1199 FF. This is probably from OE *hīgna-tūn*, 'farm of the *hīwan*,' *v.* higna, tun. The *hiwan* might be members of any household, not necessarily a monastic one, though that is the commonest use of the term.

WARDEN GRANGE was a farm (*Grangia* c. 1175 Wardon) of the monks of Warden Abbey (Beds). WOODFORDHILL. Cf. *super montem de Wodeforde* 1330 *Ass.*

III. GREEN'S NORTON HUNDRED

This was earlier known as *Voxle* a. 1076 Geld Roll, *Foxele*, *Foxle*, *Foxelea*, *Foxleu*, *Foxeslau*, *Foxeslea*, *Foxesle*, *Foxhela* 1086 DB, from Foxley in Blakesley *infra* 40. It is first called *Hundred de Norton* in the 12th cent. Survey. The meeting-place may have been near the fields now called *Modley* Gate in Green's Norton, on the Towcester-Litchborough road, to the west of Field Burcote. Modley is probably for OE *(ge)mōt-lēah*, 'moot-clearing,' cf. Mutley PN D 235. These fields are on the highest ground in the neighbourhood, with old tracks leading to them.

Adstone

ADSTONE [ædsən] 83 F 7

> *Atenestone, Etenestone* 1086 DB
> *Attelestuna* t. Hy 2 AD i, *-ton* 1294 *Ass*, 1298 Ipm, 1356 *Ass*, *Attleston* 1258 FineR
> *Atteneston* 12th Survey *et passim* to 1330 FA, *Ateneston'* 1206 Cur
> *Ataneston'* t. Ric 1 Cur, *Attanestone* 1206 *FF* (p), 1220 Fees
> *Ettoneston* 1199 Cur, *Etteneston* c. 1200 BM
> *Atteneston et non Attereston* 1299 *Ass*
> *Atneston* 1314 Ipm *et freq* to 1417 AD ii
> *Atteston* 1319, 1342 AD i
> *Adneston* 1522 AD iii, (*al. Adston*) 1550 Pat, (*al. Addeston*) 1578 *FF*
> *Adson* 1681 DKR xl, 1702 Poll, 1779 F

'*Ættin*'s farm,' *v.* tun. Cf. Ekwall, *Studies* 4.

Canons Ashby

CANONS ASHBY 83 F 6

Ascebi 1086 DB with the same run of forms as for Ashby
St Ledgers *supra* 9

Canounes Hessheby 1287 Cl, *Essheby Canons* 13th AD ii,
Assheby Canonicorum 1320 Ipm, *Chanons Assheby* 1506
AD iii

Assheby in the Wodende 1371 Cl

Coopesassheby al. Cannonsassheby 1542 AD vi, *Copesashebye*
1573 AD iv

v. Ashby *supra* 9. It is the most southerly place-name in
by in the Midlands. *Canons* from the priory founded here in
the mid 12th cent. (VCH ii, 130). John *Coope* is mentioned in
connection with the place in 1542 (AD vi). Woodend (*infra* 46)
is three miles away. It was probably so called as the western
limit of Whittlewood forest.

CONDUIT COVERT (6″). Cf. *le Cundite Close* 1537 LP. Bridges
(i, 223) says that within a little distance of certain ponds in the
park is the spring that was formerly called *Morwelle* whence
water was conveyed by pipes into the convent. EAST FM may
correspond to *Estfeld*, 1537 LP. WARDS COPSE (6″) is to
be associated with the family of John *le Warde* (1316 AD i).

Blakesley

BLAKESLEY [breiksli] 83 F 8

Blaculveslei, -lea, Baculveslea (sic), *Blachesleuue* 1086 DB

Blacculfeslea 1175 P (p), *Blaculf-* 1190, 1191 P (p), *Blaculfesle*
1242 Fees

Blaculueslea, -ley, -lee 1185 P (p) *et freq* to 1352 Cl, *Magna
Blacculueslee* 1197 FF, *Blachuluesley* 1219 FF, *Brode-
blaculueslee* 1262 FF

Blacolvesle 12th Survey *et freq* to 1428 FA, *Blacovisle* 1277
Ipm, *Blacovesle* 1284 FA, *Blacouvesle* 1305 Ipm

Blacoslegh 1330 QW, *Blakeslee* 1386 Cl, *-ley* 1468 AD iv,
Blakesley al. Blackolvesly 1566 FF, *Blaxley* 1702 Poll, 1776
Recov

'*Blæcwulf*'s clearing,' *v.* leah. This pers. name is not on record but would be a regular formation. The little stream on which Blakesley stands is known locally as Black Ouse (LG 74). This is doubtless a back-formation made at the time when the name was still pronounced as a trisyllable. 'Brode' to distinguish from Little or Wood Blakesley, now Woodend *infra* 46. Cf. Bradbury (PN D 338).

Foxley is *Foxeslea* 1086 DB, *Foxlea* 1190 P (p) *et passim* with variant spelling -*le*(*ye*), *Foxele* 1230 P, 1299 *Ass* (p), 1316 FA. 'Fox clearing or wood,' *v.* leah.

Quinbury End is so called in 1761 (*EnclA*).

Seawell Fm is *Sewell*(*e*) 1086 DB *et freq* to 1823 B, *Sewewell* 12th Survey, *Seuewell* 1220, 1235, 1242 Fees, *Seuwell* 1337 Pat, *Seywell Close*, *Seawell Coppice* 1681 *Rental*, *Se*(*y*)*well* 1761 *EnclA*, *Seywell* 1930 Kelly. There are numerous springs in the neighbourhood, and this is probably for *seofonwiellan*, 'seven springs.' A tradition of seven springs is common in place-names, cf. *seofenwyllas* (BCS 165), Sinwell (Gl), 1248 *Ass Suvenewell*, Sowell (PN D 565), Seven Wells Fm in Stoke Doyle and Seven Springs nr. Coberley (Gl), the reputed source of the Thames, a field called *Seven Wells* in Apethorpe (Nth), and possibly Sewell's Pond *supra* 23. See also Sywell *infra* 139.

Bradden

Bradden 83 F 9

    Braden(*e*) 1086 DB, 1195 P, 1203 Cur, *Bradden*(*e*) 12th Survey *et passim*
    Bradenden(*e*) 1185 P (p), c. 1225 Abingdon, 1227 Ch, *Bradedene* 1272 *FF* (p)
    Breddene 1300 AD vi, 1301 Cl
    Bradwyn al. Braden 1550 Pat

    'Wide valley,' *v.* brad, denu.

Bury Brake (6"). Cf. William *ate Bury de Braddene* (1297 *For*) and Agnes de *Bery* (t. Ed 3 *SR*), *v.* burh. The term is probably manorial here.

Maidford

MAIDFORD 83 E 7

Merdeford (sic) 1086 DB
Maideneford 1166 P (p), *Maydenford* 1285, 1312 *Ass*
Maideford, -y- 1175 P (p) *et passim* to 1453 AD iv
Maydenforth c. 1200 *Ashby*
Meideford 1200 Cur *et freq* to 1232 Cl, *Medeford* 1307 Ipm
Madeford 1359 Ipm

'The maidens' ford,' cf. Maidenford (PN D 26) and Medbury (PN BedsHu 71).

BURNTFOLD COPSE. Cf. *Burn(t)fold* 1779 *EnclA*.

Moreton Pinkney

MORETON PINKNEY 83 F 6

Morton(e) 1086 DB *et passim*, (*juxta Assheby Canonicorum*)
    1317 *Ass*, (*Pynkenye*) 1346 Cl
Geldenemortone 1219 WellsR, *Guldene-* 1225 WellsR, 1341 Cl,
    Gildene Mortone 1226 WellsR, *Gilden Moreton* 1296 Cl,
    Guyldenmorton 1343 Ipm
Moreton al. Moreton Pynckney al. Gyles Moreton 1590 *Recov*

'Farm by the marshy place,' *v.* mor, tun. The family of *Pinkeni* is first mentioned in connection with the place in 1199 (FF). It borders on Weedon Lois or Pinkney which was the head of the Honour of Pinkney. The family of *Pinchengi* (DB) came from *Picquigny* in Picardy. The change from *Picquigny* to *Pinkney* is of interest, for, as Round notes (VCH i, 291–2), the pronunciation of this name was a test-word for the English, who were never able to pronounce it. It was used as such for their recognition when they were expelled from Ponthieu and, as late as 1489, a Frenchman, employed in London, writes

> "Anglais aussi tant soit cure
> Ne formera bien Pinqueny."

No certain explanation of *Geldene-*, *Guldene-*, *Gildene-* can be offered. It may be that we should take it to be the common adj. *gylden*, 'golden,' in which case, as Professor Ekwall suggests, it might perhaps denote a specially wealthy manor, cf. Addenda, *supra* lii *s.n.* Peterborough[1].

CANADA was named after Dr Oxenden, Metropolitan of Canada (1869–78) (Kelly). FOXHALL FM (6″), cf. *Foxholewey* c. 1200 *Ashby*, *Foxolewey*, *Foxoledene* 1356 AD ii, *Long Foxehooles* t. Eliz *Rental*. Self-explanatory. LAWNHILL FM. Cf. *The Launde* 1602 *Terrier*, *v.* Beanfield Lawn *infra* 155.

Green's Norton

GREEN'S NORTON 83 F 9

> *Norton(e)* 1086 DB *et passim*, *Nortune* 1187 P (p), *Northton* 1191 P, *Norton Davy* 1329, 1369 Cl, *Norton-near-Toucestre* 1325 Cl
> *Grenesnorton* 1465 *FF*, *Greynsnorton* 1541 Statutes, *Norton Davye al. Grenes Norton* 1580 *FF*

'North farm,' *v.* tun. It lies north-west of Towcester. Henry *Grene*, Knight, held the manor jointly with Thomas his son in 1369 (Cl), and the association of the family continued for many generations. *Davye* may have reference to the holding of the manor in the 13th cent. by *David*, son of Griffin (Bridges i, 239).

FIELD BURCOTE is *Burecot* 1200, 1204 Cur, *Bulecot'* 1200 Cur, *Burcot(e)* 1204 Cur, 1256 FineR, *Borcote* 1316 FA, *Feldenburcote* 1330 *Ass*, *Burcote feelde* 1500 *Ct*. We may compare Burcot's Fm in East Stratton (Ha), BCS 602 *Burcote* and Burcott (So), KCD 816 *Burcotan*. This is fairly common as a place-name, and it is probably in most cases a compound of bur and cot(e). Ekwall (PN Bk xxxii) compares the OE *būr-cote*, 'bed-chambers.' This is presumably a derivative of OE *būr*, 'bower,' and the change of sense is a little difficult to explain. Possibly *Burcott* as a place-name is rather a compound of OE *būr*, 'peasant,' hence 'peasant cottages,' or, if the true form is *būra-cot(e)*, 'peasants' cottages.' For such a name cf. Sannacott (PN D 345). *Field*, i.e. 'in the open country' (*v.* feld), to distinguish it from *Wood* Burcote *infra* 95.

---

[1] The suggestion as to a possible etymology made in PN Wo 125 should be withdrawn.

CASWELL is *Kerswell'* 1200, *Karswell* 1204 Cur, *Carsewell* 1299 Cl, 1302 *FF*, *Kereswell* 1316 FA, *Cassewell* 1359 Ipm, *Carswell* 1823 B. 'Cress spring,' *v.* wielle.

DUNCOTE is *Dunecote* 1227 *FF*, 1305 *Ass*, *Donecote* 1253 *Ass* (p), 1256 FineR, 1316 FA, *Doncote* 1276 BM, *Dunnacote* 1287 *Ass* (p), *Duncote* 1302 *FF*. As Duncote is in a hollow by a stream, it cannot have anything to do with dun. It must be '*Dunna*'s cottages,' *v.* cot(e).

KINGTHORN WOOD and MILL are *mill of Kingesthorn* 1274 Pat, *boscus de Kynghthorn* t. Ed 1 *PeterbB*, *Kingethorne Mylne* 1551 Pat, *Kingshornewood* 1726 *Recov*. The manor of Green's Norton was held by the king in DB.

GREEN'S NORTON PARK is *Grenesnorton park* 1546 LP.

Plumpton

PLUMPTON 83 F 7
    Pluntun(e) 1086 DB, 1162 P (p), 1217 ClR (p)
    Plumton(e) c. 1160 *Add* (p) *et freq* to 1377 Cl, (*juxta Wedone Pynkeny*) 1289 *FF*, (*al. Plumpton*) 1304 Ipm, *Plumpton* 1220 Fees *et passim*, (*Seint Johan*) 1341 AD iv
    Plomton 12th Survey, 1377 Cl

'Plum farm,' *v.* tun. William de *Seynt John* had a holding here in 1304 (Ipm).

OAKLEY BANK is *Hocle, Hockle, Oclee* c. 1200 *Ashby, wood called Hockle* 13th AD ii, *Hokelee* 1324 AD i, *Oakley Banks* 1779 F. This is probably a compound of hoc and leah, with later folketymology. The hill here is irregular in shape and the hoc may have reference to the spurs of the hill.

PLUMPTON WOOD is *boscus de Plomton* c. 1220 *For*.

Silverstone

SILVERSTONE [silsən] 83 H 9
    Silvestone, -y- 1086 DB, 1207 ClR, 1216 FineR, 1252 Cl *et freq* to 1823 B
    Selveston(e) 1086 DB *et passim* to 1314 Ch

Sulvestun 1221 ClR, *-ton* 1360 Ipm
Shelveston 1237, 1244 Cl, *Shulveston* 1243 Cl, 1371 *For*
Silvereston 1253 *Ass*, *Silverstone* 1260–90 Ch, *Solverston* 1305 Ipm, *Sulverston* 1339 Cl
Sylson 1484 AD iii, *Silleston* 1495 AD iv
Silveston al. Silston t. Eliz ChancP, 1657 NRS i, 1675 Moulton

This is probably from *Sigewulfes-tūn*, ' *Sigewulf*'s farm,' *v.* tun. *Siulf* is common as a contracted form of this name already in the OE period. The forms with *r* are due to ready confusion with the common word *silver*, ME *silvre*, *sulvre*. For the forms with *sh*, cf. Syresham *infra* 58.

OLNEY is *Anelegh, boscus de Aneleg*' c. 1220 *For*. If this identification is correct, the interpretation may be 'lonely clearing or wood,' from OE *ān(a)*, 'one, alone, single, solitary.' *v.* leah.

CATTLE END is *Kettle End Green* 1790 Woods Rept. FOXHOLE COPSE is *le Foxholes* 1365 *For*, *Foxehall al. Monckes* 1612 BM, representing the land in the parish held by the monks of St Andrew's Priory, Northampton. LITTLE LONDON (6″) is a jesting name found in various parts of the country. SILVERSTONE FIELDS FM cf. *campo de Selveston* c. 1220 *For*, *le Westfeild, Felde Grove* 1553 *Deeds Enrolled*. WILD WOOD is *Wildwood Coppice* 1790 Woods Rept. Cf. Wildwood Fm in Alfold (Sr), *Wildewode* 1391 Cl, *Wyldewode* 1436 FF.

Slapton

SLAPTON 83 G 8

Slapton(e) 1086 DB *et passim*
Slapetorn 1203 FF
Slepton c. 1220 *For*, 1253 *Ass*

'Farm in the slippery place,' *v.* slæp, tun and cf. Slapton (PN Bk 100). For the confusion in the second element cf. Hardingstone *infra* 147.

SLAPTON MILL was the home of Peter *de molendino* t. Ed 3 *SR*.

Weedon Lois

WEEDON LOIS [wiˑdən lɔi], [lɔi wiˑdən] 83 G 7

Wedon(e) 1086 DB *et passim* to 1316 FA
Suthwedon 1261 *FF*
Wedune Pynkeny 1282 AD ii, *Wedenpynkeney* 1285 *Ass*,
    Weedon Pynkenye 1301 Cl
Leyes Weedon 1475 *Knightley*, *Loyeswedon* 1524 *SR*, *Levis*
    Wedon 1526 SR, *Wedon Pynkney al. Loveswedon* 1542 LP

v. Weedon Beck *supra* 30. The manor was the head of the
Pinkney Honour. *South* in contrast to Weedon Beck. Bridges
(i, 254) says there is a well at the west end of Weston in Weedon,
sometimes called 'St Loys' or 'St Lewis,' and that hence the
village is sometimes called 'Loys' Wedon' or 'Wedon St Lewis.'
According to Morton (283) it specially cured the blind and
leprous.

MILTHORPE is *Middiltrop* c. 1200 *Ashby*, *Mideltorp* t. Ed 3 *SR*
(p), *Milthrope* 1562 *FF*, *Middlethropp* 1624 *Recov*. 'Middle
village,' *v.* þorp. It lies between Weedon and Weston.

WESTON is *Weston(e)* 1162 P *et freq* to 1304 Cl, (*juxta Wedon
Pynkeny*) 1292 *FF*, *Weston Pynkeny* 1311 Ipm, (*by Wedon*) 1343
Ipm. 'West farm,' *v.* tun. It is at the west end of the parish.

Whittlebury

WHITTLEBURY 83 H 10

Witlanbyrig c. 930 (c. 1100) Laws
Witleberia, -y- 1185 RotDom *et passim* to 1369 Cl
Wittlebir, 1255 *For*, *Wyttlebiry* 1269 Ch (p)
Wytelbur(y) 1275 RH, 1399 Cl, *Wyttelbury* 1307 Ch, *Wittel-*
    1326 Cl, *Wittil-* 1369 Cl, *Wittul-* 1391 Cl
Witteleburi 1281–9 Ipm (p)
Wytelesbyry 1294 *Ass*
Whittlebury 1316 FA, *Wutlebury* 1320 Cl, *Whittleberry* 1675
    Ogilby

It is clear that the burh of Whittlebury and the wood of the
neighbouring Whittlewood (*supra* 2) take their name from the
same person. Only once in the spelling of each name do we

find a trace of any form which suggests initial *Hw-*, so we are probably right in assuming a weak form *Witela* of the name *Witel*, which is on record. Cf. Whittlesey (PN BedsHu 191).

CATTLEHILL WOOD is *Cattwell Hill* 1672 *LRMB*. 'Wild cat spring,' *v.* wielle.

THE GULLET is *Golet in Estpirie* 1330 *Ass*, *le Golet* 1337 *Ass*, *le Gullett* 1631 NRS i. It is the name of a shallow depression with a stream running through it. For *Estpirie v. infra* 105.

BUCKINGHAM THICK COPSE is *Bukyngham Thyk* 1538 *CtAugm.* For *thick v. infra* 206. CHAMBER'S SALE COPSE is *Chambersale Coppice* 1790 Woods Rept, and is probably to be associated with the family of Adam *de la Chaumbre* (1275 Fine). For *sale v.* Britain Sale *infra* 156. CLAYDON'S BARN (6″) is to be associated with the family of William *Cleydon* (1570–77 Wills). COLDTHORN is *Cold Thorn* 1790 Woods Rept. FARTHING COPSE (6″) is *Ferthing* t. Ed 1 *PeterbB.* *v.* feorðung. LORDSFIELDS FM is *Lord Feilds* 1663 *Lumley*. LONGHEDGE WOOD (6″) is *Longhegge* 1383 Cl. PORTERSWOOD FM is *Porters wood* 1650 *ParlSurv*, *coppice called Porters Wood* 1672 *LRMB*, and is possibly to be associated with the family of John *le Porter* de Burcote (1297 *For*). SHOLEBROKE LODGE is *Shoulbrooke Land* 1650 *ParlSurv*, *Sholbrook* 1790 Woods Rept. 'Shallow brook,' *v.* sceald, broc. SMALLADINE COPSE (6″) is *Smallydene* 1287 *For*. 'Narrow valley,' *v.* smæl, denu.

Woodend

WOODEND 83 F 8

> *Little Blacolvesle* 12th Survey, *Parva Blakoluesl'* 1275 RH
> *Wodeblakolesle* 1247 *FF*, *Wudeblakolvesle* 1247 *Ass*, *Wodeblacolveslee* 1384 Cl
> *Wodende* 1316 FA, 1371 Cl, *Wodendeblacolvesley* 1420 *FF*, *Woodende al. Woodblakesley* 1522 LP, *Wodynde* 1539 LP

Self-explanatory. It was originally a hamlet of Blakesley *supra* 39.

KIRBY GROUNDS is *Kerby* 1316 FA, 1330 *Ass*, 1386 IpmR, *Kereby* 1341 Pat (p), *Kirkeby* 1583 *Depositions*, *Kerby Grounds*

1781 *EnclA*. This may be '*Kæri*'s by,' *v*. by and cf. Cold Kirby (PN NRY 197). For *grounds v*. Newbold Grounds *supra* 17.

CATHANGER FM is *Kathang'* c. 1200 *Ashby, Catteanger* 1593 *Map*. 'Wild cat slope,' *v*. hangra. GREEN'S PARK is *Greens Park* 1781 *EnclA*. SOUTHFIELDS is *South Field* c. 1825 O.S. It is at the south end of Kirby Grounds estate. WAR'S FARM is to be associated with the family of Robert *War* of Sulgrave (1631 NRS ii).

IV. KING'S SUTTON HUNDRED

Suttunes a. 1076 Geld Roll, *Sutone, Sudtone* DB, *Sutton* 1195 P, *v*. King's Sutton *infra* 58. The north-eastern part was originally an independent hundred and was named *Eadboldestowe* a. 1076 Geld Roll, *Edboldeston, Edboldestou, Alboldestou* 1086 DB, 1156 P, *Albadesto* 1161, *Albodesto* 1162 P, *Albodestow* 1181 P, *Abbotestan* 1230, 1241 P. '*Ealdbeald*'s place,' *v*. stow. For such a use of stow in a hundred-name, cf. *s.n*. Wixamtree (PN BedsHu 87–8). The traditional meeting-place of the hundred of *Alboldestou* was in the *Gallows*-field of Stuchbury on a small hill (Bridges i, 203).

Astwell with Falcutt

ASTWELL [æstəl] 83 H 8

> *Estwell(e)* 1086 DB, 1189 P (p), 1190, 1191 P, 1216 ClR, 1242 Fees
> *Astwell* 1253 *Ass et passim, Astewelle juxta Wapenham* 1294 *Ass, Astewell(e)* c. 1300 AD vi, 1304 Cl

'East spring,' *v*. wielle.

FALCUTT [fɔ·kət]

> *Faucot(e)* 1220 Fees *et freq* to 1428 FA with variant spelling -*kote*, (*by Wappenham*) 1316 Ipm, *Faucutt* 1702 Poll
> *Falcote* 1268 *Ass*
> *Fawcote* (*al. Falcot*) 1659 *Clayton*, 1694, 1745 *Recov*, 1823 B

v. cot(e). The first element may be OE fag, 'variegated,' with some reference to the building material of the original dwellings. In that case the spelling with *l* is an inverted one. OE *fealu*, 'reddish-brown,' is also possible, but in that case we should have expected some early forms in *Falwe-*.

STOCKINGS FM, cf. *le Netherestokking* c. 1300 *For. v.* stocking.

Aynho

AYNHO 94 B 4

> *Aienho* 1086 DB, *Aenho* c. 1175 *Magd*, *Aieynho* 1226 ClR, *Ayngho* 1319 Misc
>
> *Ayno* 12th Survey, -*ho* 1243 Cl *et freq*, *Ainho* c. 1185 *Magd*
>
> *Einho*, -*y*- c. 1195 *Magd*, 1215 WellsR *et freq* to 1375 Cl with variant spellings -*hoo*, -*hou*, *Eyno* c. 1210 Eynsham, *Enoo* 1549 *SR*

'*Æga*'s hoh,' *v.* Eydon *supra* 35. It stands on a well-marked hill.

PESTHOUSE WOOD preserves the name of the old Pest House in the neighbouring parish of Newbottle, marked *Pest Ho* in 1823 (B).

SMANHILL COVERT (6″) [smænəl] is *Smethenhulle* c. 1260 *Magd*. 'Smooth hill,' *v.* smeðe, hyll.

AYNHO GROUNDS is so named in 1823 (B). Cf. Newbold Grounds *supra* 17. COLLEGE FM (6″) is so called from its owners, Magdalen College, Oxford. FIELD BARN (6″), cf. *le Oldefeld* 1330 *Ass*. FRIAR'S WELL (6″) is *Frier's Well* 1792 *EnclA*. GOSPEL WELL (6″) may be the *Haliwelle* of a Magdalen Deed of 1318. 'Holy well,' *v.* halig. NELL BRIDGE was *Neiel bridge* in 1506 according to Bridges (i, 134). NORTHCOTEHILL COVERT. Cf. *Northcote Hill* 1792 *EnclA*. OLD DOWN (6″) is recorded in 1792 (*EnclA*). PUCKWELL (6″) is mentioned in 1712 by Morton (282). 'Puck or goblin spring,' *v.* puca, wielle, and cf. Polebrook *infra* 209.

Brackley

BRACKLEY[1] 94 A 7

Brachelai 1086 DB, *-le* 1192 P, 1208 Fees, *Brachal* c. 1154 BM, *Braccalea* c. 1170 *Harl*, *Brachkelea* 1172 P (CR), *Bracchelea* 1181 P

Brakele 1156 (1318) Ch *et freq* to 1415 AD iii with variant spellings *Bracke-*, *Brakke-* and *ley(e)*, *-lee*, (*Vetus*, *Nova*) 1316 FA

Brakleye 1292–1301 Ch, *Brackleye* 1316 Ch, *Olde Brakley* 1549 *SR*

Perhaps '*Bracca*'s clearing' or 'woodland,' *v.* leah. For this pers. name cf. *s.n.* Bragenham (PN Bk 83) and note also OGer names *Brachio* and *Brachila* (Förstemann, PN 1638). The traditional etymology first noted by Camden (505), 'a place full of *Brake* or *Ferne*' does not suit the forms very well, but certainty is impossible to attain in view of our ignorance of the history of the word *brake* itself. That word may well go back to OE times. Toller (BT Supplt *s.n. fearn-bracu*) suggests that in the phrase *on fearn-braca* (BCS 624) we have an example of the word *ferne-brake*, not otherwise recorded before the *Promptorium*.

GOLDEN SPRING (6″) is *Goldewelle* c. 1175 *Magd et passim*, *Goldwell* 1791 Bridges. Cf. *Goldwellehul* (13th AD ii) in Chalcombe, *Goldewelle* (15th *Daventry*) in Daventry, and Goldwell Fm in Charlton Abbots (Gl), 1377 *Ass Goldwell*. The reason for the name is not known.

HALSE [hɔ·z]

Hasou 1086 DB, *Hasho* 1229 Pat

Halsou c. 1160 *Magd*, t. Ric 1 BM, *Halsho* 1202 P, 1220 Fees, 1247 *Ass*, 1314 Fine, Cl, 1346 FA, *Alsou* 1318 Ch

Hausho 12th Survey, c. 1240 *Magd*, 1296 Ipm, *Hauso* 1236 Cl, *Hawesho* 1285 *Ass*

---

[1] In the deeds relating to Brackley in the possession of Magdalen College we find the following old street and lane names: *Bassateslane* (c. 1250), *Beneites lane* (c. 1235) from medieval owners, *Castle lane* (c. 1255), *Gameleslane* (c. 1260) from the Scand. pers. name *Gamel*, *in venella Horn* (c. 1240), *Hornes lane* (1315) from the family of Richard *Horn* (c. 1260), *the Ratoun Rewe* (1365), a common term of contempt, 'rat row,' *Smetheslane* (1402), 'smith's lane' and *Soudoneslane* (1376) from the family of Laurence *Soudon* (1381).

Hals 1284 FA *et freq* to 1349 Cl, *Halse* 1485 AD iii, *Hawlsse*
    1549 *SR*
Hawes 1657 NRS i, *Halse al. Hawse* 1673 *Recov*, *Halse or*
    Hawes 1823 B

Halse stands on a high neck of land between two valleys and
the name is a compound of OE *h(e)als*, 'neck,' and hoh. Cf.
Halse (PN D 360).

OLD TOWN. Cf. *Heldetunfeld* c. 1260 *Magd*, *le Eldetonfeld*
c. 1290 ib., *Old townmylne* 1425 ib., *le Oldtonfeld* 1426 ib. 'Old
farm or enclosure,' *v.* tun, with interesting abandonment of
southern *eld* for StEng *old* from OE eald. Cf. Introd. xxxi.

ANTELOPE HILL (6″) is so called in 1839 (*EnclA*). Cf. 'the house
called the *Antyloppe* in the town of Brackley' 1536 *Magd*.
BURWELL FM (6″). Cf. *Burchwellebalke* 1403 *Magd*, *Burwell-
furlong* 1457 ib., *Burwell waie* 1550 *Ct.* *v.* burh, wielle. *Burwell*
is presumably the 'borough (or town) well.' *Burwell waie* is the
road now called Burwell Hill. HILL FM is *Brakkelehil* c. 1300
For. ST RUMBALD'S WELL (6″) is mentioned by Leland (ii, 37)
as 'S. Rumoaldes Welle, where they say that within a fewe days
of his birth he preched.' According to the same authority the
saint was born in King's Sutton (*v. infra* 59). TOWN FM
(Kelly). Cf. *Tunfurlong* 1258 *Magd*. *v.* tun.

Chalcombe

CHALCOMBE [tʃeikəm] 83 H 4

Cewecumbe 1086 DB
Chaucumba 1178 P (p) *et passim* to 1371 Cl with var. spelling
    -*cumb(e)*, *Caucumba* 1179, 1190 P (p), *Chawcumbe* 1317–25
    Ipm
Sawecumb 1198 P
Chacombe, -a 12th Survey *et freq* to 1428 FA
Chalcumbe 1308 Ipm, 1399 Cl
Chakeham 1537 AD ii, *Chacombe al. Chalcombe* 1583 *Recov*,
    Chacombe 1823 B, 1826 G

This name would seem to contain the same pers. name as

Challow (Berks), BCS 833 *ceawanhlæw*[1], and Chawridge (Berks), BCS 775 *ceauuan hrycg*, and denote 'Ceawa's valley' (*v.* cumb). In that case the spellings with *l* are inverted spellings.

CHALCOMBE HILL FM. Cf. William *at Hul* (t. Ed 3 *SR*) and *le Overhill, le Farre Hylles* 1552 Pat.

Croughton

CROUGHTON [krouten] 94 B 5

Creveltone, Criweltone, Cliwetone 1086 DB
Creulton 1174–83 *Magd*, 1194, 1195 P, 1292 Ipm, *Creuulton* c. 1200 *Magd, Creuleton* c. 1210 *Magd*, 1300 Ipm
Creueltune c. 1200 *Magd*
Crouelton 12th Survey, *Croulton* 1202 Ass *et freq* to 1428 FA, *Crowelton* c. 1210 WellsR *et freq* to 1401 Cl, *Crowlton* c. 1240 *Magd*, 1381 Cl
Crewelton 1200 FF, 1241 P, 1247 *Ass*, c. 1255 *Magd, Crewulton* 1269 FF
Cruelton c. 1212 *Magd, Cruwelton* 1241 FF
Crouleton 1215 WellsR, 1296 FF, 1298 Ipm
Craulton 1234 Cl, *Crowlton al. Crofton al. Crowton* 1556 FF
Crowton 1526 FF, (*al. Croton*) 1691 Recov, *Croton* 1549 SR
Crofton 1553 BM, 1573 FF, *Croughton oth. Crolton* 1618 FF
Shroughton al. Craughton 1675 Ogilby

Croughton lies on a much broken hill between two streams, and Professor Ekwall and Dr Ritter agree in suggesting that the first element is a lost OE **creowel*, the cognate of OHG *crawil*, MLG *krouwel*, OFris *krawil*, denoting 'a fork.' This would describe the situation of the place, and OE *creowel* would give ME *crewel* and *crowel*. Hence, 'tun on the fork of land.'

ROWLERS FM is *Roulowe* c. 1260 *Magd, Rowler* 1808 *EnclA*. 'Rough hill,' *v.* ruh, hlaw. Kelly gives the name as Rowler Fm, which is probably more correct, the *s* being pseudo-manorial. The 1″ map has POWLERS FM, a printing error.

---

[1] The *ceawwan leage* of BCS 476 must not be brought into account if, as suggested by Grundy (*Saxon Charters of Somerset* First Series 12), this is to be identified with Chipley (So).

COLLEGE BARN (6″) is the property of Magdalen College, Oxford.
THE GREEN (6″) is *le Grene* 1318 *Magd.*

Culworth

CULWORTH [kʌləθ] 83 G 5

Culeorde 1086 DB, *-wurda* 1184 P *et freq* to 1371 AD i, with
variant spelling *-worth(e)*, *Culleworth* n.d. AD i
Colewyth 12th Survey, *Coleworth* n.d. AD i *et passim* to
1376 Cl, *Coleswrth* 1235 Fees
Collewrth n.d. AD i, *-worth* 1380 Cl, *Colworth* 1331 Ipm,
1378 Cl

'*Cula*'s enclosure,' *v.* worþ, cf. Culham (O), *Culanham* BCS
759. The derivative *Cul(l)ing* is on record. A lost part of Culworth is *Cotes* c. 1200 *Ashby*, *Coton* 1438 Cl, *Cote Culworth*
1535 VE, *Cotes Culworth al. Cotton beside Culworth* (1543 LP),
v. cot(e).

BERRY CLOSE HILL (6″) is marked by the remains of an ancient
manor-house (Bridges i, 162), *v.* burh. BLACKBIRD HILL FM is
Blackbird House 1823 B. CULWORTH GROUNDS is so named c. 1825
O.S., *v.* Newbold Grounds *supra* 17. D'ANVERS HO (6″). The
Danvers family held the manor from the 15th century onwards.
FULFORD FM (6″) may have been near *Fulebroc* (c. 1200 *Ashby*).
'Muddy stream and ford,' *v.* ful, broc. WADGROUND BARN is
The Oad or Woad Ground 1771 *Lumley*, and is so called from
the growing of woad, *v.* wad and *infra* 273.

Evenley

EVENLEY [imli], [emli], [evənli] 94 B 7

Evelaia, Avelai 1086 DB, *Eveleia* 12th Survey
Euenlai 1147 BM *et passim* with variant spellings *Even-* and
-lee, -ley, -leg, Evenle by Brakle 1386 Cl
Ivenle 1306 *FF*, *Ivynle* 1384 Pat
Evenele(gh) 1330 FA, *Ass*, 1331 Ipm, 1390 Cl
Yevynle 1427 *Magd*, *Yevenley* 1536 *FF*
Imley al. Evenley t. Jas 1 ECP, *Emly* 1657 NRS i, *Evenley*
al. Emley 1702 *Recov*, *Imly* 1719 Croughton ParReg

'The level leah,' the reference probably being to the broad stretch of country west and south of the present village. Cf. *emnan* (i.e. *efnan*) *leage* BCS 748 and Emborrow (So), *Emnebergh* 1238 Ass.

ASTWICK is *Estwic* c. 1195 *Magd*, 1200 FF, 1208 Cur, 1221 Bracton, -*wyk* 1261 *FF*, *Astwik* 1248 *FF et freq*, *Astewyk(e)* 1347, 1390 Cl, *Estwyke al. Astwyke* 1536 *FF*. 'East farm,' v. wic. *East* with reference to Croughton.

PLOWMAN'S FURZE was usually called *Plummer's Furze* according to Bridges (i, 168), and it is still PLOMER'S FIRS on the 6″ map. In a Brackley deed of c. 1255 (*Magd*) we have John *le Plomer*, and Robert *Plom(m)er* in another of 1381. Probably this was the family which gave name to the Furze.

GROVE FM (6″), cf. *le Grofhey* c. 1275, *Grovesende* 1317 *Magd*, v. graf(a), (ge)hæg. MIXBURY BARN (6″), cf. *Mixburyfeld* t. Hy 8 *Rental*. It takes its name from the neighbouring parish of Mixbury (O). SLADE FM is *Astwik Slade* t. Hy 8 *Rental*, v. slæd. WHITE HOUSE is so named in 1779 (F).

Farthinghoe

FARTHINGHOE [fɑˑnigou] 83 J 5

> *Ferningeho* 1086 DB, 1194 P, 1232 *FF*, -*minge*- 1195 P
> *Feringeho* 1195 P, c. 1200 *Magd*, *Feringho* 1232 Cl, *Farringeho* 1278 RH, *Faryngho* 1316 FA
> *Furningho* 12th Survey
> *Ferningho* 1195 P, 1229 Cl, *Ferlingho* 1203 ChR, *Fernynghoo* 1380 Ch
> *Ferthingo* 1198 P
> *Farningho* 1220 Fees *et passim* to 1406 Inq aqd with variant spelling -*yng*, *Farningehou* c. 1210 *Magd*, 1318 Ch, *Farnynhou* 1301 Ch
> *Farthinghoe* 1580 AD iii, *Farnigo al. Farthingho* 1595 FF, *Farninghoe al. Farthinghoe* 1618 FF

'The hoh or hill of the dwellers in the bracken,' v. fearn, ing. Cf. *fearninga leage* BCS 1076, and *fearninga broc* BCS 926.

OUSE WELL (6″) is the source of the Ouse.

Helmdon

HELMDON 83 H 7

Elmedene 1086 DB, 1235 Fees
Halmeden 1162 P (p), *Hameldene* 1162 P (CR) (p), *Hemelden* 1222 Bracton
Helmesden a. 1166 BM, 1166 P
Helmenden(e) 12th Survey, 1284 FA, 1285 *Ass*, 1327 *FF*, 1428 FA
Haumedon' 1202 Ass, *Heumeden* n.d. AD iii
Helmedon' 1220 Fees, 1275 Cl
Helmeden(e) 1224 Cl *et passim*

'*Helma*'s valley,' v. denu, and for the pers. name cf. *s.n.* Helmsley (PN NRY 71).

ALLITHORNE WOOD is *Allithorn Wood* 1759 *EnclA*, *Alley Thorne* 1823 B. Cf. *Allibridge* and *Ford* (1759 *EnclA*), close at hand. FATLAND BARN (6"). Cf. *Fatland Furlong* 1759 *EnclA*. GRANGE FM is *Grounds Farm* in 1823 B. If this is an early form of the name, we may compare Newbold Grounds *supra* 17.

Hinton in the Hedges

HINTON IN THE HEDGES 94 A 6

Hintone 1086 DB *et passim* with variant spelling *Hyn-*, (*Helye*) 1166, 1175 P, (*juxta Brackele*) 1281 *FF*, *Hynton juxta Brakele* 1285 *Ass*, *Hynton in the edge* 1549 SR, *Hinton oth.* Hinton in the hedges 1754 *Recov*
Hentone 1403 AD iii

This, like Hinton in Woodford *supra* 37 is probably from OE *hīgnatūn*, but we have no record of monastic possession. In 1166 it was held by *Elias* of William de Mandeville. For HINTON GROUNDS, a farm in the parish, v. Newbold Grounds *supra* 17.

Marston St Lawrence

MARSTON ST LAWRENCE 83 H 5

Merestone, -a 1086 DB, 1121–9 France, 1336 AD i
Merston(e) 1181 P *et freq* to 1316 FA, (*by Bannebury*) 1396 Pat

Mersshton Scī Laurencii 1330 QW, *Mersshton* 1383 Cl
Lawrence Marston t. Hy 8 AD iii, *Larrens Marston* 1539 LP

'Marsh farm,' *v.* tun. *St Lawrence* from the dedication of the church.

COSTOW HO is *Costowe* 1221 ClR, 1261 *Ass*, 1324 Ipm, *Cotstowe* c. 1250 *NthStA*, 1255 *FF*. 'Cottage place,' *v.* stow, and cf. *cotstow* BCS 919, 1183 and 1292, the last two referring to the same place.

WESTHORP is *Westhrop, Westthrop* 1219 *FF*, *Westrop* 1316 FA, *Westthrop juxta Merston Sci Laurencii* 1317 *Ass*. 'West village,' *v.* þorp. It is west in relation to Greatworth, not to Marston.

DEAN BARN (6″) probably takes its name from the holding of the Dean and Chapter of Lincoln in the Parish. There is no denu or valley here. MARSTONHILL FM is *Merschtonehil* c. 1300 *For*.

Middleton Cheney

MIDDLETON CHENEY 83 J 4

Mideltone 1086 DB, *Middelton* 12th Survey *et passim*
Mid(d)elinton 1215, 1216 ClR
Middelton Curcy 1224 ClR, *Chirchemiddleton* 1328 Orig,
 1330 QW, *Middelton juxta Chaucombe* 1330 *Ass*, *Middelton*
 Cheyndut 1342 Cl, -*duit* 1343 Ipm, *Middleton Cheynie* 1558
 AD v

'Middle farm,' *v.* tun. Possibly so named because midway between Purston (Nth) and Wardington (Wa). Simon de *Chendut* held the manor in the 12th Century Survey. John de *Curci* held a part in 1205 (ClR). Distinction is also made (Bridges i, 184) between *Upper* or Church Middleton and *Nether* Middleton (*Nethere middelton* 1287 *Ass*) a hamlet a quarter of a mile to the east.

THE HOLT (6″) is *le Holte* 1551 Pat, *v.* holt.

OVERTHORPE is *Trop* 1235 Fees, (*juxta Bannebyr*) 1242 Fees, *Thorp near Charwell* 1299 Cl, *Overthorp(e)* 1330 *Ass*, 1497 *FF*, *Overthropp* 1524 AD v, 1542 LP, *v.* þorp. The place stands high on a hill above Banbury.

Newbottle

NEWBOTTLE 94 A 5

Neubote, Niwebotle 1086 DB, *Neubotha* 1121–9 France,
Neubote 1166 LN
Neubotl(e) 1148–66 Dunstable *et passim* to 1331 Ipm with
variant spellings *New-, Niwe-, Newe-* and *-bottle*
Neubothle 1205 Pap, 1256 Dunstable, 13th AD ii, *New-
bolthl(e)* 1242 Fees
Neupotle 1210–12 RBE
Newebaud 1247 *Ass*

'New building,' *v.* niwe, boðl. Cf. Newbold *supra* 17, and
Nobottle Grove *infra* 78.

CHARLTON

Cerlintone 1086 DB, *Cherlington* 12th Survey, *Cherlenton
juxta Sutton* 1297 *Ass*
Cerletona 1148–66 Dunstable, *Cherleton(a)* c. 1190 (ib.) *et
passim*, (*near Aynho*) 1311 Cl, *Cherilton* 1235 Fees, *Sherlton*
1304 Ipm
Chorlton 1247 *Ass*, 1432 AD iv, *Chorleton* 1446 AD iii, 1524 *SR*
Charleton 1316 FA, 1346 Cl, *Carleton* 1675 Ogilby

This may be for OE *ceorlena-tūn*, rather than the normal
ceorla-tūn, 'farm of the *ceorls*' (cf. Charlton PN BedsHu 92
and Charlton PN Wo 105), but the *ing-* forms are found here
much earlier than in those names. *v.* ceorl.

FORCELEAP COPSE (6″) is *Fourslips Copse* c. 1825 O.S. RAINS-
BOROUGH CAMP is *Rainsborough Hill* 1712 Morton, *Raynesbury*
1739 Camden (Gough), 1779 F, *v.* burh. There is an ancient
camp here.

Radstone

RADSTONE 83 J 7

Rodeston(e) 1086 DB *et passim* to 1415 AD iii, (*Overe and
Nethere*) 1259 Ipm, *Rodiston* 1253 *FF*
Rodestun 1166 P (p), c. 1195 *Magd*, 1223 Pat
Rudstan 1198 P
Roddeston(e) 1200 Cur, 1220 Fees, c. 1225 *Magd*, 1329 Pat,
1381 Cl

Rodestan 1201 Cur, 1227 Pat
Rudeston 1225 ClR, *-tun* 1244 Cl
Reddeston 1227 Cl
Radeston 1288 Ipm, *Radston* 1629 *SR*
Rodestayn 1295 Pat
Rowston 1428 FA
Rodston al. Rodeston al. Raddeston al. Rudston 1572 *FF*
Rodson 1623 *Ipm, Radson* 1730 Poll

This is a difficult name. If the second element is stan we may have an exact parallel in the *Rodestan* of BCS 1127 (a Wiltshire Charter), which is again mentioned in a perambulation of 1575. This may be a compound of rod, 'clearing,' hence 'stone in a clearing,' or much more probably, it denotes a stone used as the socket of a rood (OE *rōd*) or cross.

COLDHARBOUR FM is *Cold Harbour Farm* c. 1825 O.S.

Steane

STEANE 83 J 6
Stane 1086 DB
Stanes 12th Survey *et freq* to 1294 Ch, *-nis* late 12th BM
Stenes 1249 WellsR, 1285 *FF*
Stene 1293 BM *et passim* to 1504 AD iii
Stone 1326 Fine
Stein 1335 Ch, *Steyn* 1526 SR

'At the stone.' For the plural form cf. Staines (Mx). We are well out of the Scandinavian area here and it can only be suggested that we have early confusion between stan and the lost OE *stǣne*, 'stony-place,' discussed under Steine (PN Sx 292).

COLEREADY FM is *Collready, Coleready* 1618 *Clayton, Collerdy* 1773 *EnclA, Cold Readie* 1826 G. No very early forms have been found, but the name is doubtless a compound of col, 'cool' and riðig, 'stream.' There is a small stream here. For the form of the second element cf. Cropredy (O).

STEANE GROUNDS FM. Cf. Newbolds Grounds *supra* 17. WALLTREE FM is *Wall Tree* c. 1825 O.S.

Stuchbury

STUCHBURY 83 H 6

> *Stoteberie* 1086 DB, *-byr(e)* 12th Survey
> *Stutesbiria* 1155–8 (1329) Ch, *-buria* 12th Ord, *-burie* 12th
> 　　AD iii, *Stwtysbury* 1428 FA
> *Stuttebyri* 1227 WellsR, *Stuttesburi* 1288 Ipm
> *Stutebiry* 1229 WellsR, *-byr'* 1244 ib., *-bire* c. 1250 MP
> *Stotesburi* 1284 FA *et freq* to 1372 Cl with var. spellings *-biry*,
> 　　*-ber'*
> *Stoutesbury* 1374 Pat
> *Stuttesburie al. Stuchburie* 1621 DKR xxxviii

We probably have here OE *stūt*, 'gnat, midge,' used as a pers.
name, hence '*Stūt*'s burh.' There can be no question of the
word **stūt*, 'hill,' postulated in PN D 192 *s.n.* Brimpts, for the
place lies in a valley, with no prominent hill near.

King's Sutton

KING'S SUTTON 94 A 4

> *Sudtone* 1086 DB, *Sutton(e)* 1155 P *et passim*
> *Suttun Regis* 1252 Ch, *Kinges Sutton* 1294 Cl

'South farm,' *v.* tun. *South* possibly with reference to
Purston. King William held the manor in 1086.

ASTROP is *Estrop* 1200 Cur, 1247 *Ass*, 1269 Ipm, *-torp* 1201 Cur,
Estthorp' t. Ed 3 *SR* (p), *Astrop* 1269 Ipm, 1284 FA, *Astthrop
juxta Kyngessuttone* 1306 FF, *Astethorp* 1316 FA, *Astropp al.
Ostropp* t. Jas 1 ECP. 'East village,' *v.* þorp. It lies just east of
Sutton.

GREAT PURSTON is *Prestetone* 1086 DB, *Preston* 12th Survey,
Purston 1220 Fees *et passim*, *Great Purston* 1791 Bridges.
'Priests' farm,' *v.* tun. Little Purston is now Buston *infra* 59.

TWYFORD FM (6″) is *Twiford* 1200 Abbr, 1202 Ass, *FF*, *Twyford*
1282 *FF*, *Twyford(s)myll* 1413 Cl, 1452 IpmR. 'Double ford,'
v. twi.

WALTON GROUNDS is *Waleton(e)* 1086 DB, 1331 Ipm, *Walton(e)*
1086 DB *et passim*, (*juxta Sutton Regis*) 1306 *FF*, *Waltun* 1203–6
BM. This lies on the old Port Way. There are Roman remains

in the neighbourhood (cf. VCH i, 201) and it may be that this is from OE *weall-tūn*, 'wall-farm,' rather than *wēala-tūn*, 'serfs' farm,' v. **wealh**. See further Aston le Walls *supra* 32. For *Grounds v.* Newbold Grounds *supra* 17.

BUSTON FM is *Buston* 1775 *EnclA*, *Little Purston* 1791 Bridges, *Burston* c. 1825 O.S. The modern form is corrupt. It should really be *Purston* or *Little Purston* in contrast to Great Purston *supra* 58. LANGLANDS (6″) is *Longlands* 1823 B. ROSAMOND'S BOWER is so named c. 1825 O.S. ST RUMBALD'S WELL. For the association of St Rumbald with King's Sutton, *v. supra* 50.

Syresham

SYRESHAM [saisəm], [səˑrsəm], [sairəsəm] 83 J 8

Sigresham 1086 DB, c. 1147, 1155 BM, 1318 Ch, -*ris*- 1150 BM, *Sigeresham* 1150, 1153 BM, 1179 P, *Sigheresham* c. 1220 WellsR

Sigreham 1086 DB

Shiresham 1162 P *et freq* to 1361 Cl with var. spellings *Sch-*, *Sc-*, *Ch-*

Siresham 12th Survey *et passim* with var. spelling *Syr-*, *Syresham al. Sigresham* 1583 Recov

Sisheham 1526 SR, *Sursame* 1542 LP, *Syresham al. Syseham* 1600 Recov, *Sesham al. Siresham* 1605 Recov, *Sisam* 1702 Poll

'*Sigehere*'s ham(m).' For *s(c)h*-forms cf. Silverstone *supra* 43–4.

BIRCHENHOE (lost) is *Bycchenho* c. 1220 *For*, *Bichenhofeld* c. 1255 *Magd*, *Bicchenho* t. Ed 1 *PeterbA*, *Bichenho* 1287, *Bychen*- t. Ed 3 *For*, *Birchenhoe* 1781 *Recov*. '*Bicca*'s hill,' *v.* hoh. For the pers. name cf. Beachendon (PN Bk 138) and *Beachampstead* (PN BedsHu 268).

FERNILY (lost) is *Fernyleye* 1365, 1377 *For*, *Little Fernily coppice* 1790 Woods Rept. 'Ferny clearing or wood,' *v.* leah.

HAZELBOROUGH LODGE (6″) and WOOD is *Heselebur'* c. 1220 *For*, -*burgh* 1248 Cl, -*berwe* 1272 *For*, *Haselberegh'* 1224 ClR, 1238 Cl, *Haseleberg'* 1244 Cl, *Haselberwe* t. Ed 1 *PeterbB*, -*burwe* 1278 Seld 13, -*bergh* 1341 Cl. 'Hazel hill,' *v.* beorg.

WETLEY'S WOOD is *Weteley* 1287 *For*, *Whetelegh* 1292 Pat, *Whatele* c. 1300 *For*, *-lye* 1346 *For*, *Whitelegh* 1337 Orig, *Wetleys Wood* 1839 *EnclA*. Probably 'wheat clearing,' *v*. leah, the *s* being pseudo-manorial.

WHISTLEY FM (6″) and WOOD is *Wisselai* c. 1200 *Magd*, *Wysseleg* 1287 *For*, *Wyssele* 1367 *For*, *Whistle Wood* 1839 *EnclA*. 'Clearing in soft ground,' *v*. wisce, leah, and cf. Whistley (Berks), *Uuisclea* BCS 1226, Wistley (Gl), *Wisleage* BCS 187, Wisley (Sr), *Wiselei* 1086 DB, *Wys(c)hele(g)* 1246 Ipm, 1272 FF, and Westley PN D 502.

WILD HO is (*in*) *waldis de Wappenham* c. 1220, *Wapenham Wold* 1287 *For*, *Wapenham Weld* 1550 *Ct*, *Wapenham Wilde* 1651 *Lumley*, *v*. weald. Cf. Wild Fm in Aldenham (Herts), *Waldo* 1199 *FF* (p), *ate Welde* 1294 *SR* (p), *the Weilde* 1636 ParReg, and Introd. xxxi.

ABBEY WAY HO is on the road to Biddlesden Abbey (Bk). BLACK HEDGES (6″) is *Blakehegges* 1287 *For*. BRACKLEY HATCH was formerly a detached part of Brackley parish in Whittlewood Forest. It was transferred to Syresham in 1884 (Kelly). *v*. hæcc. BUTTOCKSPIRE WOOD is so called in 1839 (*EnclA*). CROWFIELD is *Crowefeld*, *-feud* 1287 *For*. Self-explanatory. EARL'S WOOD is *Erleswod(e)* 1285 *Ass*, 1469 Pat. The *Earl* of Leicester held land in the parish from the time of Henry II (Bridges i, 194). FARTHING WOOD (6″) is so called in 1839 (*EnclA*), cf. Farthing Copse *supra* 46. HOPPERSFORD FM is so named in 1826 (G) and is probably to be associated with the family of Thomas *le Hoppere* of Steane (t. Ed 3 *SR*). KINGSHILL is *Khingeshil* t. Hy 2 BM, *Kyngyshille* 1269 ib., *-hulle* 1283 *FF*. It is not known what king is here referred to. LANGLEY FM (6″), cf. *Langelesike* t. Ed 1 *PeterbB*, *v*. lang, leah, sic. LITCHLAKE is *Lyche Lake copp*' c. 1550 *AOMB*, *v*. lacu. LODGE COPSE is *Loggecoppis* 1367 *For*. It adjoins Hazelborough *supra* 59, one of the forest lodges. MARY WOOD (6″) is *Marywode* c. 1220, *Maryewod* 1287 *For*. MONK'S WOOD is *Monkeswode* t. Ed 1 *PeterbB*, *Monekeswod* 1287 *For*, and is so called from the monks of Biddlesden Abbey. NEEDLES HALL (6″) is *Needless Hole* 1779 F, *Needle's Hole* 1839 *EnclA*. PENTIMORE WOOD is so called in 1839 (*EnclA*). PIMLICO is so called in 1791 (Bridges), and is no doubt named from the London district of the same name, the origin of which is not known. SANDYHURST COPSE (6″) is *Sandyhurst coppice* 1790 Woods Rept, *v.* hyrst. SHIPLANDS COPSE (6″) is *Sheeplands Copse* c. 1825 O.S. SHORTGROVE WOOD is *bosc. de Shortegrave* 1286, *Schortegrave* c. 1300 *For*, *v.* grafa. SWALLOWTAIL WOOD (6″) is so called in 1823 (B). WINTER HILL (6″) is so called in 1790 (Woods Rept).

Thenford

THENFORD 83 J 5

Teworde, Taneford 1086 DB

Tanford(a) c. 1130 OxonCh, 1185 RotDom, 1267 Ch, *Thaneford* 1220, 1235 Fees

Thayniford 12th Survey

Teinford 1175 P *et freq* to 1285 *Ass* with variant spelling *Teyn-, Teineford* 1195 P, *Theinford* 1349 Ipm

Teneford 1184 P, 1235 Fees, *Tenford* 1235, 1242 Fees

Tinford' 1201 Seld 13, *Thinford* 1240 *FF*, *Thingford* 1712 Morton

Thenford 1242 Fees, 1275 Cl, RH, 1313 Ipm

Theneford 1301 Ipm, 1309 *FF*, 1312 *Ass*, 1314 *Deeds Enrolled*

Fenfforde 1546 BM, *Fenford al. Thenford* 1567 *FF*, *Thenford al. Fenford* 1596 *FF*, 1707 *Recov*

This would seem to be from OE *þegn(a)-ford*, 'ford of the thegn or thegns.' Bridges (i, 203) hazards this suggestion. The reason for the name is unknown.

THENFORD GROUNDS FM. Cf. Newbold Grounds *supra* 17. THENFORD HILL CAMP is called *Arbury* by Bridges (i, 203). For this name cf. Arbury Hill *supra* 13.

Thorpe Mandeville

THORPE MANDEVILLE 83 H 5

Torp 1086 DB, *Thorpe* 12th Survey, *Trop* 1220 Fees

Throp Mondeville 1300 AD vi, *Thorp Mondevill* 1301 Cl, *Thropmundeville* 1315 *Ass*, *Thorp Mandevill* 1316 FA, *Thropmundevile* 1345 AD ii

Thrupmounfeld 1539 LP, *Thropmandefelde* 1547 Pat, *Thrup Mandeville* 1702 Poll

v. þorp. The family name appears first as *Amundevill* in 1252 (Ch), and that is the correct form, though subsequent records show no initial *a*.

MAGPIE FM is *The Magpye* 1779 F, *The Magpie* c. 1825 O.S. suggesting that there may formerly have been an inn here of this name.

Wappenham

WAPPENHAM [wɔpnəm] 83 G 8

Wapeham 1086 DB, 1162 P, 1205 Cur, 1284 FA, *Wapham* 1254 Ipm, 1283 Fine
Wappeham 1175 P, *-hamm'* 1220 Fees
Wappenham 12th Survey *et passim*
Wapenham 1203 Cur, 1204 *FF*, 1242 Fees, 1263 Ch
Wappingham 1316 FA, 1702 Poll
Wapnaham 1503 *FF*, *W(h)apnam*, *Wapneham* 1542 LP, *Wapnam* 1576 *Recov*

'*Wæppa*'s ham(m).' Cf. Wephurst, Wepham, Wappingthorne (PN Sx 108, 167, 237) and Wappenbury (Wa).

THRIFT BARN (6″) is *le Fryht in bosco de Wappenham* 1287 *For*, *Thrift or Frith Wood* 1762 *EnclA*, *the Thriffs* 1791 Bridges, v. fyrhðe. For the form cf. Salem Thrift and Marston Thrift PN BedsHu 30, 80.

BLACKMIRE'S FM is *Blakemerewode* c. 1200 *Ashby*. 'Dark pool,' v. mere. The *s* is pseudo-manorial. COCKERELL'S COPSE (6″) is to be associated with the family of Elizabeth *Cockrill* (1716 ParReg). POTASH is *Potash Farm* (1826 G), and was so called from the making of potash here. Cf. Potash Close (1761 *EnclA*) in Sulgrave and Pot Ash (1747 *EnclA*) in Cosgrave, also in old woodland country. PRIESTHAYWOOD FM is *Prosthey* 1316 Ipm, *Presthey* 1330 *Ass*. 'Priests' enclosure,' v. preost, (ge)hæg. RADMORE FM is *Redmore* 1247 *FF*, *-mour* 1373 Pat, *Radmore Feild* 1681 *Lumley*. v. mor. The first element is either read, 'red,' or hreod, 'reed.'

Warkworth

WARKWORTH[1] 83 J 4

(*Wauerc*)*uurt* 1153 RegAntiquiss, *Wauercurt* 1206 *FF*, 1208 Cur, 1219 *FF*, t. Hy 3 BM

Wauencurt c. 1156 (13th) RegAntiquiss

Wauercheurda c. 1180 MertRec, *Wauerkeworth*(*e*) 1219 WellsR, 1220 ib.

Warcw(*o*)*rth* 1257 Ipm, 1284 FA, *Warkewrthe* 1274 Ipm, -*worth* 1321 Pat, 1329 AD i, 1347 Cl, *Warkworth* 1316 FA

Warecurthe n.d. AD i, *Warcourth* 1332 AD i

This name has already been commented upon in PN D 349 (*s.n.* Warkleigh). The first element would seem to be a lost OE **wæferce*, 'spider,' but if so, it should be noted that except possibly for Beauworth (Ha), *Beowyrð* BCS 731, this is the only example we know of wor**þ** compounded with the name of a spider or any insect, and such a compound does not in itself seem very probable. Dr A. H. Smith suggests the possibility of a pers. name *Wæferce*, derived from *wæfre*, 'wavering, unsteady.'

BLACKPITS FM (6″) is *Blakepittes* 1330 *Ass*

FRANKLOW KNOB FM is *Frankelowe* 1543, 1544 LP. Probably '*Franca*'s mound or tumulus,' v. hlæw. Cf. Frankley (PN Wo 346). 'Knob' must refer to the small round hill here.

GRIMSBURY is *Grimberie* 1086 DB, *Gremesbir*' 12th Survey, *Grimesberi* 1198 P, *Grimesbir*' t. John BM *et freq* with variant spellings *Grymes-* and -*beri*, -*buri*, *Grynnsburye* t. Eliz *FF*, *Grynncebury* 1610 *Pat*. '*Grim*'s burh.'

HUSCOTE HO is *Hussecote*, *Husecote* t. Ed 3 SR (p), *Huscot*(*e*) 1497 *FF*, 1531 Recov, *Hiscote* 1498 *FF*. Personal names *Hussa* and *Husa* are alike on record, hence '*Hus*(*s*)*a*'s cottages,' v. cot(e).

NETHERCOTE is *Nerthercote* 1202 Ass (p), *Nethercot*(*e*) 1290 Abbr, 1346 AD iii, (*by Bannebury*) 1392 IpmR, 1497 *FF*. 'Lower cot(e).' It lies below Overthorpe *supra* 55. The first form is corrupt.

---

[1] Part of this parish, including Grimsbury, Huscote and Nethercote, was transferred to Oxfordshire in 1889.

SPITAL FM. 'The *Spittle*-house, formerly an infirmary or hospital for lepers. In old times called The Hospital of St. Leonard near Banbury' (Bridges i, 220).

Whitfield

WHITFIELD 83 J 7

> *Witefelle* 1086 DB *et freq* to 1293 Ipm with variant spellings *Wyte-* and *-feld, -feud*
> *Withesfeld* c. 1150 BM, *Withefeld* c. 1220 *Magd*, *-y-* 1238 *FF*, 1285 *Ass*
> *Hwitefeld* 1185 RotDom, *Parva Whitefeud* 1209–35 WellsR, *Whitefeld* 1220 Fees *et freq* to 1307 Ch with variant spelling *Whyte-, Whitfeld* 1381 *Ass*
> *Watfeld* 1194 P, *Wetefeld* 1208 Fees, *Wutefeld* 1236 Cl
> *Wittefeld'* c. 1220 *Magd*, 1241 P, *Wyttefelde* 1239 Eynsham
> *Quitefeld* c. 1240 MertRec (p), *Qwytefeld* 1285 *FF*

'White open land,' *v.* feld. For a more detailed interpretation *v.* Whitefield (PN D 52).

WHITFIELD MILL. Cf. *Mulnecroft, Mulnehyl* c. 1240 *Magd*.

V. GUILSBOROUGH HUNDRED

Gildesburh a. 1076 Geld Roll, *Gildesboru* 12th Survey, *Gisleburg* 1086 DB, *Gildeburc(h), -burg* 1185–7 P, *Gildesburc* 1202 Ass, *Giltesburgh* 1220 Fees. *v.* Guilsborough *infra* 70.

Cold Ashby

COLD ASHBY 73 G 9

> *Essebi* 1086 DB
> *Caldessebi* c. 1150 BM, *Kald-* 1205 *FF*, *Caldeassheby* 1401 Cl
> *Chaldessebi* c. 1160 *AD* B 8540, *-by* 1212, 1219 *FF*, *Chald Asseby* early Hy 3 BM
> *Coldessebi* 1199 FF, *-by* c. 1230 AD i, 1235 Ch, *Colde Assheby* 1359 Ipm
> *Haldaskebi, Kolekebi* 1200 Cur, *Asheby* 1233 Cl, *Cole Ashbye* 1631 NRS i, *Cole Ashby al. Cold Ashby* 1780 FF

'**By** by the ash-tree,' cf. Ashby St Ledgers *supra* 9. *Cold* 'from its high and exposed situation' (Bridges i, 550). Distinctive adjectival epithets are seldom added as early as the 12th cent.

CHILCOTE'S COVER[1] (1825 O.S.) is the last trace on the map of the DB manor of *Cildecote*, referred to also as *Childecote* 1235 Ch, c. 1250 *PipewellB*. 'Cottage(s) of the young men or servants,' *v.* cild, cot(e).

PORTLY FORD BRIDGE. *Portly* is possibly a corruption of *Portway*. The main road here is referred to as *le Porteweye* in 1439 (HMC Hastings 255).

Long Buckby

LONG BUCKBY 83 A 8

Buchebi 1086 DB, 1190 P, *Buckebi* 1175 P (p) *et passim* with variant spellings *Bukke-*, and *-by*, *Buckby* 1284 FA

Bukebi 1189 P (p) *et freq* to 1361 Cl

Bokeby 1264 Ipm, 1316 FA

Bockeby 1291 AD v, 1310 Ipm, 1344 Pat, *Bokkeby* 1391 AD iv

Longe Bugby 1565 Recov, *Longbuggbeye* 1595 NRS iii, *Longbugby* 1599 Recov, *Bugbey* 1702 Poll

The first element here is probably a pers. name. We have in ON a pers. name *Bukkr*. This should give Late OE *Bukke* with gen. *Bukkes*. Possibly the existence of a weak Old English name *Bucca* led to the development of a would-be weak form in the Anglo-Scandinavian name. The alternative is to believe that *Buckeby* has replaced earlier *Buccanbyrig*, cf. Badby *supra* 10 and Introd. xxii. In 1437 (*Ct*) we have mention of a *Bukwelsyde* in Buckby. The village is so called from its length (Bridges i, 564).

COTTON END (6″) is *Coten* 1324 Ipm, *Cottonend* 1544 *FF*, *Cotton Inde* 1550 Pat. 'At the cottages,' *v.* Claycoton *infra* 66.

HOBOROUGH HILL is *Houberwe*, *Hoberwe*, *Houberewe* c. 1250 *PipewellA*. 'Hollow hill,' *v.* holh, beorg, doubtless from the two deep hollows which almost cut it in two. Cf. Hobberill *supra* 31.

---

[1] Still surviving in fields called *Chilcotes*, in Thornby.

MURCOTT (6″) is *Morcot(e)* 1220 Fees *et freq* to 1428 FA, *More-cote* 1268 *Ass*, *Murcote* 1334 Ch, 1444 *Ct*, *Moorcote* 1481 *FF*. 'cot(e) in the swampy place,' *v*. mor. Cf. Morcott (R), *Morcot(e)* 1086 DB, 1232 Ch.

RYEHILL FM is *Est Ryenhull* 1295 AD iii, *Ruhulle* 15th *Daventry*. Morton (35) tells us that in each of the three fields into which the open-Field lordships were divided, there was a parcel of sandy or looser soil, which they usually called *Rye-Hill* from its elevated site and its fitness for that sort of grain.

SURNEY BRIDGES and LODGE is *Sutheneybrugge* 1437, *Southeney* 1444 *Ct*, *Cerney Lodge* 1823 B. This may be for earlier ME *bysouthen ey*, 'south of the eg or well-watered land.' For the modern form cf. Surbiton (Sr), earlier *Subertone*, which is doubtless for *Suthbertone*.

BOTTOM MILL (6″). Cf. *le Nethermylle* 1444 *Ct*. GREENHILL FM was the home of Simon de *Grenehille* (1330 *Ass*). LEIGHTON LODGE (6″). Cf. *Leyghtondole* 1458 *Ct*. This is OE leactun, 'vegetable-enclosure, garden.' For *dole*, *v*. dal. PATFORD BRIDGE [pæpfəd bəˑdʒ] must be identical with *Patbroc bridge* 1591 *DuLaMiscBks*. For the local pronunciation *v*. Introd. xxxii. ROCKHALL HILL is *Rokwelhyl* 1460 AD vi. 'Rook-spring hill,' *v*. wielle. RODWELL SPRING (6″) is *Rodewelle lynche* 1366 AD iv, perhaps 'spring by the reeds,' *v*. hreod, wielle, hlinc.

Claycoton

CLAYCOTON 73 G 7

> *Cotes* 1175 P, 12th Survey, 1220 Fees, (*juxta Lilleburne*) 1285 *Ass*
> *Cleycotes* 1284 FA, 1360 AD iv, *Clay-* 1330 FA, 1361 Cl
> *Claycoten* 1330 QW, *-ton* 1427 AD iii, *Cleycoton* 1388 AD v
> *Claycotton* 1521, *Claycotten al. Claycoates* 1684 *Recov*

'At the cottages,' the earliest forms going back to the OE strong plural, the later and modern probably to the weak plural. According to Bridges (i, 548) it is named Claycoton from its soil, to distinguish it from the adjacent Coton *infra* 67.

BLACKDOWN (6″) is *Blake Downe* 1587 *Map*.

Coton

COTON 73 H 9

Cota, Cote 1086 DB

Cotes t. Hy 2 BM *et passim* to 1428 FA, *Cotes Goldinton* 1220
Fees, *Cotis* 1235 Fees, 1252 Ipm

Cotene juxta Gildeburg' 1285 *Ass, Estcoton by Gildesburgh*
1369 Cl

Cotton subtus Gyllesburroughe 1581 *FF*

'The cottages,' *v.* Claycoton *supra* 66. *East* with reference
to that place. Peter de *Goldinton* is mentioned in connection with
the place in 1191 (P).

Cottesbrooke

COTTESBROOKE [kɔtizbruk] 73 H 10

Cotesbroc 1086 DB *et passim* to 1342 Cl with variant spelling
-*brok*

Codesbroc 1086 DB, *Codebrok* 1251 Cl, (*Cotesbrok al.*) 1304
Ipm

Cottesbroc 1219 WellsR, -*broke* 1575 AD v

Catesbrok 1332 Cl

Cottesbrooke al. Cosbrooke 1639 NthNQ i

Cottesbrooke al. Codgbrooke 1684 *Recov, Codgebrooke* 1657
ParReg

There is good evidence for an OE pers. name *Codd, v.* Cuts-
dean (PN Wo 120). In Cottesbrooke we probably have an unvoicing of *d* to *t* before following *s* in spite of the immediately
following *b*. Hence, '*Codd*'s brook.' The alternative would be
to derive it from the strong form *Cott* parallel to the weak *Cotta*,
cf. Cottesmore (R), *Cottesmore* (10th Hyde), Cossall (Nt) DB
Coteshale, Cottesloe (PN Bk 87), Cotesbach (Lei) DB *Cotes-
bece*, and *Cotteshyrst* (BCS 1085) in Sunbury (Mx).

CALENDER FM (6") is *lands called Kalendre* 1541 LP. Bridges
(i, 557) says that *Kalender* is named from *Kaylend* in the meadow-
land of Cottesbrooke, given to the abbot and convent of Sulby,
who placed here a cell. The form *Kaylend* cannot be explained
and looks unlikely.

MITLEY SPINNEY is *Mittelowehul* t. Hy 3 *Brudenell*. The name *Mittelhul* (1416 AD iii) in Yelvertoft is probably for *Middelhul*, and suggests that the name here may really be *Middellowe*, 'middle hill.' The ground is much broken.

PITMOREHILL SPINNEY. Cf. *close called Pittmore* 1618 *Clayton*.

Creaton, Great and Little

CREATON, GREAT and LITTLE 73 H 10

> *Craptone* 1086 DB, *Creptone* ib.
> *Creton(e)* 1086 DB *et passim* to 1484 AD iv, (*Magna*) 1202 Ass, (*Parvam*) 1284 FA, (*Grosse*) 1405–24 ECP, (*Mich*) 1477 AD iv
> *Cretton* 1176 P (p), 1235 Fees
> *Creiton* 1202 Ass (p), *Creyton* 1526 SR, 1563 *FF*
> *Cratton'* 1285 *Ass*
> *Greate Creaton* 1657 NRS i
> *Critton* 1687 StJ

The history of this name is not made easier by what are clearly eccentric forms in DB. Topographically the chief feature of Creaton is that it stands on the top of a high ridge which slopes steeply down on two sides. The most likely possibility is that it is named from the hill on which it stands, and that that was called *Cre(i)c*. For such a hill-name, *v*. Crick *infra*. Hence, 'farm on the hill,' with early assimilation of *k* to *t*. The DB forms may be attempts to wrestle with the difficult *ct* combination. Creeton (L), with early forms *Cretun*, *Cretone* and two late forms *Cretton* may be a parallel, but no certainty is possible. It lies at the foot of a steepish hill in the valley of the Glen.

Crick

CRICK 73 H 7

> *Crec* 1086 DB *et passim* to 1331 Cl with variant spelling *Crek*
> *Kreic* 1201 Cur, *Creyk* 1300 Ipm, 1322 Ch, 1330 *Ass*
> *Creke* 1284 FA, 1385 Cl
> *Criek(e)* 1328, 1391 Cl
> *Creek(e)* 1340 Ch, 1343 Ipm, 1583 *FF*, *Creake* 1346 FA
> *Kreke* 1517 DBE, *Creke or Cricke* 1598 Moulton, *Creek* 1610 Camden, *Creeke al. Crick* 1613 Recov, *Crieke* 1618 *FF*

This is a difficult name. From the point of view of form it would seem clearly to be the same name as Crayke (PN NRY 27). Half-a-mile north-west of Crick there is a prominent isolated hill of a pointed character, of a type that is exceptional in this county. It is possible that Crick takes its name from this hill, but it should be pointed out that there are two difficulties, (1) that, topographically, village and hill are not immediately adjacent, and (2) we have no reference to Crick Hill by name earlier than the 19th century, so that one cannot be certain whether the hill was not named from the village, rather than the village from the hill. The village is itself on a hill on a knob which forms part of a ridge, and it is possible that this knob may itself have given rise to the village name (but see further *s.n.* Crack's Hill *infra*).

Similar forms are to be found for North and South Creake (Nf), but the topographical connection is less clear. They lie in the same river-valley, and though the ground round is somewhat broken, it is difficult to see from what hill or hills the places could be named. Ekwall (*Scandinavians and Celts* 105) notes what seems to be (from form and topography alike) another example of this hill-name in Blindcrake (Cu), which must be named from the prominent hill at the foot of which it stands. Different from these, at least on the topographical side, is the River Crake in Lancashire over the Sands, of which the early forms (RN 102) are in close agreement with those for the name just dealt with. The hill-names are certainly Celtic and allied to OW *craig*, 'rock.' The stream-name, as suggested by Lindkvist (*loc. cit.*) may be Scandinavian in origin, from a lost **kreik* (cf. Lakeland dialectal *creyke*, 'nook or opening formed in the sand or marshes by the tide'), the root-idea being that of 'bend, nook, or narrow valley.' The Norfolk Creakes may take their name from the stream which joins them, but it is not a particularly winding one. The Crake on the other hand has a tortuous course.

CRACK'S HILL was known as *Crick Hill* in 1839 (cf. a list of field-names of Crick made in that year by John West of Little Bowden). The form *Crackshill* or *Craxhill* seems to be of later date.

FLAVELL'S LODGE is probably to be associated with the family of Andrew *Flavel* of Kilsby (1621 Wills).

Elkington

ELKINGTON 73 G 8

> *Eltetone* 1086 DB, *Heltedune* 1200 Cur, *Eltedon* 1247 *Ass*
> *Heldendun* c. 1160 *AD* B 8540
> *Eltindon(e)* 1184 BM, 1219 Bracton, 1247 *Ass*, 1283 Ch,
>   *Elten-* c. 1190 *PipewellA*, t. Hy 3 AD ii, 1235 Ch, 1240 *Ass*,
>   *-den* 1275 RH
> *Eltesdon* 12th Survey, 1240 *Ass*
> *Eltyngdoun* 1394 Cl, *Eltington oth. Eltingdon* 1656 *FF*
> *Eltington al. Elkington* 1617, 1767 *Recov*, *Eltington* 1791
>   Bridges

This is a difficult name. The second element is clearly dun. Ekwall takes the first element here, and probably also in Eltham (K), to be a pers. name **Elta*, of which we have a strong form in Eltisley (C) and, it may be added, in one or two of the forms noted here. It is clear that Elkington can have no connection with OE *ielfet*, 'swan,' which Wallenberg (KPN 361) would take to be the first element of Eltham, neither can Eltisley. Hence, probably, '*Elta*'s hill,' v. dun, ing. Interchange of *k* and *t* is fairly common, cf. EDG 283.

COT HILL is *Cotehill* 1285 *Ass* (p), 1553 Pat, *Cothill, Cockhill* 1540 *LRMB*, *Cock(e)hill* c. 1660 *Clayton*. v. cot(e), with the same confusion of *c* to *t* in the 1540 form as in the name of the parish. Cf. Cotterells Fm in Shere (Sr), *Cot(e)hull(e)* 1279 *Ass*, 1413 *Ct*, *Westcotell'* 1521 *Ct*, *Cottles in Shere* 1599 Surrey Wills.

HONEY HILL is *Grethonehill* 1540 *LRMB*. It is just possible that this is really 'great hone hill,' the first element being *hone*, 'stone, rock' (OE *hān*). Morton (99) speaks of 'cemented masses of gravel as hard almost as flint standing out above the surface,' in the neighbouring parish of Welford.

Guilsborough

GUILSBOROUGH 73 H 9

> *Gisleburg* 1086 DB
> *Gilleburc* 1160 P
> *Gildeburch* 1194, 1195 P, *Ghildeburc* 1209–35 WellsR, *Gilde-*
>   *burg* 1226 ClR

Gildesburc late 12th BM *et passim* with variant spellings
-*burgh*, -*burg*, *Giltesburgh* 1220 Fees
Geldesburg' 1228 *FF*, -*bur'* 1290 Ipm, *Geldeburg* 1242 Fees
Guldesburgh 1316 FA
Gylesburgh 1367 Cl, *Guillesborow* 1596 *FF*, *Gilsborowe* 1610
Recov

OE *Golda* is recorded as a pers. name, and there may have been a corresponding strong *i*-form *Gyldi*, which would yield OE *Gyldesburh*, 'the burh of one *Gyldi*.' Most *borough*-names go back to OE beorg, but this is clearly a burh-name. Bridges (i, 566) says that on the top of *Burrows* or *Borough* hill were still to be seen remains of the encampment which gave rise to the name. See further Morton 524.

NORTOFT GRANGE is *Nortot* 1086 DB, -*toft* 1175 P *et passim*, *Northtoft* 1175 P, 1211 *FF*, *Norththoft juxta Gildesburgh* 1291 *Ass*, *Northtoftes* 1314 Cl, *Nortaft* 1665 Renton. 'The north topt,' cf. the same name *supra* 25.

BLACKPITS SPINNEY (6″) is *Blackpitte* c. 1650 *Clayton*. KETCH-LOW FM (6″). Cf. *Cattsloe ground* c. 1650 *Clayton*, *Catslo grounds* 1764 Renton. LINDOW SPINNEY (6″). Cf. *Lindoe* 1684 Renton. Probably 'lime-tree hill,' *v.* lind, hoh. RYE HILLS (6″) is *the Rye Hille* c. 1650 *Clayton*. Cf. Ryehill *supra* 66.

West Haddon

WEST HADDON 73 H 8
E(d)done 1086 DB
Westhaddon 12th Survey *et passim*, *West Haddoun* 1388 Cl

'Heath hill,' *v.* hæð, dun, and cf. East Haddon *infra* 83. Morton (10) notes that the sheep 'upon the heaths' at West Haddon are specially healthy.

OSTOR HILL (6″) is *Ostrou* 13th *PipewellA*. Cf. also *Ostrouweye* in the same document and in the Daventry Cartulary (15th). There is a tumulus here, and it would seem most likely that the name goes back to OScand *austr*, 'east,' and haugr, hence 'eastern barrow.' For other similar spellings of compounds of *austr*, *v.* Lindkvist 151–4. If these forms contain *austr*, the preservation of the inflexional *r* in this, as in some other names quoted by Lindkvist, is noteworthy and exceptional. Possibly the comparative form *øystri*, often used in p.n.'s, which would keep its *r* and become *estre*, has been replaced by an analogical formation with the vowel of the positive form and the *r* of the comparative. Antiquaries have associated the hill with *Ostorius* Scapula (Bridges i, 599). There is as little authority for this as for a similar attempt to associate him with Austerfield (Y), *v.* Lindkvist 151 n. 3.

FOXHILL is *Fox Hill* 1805 NthNQ ii. HUNGERWELL BARN (6″) is *Hungerwells* ib. This is probably a piece of folk-etymology for *Hangerwell*. There is a little stream here running down a steep slope, *v.* hangra, wielle. NENMOOR SPRINGS (6″) is *Nenmore Springs* 1791 Bridges. One of the reputed sources of the Nene (*supra* 3). Morton (3) notes that 'to confirm their Pretences they have there a groundless Tradition that the Monks of Peterborough, a City seated on the Nene, had in one of their Officials (? offices) a Petition that the Spring on Nenmoor might never fail.' *v.* mor. REDMORE FM (Kelly) is *Rodemor* 13th *PipewellA*. Probably 'reed marsh,' cf. Rodmore in Watford *infra* 76, and Rodwell Spring *supra* 66.

Hollowell

HOLLOWELL 73 H 10

> *Holewell(e)* 1086 DB *et passim* to 1348 Cl, *Hollewelle* 1166 RBE, n.d. AD iv, *Holwell* 1284 FA, 1347 Cl
> *Holowell juxta Gildesburgh* 1317 *Ass*, *Hollowell* 1701 *Recov*
> *Hollywell* 1595 *FF*

'Spring in the hollow,' *v.* holh, wielle.

Lilbourne

LILBOURNE 73 G 5

> *Lineburne* 1086 DB
> *Lilleburne* 1086 DB *et passim* to 1437 AD v with var. spellings -*bourne* and *Lylle-*, *Lilburne* 1393 Cl

'*Lilla*'s stream,' *v.* burna. Cf. Lilford *infra* 185, and Lilly Brook (PN D 8).

Dow Bridge is *pons de Douuebrigge in Watlingstrete* 1330 *Ass*, *Dowbridge* 1610 Camden, *Dobridge* 1657 NRS i, *Dow Bridge* or *Dove Bridge* 1826 G. The bridge was apparently named 'Dove-bridge.' It may contain either the bird-name or, as Professor Ekwall suggests, the recorded 12th century pers. name *Duua*. *dow* is a common dialectal form of *dove*, though not recorded from Northants (*v.* EDD). Close at hand is Dow Boards Covert. *Boards* is probably due to an attempt to preserve the dialectal pronunciation [bə·dʒ] of *bridge*, *v*. Introd. xxxii. In both names the *v* would readily be lost before following *b*.

Naseby

Naseby 73 F 10

> *Navesberie* 1086 DB
>
> *Nauesbi*, *-y* 1166 P, c. 1190 *Add et passim* to 1475 AD vi, with variant spellings *Naves-*, *Naveseby* 1305 Fine
>
> *Naveneby* 1253 *Ass*, *Navenesby* 1275 RH
>
> *Naseby* 1447, *Nasby* 1481 AD iv

This is apparently one of the names in which an OE p.n. has been partially Scandinavianised. The OE name was clearly *Hnæfes-burh*, i.e. 'the fortified place of one *Hnæf*,' a name recorded in the heroic poetry, but not hitherto noted elsewhere except in *Hnæfes scylf* in a Hampshire charter (BCS 307). The third series of forms show the influence of the ON pers. name *Nafni*, which has given us Navenby (L), DB *Navenebi*. We can hardly start from that name here, as it is unlikely that it would be compounded with burh, and would leave the genitival *s* unexplained.

Shuckburgh Fm is *Shukbourgh* 1540 *LRMB*. A Thomas *Shukburgh* is associated with Naseby in 1476 (AD vi) and the family remained here till the 17th century (Bridges i, 574). The name is probably manorial in origin, the family having come from Shuckburgh (Wa).

Avon Well (6″) is the source of the Avon river. Cromwell Ho is a modern name suggested by the battle of Naseby (1645), cf. Prince Rupert's Fm *infra* 121. Nutcote is *Knutcoat* 1792 Mastin. Broad Moor, Fenny Hill and Mill Hill are all shown in a 17th century plan (Mastin) of the battle of Naseby.

Stanford on Avon

STANFORD ON AVON 73 F 7

> *Stanford* 1086 DB *et passim*, (*abbatis de Selebi*) 1190 P, (*juxta Lilleburne*) 1242 Fees, *Staneford* 1275 RH, 1483 AD v
> *Stanfort* c. 1125 BM
> *Stanford super Hauen* 12th Selby, (*Aven*) 1367 *Ass*, *Stanford upon Aven* 1540 LP

'Stony ford,' *v.* stan. *On Avon* probably to distinguish it from Stamford *infra* 242. Already in DB the Abbot of Selby had land here.

CHURN SPINNEY (6"). Cf. *Churne ground* 1645 *Deed*.

DOWNTOWN HILL is *Duna* 12th Selby, *la Doune* 1317 *FF*, 1330 *Ass* (p), *Downe* 1540 LP, *Down Town* 1645 *Deed*. *v.* dun. There was formerly a village here, now depopulated (Bridges i, 578).

Thornby

THORNBY 73 G 9

> *Torneberie* 1086 DB
> *Thirnebi* c. 1160 *AD* B 8540, -*by* 1236, 1242 Fees, 1379 Cl, *Thyrneby* 1261 *Ass*, 1316 FA
> *Turnebi*, -*y*- 1175 P (p) *et freq* to 1242 Fees
> *Thurnebi* t. Ric 1 BM *et freq* to 1361 Cl with variant spelling -*by*
> *Turlebi* 12th Survey
> *Thurleby* 1226 WellsR
> *Thornby by Sulby* 1418, *Thorneby* 1419 Pat
> *Thurnebye al. Thornbye* 1582 *Recov*, *Thornby* 1633 *Ipm*
> *Thurnby al. Thynby* 1648 *Recov*, *Thurnby* 1791 Bridges

If we lay stress on the first form of this somewhat difficult name, we might take it to be an exact parallel to Thornbury (Gl, He), *þornbyrig* in BCS 574 and 1317, denoting a burh by a thorn-tree, or possibly a burh of which a thorn-hedge formed part of the defences. In view, however, of the great preponderance of *i* and *u* forms from the 12th to the 14th century, we should probably be right in following Professor Ekwall's suggestion that the first element is really OE *þyrne*, 'thorn-bush,' hence 'by by the thorn-bush,' and take the

DB form as showing *o* for normal *u*. The 15th and 16th century forms at times show confusion, such as might readily arise, with the more common *thorn*. For the somewhat rare development of OE *y* to *u* in this county, we may compare the history of Thurning *infra* 221 and the field-name *Thurne-wong* in Sibbertoft (14th *NthStʒ*).

FIRETAIL COVERT (6″). *firetail* is a dialectal name for the red-start (NED *s.n.*).

Watford

WATFORD 73 J 6

> *Watford* 1086 DB *et passim*, (*near Daventre*) 1299 Cl, *-forth* 1307 Ipm
> *Wadford* 1176 P (p), *Wadforð* 1177 P (p)
> *Wateford* 1235 Fees, *Watteford(e)* 1285 *Ass*, 1291 Cl, 1302, 1364 AD iv, 1401 Cl
> *Wathford* 1238 WellsR, 1290 Ch, *Watford juxta Buckeby* 1280 *Deeds Enrolled*, n.d. AD v

This name would seem to be identical with Watford (Herts), *Watford* 944–6 (c. 1250) BCS 812, 1007 Crawf 11 *et passim*, except *Wetford* 12th AD iii, *Wathford(a)* 1188 MP, 1219 Pap, 1225 Bracton. It is not an easy name. It should be noted that the two OE forms respectively come from a late cartulary in which the forms are hardly to be relied upon, and from an 11th century original. The spellings with *Wad-* and *Wath-* suggest that the *t* may not be original, but due to later assimilation of *d* or *th* to the following *f*. One possibility is that the first element is OE wæd, 'place for wading,' hence perhaps *wæd-ford*, 'a ford which can be crossed by wading.' The other is that the first element is OE *wāð*, 'hunting.' Hence perhaps 'ford used by hunters.' The *wæd* interpretation is the more likely, for there is more pro-bability of *d* being unvoiced to *t* before following *f*, than of *th* becoming *t* before *f*. An early *wāð-ford* would probably have given *Wafford*.

SILSWORTH LODGE

> *Silvesworth* 1213 ClR
> *Sivelesworth(e)*, *-y-* 1220 Fees *et passim* to 1330 QW, (*juxta Watford*) 1305 *Ass*

Sillesworth, -y- 1284 FA, 1399, 1430 AD iv
Sevelesworth 1287 *Ass* (p), (*juxta Watford*) 1330 *Ass*
Sulesworth 1367 AD i, *Sullesworth* 1393 Cl, 1398 AD iii,
    Sunelesworth (sic) 1438 AD iii
Silsworthe 1482 AD iv
'*Sifel*'s worþ,' cf. Silsoe (PN BedsHu 161).

BRIDGE HO (6″). Cf. *Briggefurlong* 13th *NthStʃ*. BURNHAM'S
BARN (6″) is to be associated with the family of Ralfe *Burnham*
of Buckby and Richard *Burnam* of Watford (1560–66 and 1603–
52 Wills). LANGBOROUGH is *Langeberuwe* 15th *Daventry, -burgh*
1444 *Ct.* 'Long hill,' *v.* beorg. RODMORE LODGE (6″) is *Rodmor*
13th *NthStʃ*, 15th *Daventry, Rodemor* 1366 AD iv. Probably
'reed marsh,' *v.* hreod, mor.

Welford

WELFORD 73 F 8

Wellesford 1086 DB
Welleford(ia), -e 1155–8 (1329) Ch *et passim* to 1483 AD iv,
    Welliford 1235 Fees
Weleford 1166 P (p), 1201 Cur (p), 1223 ClR, *Welford* 1347 Cl
Wileford 1200 Cur (p), 1222 Bracton (p)

'Ford by the spring or stream,' *v.* wielle, ford.

HALLFIELD COTTAGE (6″) is *Hallefeld* 1540 *LRMB*.

HEMPLOW HILLS, THE HEMPLOE is *Hindeplewe* 13th Selby,
Hemploe 1587 *Map*, *Hempley hill* 1645 *Deed, Hemply Hills* 1791
Bridges. This is a difficult name. The early form is almost certainly corrupt. It is unlikely in itself, and could not give rise to
the modern form. Ekwall (PN La 265) quoted the early form,
though he was unaware of its identification, as a parallel to the
Lancashire and Yorkshire p.n. Deerplay. The early forms for
these last names are *Derplaghe, Derplawe* (13th and 14th centuries) from OE *dēora-plaga*, 'play-place of the animals,' with
early forms going back to OE *plaga*, and late forms showing the
influence of ME *pleie*, from OE *plega*. *Hemplo(w)e* must go
back to OE *hinda-plaga*, 'play-place of the hinds.' This would
give ME *hindeplawe* which, by confusion with ME *hindepleie*,
might give a form *hindeplewe*, and, by reason of the common

transition of ME *lawe*, 'hill,' to ModEng *lowe*, might give ModEng *Hemplo(w)e*. For variant ME *plawe*, *pleie*, *v.* Plaw Hatch (PN Sx 329).

Winwick

WINWICK [winik] 73 H 8

 Winewican 1043 (14th) KCD 916, *Winewiche*, *-y-* 1086 DB *et passim* to 1446 AD iii with variant spellings *-wik(e)*, *-wyk(e)*, *-wich*, *Wynnewyk*, 1291 *Ass*
 Winewincle 1189 (1332) Ch
 Wilewik 1267 Ch
 Winwik 1284, 1346 FA
 Wenewyk 1285 *Ass*, 1316 FA, 1319 *FF*, *-wik* 1287 Ipm
 Wynewigg' 1288 *PeterbA*, *Wenewyg* 1428 FA
 Wyneweke 1416 AD iv, *Wynweeke* 1620 *FF*
 Wynthyck 1565 *Recov*, *Windwicke* 1612 *FF*, *Wynnycke* 1627 *FF*

 '*Wina*'s dairy farm,' *v.* wic, as in Winwick (PN BedsHu 251).

FLINTHILL is *Flint-hill* 1684 Renton. Cf. Flimborough *infra* 280.
WOLD FM (6″). Cf. *Woldfurlong* 13th *PipewellB*, *v.* weald.

Yelvertoft

YELVERTOFT 73 G 7

 Celvrecot, *Gelvrecote*, *Givertost* 1086 DB
 Gelvertoft(e) 12th Survey, 1203 *FF*, 1220 Fees, *Gelvre-* c. 1220 WellsR, *Gyeluer-* 1223 Bracton, *Gever-* 1235 Cl, *Gerver-* 1243 Cl, *Ghelver-* 1247, 1253 *Ass*
 Chelvertoft 1206 Cur, *Chelveristoft* n.d. AD iv
 Gyluertoft 1222 Bracton, *Gilver-* n.d. AD v
 Jelvertoft n.d. AD iii, 1235 Fees, 1276 Cl, *Jerveltoft* 1244 Cl
 Ylverestot (sic) 1247 *Ass* (p), *Ilvertoft* 1294 *Ass*
 Yelvertoft 1276 Cl *et passim*, (*al. Jelvertoft*) 1290 Ipm
 Zelvertoft 1314 Ipm, *Zelver-* 1315 Cl, *Zelurtoft* 1370 *AD* A 3465.
 Jellerthopt 1321 AD iii
 Helurtofte 1328 AD iii
 Gilverestoft 1388 Pat
 Yellowtoft 1517 DBE, 1584 *FF*, (*Yelvertoft al.*) 1609 *Recov*, *Yellowtaft* 1714 St Peters Nth ParReg

This is a difficult name. With the Scandinavian second element topt one would have expected a Scandinavian first element, but no known word or name can be suggested. An English pers. name *Geldfrith* or *-ferð* is a possible formation (cf. OE *Geldwine* and OGer *Geltfrid*, Förstemann PN 640). This name would explain the name Yelvertoft, provided we assume, as is sometimes the case, that in a name of this type all traces of genitival *s* may have disappeared. If this is the history of the name, it is very likely that at an earlier stage it had an English second element, later replaced by *toft*. That second element may well have been cote, and this would account for the hesitation in DB.

SPELLER FM (6″) is *Longespellowe* 1361 AD iii, *Spellowe* 1662 *Clayton*. 'Speech-hill,' v. hoh. Cf. Spella Ho *supra* 33 and Spelhoe Hundred *infra* 131. There is a long hill here with old paths and roads in the neighbourhood, such as would have made it a good place of assembly.

VI. NOBOTTLE GROVE HUNDRED

Neowbotle grave a. 1076 Geld Roll, *Niuebotlegrave, Neubotla-grava, Niwebotle, Niwebold, Niuebote* 1086 DB, *Newebotleagraua* 1181 P, *Newebotlesgrava* 1195 P. The form *-grove* appears first in 1316 FA. The hundred must have taken its name from a *grove* (*v.* grafa) near Nobottle in Brington *infra* 80. For possible further light on the exact meeting-place of the hundred, *v. infra* 280.

Althorp

ALTHORP [ɔ·ltrəp] 83 A 10

Olletorp 1086 DB, *Olethorp* 1208 Cur, 1284, 1285 Ipm, *Olesthorp* 1242 *FF*

Holtrop 12th Survey, *Holthorpe, -throp* 1300 Ipm

Olthorp 1208 Cur *et passim* to 1475 AD v with variant spelling *-throp*, *Oltrop* 1524 *SR*

Aldrop 1320 *FF*, *Allthroppe* 1558 AD vi, *Allthrope* 1662 Fuller

Oldethorpe al. Althorpe 1562 *Recov*

This is probably a compound of þorp and an OE pers. name *Olla*, perhaps a pet-form of *Ōslāf*. Cf. Olney PN Bk 12.

Chapel and Church Brampton

CHAPEL and CHURCH BRAMPTON 83 A 11

Branton(e) 1086 DB *et freq* to 1255 FineR, (*Minor*) 1242–3 Fees, *Braunton* 1253 Ch

Bramton(e) 1194 P, 12th AD ii, 1200 Cur, 1202 Ass, 1203 Abbr

Brampton(e) 12th Survey *et freq*, (*Little*) 13th AD ii, (*Magna*) 1275 RH, (*Chyrche*) 1287 *Ass*, (*Chapell*) 1474 BM, *Brambton* 1228 Cl

Bromton 1215 ClR

The history of this p.n. is the same as that of Brampton (PN BedsHu 234). It is from brame and tun, hence 'brier' or 'bramble farm.' There are no remains of the chapel which gave name to Chapel Brampton and very imperfect traditions of it (Bridges i, 493).

CANK COVER (6″) and LODGE is *Cank(s) Cover* 1823 B, c. 1825 O.S. HOE HILL is so named c. 1825 O.S. There is a spur of land here, *v.* hoh.

Great Brington

GREAT BRINGTON 83 A 9

Brinintone 1086 DB

Brinton(e), -y- 1086 DB *et passim* to 1334 Cl, (*Little*) 1284 Ipm, *Chyrchebrynton* 1312 *Ass*, *Greate Brinton* 1657 NRS i

Brunton 1248 Ch, 1284 FA, 1288 Ipm, *Bruynton* 1253 Ch, 1298 Ipm

Bryngton, -i- 1325 Ipm *et freq*, *Brynkton* 1330 FA, *Brynketon* 1350 Cl

Churche Bryngton al. Moche Bryngton 1559 *Spencer*

'*Brȳni*'s farm,' *v.* ingtun. Cf. Brington PN BedsHu 235.

GAWBURROW HILL is *Calberwe* c. 1300 *Buccleuch*, *Corber Hill* 1823 B. This is probably 'cold hill,' *v.* cald, beorg.

NOBOTTLE is *Neubote* 1086 DB, *Neubottle* 12th Survey *et passim* to 1511 *FF* with variant spellings *Niwe-*, *Newe-*, and *-botle*, *-botel*, *Neubotlegrave* 1322 Ipm, *Neuboltegrave* 1322 Cl. 'New building (grove),' *v.* boðl, grafa, cf. Newbold *supra* 17.

ALTHORP MEER (6″) is *Althorpemere* (1398 *Spencer*), and is on the boundary of Brington and Althorp. *v.* (ge)mære. CHINK-WELL SPINNEY (with CHINKWELL CLUMPS in Althorp and CHINKWELL BELTS in Harlestone, both 6″) is *Close called Chynk-well* 1486 *Spencer*, *greate Chinckwell*, *Chinckwell meadowe* 1580 NthNQ i. Presumably this refers to a spring which comes out of a *chink* in the ground. LANGLAND'S PLANTATION (6″) is *Langeland* t. Ed 3 *Ct*, *Langland feilde* 1580 NthNQ i. MOOR FM (6″) was the home of Roger de *la More* (1289 *FF*), *v.* mor. NOBOTTLE WOOD is *Newbotlewode* 1396 *Spencer*. THORNBURROW HILL is *Thirnebeurew* (sic) 13th *PipewellA*, *Thumber Hill* in 1823 (B). *v.* þyrne, beorg. WASHINGTON'S HO (6″) is so called from Lawrence Washington and his family who settled here in 1616, having come from Sulgrave, the seat of the main branch of the family (Kelly). WAYDALEHILL is *Wade Hill* 1823 B. WOODCLOSE PLANTATION (6″) is *the wodde close* 1580 NthNQ i.

Brockhall

BROCKHALL [brɔkəl] 83 B 8

Brocole 1086 DB, *Brochole*, *-k-* 1220, 1242 Fees
Brockehole 12th Survey, *Brockhole* 1316 FA, *Brokhold* 1494 Ipm *Brockhall* 1567 *FF*

'Badger hole,' *v.* brocc-hol.

ROUGH MOOR FM (Kelly) is *Roughmyre* 1582 *FF*, *-mire* 1618 Recov, *Rumour* 1823 B. 'Rough miry spot,' *v.* ruh, myrr. A late hybrid name.

Bugbrooke

BUGBROOKE 83 D 9

Buchebroc 1086 DB *et passim* to 1359 Ipm with variant spellings *Bucke-*, *Bukke-*, and *-brok*
Buchebroch 1086 DB
Buttebroc c. 1175 Dunstable, *Butebroc* 1194 P, 1206 Cur

Buddebroc 1195 Abbr
Bockebrok 1247 *Ass*, 1293 Ipm, 1330 FA
Bukbrok 1332 Cl, *Bucbroke* 1428 FA
Boogbrooke 1595 NRS iii, *Bugbroke al. Budbroke* 1598 *Recov*

'Brook of the bucks' (*v.* bucc) or 'of the goats' (*v.* bucca), or of a man named *Bucca.*

BUGBROOKE DOWNS is *pasture called le Dounes* 1293 Ipm. CORPORATION FM is in the possession of the Corporation of Northampton. LITTLELIFT FM (6″), cf. *Littliff Leys* 1780 *EnclA*. Probably for 'little-lithe,' *v.* hlip and cf. Life *infra* 285.

Dallington

DALLINGTON 83 B 11

Dailinton(e), *-y-* 1086 DB *et passim* to 1332 Ch with variant
spelling *-ing-, Dayllington* 1284 Cl, *Daelyngton* 1313 Pat
Deilintone 1141 Eynsham
Dalinton 1189 (1332) Ch, *Talinton* 1208 BM, *Dalyngton* 1316
FA, 1379 Cl, 1428 FA, *Dall-* 1346 Ipm
Del(l)inton' 1201 Cur

'The farm of one *Dægel*,' *v.* ingtun. For this pers. name cf. Daylesford (PN Wo 121).

GRANGE FM is *Granga* (sic) 1199 FineR.

HOPPING[1] HILL is so called in 1764 (*EnclA*). Cf. Hoppin Hill *infra* 117, Hopping Hill (field) in Coton and Guilsborough (1764 *EnclA*), as also *Hoppyngfeld* (13th *NthStA*) in Quinton, and *le Hoppynges* (c. 1300 *For*) in Preston Deanery. A further possible parallel is Hoppingwood Fm in Kingston (Sr), *Hopping-mede* 1536 MertRec, which is very likely identical with *biweste hoppinge* (i.e. 'west of *hoppinge*') in the bounds of Merton (BCS 1196, ME version), since it lies near the Merton border. The last reference shows that the word is of great age, but it is impossible at present to offer any explanation of these names.

[1] Mr F. Williamson calls our attention to the occurrence in Derbyshire of uncompounded *Hopping* (twice), and of its use in conjunction with Hill, Hole, Mill and Lane. See also Addenda lii.

Duston

DUSTON 83 B 11

> *Duston(e)* 1086 DB *et passim*
> *Doston* 1303 AD iii

There is a Dust Hill in Sibbertoft *infra* 121, and a *Dusthul* (13th AD ii) which survives as a field-name *infra* 282, and a late *Dustholme* (1624) in Barton Seagrave, and the first element here must be the common word *dust*, though no such p.n. element has been noted elsewhere. The term has various meanings in dialect, e.g. *chaff* (EDD *s.v.*), and the sense need not be that commonly found in StEng. Baker (i, 138) favours the common dust etymology, and speaks of the light pulverising value of the soil here.

Another possibility is that we have to do with a lost OE **dus*, allied to the word *dûs*, 'heap,' found in Westphalian p.n.'s (cf. Jellinghaus 57) and in other German place-names (cf. Förstemann ON i, 779–80). Falk-Torp (*s.n. dysse*) associate the word with ON *dys*, 'stone grave-how,' Norwegian dialectal *dussa*, 'irregular heap,' and, with different vowel-grade, OFris *dûst*, 'confused mass.' Duston is on a hill and, if that is the first element, might take its name from the hill or from some lost barrow.

Floore

FLOORE [fluˑə] 83 C 8

> *Flora* 1086 DB, 1155–8 (1329) Ch, *Flore* 1086 DB *et passim*
> to 1472 AD iv
> *Floure* 1330 Cl, *Flower* 1535 VE, 1675 Ogilby, 1702 Poll,
> 1779 F, *Flore al. Flower* 1685 *Recov*

It is tempting to believe that this place was named from some forgotten Roman *flor* or tessellated pavement (IPN 143). The parish is bounded by Watling Street, and in the south of the neighbouring parish of Nether Heyford such a pavement has been unearthed (Morton 527–8). Cf. also Flower Fm in Godstone (Sr), *le Flore* 13th AD ii, *Flore* 1274 FF, 1332 SR (p), *Flower al. Flore* 1738 *Recov*, near which is a place called Stratton and an old Roman road. The spelling *flower* represents the regular dialectal pronunciation of *floor*.

GLASSTHORPEHILL

Clachestorp 1086 DB, 1201 Cur, *Clachetorp* 12th Survey
Clakestorp 1178 P, 1200, 1205 Cur, *-trop* 1198 Cur, *Claxthorp*
   1208 Cur
Clacstorp' 1220 Fees, *Claxthrop* late 13th BM
Clasthorp 1316 FA, 1353 Cl, *-tropp* 1660 *Recov*
Claxthorp al. Clasthorpe 1548 *FF, Glastroppe al. Claxthorp*
   1551 *Deeds Enrolled, Glasthorp al. Claxthorpe* 1562 *Recov*

'*Klak*'s village,' *v.* þorp. For the Danish name *Klak* or *Klacki*
(ON *Klakkr*, OSw *Klakker*) *v.* NP 81. There is mention of more
than one *Clac(c)* in the list of Peterborough sureties (BCS 1130).
The p.n. is identical with *Klastorp*, found twice in Sweden.

FLOOREFIELDS FM. Cf. *in campo orientali, occidentali* 1203 *FF.*
For the *field(s) v.* Braunston Fields *supra* 16. GREENWAY
SPINNEY (6″), cf. *Greenway Gate* 1779 *EnclA.*

East Haddon

EAST HADDON 73 J 9

Ed(d)one 1086 DB
Hadone 1086 DB, *Haddun* 1185 RotDom, 1187 P, *Haduna*
   12th AD iii (p), *Haddon* 1195 P, *Esthaddon* 1265, 1279,
   1305 Ipm
Hed(d)on(e) 1230 P

v. West Haddon *supra* 71.

WASHBROOK BRIDGE (6″). Cf. *Wasschebrook* t. Ric 2 *Ct*, a compound of broc and OE (ge)wæsc, 'ground washed over by water.'

Harlestone

HARLESTONE[1] [hælsǝn] 83 A 10

Herolvestone, -tune 1086 DB, *Heruleston* 13th *Brudenell*
Erlestone 1086 DB, *Herleston(e)* 1169 P *et passim* to 1372 Cl,
   Herliston 1328 Cl
Herlestune 1231 Bracton

---

[1] For information with regard to the minor names in this parish we are
much indebted to Miss E. W. Hughes.

Harleston 1367 Cl, *Harlston* 1482 AD iv
Halstone 1675 Ogilby, 1712 Morton

'Farm of *Herewulf* or *Heoruwulf*,' v. tun.

DUDMAN'S PLANTATION (6″). Cf. *Dodemones Croft* c. 1320 H de B, *Deadman's Slade* 1766 *EnclA*, *Dudman's Close* 1926. This contains the OE pers. name *Dudeman*.

FLEET FM (Kelly) probably corresponds to *fflitlond* 1312 H de B, *Flitland* 1766 *TAB*, *Fleetland* 1828, *Flitland* 1926. If this is correct then the early name meant 'land in dispute' (cf. NED *s.v. flite*), and the modern form is corrupt. Cf. *Flytlond* in Benefield (1253 *FF*), *Flyttelondes* in Easton (c. 1400 *Rental*), *Flithul* in Braybrooke (c. 1250 *PipewellB*), *Flitehyl* in Isham (14th *NthStA*), *Flithil* in Boughton (1250), *Flytehil* in Irthlingborough (14th) and Flitnell Barn *infra* 85.

SOWDITCH THICKET (6″). Cf. *Suzdik* c. 1312 H de B, *Sowditch* 1828. 'South ditch.' The reference is to a deep ditch still to be found in the woodland here.

STANDING WELL (6″). The field-name *Stanhul* c. 1312 H de B gives rise to *Stanhill Thorns* 1766 *TAB*, *Standing Thorns* 1828, 1878, 1926, and it may be presumed that *Stanewelle* c. 1312 H de B, *Stanwell* 1791 Bridges in the same way has given us *Standing Well*. Cf. also Stangrove (*Stangrave* 1269 Ipm) *al.* Standing Grove, a field-name in Latton (Ess).

HARLESTONE HEATH is *Herlestonheth* 1287 *For*. OLDFIELD THICKET (6″). Cf. *Oldefeld* c. 1312 H de B.

Harpole

HARPOLE [ɑ·pəl] 83 C 10

Horpol 1086 DB *et passim* to 1580 *Pat* with variant spellings -*poll(e)*, -*pull*
Horepol 12th Survey *et freq* to 1270 Ipm
Harepol 1258 Ipm, 1545 LP, *Harpole* 1307, 1314 Inq aqd, 1556 *Pat*
Happall 1557 *Pat*

'Dirty or muddy pool,' v. horh, pol.

FLITNELL BARN (6″). No early forms have been found but we may compare the field-names *Fletynhyll* t. Hy 7 (Rothwell), *Flittenhill* 1650 (Green's Norton), and Flitnells in Gayton *infra* 91. All these seem to be compounds of OE *(ge)fliten*, 'disputed,' and the meaning must be 'hill over which there was some quarrel or dispute as to ownership.' Cf. Flitteridge (PN Sx 346) and Fleet Fm *supra* 29.

BLACKWELL'S FM is to be associated with the family of *Blackwell* found in the parish from 1760 (ParReg). HARPOLE COVERT. Cf. *Horpolegrove* 1460 *FF*. HARPOLE MILL is *molendino de Horepol* 1219 *FF*. HEATH FM, cf. "le croppe of heath called le ffurres...in Harpole" (1550 Pat). WOOD FM. Cf. *boscum de Horepol, cultura de Bosco* 13th *NthStJ*.

Heyford, Upper and Nether

HEYFORD, UPPER and NETHER [hefəd] 83 C 9

> *Haiford, Heiforde* 1086 DB
>
> *Heiford, -y-* 1178 P *et passim* to 1405 AD iv, (*Little*) 12th Survey, (*Superiore et inferiore*) 1220 Fees, (*Nether-*) 1240 *FF*, (*Over-*) 1253 *FF*, (*Great*) 1283 Cl
>
> *Haiford, -y-* 1178 P *et freq* to 1362 Cl, *Haieford* 1199 FF, (*Norhtthere*) 1285 *Ass*
>
> *Hieford* 1235 Ch, *Heghford* 1334 Cl, *Heafford* 1657 NRS i *Hefford* 1754 ParReg

The first element may be either OE (ge)hæg or hege or heg. The first two would mean 'ford by the enclosure' or 'by the hedge,' the last would mean 'hay-ford,' i.e. one over which hay was often carted. We have a parallel for the last in Heyford (O), *Hegford* KCD 1289, and in *higford* (BCS 782 and 1093).

BROOK FM (6″). Cf. *Brocmede, Brokmede* 1382 *Ct*. THE GREEN (6″) was the home of Hugo *attegrene* (1247 *Ass*) and John *atte Grene* (1253 *Ass*). WHITE HALL is so named in 1823 (B).

Holdenby

HOLDENBY [houmbi] 73 J 10

> *Aldenesbi* 1086 DB, *Aldenebi* 1184 P, *Audenebi* 1200 Cur
>
> *Haldenebi* 1169 P (p) *et passim* to 1317 AD iv with variant spelling *-by*, *Haudenebi* 1200 Cur, *Haudenesby* 1201 PatR

Haldaneby 1247 *Ass*
Haldenby 1298 Ipm, 1306 Ch, 1428 FA
Holmby al. Holdenbye 1568 *FF, Holmeby al. Holdenby* 1607
  Recov
Holmby, Homby 1675 Ogilby

'*Halfdan*'s by.' The pers. name *Halfdan* or *Haldan* was very common in all the three Scandinavian kingdoms, and was borne by one of the chief leaders of the Viking invasions of this country. The local pronunciation *Holmby* is familiar to us in *Holdenby* or *Holmby House*, where Charles I was a prisoner in 1646.

If *Aldenestone* (DB) is Holdenby, we may have a variant form of this name with second element tun rather than by. (Cf. VCH i, 328 n., 378 n.)

DELF SPINNEY (6″), cf. *The Delfe close* 1587 *Map, Delfe meadow* 1650 *ParlSurv,* v. (ge)delf. TWIGDEN SPINNEY (6″) is *Twigden(s) meadow* 1650 *ParlSurv,* and is perhaps to be associated with the family of George *Twigden* of Brampton (c. 1650 *Finch-Hatton*).

Kislingbury

KISLINGBURY 83 C 10

Cifelingeberie 1086 DB
Ceselingeberie 1086 DB, *Cheselinberi* 1166 P (p), *Cheselingeberi*
  ib. (CR)
Kiselingeberia, -y- 1175 P (p) *et freq* to 1278 RH with variant
  spellings *-bury, -biry*
Kyselingbyr', -i- 12th Survey *et freq* to 1360 Ipm with variant
  spellings *-bury, -byr(i), Kiselengberi* 1202 Ass
Kislingebir 1235 Fees, *Kyslyngbury* 1308 AD vi
Chilesengebur' 1247 *Ass*
Kyselingham 1305 Ipm, *-y-* 1316 FA
Keselingbury 1326 Fine, *-yng-* 1348 Cl
Killingeberia 1329 Ch, *Kislenbury* 1657 NRS i

The soil here is partly clay, partly gravel, and the village may take its name from the original burh on a patch of gravel. An OE name *ceosolinga-burh,* 'burh of the dwellers on the ceosol or gravel,' should have given *Chesling-* or *Chislingbury* and in that case the form with initial *k* must be due to

Scandinavian influence, cf. Introd. xxiii. Professor Ekwall would take the name to be from OE *Cȳselingabyrig*, 'burh of the people of *Cysel*,' this name being an unrecorded diminutive of the 8th cent. OE name *Cūsa*.

BLY LANE (6″). Cf. *Blythefurlong* 14th *NthStA*. Presumably Bly lane, which comes up from Banbury Lane, crosses a nameless tributary of the Nene, and goes to the Nene itself, lay near this furlong. Both alike must have been named from this nameless stream which was clearly another *Blithe*, *v. supra* 12 n. A further reference to this stream is to be found in *pontem de Blye* (1253 *Ass*), *aquam de Blythe* (1285 *Ass*), *le Blythegrene* (1330 *Ass*), all in the hundred of Wymersley. The lane comes up from Rothersthorpe parish which is in that hundred.

HILL FM is *le Hille* (14th *NthStA*) and was the home of Dionis de *Hulle* (1285 *Ass*). HOLLOWELL HILL FM is *Halywellhille* 14th *NthStA*. 'Holy spring,' *v*. halig, wielle. STOCKALL FM (F) is *Stokwell* 14th *NthStA*. 'Spring by the stump,' *v*. stocc, wielle.

Ravensthorpe

RAVENSTHORPE [rɔ·nstrəp] 73 J 9

> *Ravenestorp* 1086 DB *et passim* to t. Hy 6 AD vi with variant spelling -*thorp*(*e*)
> *Raunestorp* 1247 *Ass*, *Raunsthorp* 1346 FA, *Rawns*- 1477 AD iv, *Rawnesthorpe* 1539 LP
> *Rounsthorp* 1486–93 ECP
> *Ransthorpe* 1539 LP, *Raunsthorp al. Ranstrope* 1731 *Recov*, *Rawnstruppe* 1631 NRS i

'*Hrafn*'s village,' *v*. þorp. Absence of any early spellings in -*throp* suggests that this is a Scandinavian name in the strictest sense.

CHORLEY COP is *Sharley Cop* in Kelly and is still found as the field-name *Sharley Coppice* 1796 *EnclA*.

Teeton

TEETON 73 J 10

Teche 1086 DB, *Theche* c. 1160 NRS iv

Teacne 1195 P (p)

Cheta 12th Survey

Tecnat t. early Hy 3 BM, *Tekne* 1220 Fees *et freq* to 1326 AD i
  with variant spelling *Tecne*, *Teghne* 13th AD ii

Thekene 1221 Bracton, *Tekene* 1227 *Ass et freq* to 1386 Cl,
  Tekyn 1414 AD i, *Teken* 1467 AD v

Tokene 1275 RH

Tetene 1316 FA

Tikene 1346 FA

Teton 1551 *FF*, *Tecon al. Teton* 1647 *Recov*

Teeton is a difficult name. From the point of view of form it
is to be noted that the second consonant was originally clearly
a *c* rather than a *t*, the present form being due to common confusion of *t* and *k*, and the influence of the neighbouring Creaton.
Topographically, it is to be noted that it stands high, with the
ground falling sharply away on three sides. Form and topography alike make association with OE *tācn*, 'token, sign, signal,'
virtually certain, the name perhaps being given from some
prominent landmark here. This is a district in which Scandinavian influence is fairly prominent, and OE *tācn* may have been
Scandinavianised to *tekn*, under the influence of OSc and *teikn*.
The process would have been assisted by the fact that derivatives
of OE *tācen*, like *tǣcnan*, 'to show,' (*earfoð-*)*tǣcne*, 'difficult to be
shown,' have an *ǣ* vowel in OE itself. Professor Ekwall would
prefer to take it as coming from a lost OE *tǣcne* (sb.), 'beacon.'

TEETON MILL is *molendinum de Theche* c. 1160 NRS iv.

Upton

UPTON 83 C 11

Opton(e) 1086 DB *et freq* to 1317 *FF* with variant spelling
  Up-, *Oppeton* 1194 P

Upeton 1158, *Uppeton* 1159 P, *Uppetona juxta Norðħ* 1175
  BM, *Upton juxta Norhampton* 1317 FF

Ufethona 1190 BM

'Up farm,' *v.* uppe, tun. Probably because a little farther up the Nene than Northampton, though it may be 'high' farm because on a hill.

BERRYWOOD FM (6″) is *wood called Berry-wood* 1791 Bridges. UPTON MILL was the home of Henry *del Milne* (1261 *Ass*).

Whilton

WHILTON 83 A 8

Woltone 1086 DB, *Wlton* 1247–50 AD i
Whelton 12th Survey *et passim* to 1401 Cl, *Wheelton* 1382
    AD iv, *Wheleton* 1408 AD iv, 1428 FA
Whywelton 1282 Ipm
Weulton, Welton 1295 Ipm

The forms make it likely that this is a compound of OE *hweogol*, 'wheel' and tun, *hweogol* appearing in ME as *weole, wel, whewel.* If so, the place probably took its name from the circular hill on which it stands, lying between two streams, or it may be that the term *wheel* was part of the name of the curving stream here, cf. *hweol-riðig* (BCS 216). For *wheel* in place-names cf. Wheelden (PN Bk 212) and Whilborough (PN D 515). We may note also *hweogol weg* (BCS 246) and *sceard hweogol* (BCS 782), but these cannot be identified, and it is not certain that they are applied to topographical features.

VII. TOWCESTER HUNDRED

Tovecestre Hundred 1086 DB, *v.* Towcester *infra* 94. According to Bridges (i, 258), the hundred-court was usually held at Foster's Booth *infra* 93.

Abthorpe

ABTHORPE [adθrəp] 83 G 9

Torp 1086 DB
Abetrop 1190 P (p), 1203 Cur, -*throp* 1329 Ipm, -*thorp* 1384
    Cl

Abbetorp 1200 Cur, 1202 Ass (p), *-thorp* 1230, 1241 P, *-throp*
 1276 Pat, *Abbeythorp* 1625 *FF*
Abpthrop 1255 Seld 13, *Abthorp* 1384 Cl
Apethorp 1354 Ipm, *Apthorp* 1384 Cl
Adthrop 1601 NthNQ ii

'*Abba*'s village,' *v.* þorp, the name of a former holder having
been added in later times, as in Payhembury (PN D 566) and
Rothersthorpe *infra* 151.

BUCKNELL WOOD

Boggenhul c. 1220, 1250 *For*
Bokenhil 1285 *Ass* (p), *-hull(e)* 1287 *For*, 1324 Ipm
Buckenhulle 1309 Pat, *Buckenell woode* 1535 *LRMB*
Bukenhull(e) 1309 Pat, (*le Frethe de*) 1309 Cl, *Buknell* 1511
 AD vi

v. hyll. The first element is uncertain, but it is most likely to
be *bōcen*, 'beech-covered.' *Frethe* is OE fyrhðe, 'woodland.'

CHARLOCK FM is *Chaldelacke* 1250 BM, *-lak(e)* 1261, 1294 *Ass*,
Challake 1490 Pat, *Chalocke* 1535 *LRMB*, *Challock* 1578 *Recov*,
1791 Bridges. 'Cold streamlet,' *v.* cald, lacu.

FOSCOTE is *Foxcot(e)* 1200 Cur, 1247, 1261 *Ass*, *Foxscote* c. 1220
Magd, (*juxta Toucestre*) 1285 *Ass*, *Foscote* 1391 AD i, 1404 AD
iii, *-kott* 1638 *Recov*, *Foscutt*, *Foskett* 1672 *LRMB*. 'Fox-
cottages' or perhaps better 'fox-burrows,' *v.* fox, cot(e) and
PN Wo xxxix.

HAYES FM is *Heymulne sub parco de Hanle* 1330 *Ass*, *Haunele hay*
1331 Pat, *The Hayes* 1609 *Terrier*, and was the home of Thomas
ate Hey (1287 *For*). 'Enclosure,' *v.* (ge)hæg and Handley *infra*
90.

Gayton

GAYTON 83 E 10

Gaiton(e) 1162 P *et passim* with variant spelling *Gay-*
Gainton 1166 P (CR)
Gauton (sic) 12th Survey
Garton (sic) 1269–71 Ch
Geyton 1227 *FF*, 1241 P, 1247 Misc, n.d. AD v, (*Gayton al.*)
 1322 Ipm

One is tempted to take this as the same name as that found in Gayton-le-Wold and Gayton-le-Marsh (L) which might in their present form go back to ON *geit(a)-tūn*, 'goat(s) farm,' and Gayton (Ch) which is in the strongly Scandinavianised district of Wirral and might have the same history. Gayton (St) and Gaydon in Chadshunt (Wa) are however in districts which do not show Scandinavian influence and the same is true of the Northamptonshire Gayton. Further, it is to be noted that the forms *Gauton* (*sic* for *Ganton*), *Gainton*, and *Garton* (whatever that may stand for) are hardly compatible with that etymology. We have in an Oxfordshire charter (KCD 1292) place-names *geganstede*, *gegandene*, which point to an OE personal name *Gæga*. This would explain the forms.

FLITNELLS FM (local). Cf. *Flitten Hills* 1772 *EnclA*. See further Flitnell *supra* 85. GAYTON WILDS is *Wild Farm, The Wild* 1823 B. Cf. Wild Ho *supra* 60. GAYTON WOOD Ho. Cf. (*in*) *bosco de Gayton* 1292 *For*. OLDFIELD [oufəl] is *Westoldefelde* 14th *NthStA*.

Cold Higham

COLD HIGHAM 83 E 9

> *Hecham* 1086 DB, 1176 Dunstable, 1198 Fees, 1205 Pap, *Heccham* 1176–90 Dunstable
>
> *Hegham* 1316 FA, 1335 Ch, 1338 Cl, *Heygham* 1350 Ipm, *Heigham juxta Patteshull* 1362 IpmR
>
> *Little Hygham* 1401 Cl, *Colehigham* 1541 Statutes, 1672 LRMB, *Coldhigham* 1616 FF, *Could-* 1632 FF

'High ham.' It stands high and exposed. Formerly named *Hecham-parva* or *Little-Higham* (Bridges i, 259), presumably in relation to the more important Higham Ferrers *infra* 191.

GRIMSCOTE is *Grimescote* 12th Survey *et freq* to 1349 Ipm with variant spelling *Grymes-*, *Grimmescot* 1242 Fees, 1269 Ch, *Grimscote* n.d. AD ii (p), *Gremescote* 1499 FF, *Grimestorp* 1235 Fees, and *Grinscutt* 1702 Poll. '*Grim*'s cot(e), or *Grímr*'s.'

POTCOTE and POTCOTE FM is *Potcote* 1202 Ass (p) *et freq* to 1317 Ass, *Potecote* c. 1220 *Magd* (p), 1304 Ipm, 1397 Cl, *-kote* 1316

FA, *Patkote juxta Hecham* 1285 *Ass*, *Pottecote* 1359 Ipm. Potcote Fm is probably the older settlement. It lies in a well-marked hollow and the whole name may well mean 'cottages in a *pot* or depression.'

Pattishall

PATTISHALL [pætʃɔ·l] 83 E 9

> *Pascelle* 1086 DB
> *Patesshille* t. Hy 2 BM, *Pateshulle* 1176–81 Dunstable *et passim* to 1675 Ogilby, -*hella* 1190 P (p), -*hill*(*e*) 12th Survey, 1200 *FF*, 1206 FineR, 1220 WellsR, -*hylla* 1190 P
> *Patteshull'* 1255 Seld 13, (*Patheshull al.*) 1304 Ipm, -*hill* 1457 Ch
> *Patsell* 1542 LP, *Patteshull al. Patteshall al. Patteshill* 1608 FF
> *Patchall* 1657 NRS i, *Pachel* 1693 ParReg, *Patchell* 1702 Poll

'*Pætti*'s hill,' *v.* hyll, and for the pers. name cf. Patsford PN D 52

ASTCOTE

> *Aviescote* 1086 DB, *Auichescote* 1248 *FF*
> *Hauekescote* 1198 P, *Hauescote* 1316 FA
> *Acheskot* 1277 BM
> *Auescot*(*e*) 1300 Ipm *et freq* to 1591 *FF*, *Auyscote* 1343 *FF*, (*juxta Pateshull*) 1381 *Ass*[1]
> *Auenescote* 1368 Cl
> *Ascott* 1542 Statutes, *Ascoat* 1702 Poll, *Ascote* 1791 Bridges

'The cottage(s) of one *Aefic.*' This pers. name is on record. It is the name of the monk of Evesham to whom the grant of Newnham (*supra* 26 n) was made. Cf. Adgestone (Wt), DB *Avicestone.*

DALSCOTE [dɔ·lskət]

> *Derstanescote* 1203 FF, *Derstescote juxta Pateshull* 1294 *Ass*
> *Derlewescote* 1247 *Ass*, *Derlescote* 1297 *Ass et freq* to 1428 FA, (*juxta Patteshull*) 1381 *Ass*, *Derscote* 1404 *FF*

---

[1] Some of these forms have been transcribed with *n* for *u* in earlier printed documents.

Darlescote 1368 Cl, 1730 Poll, Dawlescote 1653 Recov, Dolscot
1657 NRS ii

'The cottages of one Dēorstan or Dēorlāf,' v. cot(e). This is
possibly a case of successive holders bearing similar names. Less
probably the names have actually been confused.

EASTCOTE [jeskət]

Edeweneskote 1277 BM, Edwynescote 1287 FF, 1315 Ass (p)
Ednescote 1359 Ipm, 1394 Ass, Edenescote 1381 Ass, 1392 Cl,
Edmescote 1408 AD iv
Edescote 1404 FF, Escott 1541 Statutes, 1597 FF, Eascott
1631 NRS i, Escoat 1702 Poll

'Ēadwine's cot(e).'

FOSTER'S BOOTH, locally THE BOOTH, is Fosters booth, Forsters
booth 1675 Ogilby. According to Bridges (i, 262) "it was originally the hut of one Forster, a poor countryman, but grew by little
and little to a fair street of inns."

CORN HILL is Cornhill 1650 ParlSurv. DEBDALE FLATS (B) is
Depedale c. 1500 Easton Neston, Debbdell Plaine, Dibdaill Hill
1650 ParlSurv. 'Deep valley,' v. dæl.

Tiffield

TIFFIELD [tifəl] 83 E 10

Tifeld(e), -y- 1086 DB et freq to 1275 RH with variant
spelling -feud
Teiffeld 1162 P (CR)
Tiffeld, -y- 1182 P (p), 12th Survey et passim with variant
spelling -feud, Tiffil 1675 Ogilby
Tythefeld al. Tyghfelde 1551 Pat, Tithfield 1613 Pat, Tighfield
al. Tiffield 1695 Recov
Tiffield al. Tighfield al. Tithfield t. Geo 3 FF

This name is probably a compound of OE feld and tig or tih.
That word is found in the OE compound tūn-tih, and is
clearly the same as the tig of OE foretig, forðtig, 'forecourt' (see
Wallenberg, KPN 106) and probably also found in the compound tigwellan (BCS 1023). We know nothing definite as to its
meaning in OE. Hellquist (s.v. teg) takes it to be identical with

OHG *zich*, MHG *tig*, 'public meeting-place in a village.'
Hellquist and Torp (*s.v. teig*) agree in taking the original stem
to be Indo-Ger **dic*, 'direction,' but no precise definition of the
meaning of the word in English is possible. It is not the same
word as OE *tēag*, dialectal (Ess, K, Sx) *tye*, used variously
to denote (*a*) 'common pasture or field,' (*b*) 'close,' 'enclosure.'
Tiffield is therefore 'open land marked by the presence
of a *tig*,' but what precisely that was, we cannot say. See
further Jellinghaus, *Die Westfalischen ON*, *s.v. ti* on this word
and its distribution in north-west Germany, *v.* Addenda lii.

BURN WOOD (6″) is *Burnwood Close al. Burnwood Coppice in
Tiffield* 1699 *Lumley*. TIFFIELD WOOD FM is *Tighfeild al. Tith-
feild Woods* 1681 *Lumley*.

Towcester

TOWCESTER[1] [toustə] 83 F 10

   Tofeceaster c. 925 ASC (Ā) *s.a.* 921, *Tofcestre* 1266 Pat
   Tovecestre 1086 DB, *Touecestr(e)* 1157 P *et passim* to 1404
      AD iii, *Thoue-* 1234 Cl, 1241 P
   Toucestr(e) 12th Survey, *Tuu(e)cestre* c. 1220 *For*
   Towecestre t. John, c. 1220 *For*, *Towcestre* 1498 AD iii
   Touchestre 1294, 1297, 1299 *Ass*, *-ter* 1294 *Ass*, *Towchester*
      1577, 1596 *FF*, *Touescestre* 1335 *Ass*
   Taucestre 1387 Pat, *Tawsythur* 1523 HMC Middleton
   Towsetour 1499 AD iii, *Towcetre* 1510 LP, *-cettour* 1550 Pat
   Tocester 1511 AD vi, *Tossetour* 1541 Statutes, *Toceter* 1564
      FF, *Tocester* 1595 NRS iii
   Tossiter 1657 NRS i, *Towcester vulg. Tosseter*, *Toster* 1675
      Ogilby

'The *chester* or Roman camp on the river Tove' *supra* 4,
v. ceaster. Towcester is on the site of the Romano-British settlement *Lactodurum*, the second element of which is the same
British word for 'fortress' noted under *Durobrivae infra* 232.
The meaning of the first syllable is uncertain. Professor Ekwall

---

[1] CHURCHYARD. Cf. *Chirchelane* 1451 Pat. MILL LANE is *Myllelane* 1449
Easton Neston. PARK STREET is *Parklane* 1404 ib.

suggests that it may be an ablaut form of Welsh *llaith*, 'damp, moist,' being possibly the earlier Celtic name of the Tove.

WOOD BURCOTE is *Burchot* 1200 *FF*, *-cot(e)* 1208 BM, 1324 Ipm, *Burecot(e)* 1219 *FF*, c. 1220 *For*, 1230 Cl (p), 1274 *Ass*, *Wodeburcote* 1274 *Ass*, *Odeburcote* 1511 *FF*, *Wood Burket(t)* 1657 NRS i, 1666 *Recov*. *v*. Field Burcote *supra* 42.

BURY MOUNT (6") or *Berrymount-Hill* (Morton 508–9) is surrounded with a trench filled with water from the rill that encloses the town on the north. Its date is a matter of dispute.

CALDECOTE [kɔ·kət] is *Caldecot(a)* 1203 Cur (p) *et passim* with variant spelling *-cote,* (*juxta Toucestre*) 1287 *Ass*, *Coldecot(e)* 1274 *Ass*, 1657 NRS i, *Calcote* c. 1460 ECP, *Cawcote* 1595 NRS iii, *Chaldecott al. Calcott* 1621 *Recov*, *Caucote* 1791 Bridges. 'Cold cottages,' *v*. ceald, cot(e).

COSTWELL FM is *Kerswell* 1247 *Ass* (p), *Carswelle* 1299 *Ass* (p), *Carsewell* t. Ed 3 *SR* (p), *Creswell* 1330 *Ass* (p), 1331 *FF* (p), *Castwell* 1650 *ParlSurv*, *Costwell* 1763 *EnclA*. 'Cress spring,' *v*. wielle. Cf. Caswell *supra* 43.

HANDLEY

   Hanle, -egh, -ey 1220 ClR *et freq* to 1290 Cl
   Henle 1234 Ch *et freq* to 1286 Cl with variant spellings *-legh, -ley*
   Haunle(g') 1234 Ch, 1301 Cl
   Hanele(g) 1237 Cl *et freq* to 1281 Cl
   Heinl' 1243 Cl, *Haynle* 1253 Cl
   Henneleye juxta Selveston 1245 Cl, *Henele* 1281 Cl

'At the high clearing,' *v*. heah, leah.

PARK FM takes its name from *parco regis de Hanl'* 1229 Cl.

RIGNALL (6") is *Wriggonhale juxta Hanle* 1375 *For*, *Upper Rignall* 1713 *Terrier*.

VIII. CLEYLEY HUNDRED

Klegele a. 1076 Geld Roll, *Claveslea, Claislea, Claile, Claiesle, Claieslea, Clailea, Clailæ, Clailei* 1086 DB, *Claislund* 1086 DB, *Cleile(y)*, *-y-* 1185 RotDom *et freq* to 1346 FA, *Claile* 1202 Ass, *Clayl'* 1235 Cl, *Cleyele* 1275 RH, *Cleilley* 1428 FA. The hundred meeting-place was at Cleley Well in Potterspury (*infra* 105), now misprinted *Cheley* on the maps (Bridges i, 316). There are several old foot-paths here, leading to the meeting-place. The form *Claislund* shows assimilation to a common type of hundred-name, *v.* Huxloe Hundred *infra* 176–7.

Alderton

ALDERTON

> *Aldritone* 1086 DB, *Aldrinton* 1184 P, 12th Survey *et freq* to 1279 Ipm
>
> *Aldringthune* c. 1200 AD iii, *Alderingtune* c. 1270 Gerv, *Aldrington* 1278 Ch, 1279 Ipm, 1283 Ipm, 1304 Cl, *Auderingthon'* 1284 FF
>
> *Aldington* 1283 Cl, Fine
>
> *Alderton* 1316 FA, 1386 Cl, *Altherton* 1347 Cl

'*Ealdhere*'s farm,' *v.* ingtun.

TWYFORD (not on map), *Twyfordfeild* 1650 *ParlSurv* is an old ford (and bridge) over the Tove near the entrance to Stoke Park. 'Double ford', *v.* twi-.

Ashton

ASHTON 83 F 12

> *Asce* 1086 DB
>
> *Essa* 1166 P, *Esse* 12th Survey, 1242 Fees, 1284 FA
>
> *Aisse* 1176 P (p), *Eysse* 1220 Fees
>
> *As(s)hen* 1296 AD i *et freq* to 1490 AD i, *Aschenne* 1316 Cl, *Asshene* 1324 Cl, 1333 Ipm, *Hasshehen* 1367 BM
>
> *Esshen* 1311 FF, *Essen* 1351 BM
>
> *Ayshene* 1311 FF, *Asshen al. Asheton* 1579, *Ashen al. Ashton* 1602 FF

This is OE (*æt ðæm*) *æsce*, 'at the ash' and (*æt ðām*) *æscum*, 'at the ashes,' dat. pl. (ME *atten ashen*). In late times the name was assimilated to a more common type.

Gun Hole (6″) is *Gunhole* 1672 *LRMB*. It is very likely that it is by the spot called *Gunnildebrege* in the 14th century (*NthStʒ* 120 f.). This would become *Gunnelbridge*. *Gun Hole* lies by a small stream, and *Gun Hole* is probably a corruption of the name of the onetime owner of the bridge, a woman bearing the Anglo-Scandinavian name *Gunhild*.

Ashwood Fm is *Asshewode* 1337 *For*. Rowley Wood is *copic' voc. Rowley* t. Eliz *LRMB*. 'Rough wood,' v. ruh, leah.

Cosgrove

Cosgrove 83 H 13

> *Covesgrave* 1086 DB *et passim* to 1328 Ipm with variant transcription *Coues-, -grove* 1600 AD iv
> *Colesgrave* 1199 FF, (*Couesgrave al.*) 1338 Ipm
> *Cogesgrave* (sic) 1253 *Ass*
> *Cosegrave* 1275 Fine, 1445 AD iii, *Cousgrave* 1300 Ipm
> *Coueresgrave* 1326 *FF*
> *Couwesgrave* 1330 FA, 1361 Cl
> *Gosgrave or Couesgrave* 1341 Ipm, *Govesgrave* 1345 Cl, *Goosegrave* 1675 Ogilby
> *Cosgrave* 1401 *FF*, *Coddesgrave al. Cosgrave* 1562 *FF*, (*Covesgrave al.*) 1608 *Recov*

'The grove of one *Cufel*,' v. graf. For the pers. name *Cufel* cf. Cowsden (PN Wo 230). OE græf, 'pit, ditch,' would perhaps suit the forms rather better, but there is no evidence for such a feature here.

Isworth is *pratum de Hutchesworthe* 1287 *Furtho, Huseworthe-diche, Hyehuseworthe* 1364 ib., *Huseworth* 1374, 1378 ib., *Hiʒehuseworthe* 1378 ib., *Hisworth* 1650 *ParlSurv*, *High Hisworth, Hisworth mead* 1672 *LRMB*. This name may contain a pers. name *Hycgi, the strong form corresponding to the weak *Hycga found in Hughenden, Hitcham and Hedgerley (PN Bk 182, 229, 238). Hence '*Hycgi*'s worþ or enclosure.'

Old Stratford is *Westratford* 1278 Seld 13, *Forstratford* 1330 FA, 1361 Cl, *Oldstratford* 1498, 1503 AD iii, *Oldstretford* 1523 *SR*. This is the part of the town of Stony Stratford that lies west of Stony Stratford (Bk), across the Ouse. *For-*, perhaps because it lies on Watling Street in front of Stony Stratford.

THE GREEN is *Cosgrave Green* 1767 *EnclA*, and was the home of John de *la grene* (t. Ed 3 *SR*). ST VINCENT'S WELL (6″) is so called in 1767 (*EnclA*), and was at one time corruptly called *Finche's well* according to Bridges (i, 285).

Easton Neston

EASTON NESTON [iˑsənnesən] 83 F 10

Adestanestone, Estanestone 1086 DB
Estaneston 1196 P (p), 1220 Fees
Esteneston 12th Survey *et passim* to 1273 Ipm
Estenstona t. Hy 3 AD ii, *-ne* c. 1226 AD iii, *Estonston* 1240 Cl
Astaneston c. 1220 WellsR
Estneston 1300 Ipm *et freq* to c. 1480 ECP
Eston 1316 FA, (*by Toucestre*) 1379 Cl, *Esteston* 1328 AD ii
Eston Nesson 1610 Camden, *Eston-Neston* 1791 Bridges

'*Aeþelstān*'s or *Ēadstan*'s farm,' *v.* tun. The pers. name *Aeþelstan* appears in DB as *Estan*.

HULCOTE

Halecote, Hulecote 1086 DB, *Halecot* 1235 Cl
Hulecot(a) 1189 P (p) *et freq* to t. Ed 3 AD ii
Hulcote c. 1226 AD iii *et freq* to 1321 Cl, (*by Toucestre*) 1335 Ipm
Holecote 13th AD ii, 1275 RH, 1281 AD i, *Holcot(e)* 1300 Ipm, 1316 FA
Ulecot' 1230 Cl (p), 1237 Cl, *Ullecot'* 1232 FF
Hullecot(e) 1237 Cl, 1256 FF

The persistent *u* in the forms of this name suggests that here, as in Hulcott (PN Bk 151), we have a compound of OE *hulu*, 'hull, husk, hovel,' or the derivative *hulc*, and cot(e), hence 'hovel-like cottages.'

NUN WOOD is *Nonewode* 1287 *For*, with reference to the nuns of Sewardsley priory near by.

SEWARDSLEY [ʃouzli] is *Sewardeslega, -le(ye)* 1179 P *et passim* to 1371 AD ii, *Seuuardeleye* n.d. AD i, *-lia* 13th AD ii, *Sywardisle, -y-* 1319 Ipm, 1378 AD ii, *Sywardeslee* 1382 AD ii, *Shoresley* 1541 Statutes, *Sewardsley al. Shewesheley* (sic) 1566 FF, *Shewarsley* 1579, 1585 Recov, *Shoasley* 1779 F, *Shewdesley* 1826 G. '*Sigeweard*'s clearing or woodland,' *v.* leah. The local pronunciation is preserved in the name of the adjacent SHOWSLEY BELT (6″), a wood, and in a field called *Showsley Ground*.

WATERHALL (6″) is so named in 1512 LP.

Furtho

FURTHO 83 H 12

> *Forho* 1086 DB *et freq* to 1315 Cl with variant spellings *-hou, -how, Forreho* 1235 Cl
> *Fortho* 12th Survey *et freq* to 1428 FA, *Fordho* 1220 Fees, *Forthoo* 1341 Ipm
> *Furthoo* 1600 AD iv, *Furtho al. Fortho* 1622 FF

'The projecting hoh,' cf. Forty Green (PN Wo 202) for similar compounds of *forth*. The church and manor house stand on a low spur of land.

KNOTWOOD FM is *Notwod(e)* 1367, 1374 For, *Nottewode* 1373 Pat. Cf. also *Nottepokesle* (*boscus*) t. Ed 1 PeterbB, which must have reference to the same wood, as Puxley (*infra* 102) is close at hand. OE *hnott*, 'bald, close-cut,' is applied to a thorn in *hnottan ðorn* (BCS 789), and to a willow in *hnottan seale* (BCS 674), doubtless with the sense 'cut, pollarded.' So here, 'pollarded wood.'

Grafton Regis

GRAFTON REGIS 83 G 12

> *Graston(e)* 1086 DB, 1284 FA
> *Grafton(e)* 1166 P *et passim*, (*juxta Aldrynton*) 1312 Ass, (*by Yerdele Gobyon*) 1366 Cl, (*Wydevyle*) 1465 Ch

'Grove farm,' *v.* grafa, tun. Robert de *Wivill* held the manor in 1204 (Cur), the surname being spelt *Wydivyll* in 1339 (Cl). *Regis* because it belonged to the crown (Bridges i, 298).

GRAFTON FIELDS. Cf. *North-*, *Suth-*, *Estfeld* 1315 *FF*, and Braunston Fields *supra* 16.

Hartwell

HARTWELL [hɑ·təl] 83 F 13

   Hertewell(e) 1086 DB, 1177 P, 1275 RH, 1293 Ipm (p)
   Hertwell(a) 1148–66 NRS iv, 12th Survey *et freq* to 1498 Ipm
   Herteswella 1168 P
   Hurtwell 1175, *Hurtewella* 1177 P (p)
   Harwell 1675 Ogilby

'Harts' spring,' *v.* wielle. Bridges (i, 302) says that 'from its situation (it) had formerly the name of *Wold-Hartwell*.'

BOZENHAM MILL [bouznəm] is *Bosenhou* 1148–66 NRS iv (p) *et freq* to 1333 Ipm with variant spelling *-ho*, *Boseho* 13th AD ii, *-hou* 1284 *FF*, *Bossenho* 1341 *FF*, *Ouerbosenho* 1430 BM, *Bosnoe feild* t. Eliz *LRMB*, *Bosnome Mill*, *Bosnum field* 1672 *LRMB*. '*Bosa*'s spur of land,' *v.* hoh. For the pers. name cf. Bosham (PN Sx 57) and Bozeat *infra* 189. The forms *Bosnum*, *-nome* may be due to the combination *Bosnoe Mill*, which would readily be corrupted to *Bosnome Mill*, and give rise in turn to a polite spelling *Bosenham Mill*.

LAYTHICK COPSE (6″) is *Lay Thick Coppice* 1790 Woods Rept. For *thick v.* Blackmore Thick *infra* 206. Possibly the first syllable is to be associated with *Leye* t. Ed 3 *For* and the field-name *Ley Stocking*, found in the parish in 1672 (*LRMB*), *v.* leah, stocking.

WIKE (lost) is *Wyk juxta Hertwell* 1285 *Ass*, *Wyke Hertwell* 1289 Ipm, *Wikehertwell* 1290 Cl, *Hertewellewyk* 1299 Pat, *Wyke juxta Rode* (i.e. Roade *infra* 106) 1315 *FF*. 'Dairy farm,' *v.* wic.

CHAPEL FM is *Chappelfeld* t. Eliz *LRMB*, *Hartwell Chappell* t. Eliz ChancP, *Chappell farme* t. Eliz *LRMB*. Hartwell was a chapelry of Roade. HARTWELL END FM is *Harwell al. Hartewell End* 1538 *AD* B 12135. PARK FM is *le parke feld*, *Parkfeld* t. Eliz *LRMB*. PRENTICE COPSE (6″) is *Prentys copp'* c. 1550 *AOMB*. RAWLESMERE COPSE (6″) is *Rolles Mere Copse* 1823 B. *mere* may be OE (ge)mære, 'boundary,' since the wood is on the county border. SANDPIT COPSE is *Sandpittes* t. Ed 1 *PeterbA*,

Sandpitt furlong 1672 *LRMB*. STONEPIT FM (6″), cf. *the Stone-pitts, the Stonepitt furlong* 1672 *LRMB*.

Passenham

PASSENHAM [pɑˑznəm] 83 J 13

    Passanhamme c. 925 ACS (Ā) *s.a.* 921

    Passonham, Passeham, Paseham 1086 DB

    Passeham t. Hy 2 (1383) Pat, 1242 Fees, 1252 Cl, *Pasham* 1262 *Ass*

    Bassenham 12th Survey

    Pasenham 1277 Ipm, 1702 Poll, *Passenham* 1284 FA *et passim, Passingham* 1675 Ogilby

    Passhenham 1327 Ipm

    Pasnam 1568 *FF, Parshnam* 1595 NRS iii, *Parsenham* 1657 NRS i, 1730 Poll, *Parsnam al. Passenham* 1675 Ogilby

'*Passa*'s hamm.' Cf. the reference in 1327 (Ipm) to a meadow there, called *le Hamme*, on the bank of the Ouse.

ASHALLS COPSE is *boscus de Asswell* c. 1220 *For, Ashwells Coppice* 1790 Woods Rept, 1823 B. 'Ash spring,' *v.* wielle.

DENSHANGER[1] [densæŋə] [dʌnsæŋə] [dinsæŋə]

    Dinneshangra 937 BCS 712

    Daneshongr' 1202 Ass, *-hanger* 1312 *Ass*, 1330 QW

    Duneshangr' 1227 *Ass* (p), 1261 *Ass, Dunehanger* 1241 Cl

---

[1] BCS 712 is a grant of land at *Niwantune*, which was near a river Ouse and contained a place called *dinneshangra*. Ekwall (*Studies* 23 n. 1) first suggested that this might be Denshanger, and there is little doubt that he is right. The boundaries run from *stanweg* along the *slæd* to the foul *rod*, thence along the *slæd* to Denshanger and out through *Denegyð*'s grove to the haw-thorn, thence to the *hlæw* and so to the elder-tree and to the bank of the Ouse by *Ealferhþ*'s *hlæw*, thence to *suðfeld* and so by the *wyrtwalu* to the *efsan* (probably 'edge of the wood'), thence to the withy and so by the *wyrtwalu* to the boundary-thorn on the east side of *branteswyrð* and thence to the *stanweg*. The name Newton is completely lost, and clearly the unit to which it gave name did not correspond to any modern parochial unit. Watling Street, however, still forms the eastern boundary of Passenham parish and is pre-sumably the *stanweg* of the charter, while the Ouse bounds it on the south. There is much likelihood that Brownswood Cottage *infra* 105 gives us a last relic of *branteswyrð*. It lies just by the Passenham-Potterspury boundary. Just to the east of Brownswood, between it and Watling Street, the bounds of Potterspury make a curious rectangular projection into Passenham and this may be the second *wyrtwalu* of the charter (cf. *supra* 11 n.).

Deneshangre 1252 Cl *et freq* to 1336 Ipm, *Denys-* 1268 *Ass*,
  Denshangre 1327 Ipm, 1332 Cl, *Densager* 1541 Statutes,
  Densanger 1545 LP, 1702 Poll, *Deanshanger* 1640 *Ipm*
Doneshangre 1285 *Ass*, *Donsha(n)g(er)* 1316 FA

'*Dynne*'s slope,' *v.* hangra.

GRUB HILL (lost) is *Grobihill in balliva de Wakfeld* 1337 *For*,
Grobyhill 1339 Orig, *-hul* 1346 *For*, *Groobhill* 17th *Furtho*,
Grubb Hill 1653 ib., *Grubhill Coppice* 1790 Woods Rept, *Grubby
Hill* 1823 B. This may be a compound of *hill* and the adjective
grubby, 'infested with grubs,' though that adjective has not
hitherto been noted before the 18th century.

HANGER LODGE is *le Hanger* 1346, 1349 *For*, *v.* hangra.

KINGS STANDING OAK (6″). Cf. *the kinges standing furlong* 1566
Rental. standing here denotes 'hunter's station from which to
shoot game,' cf. King's Standing (PN Sx 392).

PUXLEY

Pocheslei, -lai 1086 DB, *-lea* 1161 P, *Pokesle(am)* 1193 P *et
  passim* to 1362 IpmR with variant spellings *-legh*, *-ley*,
  Pockesle 1261 *Ass*
Pokelesleam 1194, 1195 P
Pokel(e) 1206 ClR, 1284 Cl, *Pochele* 1235 Cl
Poghel(e) 1224 ClR, 1238, 1252 Cl, *Poghl'* 1227 ClR
Pukesl' 1234 Cl, *Poukesle(ye)* 1332 Cl, 1356 Ipm, 1362 IpmR,
  Powkesley 1501 AD iii, 1773 *EnclA*
Powel' 1237 Cl

'Goblin's leah,' from OE *pūcel*, 'goblin, sprite.'

SHROB LODGE

Shirope 1220 ClR
Scrob c. 1220 *For*, 1230 Cl, 1250 *For*, *Pokelescrob* 1223 ClR
Srubbe 1224 ClR, *Shrob* 1235 Cl, *Shrub(be)* 1237 Cl, *Schrobbe*
  t. Ed 1 *PeterbB*
Scrubbe 1235 Cl
Srubbes 1252 Cl, *Shrobbes* 1346 Pat

shrub is commonly derived from OE *scrybb*, but the forms for
this name, with no ME *shribbe* forms, tend to confirm the doubts

of the NED and to support the conjecture made there that there must also have been an OE unmutated form *scrubb*. Cf. further *le Over-, Nethershrubbe* (1400) in Cottingham, *le Shrobbes* (14th) in Marholm. The earliest form shows a typical AFr spelling with interpolated vowel.

BRIARY WOOD is *Briery* 1672 *LRMB*, *Briary Coppice* 1790 Woods Rept. LITTLE LONDON is so named in 1773 (*EnclA*), *v. supra* 44. NORTHFIELDS FM is *the Northefelde* 1566 *Rental*. REDMOOR COPSE is *Rodmoor Coppice* 1790 Woods Rept. 'Reed swamp,' *v.* hreod, mor. STOLLEGE LODGE (6″) is *Stalladge yate* 1591 *DuLaMiscBks*, *Stollage Coppice* 1790 Woods Rept.

Paulerspury

PAULERSPURY 83 G 11

> *Pirie* 1086 DB, c. 1220 WellsR, *West Pyria* 12th Survey, *Pyrie* 1241 P
> *Peri* 1187 P (p), *Perie* 1199 FF, *Westpery* 1220 Fees
> *Peria al. Piry* 1251 Ipm
> *Pirye Pavely* c. 1280 AD iv, *Paueleyespirye* 1319 *FF*
> *Westpury al. Paulespury* 1410 Ch, *Westpery al. Pawlespery* 1522 *Recov*
> *Pawlerspyrry* 1535 AD iii, *Pallers Perie* c. 1550 *AOMB*
> *Pallispery* 1541 Statutes, *Pawlysbury* 1543 LP, *Palespury* 1637 StJ, *Paulsperry* 1712 Morton

'Peartree,' *v.* pyrige. Robert de *Pavelli* held the manor in 1086. *West* to distinguish from Potterspury *infra* 105. Locally the places are known simply as *Pury*.

CUTTLE MILL (6″). Cf. *Cuttel(l)ebrok* 13th *Furtho, Cuttellebrygge* 1390, *Cuttulforth* 1499, *le Cotillmylle* 1524 *Easton Neston, Cottle Myll* t. Hy 8 *Ct, Cuttle Mill, Cuttle Brooke* 1672 *LRMB*. *Cuttle-brook* is mentioned by Bridges (i, 296) as the eastern boundary of Furtho. He also mentions a Cuttle Brook (now Ockley Brook) in Aynho (i, 134). Cuttle Meadow in Evenley and Cuttle Hill in Hinton, by the same stream, furnish a further parallel to this name, and there is a Cuttle Meadow by a stream in Ravensthorpe. All these point to *Cuttle* as a possible stream-name. Professor Ekwall calls attention to the probable parallel to be found in OGer *Cuttelbeke* (11th cent.), which corresponds to a modern *Kützelbach* or *Küttelbach*, and to *Cutelbecke, Kutelbeke* (13th cent.), similar stream-names. According to Förstemann (ON i, 1766) these correspond to LGer *küötelbieke*, used of a small intermittent stream. There is also a Cuttle Brook in Temple Balsall (Wa), which may have the same history, and a Cuttle Bridge in Chilvers Coton in the same county, the home of John de *Cuttele* (1327 SR), otherwise John de *Kuttel* (1332 SR), near to which was *Cuttell Milne* (1553 *FF*), and also a Cuttle Mill in Curdworth, and a Cuttle in Long Itchington in the same county (*ex inf.* Mr F. T. S. Houghton). We may note also a *molendinum q.v. Cuttele* in Steeple Aston (O) in 1279 (RH).

HEATHENCOTE [hevənkət]

> *Heymundecot(e)* 1220 Fees, 1284 Cl, 1285 *Ass, Eymundecote* 1247, *Heyemundecote* 1253 *Ass, Heymond(e)cot(e)* 1316 FA, 1369, 1391 Cl
>
> *Hekemundecot'* 1235 Fees
>
> *Heydmundekote, Heytmundecot* 1236, 1242 Fees
>
> *Heghtmundecot'* 1242 Fees, *Heghmundecotes* 1307 Ch, *Heghtmoundcote* 1349 Ipm, *Hegmundcote* 1428 FA
>
> *Hedmondcott* t. Hy 8 AD iii, *Edmondcote* t. Hy 8 *LRMB*
>
> *Haythyncote* 1530 *Recov, Hedencote* 1551 Pat, *Hethencote* 1619 *Ipm, Heathencott al. Heueincott* 1672 *LRMB, Havencote* 1675 Ogilby, *Heavencut* 1712 ParReg, *Heathencott* or *Heavencut* 1779 F

'*Hēahmund*'s cot(e).' Cf. Hepmangrove (PN BedsHu 207).

PLUMPTON END is *Plumton'* 1275 RH, *Plumpton Pyrye* 1315 *FF, Plumptonpirie* 1330 *Ass, Plompton End* t. Eliz *Rental*. 'Plum farm,' *v.* tun. *Pyrye* to distinguish from Plumpton *supra* 43.

OUTWOOD (B) is *Outwodes* 1410 Ch. PARK FM is *Oldeparke, Newparke* 1410 Ch, *le parke clos* 1524 *Ct.* PLUMPARK is *Plumparke feelde* t. Eliz *LRMB, Plumbparke* 1650 *ParlSurv*. It is near Plumpton End *supra*. PURY END is *Perry End* 1672 *LRMB*. STOCKINGS FIELD (B) is *Stocking feild* 1650 *ParlSurv*. *v.* stocking. TEW'S END is *Tewesend* c. 1825 O.S., and is probably to be associated with the family of Hugh de *Tywe* (n.d. AD ii) and John de *Tewe* (1335 Cl), who must have come from Tew (O).

Potterspury

POTTERSPURY 83 H 12

> Perie 1086 DB et freq to 1324 Ipm with variant spellings
> Pirie, Pery, Estpirie 1229 Cl
>
> Potterispirye 1287 Ass, Pottere Pyrye 1305 Ass
>
> Potteresburi 1315 Ipm, -pury 1326 Fine, Potterspury 1498
> AD iii
>
> Estpury al. Potterspury 1552 Pat, Potters Perry, Potters Peer
> 1675 Ogilby

'Peartree,' v. pyrige. East to distinguish from Paulerspury supra 103. According to Morton (72) 'It (has) the largest as well as the oldest Pottery in all those parts. Its antiquity appears by the common appellation of the town, the name being changed long since from East Pury to Potters-Pury on this account.'

BLACKWELL END (6″) is Blakewellende 1324 AD D 8610, and was the home of Roger de Blacwell (1330 Ass) and John de Blackewelle (t. Ed 3 SR). 'Dark spring,' v. blæc, wielle.

BROWNSWOOD COTTAGE (6″) is Brownsworth Green 1649 Depositions, Browneswood gre(e)ne 1650 ParlSurv, 1672 LRMB. The first form, combined with other evidence (v. supra 101 n.) suggests that this is the branteswyrð of BCS 712, with later pseudo-etymological corruption. For the pers. name Brant involved, cf. Braunston supra 14 and v. worð.

CHELEY WELL[1] is Clayliewel feild, Cleylyfeld t. Eliz LRMB, Cleley-well 1791 Bridges. v. clæg, leah. The site of the hundred meeting-place (v. supra 96).

WAKEFIELD LAWN is Wacafeld 1086 DB, Wachefeld 1158 P, Wake- 1170 P et freq to 1281 Cl, Wackefeld t. Hy 2 (1383) Pat, 1252 Misc, 1287, t. Ed 3 For, landia de Wakefeld c. 1220 For, (bailliva de) 1337 For, the lawnd of Wakefield 1598 Depositions. 'Waca's land,' v. feld. The name is traditionally associated with the ancient oak called Wake's Oak, now perished (VCH i, 62). For this pers. name cf. Wakeham (PN Sx 43). laund is a woodland term for an open space in woodland, from OFr la(u)nde, 'wooded ground.' For bailliva, cf. Cliffe Forest supra 1.

---

[1] For the spelling see the note on the hundred-name supra 96.

Assart Fm is *the greene asart* 1650 *ParlSurv, v.* Sart Wood *infra* 166. Lady Copse is *Lady Coppice* 1790 Woods Rept.

Roade

Roade 83 F 12

> *Rode* 1086 DB *et passim, Rodes* 1224 WellsR, 1233 Cl, 1247 Fees
>
> *Roddes* 1185 RotDom
>
> *Roode* 1402 AD ii, 1541 Statutes, *Rhode* 1629 *SR, Road* 1775 *FF*

'The cleared land,' *v.* rod.

Hyde Fm is *Hida* c. 1200 BM, *La Hyde* 1289 *FF, Hide by Roda* 1336 Ch. The only example of hid in the county.

Thorpewood Fm is *Thrupp Wood House* 1662 NthNQ v, 1823 B. *v.* þorp. Wood Leys Fm was formerly the New Inn. In 1875 it was re-named Wood Leys from the adjoining field which is called *Wood Leys* in 1672 (*LRMB*)[1].

Shutlanger

Shutlanger[2] ['ʃʌtlæŋə] 83 F 11

> *Shitelhanger* 1162 P *et passim* to 1353 Ipm with variant spellings *Sitel-, Scitel-, Schitel-, S(c)hytel-, Schittel-, Scitillangel* 1202 Ass, *Siteleshangre* 1210–12 RBE, *Shittil Anger* 1541 Statutes, *Shittlehanger* 1779 F
>
> *Sutelhangra* 1184 P, *-ger* n.d. AD i, *Schutelhanger* 13th AD ii, 1281 AD i, 1329 AD iv
>
> *Schetelhangra* 1195 P (p) *et freq* to 1388 Cl with variant spellings *Shetel-* and *-hangre, -ger*
>
> *Shytenhang'* 1253, 1297 *Ass, Schuttenhangre* 1285 *Ass*
>
> *Schotellanger* c. 1282 AD iv
>
> *Skutelanger* 1290 Cl
>
> *Shetlanger* 1482 AD iv, *Shyttlanger* 1562 *FF, Shitlanger* 1678 *Easton Neston, Shettleanger* 1702 Poll

This is probably a compound of hangra and OE *scyt(t)el,* 'shuttle,' 'dart,' 'bolt.' The sense in which the latter word is

---

[1] *Ex inf.* Miss Joan Wake.
[2] Originally a hamlet of Stoke Bruerne.

used must remain uncertain. The resemblance of the hill on which Shutlanger stands to either a shuttle or a bolt is not particularly obvious. The name may be descriptive of a wood from which *shuttles*, i.e. 'gate-bars,' are cut. Cf. Mounterley *infra* 160.

Stoke Bruerne

STOKE BRUERNE 83 F 12

Stoche 1086 DB *et freq* to 1283 Ipm with variant spelling *Stok(e)*, *Stokes* 1220, 1235 Fees, *Stok in Salcey forest* 1296 Ipm

Stok(e)bruere 1275 RH, 1279, 1296 Ipm, *Stokebrewere* 1376 Cl, 1406 AD iv, *Stokebruerne* 1428 FA, *Stoke Bruin* 1657 NRS i, *Stoke-brewing* 1710 ParReg, *Stoke Brewin* 1781 *Recov*

v. stoc(c). William *Briwerre* held the manor t. John (*For*).

SHAW (lost) is *la Scage* 1202 FF, *Schawe* c. 1220 *For*, (*la*) 1240 FF, *Shaweswode* 1439 FF, *v.* sceaga.

STOKE PLAIN, PLAIN WOODS. Cf. *Plaine Close, the Plaine* 1672 LRMB, *Plane Woods* 1826 G. If, as is probable, this is a late name, we may have the ordinary word *plain*, 'flat country.'

STOKE PARK HO and STOKEPARK WOOD. Cf. *wood at Stoke* 1276 Cl, *Parkeside* 1672 LRMB. THORNY COPSE (6″) is *Thorny copise* 1535 LRMB.

Wicken

WICKEN 83 J 12

Wicha, Wiche 1086 DB, *Wika* t. Hy 1 (1267) Ch *et freq* to 1284 FA with variant spellings *Wyke, Wike*

Wyca Mainfein 12th Survey

Wykes 1209–18 WellsR

Wicne 1235 Fees, *Wykne* 1349 *For*, *Wyken* 1457 Ch, 1541 Statutes

Wykhamund 1275 RH, *Wykedyve* 1293 FF, *Wykedife* t. Hy 8 *MinAcct*

Wyken al. Wykedyve 1545 FF, *Wicken al. Wickhamond al. Wickdive* 1639 *Recov*

Wickens Ambo 1629 *SR*, *Wickins Ambae* 1702 Poll, *Wickens Ambee* 1730 ib.

The parish takes its name from two (Lat *ambo*) separate manors called **wic**. (Cf. Huttons Ambo (PN NRY 40).) These give rise to a parish name found in two plural forms, strong and weak respectively, viz. *Wikes, Wiken*. Cf. Wykin (Lei) 12th Dane *Wich, Wiken*, Wyken (Wa), and Wicken (C), with similar variations of form. One manor took its name from the family of *Hamon filius Mainfelin* (1166 P), the other from that of William de *Dyve* (1261 Ipm).

DAGNALL is *Daggenhale* 1319 Orig, *Dagnall in Wycken* 1568 *Spencer*. ' *Dagga*'s nook,' *v.* healh, with the same pers. name as in Dagnall (PN Bk 94) and *Daggeford* in Eye (1281).

MOUNTMILL FM is *Wykemulne* 1312 *Ass*, *Mill Farm* 1791 Bridges, and was the home of Robert de *molendino* t. Ed 3 *SR*. WICKEN WOOD is *boscus de Wyke* c. 1220 *For*.

Yardley Gobion

YARDLEY GOBION [gʌbinz] 83 H 12

    Gerdeslai 1166 P, *Gerdele* 1200, 1206 Cur
    Jerdelai 1166 P (CR) *et freq* to 1316 FA with variant spellings
        -le(gh), *-le(ye)*, *Jerdel al. Yerdele* 1299 Ipm
    Jeardelegh 1286 *FF*
    Yerdele(ie) 1299 Ipm, (*juxta Potterespyrye*) 1305 *Ass*,
        (*Gobioun*) 1353 Ipm, (*Gobyon*) 1363 AD iii
    Yardeley Gubbyn 1580 *FF*, *Yardley Gubbins* 1702 Poll

OE *gyrda-lēah*, 'woodland from which yards or spars are taken.' Cf. Yardley (PN Wo 231, PN D Addenda liii), *v.* leah. Henry *Gubyun* had a holding here in 1228 (Cl). The old pronunciation is preserved in *Gubbins Hill*, a field-name in Potterspury.

MOOR END is *la Mora* 1168 P (p), *la More* 1200 Cur, 1202 *FF*, *La Morende* 1304 Ipm, *Le Mourhende* 1316 Ipm, *Le Morhende* 1353 Ipm, *Moresend(e)* 1364 Pat, 1394 Cl, 1399, 1409, 1415 Pat, *Moreyend* 1498 AD iii. 'Marsh end,' *v.* mor.

QUEEN'S OAK is perhaps identical with *le Queneherberhok* 1349 *For.* Cf. also *the Queen's close in Yardley* 1454 ECP. *herber* is presumably the ME *herber*, 'shelter.' Queen's Oak is the oak under which, according to tradition, Edward of York, afterwards Edward IV, first met Elizabeth Woodville (VCH i, 62), the Woodvilles being lords of the neighbouring manor of Grafton *supra* 99.

IX. ROTHWELL HUNDRED

Rothewelle a. 1076 Geld Roll, *Rodewelle, Rodewel* 1086 DB, *Rowell* 12th Survey. *v.* Rothwell *infra* 118. The west part of the hundred was formerly known as the hundred of *Stotfalde* a. 1076 Geld Roll, *Stodfalde, Stotfald, Stofalde* 1086 DB, *Stotfolde* 12th Survey, *Stotfalde* 13th PeterbA, *Stodfalde* 1202 Ass, *Stotfald* 1220 Fees, *Stodfold* 1246 Seld 13. For a possible site of the hundred meeting-place cf. Moot Hill *infra* 121.

Arthingworth

ARTHINGWORTH 73 E 12

Narninworde, Arniworde, Arningvorde 1086 DB
Earnigwurth t. Hy 2 BM
Armingewerc 1181 P (p), *Armingworth* 1251 Cl
Aringworthe 12th Survey, *-wrth* 1235 Fees
Erningwrth' 1202 Ass, *Erningeworth* 1219 WellsR, *-wurth* 1239 FF
Arningw(o)rth' 1220 Fees, 1275 Ipm, *Arningeworthe* 1223 WellsR, *-wrth* 1266 Pat
Arthingeworth 1272 *Ass, Arthingworth* 1275 RH, 1284 FA
Ardingworthe 1530 CtWards, *Hardingworth* 1568 *FF, Ardyngworth* 1590 *FF, Arthingworth al. Ardinworth al. Hardingworth* 1805 *Recov*

'Farm of *Earn(a)* or of his people,' *v.* ing, worþ.

LANGBOROUGH WOOD (6″) is *Langeberwe* 1203 *FF, -bergh* 1225 ClR. 'Long hill,' *v.* beorg.

Little Bowden[1]

LITTLE BOWDEN [baudən] 73 C 11

> *Bugedone* 1086 DB, 1235 Fees, -*den* t. John BM, -*dune* 1228
> WellsR, *Parva Bughedone* 1220 Fees
> *Bowdon* 12th Survey, *Bowedon* 1235 Fees, (*parva*) 1253 *FF*
> *Bogedone* c. 1200 *PipewellA*, 1258 Cl *Boghedon*
> *Budune* early 13th BM, *Budon* 1304 Ch
> *Buggedone* c. 1210 WellsR
> *Parva Bukeden* 1219 *FF*
> *Parva Buwedon* 1248 WellsR
> *Boudon* 1284 FA, (*parva*) 1285 *Ass*, 1292–1300 Ipm
> *The Lasse Bouudon* 1450–3 ECP

Little and Great Bowden are on opposite sides of the Welland, and each seems to have been named from the hill on which it stands. Professor Ekwall suggests that this is from OE *Bugan-dun*, '*Buga*'s **dun** or hill.'

Braybrooke

BRAYBROOKE 73 D 12

> *Bradebroc, Badebroc, Baiebroc* 1086 DB
> *Braybroke* 12th Survey, *Braibroc,* -*y*- 1147 BM *et passim* to
> 1428 FA with variant spellings *Bray*- and -*brok(e)*, *Braiebroc*
> 1166 P (CR) (p)
> *Braebroc* t. Hy 2 *Harl* 86 C 19 (p), *Brabroc* 1197 FF
> *Breibroc* 1215 PatR
> *Bradebroke, Braybroke* 1496 DunBev

This is probably 'broad brook,' *v.* **brad, broc**, the first element having been early refashioned under the influence of the cognate Scand. word breiðr[2]. Cf. Rothwell *infra* 118 and Introd. xxiii. The relevancy of this name, unless it be ironical, is difficult to discover, as the Braybrooke is a very small stream. Bridges

---

[1] Transferred to Leicestershire in 1888.
[2] Study of the early field-names in Braybrooke parish confirms the likelihood of an etymology involving such a Scandinavianising of the name. In addition to Eckland *infra* 111 we have *Heselund, le Lound, Brakendal, Scaleberg*, which are purely Scandinavian, and *Thurulveshull* with a Scandinavian personal name, and the hybrid *Watriwong*.

(ii, 9) does however state that 'upon sudden rains it swells to a great depth.'

ECKLAND LODGE is *Aiclund, Heikelundhill* 1199 FF, *Heykelund, Eikelund* c. 1200 *PipewellA, Ekelond* 14th *PipewellB, Eagland* 1777 *EnclA*. 'Oak wood,' *v.* eik, lundr. For the change of form in the second element cf. Loatland and Mucklands *infra* 114, 237.

Clipston

CLIPSTON [klipsən] 73 E 10

Clipestune 1086 DB, *Clipeston(e)*, 1086 DB *et freq* with variant *-y-* to 1313 Cl, *Clippeston* 1315 AD iii
Clipston(e) 12th Survey *et freq* to 1316 FA with variant spelling *Clyp-*
Clypston al. Clypson 1572 *FF*, *Clipson* 1702 Poll

The first element is the ON pers. name *Klyppr* as in Clipstone (PN BedsHu 122, Nt). Hence '*Klyppr*'s farm,' *v.* tun.

LONGHOLD LODGE is *Longwoldes* c. 1250 *PipewellA, Longewolde* 1381 AD iii. 'Long wold,' *v.* weald.

NOBOLD FM (Kelly) is *Neubold* 1284, 1316 FA, (*juxta Clipston*) 1314 *FF*, *Newbold* 1344 Cl, 1381 AD iii, *Newbolt* 1461 IpmR, *Nobold al. Newball* 1778 *Recov*. 'New building,' *v.* niwe, boðl, and cf. Nobottle *supra* 80.

TWANTRY FM (6″) is *Twantr'* 1381 AD iii. This may be from OE (*æt þæm*) *twæm trēowum*, '(at the) two trees.' Cf. *Tweyn-thornes* in Brixworth (14th *NthStA*), *Tweynok* in Eye (c. 1400 *Rental*).

Desborough

DESBOROUGH 73 E 13

Dereburg 1086 DB, *-burc'* 1200 Cur, *-br'* 1202 Ass
Deresburc 1166 P (p) *et freq* to 1255 Seld 13 with variant spelling *-burg(h)*, *Dersburg* 1225 ClR, *Derisboru* 1384 Fine
Desburc 1197 FF, *-burch* 1205 Pap, *-burg'* 1246 Cl *et freq*
Deseburg 12th Survey *et passim* to 1393 Cl, (*supra Rowell*) 1255 Seld 13

Desseburgh c. 1220 *For, Deseburgh et non Desburgh* 1305 *Ass*
Desbrow al. Desborough 1705 *Recov*

'*Dēor*'s burh,' cf. Darsdale *infra* 195 and Desford (Lei), DB
Deresford. Supra Rowell is difficult to understand unless it
means 'beyond Rothwell' in relation to Kettering or, possibly,
Northampton.

HALL FM was the home of Thomas *atte Halle* (1374 Pat).

Draughton

DRAUGHTON [drɔˑtən] 73 G 12

Dractone, Bracstone (sic) 1086 DB

Drahton 1166 P, -*tun* 1170–4 BM, *Drachton(a)* c. 1170 BM,
1174 P, 1189 (1331) Ch

Draiton 1166 P (CR), *Drayton* 12th Survey, 1252 Ipm

Dracton Comitis 1184 P, *Dracton*' 1202 Ass (p), 1203 Cur,
1220 WellsR, 1228 Cl

Drauchton 1220 Fees, *Drautton* 1284 FA, *Drauhton* 1287 *Ass*,
Draughton 1317 Ipm *et freq, Drawton* 1715 ParReg

Dragton 1228 *FF, Draghton* 1297 Cl, 1316 FA, 1381 Cl

It is clear that we have here a compound of OScand drag and
tun. Draughton lies on the slopes of a hill which rises to over
500 ft. with a well-marked valley to the south and a small one
to the north-east. Rygh (*Indledning* 47) gives various senses for
drag in Norwegian place-names, including (*a*) place where boats
are drawn over a headland to avoid the passage of a river,
(*b*) place where timber is dragged down, (*c*) long island, (*d*) long
and narrow valley. None of these senses suits the topography of
Draughton. Slightly better is the sense of the equivalent Danish
word as recorded in *Frederiksborgs Amts Stednavne* 51, where it
has the sense 'small tongue of land,' hence 'farm on the tongue
of land.' It is, of course, possible that OScand drag has replaced
an earlier OE dræg. The earl (*comes*) of Huntingdon held the
manor in 1166 (P). *v.* Addenda lii.

CLIPPENDALE SPINNEY (6″) is probably identical with *Glupperes-
dale* early 15th *Finch-Hatton, v.* dæl. For confusion of initial
cl and *gl, v.* Glendon, Glapthorne *infra* 113. LEYWELL SPINNEY
(6″) is *Leywelles* c. 1300 *Rental, v.* wielle.

East Farndon

EAST FARNDON 73 D 11

Ferendon(e) 1086 DB, 1203 Cur

Farendon(e) 12th Survey *et freq* to 1337 Cl, *Farendun* 1270
Ipm, *Farindon* 1275 RH, *-yn-* 1316 FA

Farndon 1288 Ipm *et freq*, (*by Boudon*) 1300 Ipm, *Farnedoun*
1393 Cl, (*East, Est*) 1616, 1617 FF, *East Farrington al.
Farndon* 1702 Poll

Farnam 1675 Ogilby

'Bracken hill,' *v.* fearn, dun. *East* to distinguish from West
Farndon in Woodford *supra* 37.

Glendon

GLENDON 74 E 1

Clen(e)done 1086 DB

Clendon 1175 P (p) *et passim* to 1388 Cl, *Clendun* 1218 ClR,
1252 Cl, *-doun* 1401 Cl

Clandon 1184 P (p)

Glendon 1205 FineR (p), 1570 *Recov*

Clenyndon a. 1237 BM

'Clean hill,' i.e. clear of weeds or undergrowth, *v.* clæne, dun.
Cf. Clandon (Sr). Similar confusion of initial *c* and *g* is found
in Glenfield (Lei) and Glanvill (PN D 629).

BROOKSIDE SPINNEY (6″), cf. Robert *Bithebrok* (i.e. by the brook)
1247 *Ass.*

Harrington

HARRINGTON 73 F 12

Arintone 1086 DB, *-na* c. 1090 France, *Harinton'* 1166
P (p)

Hederingeton' 1184 P (p), *Hetheringtone* 12th Survey *et
passim* to 1379 Cl with variant spellings *-inton(e)*, *-yngton*

Haderington c. 1210 WellsR, *-inton* 1234 Cl, *Hatherinton*
1237 Cl

Eringtona 1225 Bracton, *Etherinton* 1275 RH

Hathrington 1526 SR, *Harrington al. Hethryngton* 1564 FF

'*Hǣðhere*'s farm,' *v.* ingtun. This pers. name is not on record but would be a regular formation. Cf. Hetherington and Hetherslaw (PN NbDu 112–13).

LOATLAND WOOD is *Loutelund* c. 1220, 1286 *For*, 1248 Seld 13, c. 1260 *PipewellA*, -*lond* 1248 Seld 13, *Loteland* 1599 *Recov.* There can be little doubt that we have here a compound of OScand *laut* and lundr, 'wood.' The first element is a rare word in Old Norse, but is recorded by Rygh (*Indledning* 64) as occurring in place-names, and denoting 'a small valley, a hollow.' Sahlgren discusses this element very fully in NoB vii, 102 f. It is found in OSw as *løt*, and survives in various senses in Swedish dialect, the chief of which are (1) a small uncultivated grass-patch, (2) pasture-land, (3) sheep-road, (4) sheep-enclosure. The word is connected with OScand *lúta*, 'to incline,' and the original idea is a sloping and then a hollow piece of ground, later a piece of pasture-land, because such land was often found in the hollows. It is impossible to be sure of the exact sense of *laut* in this compound. The present Loatland Wood is on the top of a ridge with good pasture hollows on the northern slope. Persistent medial *e* suggests that the true form may have been *lauta-lund*, rather than *laut-lund*, with the first element in the genitive plural. Hence perhaps, 'wood of the hollows.'

NEWBOTTLE BRIDGE is *Newbolthl'* 1242 Fees, *Neubotlebrigge* 1330 *Ass*, and was by the home of William de *Newebotl* (1253 *Ass*). 'New building,' *v. supra* 56.

THORPE UNDERWOOD is *Thorp* 12th Survey, *Torp* 1206 Cur, *Thorp' Belet* 1220 Fees, 1246 Cl, 1316 FA, *T(h)orp sub bosco* c. 1220 *For*, 1248 Seld 13, *Torp Underwode* 1255 Seld 13, *Thorpe Billett al. Thorpe Underwood* 1637 *Recov. v.* þorp. Hervey *Belet* held the manor in the 12th cent. Survey.

WHARF LODGE is *Harrington-warth* 1791 Bridges. The place is on a hill-top away from any water and can have no connection with the modern word 'wharf.' The 18th cent. form suggests the possibility of ON *varða*, 'cairn, heap of stones.' There are fields here called *Warth*, the local pronunciation still varying between *warth* and *wharf*.

Haselbech

HASELBECH [heizəlbitʃ] 73 F 10

Esbece 1086 DB

Haselbech(e) 12th Survey *et passim*, *-beht* 1235 Fees, *-bek* 1261
    Ass, Hasilbec 1270 Ipm, *Haselbach* 1281 Ch, *-becche* 1314 Cl,
    Hayselbeche 1316 FA, *Haselbeech* 1608 *Ipm*

Heselbech(e) c. 1220 WellsR, 1284 FA, 1300 Ipm, *-begh'*
    c. 1220 WellsR

Hasilbitche 1586 *FF, Haselbitch(e)* 1639 StJ, 1730 Poll,
    Haselbich 1712 Morton

Topographically, Haselbech is much more likely to be named
from the high ground on which it stands than from either of the
slight valleys which fall away from it on the north- and south-
west, so that we probably have the word *beche, bache,* 'hill,' as
in Burbage (Lei), rather than the better known *bache, beche,*
'valley.' See further EPN *s.v.* bæc.

BRANKLEY FM (6″). Cf. *Brankley broke* 1580 *Map.*

Hothorpe

HOTHORPE [houθɔ·p] 73 D 9

Udetorp 1086 DB, *Hudtorp* 1235 Fees

Huttórp c. 1155 Dane, 1202 Ass (p), *Huttorph* c. 1200 ib.,
    Hutthorp(e) early 13th BM, 1275 RH, *Hohttorp* 1302 Ipm

Hutorp 1203 *FF, Huthorp* 1220 Fees

Huhthorp 1242 Fees, *Huchtorp'* 1247 Ass, *Hokthorp* 1303 Pat,
    Hokyorph c. 1320 H de B, *Hucthorp* 1331 AD v

Hothorp(e) 1247 *Ass,* 1284 FA, 1295 Cl, 1313 Ipm

Houthorp' 1261 *Ass, Hoothorpe* 1617 FF, 1702 Poll

This is a difficult name. Topographically, a compound of OE
hoh and þorp, hence 'thorpe on the hill,' would suit admirably,
but the early and persistent *u* in the earliest forms has no parallel
in the numerous compounds of hoh, which have given rise to
the Yorkshire *Huttons,* the Northamptonshire *Houghtons* or the
Leicestershire *Hoby.* The DB spelling (cf. also that in Fees) is
probably an example of a common error in that document when

it attempts to deal with OE *h*, ME *gh* or ʒ. Cf. *Ludewic* (DB) for Lowick *infra* 185.

COOMBEHILL SPINNEY (6″). Cf. *Combe close* 1627 *Clayton*. One of the rare examples of **cumb** in this county.

Kelmarsh

KELMARSH 73 F 11

> *Cailmare, Keilmerse* 1086 DB
> *Chailesmers* c. 1155 BM, *Keylesmerch* 1332 *Ass*
> *Keylmers* 12th Survey, *Keilmers, -y-* late 12th BM *et passim*
>   to 1428 FA with variant spellings *-merse, -mers(c)h(e)*
> *Kelmers(e)* 1199 FF, 1223 WellsR, *-mersh* 1322 AD iv *et freq*
> *Kailmers(e)* 1201 FineR, 1204 *FF*, 1233 Bracton, 1247 *Ass*
> *Keylemers* 1242 Fees, *-merthe* 1315 AD iii, *-mersh* 1317 Cl,
>   *Keyllemerssh* 1326 Cl

This is a difficult name. Lindkvist (66) would take it to be a hybrid compound of an unrecorded OWScand *keill, or the recorded *keila*, 'rift, rent, cleft, fissure,' or OWScand *kill*, 'narrow bay,' 'wedge.' Cf. also Yorkshire dialect *keill*, 'triangular bit of ground, gore.' *kill* cannot phonologically give rise to *Keil-*, and neither word gives good sense for the topography of Kelmarsh itself. Kelmarsh is on the top of a hill. The marsh is presumably the bottom of the broad valley, full of small pools, which runs down to the Welland on the north-west. With this topographical difficulty and the further difficulty of a hybrid of a rare Scandinavian word and a common English one, it is probably better to take the first element to be an OE pers. name **Cægl(a)*. Cf. Keysoe (PN BedsHu 14–15). Hence, '*Cægla*'s marsh.'

KELMARSH FIELD FM is *Kelmarshe Feild* 1639 Kelmarsh. Cf. also *Northfeld* 1232 *FF*. It is at the north end of the parish. SHIPLEY WOOD (6″) is *wood of Shyplegh* 1257 Ch. 'Sheep wood or clearing,' *v.* **leah**.

Loddington

LODDINGTON 73 F 14

> *Lodintone* 1086 DB, 1166 RBE *et passim* to 1428 FA with
>   variant spellings *-ing-, -yng-, Lodenton* 1316 FA
> *Lodynton juxta Rothewell* 1299 *Ass*

Ludington 1305 Cl

'*Lodda*'s farm,' *v.* ingtun. Cf. Lodsworth (PN Sx 26) and Loddiswell (PN D 306).

Maidwell

MAIDWELL 73 D 12

Medewelle 1086 DB, *-wella* c. 1155 BM
Maydewell(e), *-i-* t. Hy 2 BM *et passim* to 1475 AD vi
Meidewell(e), *-y-* 1181 P (p) *et freq* to c. 1245 (1425) StFrides,
   Meydell 1227 *Ass*
Madewell' 1204 Cur (p), 1276 Cl
Maydenewell 1235 Pat, 1253 *Ass* (p), 1275 *FF*, 1287 Ipm,
   Maydenwell 1247, 1285 *Ass*
Maydwell Marie, Petri 1526 SR
Meadwell 1675 Ogilby

'Maidens' spring,' *v.* wielle and cf. Maidford *supra* 41 and Maidenwell (L), *Maidenwell'* 1212 Fees. Bridges (ii, 45) tells us that 'near the church is *Maidwell*, a very quick flowing spring.' So also he tells us (ii, 47) that 'there were anciently two churches, one dedicated to the *Blessed Virgin* the other to *S. Peter*, long since destroyed.'

BERRYDALE COVERT is *Burghdale* 13th *NthStA*, *Berydale* 1480 *Buccleuch*. This seems to be a compound of burh and dæl or dalr, hence 'valley by or with a fortification,' but no such remains here now. Cf. Borrowdale (Cu).

DALE FM (6″), MAIDWELL DALE, cf. *Dalakirwelle* c. 1270 *Buccleuch*, *Dale close* 1645 *Finch-Hatton*, *Maidwell Dale* c. 1825 O.S., *v.* dæl, æcer, wielle. HOPPIN HILL is *Hopping hill* 1684 *Rental*. Cf. the same name *supra* 81. SCOTLAND WOOD is *Scotland* 1779 F, (*Wood*) 1826 G. The land may be so called from some *scot* or payment on it, cf. Scotland (PN Sx 238, PN D 212) and in Godshill (Wt), 1354 *Add Skotland*.

Marston Trussel

MARSTON TRUSSELL 73 D 10

Mersitone 1086 DB
Merston(e) 1220 Fees *et freq* to 1361 Cl, (*Trussel*) 1235 Fees,
   1298 Ipm

'Marsh farm,' *v.* mersc, tun. Richard *Trussel* held the manor in 1233 (WellsR).

Orton

ORTON 73 F 13

Overton(e) 1086 DB *et passim* to 1316 FA
Oreton(e) 1283 Cl, 1285 *Ass*, 1306 Abbr.

'Farm on the slope or bank,' *v.* ofer, tun and cf. Overton (R). The place is on a fairly steep hillside.

Oxendon, Great and Little

OXENDON, GREAT and LITTLE 73 D/E 11

Oxendon(e) 1086 DB *et passim*, (*Parva*) 12th Survey, (*Maiore, Minore*) 1220 Fees, (*Magna*) 1249 Cl, *Oxindun* 1199 FF, -*don* 1236 Fees, *Oxon al. Oxendon* 1655 *Recov*
Oxedone 1086 DB, 1191, 1230 P

'Hill of the oxen,' *v.* dun.

Rothwell

ROTHWELL[1] [rouəl] 73 E 14

Rodewelle 1086 DB
Roewella 1152–73 St Werb, *Rowella*, -*e* 1184 P *et freq* to 1292–6 Ipm, *Rouvell(e)* 1210–12 RBE, 1273 Ipm
Rothewell(e) 1227 *Ass*, 1238 Cl, 1247 *FF*, 1253 *Ass et freq* to 1439 AD v, *Rotewell* 1251 Seld 13, *Rothewell al. Rowwell* 1274 Ipm, *Rothwell* 1314 Ipm *et freq*, *Royewell* 1298 Pat
Routhewell 1421 IpmR
Roth(e)well al. Rowell 1568 *FF*, 1678 DKR xl, *Rowell* 1634 StJ, 1712 Morton, 1730 Poll

The name Rothwell is also found in Lincolnshire and Yorkshire, the general run of forms having an *o* from DB onwards, forms with *ou* being less common, and not found before the 13th cent. Rothwell (L) is on a band of red chalk and Morton speaks (40, 137–8) of the *Red-land* at Rothwell (Nth) due to the presence of ironstone, so that topographically there is much

[1] BRIDGE ST is *Bridgstrete* 1608 *Rental*. MARKET ST is *le Markett place, Markett strete* (ib.).

in favour of Lindkvist's suggestion (160) that these are hybrid compounds of OScand *rauðr*, 'red,' and *wielle*, hence 'red spring.' Philologically, it is a little difficult however to understand the rarity of early forms in *ou*, when we compare the Rothwells with the early forms of such names as Rawcliffe, Roecliffe and Rockcliffe in Yorkshire and Lancashire.

Professor Ekwall, in explanation of this and other difficult names in *Roth-*, such as Rothley (Lei) DB *Rodole*, Surv *Rodeleia*, calls attention to a hitherto unnoted OE *roþ*, 'clearing,' cognate with OFris *rothe*, OHG *rod*, ON *ruð*. It is found in an OE Charter (BCS 737) in the form *roðe*. The place is associated with Sandon (Herts), and is to be identified with Roe Green and Wood in that parish (*la Rode, Rodewode* 1222 St Paul's DB, *la Rothe* 1307 *SR* (p), *le Rothewode, Rothegrene* 1335 *Ct*). We have noted further parallels in Herts, viz. Roe End in Flamstead (*atte Rothe* 1272–7 *Ct*), Roestock in North Mimms (*Rothstoke* 1369 *Ct*), Roe Green and Roehyde in St Peters (*la Rode* 1290 FF, *Rothhide* 1287 *Ass*). Dr Reaney notes Rothend in Ashdon (Ess) DB *Rode*, 1279 FF *Rothe*. Further we find a *Rothewellesike* (c. 1200 *Ashby*) in Moreton Pinkney, and a *Rothewell* (1404 *Magd*) in Brackley, which are in districts entirely free from Scandinavian influence.

DEBDALE LODGE is *Depedalehul* c. 1200 *PipewellA, Depedale* 1293 AD iii, *Depedale Huille* n.d. AD vi. 'Deep valley,' *v.* deop. This is clearly the (*on*) *deopandene* in the bounds of Kettering (*infra* 184 n.), with an interesting replacement of English denu by Scandinavian *dale* (*v.* dalr).

SHOTWELL MILL is *Schotewelle* 1285 *Ass* (p) (bis), *Shotelmyll* t. Hy 7 *MinAcct, Shottwell feild* t. Eliz *LRMB*. This is probably from OE *sceōta-wiell*, 'trout-stream.' Cf. the name *Shotenewell* (t. Hy 3 AD iii), a field-name in Brixworth, containing *sceōtena* the gen. pl. of *sceōta*.

HOSPITAL FM is owned by the governors of Jesus Hospital, founded in the reign of Elizabeth. ROTHWELL WOOD (6″) is *boscus de Rowell* c. 1220 *For*. WINDMILL HILL COTTAGES (6″). Cf. *Windmill feild* t. Eliz *LRMB*.

Rushton

RUSHTON 74 E 1

> *Risetone, Ricsdone* 1086 DB
>
> *Riston* 1162 P (p) *et passim* to 1329 Fine, *Ristun* t. John BM
>
> *Ruston* 12th Survey, *Ruston* 1199 FF, 1248 Seld 13, 1268
> Fine, *Ruyston* 1284 Cl
>
> *Ruchtona* 1225 Bracton
>
> *Ryshton* 1293 Cl, *Risheton beyond Rothewell* 1393 Cl
>
> *Risshton* 1305 Cl *et freq* to 1401 Cl with variant spelling
> *Rysshe-*
>
> *Russhton by Rothewell* 1343 Ipm, *Rushton* 1346 FA *et freq* with
> variant spelling *Russhe-*
>
> *Risshyngton near Rothewell* 1343 Cl
>
> *Rushton al. Ryston al. Rushon* 1614 *FF*, *Rushton al. Rishton*
> 1695 *FF*

'Rush farm,' *v.* rysc, tun.

ALDER WOOD is *Alderwood* 1611 *Depositions*.

BARFORD LODGE is *Bereford* 1086 DB *et freq* to 1316 FA, *Berford*
t. Ed 1 *PeterbB*. It is impossible to make any other suggestion
for this name than that put forward in PN BedsHu 50, viz. that
it is a common term for a ford that might carry a load of corn.

GAULTNEY WOOD is *Galklynt (wood)* t. Hy 3 BM, *Gowteney* 1611
Depositions. The second element in this name is clearly ODan,
OSw *klint*, 'steep slope by the sea, top of a bank,' allied to the
English *clent*, a hill-name discussed in PN Wo 279. The first
element is ON *goltr* or *galti*, 'boar,' cf. Galtres (PN NRY 8),
hence 'boar-slope.' Gaultney Wood is on a fairly sharp slope.
It is somewhat difficult phonologically to link the earlier and
later forms. The final *-ey* of the modern form may well represent
ME *hey* (*v.* (ge)hæg), 'enclosure,' so common in woodland
areas, and the place may at one time have been called *Galklynt-
hay*. *Galk-* may have become *Galt-* by a common confusion of
k and *t* sounds, while the original final *t* of *Galklynt* may have
disappeared after *n*. Cf. PN NbDu (Phonology § 56).

STOREFIELD WOOD. This is probably to be associated with
boscus de Storth 1198 P, *le Stordh* c. 1260 *PipewellB*, the field

having been named from a place called *Storth* (*v.* storð), denoting 'brushwood, young plantation.' Cf. also *le Storth* (1330) in Walton.

Sibbertoft

SIBBERTOFT 73 E 9

Sibertod 1086 DB, -*toft*, -*y*- 12th Survey *et passim* to 1317 Cl, *Sibre*- 1236 WellsR, 1273 Ipm, *Siper*- 1256 Fees, *Sibir*- 1285 *Ass*, *Sibur*- 1380 Cl

Sibetoft 1221 WellsR, *Sybe*- 13th Fees, *Sybbertofte al. Sibbtofte* 1564 *FF*

Sibethorp 1250 Fees, *Sybercroft* 1284 FA

'*Sigebeorht*'s toft,' *v.* topt. The absence of genitival *s* is to be noted. It may be, since the pers. name involved is English, that the original second element was tun, later replaced by the Scandinavian *toft*.

CASTLE YARD is so named in 1627 (*Clayton*). This is the name given to the remains of a motte and bailey castle here. DUST HILL is *Dusthil* 1291 *Ass*, *Dustle* 1779 F, 1826 G. See Duston *supra* 82. MOOT HILL is *The Moot hill* 1791 Bridges. This is probably 'hill of meeting,' from OE (ge)mot, possibly the meeting-place of the old *Stotfold* Hundred (*supra* 109). PRINCE RUPERT'S FM, like Cromwell Ho *supra* 73, preserves a memory of the battle of Naseby.

Sulby

SULBY 73 F 9

Solebi 1086 DB *et freq* to 1316 FA with variant spelling -*by*

Sulebi 1158 P *et passim* with variant spelling -*by*

Sulehby 1243 Cur

Seleby 1244 Fees, 1297 Cl

Sulby 1310 Cl, 1327 Ipm *et freq*

Sulleby 1347 Ipm

Sowleby 1524 BM, *Sowlbye* 1540 *LRMB*

This is probably a compound of ODan *Sule* or ON *Súla*, a pers. name, and by. Cf. Sulby (PN IOM 545), c. 1376 Chron. Manniae *Sulaby*. Alternatively it might be a compound of OE *sulh*, 'furrow, trench' (cf. Sulgrave *supra* 36 and Souldrop

PN BedsHu 42). The Abbey lies on a stream, but the valley is very shallow. The 1243 form is in favour of *sulh*.

Thorpe Lubenham

THORPE LUBENHAM 73 D 10

Torp 1086 DB, *Thorp* 12th Survey, (*juxta Lubenho*) 1220 Fees, (*juxta Lobenham*) 1285 *FF*, (*nigh Lobbenham*) 1403 AD v, *Thorpe Lubnum* 1702 Poll

v. þorp. Distinguished by its adjacency to Lubbenham (Lei).

Thorpe Malsor

THORPE MALSOR 74 F 1

Alidetorp 1086 DB[1]

Thorp 12th Survey, (*Malesoures*) 1220 Fees, *Tropmalesores* 1261 *Ass*, *Thorpmalesoveres* 1332 *Ass*, *Thorp Malsore* 1346 FA, *Thorpe Malsor al. Malsworth* t. Jas 1 *FF*, *Thorpe Malsor or Mallsworth or Malesworth* 1755 *FF*

v. þorp. Fucher *Malesoures* held the manor in the 12th cent. Survey, the name being spelt *Malesouveres* AD iv. For the form *Mallsworth* cf. Milton *infra* 150.

X. ORLINGBURY HUNDRED

Ordlingbære a. 1076 Geld Roll, *Ordinbaro, Ordibaro* 1086 DB, *Orlingberge* 12th Survey, *Orniberi* 1167 P. *v.* Orlingbury *infra* 128. Part of the hundred was known as *Malesle* a. 1076 Geld Roll, *Maleslea* 1086 DB, *Mallesl'* 12th Survey, *Maleuesle* 1202 Ass, from Mawsley *infra* 128. It included Hanging Houghton, Lamport, Scaldwell, Old, Faxton, Walgrave and Brixworth (Bridges ii, 80).

Brixworth

BRIXWORTH 73 H 12

Briclesworde 1086 DB, *Brikleswrth*(*e*) t. Hy 3 AD iii, *Bricklesuurtha* t. Hy 2 (13th) Sparke, *Bricleswurth* 1248 Cl

---

[1] This identification is made by Round in the VCH (i, 327). The first part of the early name may conceal the name of the sometime holder, possibly a woman named *Aeþelgȳð*.

Brihteswrðe 1198 P, *Brythtesworth* 1253 *Ass*
Brikelewrth 1199 FF, *Brikelesworth* 12th Survey *et freq* to
    1426 AD iv with variant spellings *Bryk-* and *-wurth, Brikil-*
    1241 P
Briglesworð 1216 PatR
Brekelesworth 1421 AD iv
Bryxworth al. Bryckelsworth 1571 *Recov*, 1780 *EnclA, Brix-*
    worth al. Woolfadge 1671 *Recov*

The first element in this, as in most *worth*-names, is a pers.
name. There are two possibilities with regard to this name. It
may be OE *Beorhtel*, as would be suggested if we lay stress on
the forms from 1198 P and 1253 *Ass*, though there is no parallel
for an otherwise uniform development of OE *Beorhtel* to ME
Bricel-, Brikel- (cf. Johnston *PN England and Wales s.n.*).
Alternatively, we might start from OE *Bricel, a diminutive of
the pers. name *Brica* found in Brickendon (Herts), *Brycandun*
in BCS 1306. See further Brigden(s) PN Sx 353, 478. In that
case we must take the two exceptional forms as due to confusion
with another and more common name.

WOLFAGE (not on map) is *Wolfhegge* 13th *NthStA*, 1287 *Ass* (p),
Wolfegge in Brykkysworth 1540 *LRMB, Brixworth al. Woolfadge*
1671 *Recov, Woolfitch* 1735 DKR xlii, *Wolfidge* 1791 Bridges.
'Wolf hedge,' with reference probably to an enclosure intended
to keep out wolves. It is a lost manor; the ruins of the manor
house were still to be seen to the south-west of the village in
Bridges' day (ii, 80). The name survives in *Wolfage Piece*, a field
just to the south-east of the village.

Broughton

BROUGHTON [ˈbrɑutən] 74 G 1

Burtone 1086 DB
Brocton(a) 12th AD vi, 1191 P (p), 1229 Cl, 1281 AD vi
Brohtune 1125–8 ChronPetro
Bructon(e) 1205 Cur (p), 1227 WellsR, 1235 Fees, *Brutton*
    1261 *Ass*
Bruchton 1220 Fees, c. 1230 *Magd*, *Bruhton* 1242 Fees
Brouton 1235 Fees, 1284 FA, *Bruton* 1349 Cl

Broghton 1275 RH *et freq* to 1428 FA, *Brohgton* 1285 *FF*
Brughton 1285, 1312 *Ass*
Browton 1310 AD vi
Broughton (*Germeyn*) 1285 *Ass*, 1316 FA, 1429 AD iv
Brouten 1657 NRS i

'Brook-farm,' *v.* broc, tun, though the many forms with *u* rather than *o* are curious. Robert de *St German* had a holding here in 1229 (Cl).

CLARKE'S LODGE (6″) is to be associated with the family of Edward *Clark* (1702 Poll).

Great Cransley

GREAT CRANSLEY 74 G 1

Cranslea bricg 956 (c. 1250) BCS 943
Cranesleg, -lea 1086 DB *et passim* to 1458 AD vi with variant
    spellings *Cranys-* and *-leye, -le, -legh, Craunisle* 1266 Ipm
Crannesley 1530 AD vi

'Clearing of the crane or heron,' *v.* cran, leah.

LITTLE CRANSLEY is *Little Crannesley* 1555 AD vi. NORTH FIELD FM (6″) is *le Northfeld* 1551 Pat. WHITE HILL LODGE. Cf. *Longwythil* t. Ed 3 *Rental*.

Faxton

FAXTON 73 G 13

Fextone 1086 DB
Fachestuna 1121 AC, *Fakes-* 12th France, *Facheston* c. 1230
    AD A 15466, *Fagestona* c. 1225 St Frides
Faxton(*a*) 1166 P (p) *et passim*, (*al. Faxon*) 1572 *FF*
Foxton 1335 Cl, 1345 Ipm
Fawxton al. Faxton 1579 *FF*

There is a rare Scandinavian name *Fákr*, found in the form *fakaR* in a Danish Runic inscription (cf. Noreen, *Altisländische Grammatik* 379) and possibly also in the Norwegian p.n. *Faxstaðr* (NG x, 353). This, in combination with tun, would account for the p.n. Faxton. It should be borne in mind, however, that there are possibilities of an OE pers. name *Fæcce*, cf. *Feaks Well*

(PN BedsHu 174) and *Fackeswell* in Clerkenwell (Mx) (1199 FF) which are hardly likely to contain a Scandinavian pers. name.

Hannington

HANNINGTON 73 H 14

Hanitone, Hanintone 1086 DB

Haninton(e) 1195 FF *et passim* to 1349 Ipm with variant spellings *Hanyn-, Haning-, Hanyng-, Hanyngton juxta Waldegrave* 1361 *FF*

Hanyton, -i- 1220 Fees *et freq* to 1376 Cl

Henigtun' 1241 Cl

'*Hana*'s farm,' *v.* ingtun.

Hardwick

HARDWICK 74 J 1

Heordewican c. 1067 (12th) AS Wills

Herdewiche 1086 DB *et freq* to 1313 Ipm with variant spellings *-wik(e), -wyk(e)*

Hardewiche 1086 DB, *-wyke* 1397 Cl, *Hardwyk* 1428 FA

Herdwyk' 12th Survey, *-wic'* 1220 Fees, *Herthwyk* 1250 *FF*

v. heordewic. The first form, if it refers to this place, is apparently in the dat. pl. form, suggesting a group of 'hardwicks.'

HARDWICK WOOD is *boscus de Hardwyc* 13th *NthStA*. MERRY-DALE LODGE (6″) is *Muridale* 1287 *For.* 'Pleasant valley,' *v.* myrig, dæl.

Harrowden, Great and Little

HARROWDEN, GREAT and LITTLE 74 H 2

Hargindone et alia Hargindone, Hargintone, Hargedone 1086 DB

Harhgeduna 1155–8 (1329) Ch

Harudon 12th Survey, 1280 Ipm, (*Magna*) 1284 FA

Har(e)wedon 1203 Cur (p) *et passim* to 1350 Ipm, (*Parva*) 1220 Fees, (*Maiore*)ib., (*Major, Minor*) 1227 BM, *Harwedenn* 1203 Cur (p)

Hareudon, -ou- 1235 Fees, 1379 Cl, *Harowedon* 1381 Cl,
　　1386 Ch, *Harodown* 1526 SR
Herowdon 1462 Pat
Haridon 1675 Ogilby

This place, like Harrowden (PN BedsHu 91), must have been
a hill marked by some place for heathen worship (*v.* hearg, dun).
We have reference in the Cartulary of St Andrew's, Northampton
(320 d), to 'the furlong callyd *Harow*,' which was in the
neighbourhood. It is tempting to think that this may preserve
record of the site of the temple or grove itself, but it may be that
the furlong was simply named from the common harrow.

FRISBY LODGE (6″). In 1282 (Cl) the sheriff of Northamptonshire was ordered to deliver Robert de Harewedon, imprisoned
at Northampton for the death of Richard Page of *Friseby*, in
bail to six men who shall mainpern to have him before the king
at Worcester at Whitsunday next. This name is probably
manorial rather than local in origin, Richard Page having come
perhaps from Frisby in Leicestershire.

BLOWHILL BARN (6″) is *Blow Hill* 1688 *Clayton*. HILL TOP is
probably identical in site with *Hilbarow, Hyl-* 14th *NthStA*.
RED HILL is *Redhill* 1688 *Clayton*. STONEBRIG LANE (6″), cf.
Stone Bridge Field 1782 *EnclA*.

Hanging Houghton

HANGING HOUGHTON　73 H 12

Hohtone 1086 DB with a similar run of forms to Houghton
　　infra 149

The additional prefix first appears as *Hangende* in 1227 (ClR).
Other forms of interest are *Hanggendehawton* 1287 *Ass, Hocghton
juxta Langeporte* 1294 *Ass*, i.e. Lamport *infra* 127. It is called
"hanging from the declining situation of the houses and enclosures on the side of an hill" (Bridges ii, 116).

CLINT HILL is *Clynthyll* 1576 *Terrier*. Cf. also *Clintesdene*
c. 1300 *Buccleuch, Clyntewellesic* 1329 Dugd iv, 208, *Clynte-
welleweye* 14th *NthStA*. There is a well-marked hill here with
springs on it, and a small stream at the foot. The 'hill' is doubt-

less the *clint* (*v.* **klettr**), the 'well' is one of the springs
which feed the 'sike,' *v.* **sic**. *Clint Hill* may be an inversion
spelling for *Clintell* from earlier *Clintwell*. The 'way' is doubtless
the old road from the west here. Cf. further *Shortclynt* (1300)
in Draughton and *Steynklint* (1315) in Teeton.

MOORWELL LEYS SPINNEY (6") is *Morall Lease* 1662 *Clayton*,
1670 *Terrier*. *v.* **læs**.

Isham

ISHAM 74 [aisəm] G 2

   Isham 974, 1077 (13th) ChronRams, 1086 DB *et passim*

   Ysham 1060 (c. 1350) KCD 809 *et passim* to 1314 Cl, *Iysham*
     1284 FA

   Hisham 1086 DB, *Hysham* 12th Survey, *Highsham* 1675
     Ogilby

   Iseham 1217 ClR, 1475 Pat

   Isam 1235 Fees, 1428 FA

   Yesham 1400 AD iii

   'ham by the river Ise' (*supra* 3).

Lamport

LAMPORT 73 G 12

   Langeport 1086 DB *et passim* to 1428 FA, *-pord* 1203 *FF*,
     -porth 1226 WellsR

   Lamp(*p*)*erd* 1553 Renton

   Langport al. Lamport 1559 *FF*

   'The long town,' *v.* **lang**, **port**. Cf. Lamport (PN Bk 48),
Langport (So), a lost *Lamport* in Eastbourne (PN Sx 430), and
possibly Landport (ib. 320). This 'town' has long since lost its
importance, like most of the other *ports*. Bridges (ii, 110) notes
"The Saxon word *Port* not always implying the Latin *Portus* an
haven or sea-port but often simply a village or town."

BLUEBERRY LODGE is *Blewberowhyll* 1503 *Isham*, *Blewbarrowe*
1548, 1567 *Deed*, *Blueborow Lodge* 1654 ParReg (St James,
Northampton). The forms are too late for certainty, but the first
element may be OE **bla**(**w**), perhaps partly influenced by the
adjective 'blue,' hence, 'cold, exposed hill,' *v.* **beorg**. The place
lies open to the east and north-east.

Mawsley

MAWSLEY[1] 73 G 13

Malesleia 1185 BM *et freq* to 1333 *FF* with variant spellings
-*le*, -*lee*
Mallesle(e) 1293 AD iii, 1299 *Ass*, 1325 Ipm, 1356 *FF*
Mawesley 1596 *FF*

v. Orlingbury Hundred *supra* 122 and Wythemail *infra* 129.

MAWSLEY WOOD is *boscum de Malesle* 1249 Seld 13, *Maleslewode*
1292 Pat.

Old

OLD 73 H 13

Walda, -*e* 1086 DB, 1166 P, 12th Survey, 1220 Fees, 1249
Seld 13
Waud(e) 1205 Cur (p), 1216 ClR, 1235 Fees, 1244 Cl, 1251
Ch, *Wauld* 1255 Seld 13
Wolde 1316 FA *et freq* to 1439 AD v
Welde 1366 Cl
Olde 1535 VE, (*al. Woold*) 1555 AD vi, *Owlde* 1567 *FF*,
Wold al. Old 1597 *Recov*, *Old* or *Wold* 1826 G
Thold 1544 *FF*, 1679 *Recov*

'Wold,' v. weald. *Thold* is a contraction of 'The Old.'

Orlingbury

ORLINGBURY [olim ɔ·libi·ə] 74 H 2

Ordinbaro 1086 DB
Orlinberg(a) 1131 P (p), *Horlinbere* 1203 Cur (p), (*H*)*orling-
burgh* 1235 Fees *et passim* with variant spellings -*ing*-, -*yng*-,
and -*ber(e)*, -*bergh*.
Ordlingber(e) 1220 Fees, *Ordlingebere* 1247 *Ass*, *Ordlingberge*
1253 *Ass*, n.d. AD vi, *Ordelingber*' n.d. AD vi, c. 1300 Inq
aqd, *Ordligeber* 1242 Fees
Orlingbery 1275 Cl, -*bir*' 1275 RH
Orlibergh 1388 Cl, *Orlingbere al. Orlybere* 1557 *FF*, *Orlingbury al. Orlebere* 1614 *Recov*, *Orlibeare* 1631 NRS i

[1] A decayed parish, now united to Faxton.

Perhaps '*Ordla*'s hill,' *v.* **berg**, with connective *ing*. The multiplicity of variant forms makes the second element uncertain. It is clear that there has been confusion between **bære, bearu, beorg** and **burh**. *Ordla* would be a regular formation from the common pers. name element *Ord-*. Cf. the cognate OGer *Ortila* (Förstemann, PN 1180).

BADSADDLE LODGE [bætsædəl]

> *Bateshasel Malesou(re)s* 12th Survey, *Batisheshell* 1313 Ipm, -*hadil* 1316 FA, *Bateshal* 1325 Ipm, *Bateshasel* 1344 *FF*, -*hasell* 1397 Cl
> *Baddeshasel* 1220 Fees, 1247 *Ass* (p), 1299 *Ass*
> *Battsadle al. Backe Sadle* 1556 *Recov*

'*Bætti*'s hazel or hazel-clump,' *v.* **hæsel** and cf. Battishill (PN D 177). Fucher *Malesou(re)s* held the manor in the 12th century Survey.

WYTHEMAIL PARK FM (WITHMALE) [wilmər]

> *Widmale* 1086 DB
> *Wismalua* 1130 P (p), *Wizmalua* 1156 P (p), *Wimalue* 1220 Fees
> *Wymale* 12th Survey, -*mall* 1284 FA
> *Wythemal(e)* 13th *PeterbB*, 1330 *Ass*, 1330 Cl, 1428 FA, *Wyth-* 1571 *Recov*
> *Wimawe, -y-* 1235 Fees, 1240 *FF*, *Wydemawe* 1247 *FF*
> *Whitmal'* 1285 *Ass*
> *Wethemale* 1316 FA
> *Wythmale al. Wymale* 1565 AD v, *Wilmer* 1791 Bridges

This is a difficult name. Possibly it should be taken with Mawsley *supra* 128, for which, when used as a hundred-name, we have an early form *Maleuesle*. Professor Ekwall suggests the association of the two names, and would take *malue* in Wythemail to be the dative of a lost OE **mealo*, gen. sg. *mealwes*, cognate with ON *möl*, fem., Swed *mal*, masc., 'stones, gravel.' Mawsley and Wythemail are a few miles apart, Mawsley being on, and Wythemail at the foot of a well marked oolite ridge. It is possible that this, from its stony character, was once called OE *mealwe* (dat.), ME *malwe*. Mawsley would in that case be the leah or clearing belonging to this ridge; Wythemail might be explained as describing the place which was *wið* or against such a ridge. No other examples of *wið*-compounds have been noted in English p.n.'s, but compounds with other prepositions such as *æt*, *bi*, *bineoðan*, are common and Marstrander (*Norsk Tidsskrift for Sprogvidenskap* vi, 125, 175) has noted similar compounds of ON *við* in Iceland and in Scandinavian p.n.'s in the Isle of Man[1]. A further example of the use of this word *malwe* is found in a field-name *le longemalewe* (now Long Mollow) in Yelvertoft (13th AD iv), presumably descriptive of a long stony field, while a *Long Mallows* survives in Clipston.

HOPCRAFT SPINNEY and LAMMAS SPINNEY (both 6″). Cf. *Hopcroft* and *Lammas* in a *Terrier* of 1809 and *v. infra* 273. MOORFIELD LODGE. Cf. *Moor Field* 1811 *EnclA*.

Pytchley

PYTCHLEY [paitʃli] 74 G 2

    pihteslea (*forda*) 956 (c. 1250) BCS 943, *Pihteslea* 1086 DB *et freq* to 1302 Ipm with variant spellings *Pyht-* and *-le*, *-legh*

    Picteslei 1086 DB *et freq* to 1249 Ipm with variant spellings *-lea*, *-le*

    Piteslea 1086 DB *et freq* to 1398 Cl with variant spellings *Pyt-* and *-le(y)*

    Pisteslai 1131 P, *-le(e)* 1205 Cur, 1237 Cl, 1284 FA

    Pichtesle 1189 (1332) Ch, *Pychte(s)le(g)* 1219 FF, 1227 Ch, 1238 Cl

    Pectesle 1198 Fees

    Pyghtesle 1316 FA *et freq* to 1391 Cl with variant spellings *Pight-* and *-lee*

    Pitchesle 1323 Ipm, *-leye* 1323 Cl, *Peychisle* 1372 Moulton, *Pycheley al. Pyghtesley* 1544 LP, *Pitchley al. Pixley* t. Jas 1 ECP, *Pichly* 1657 NRS i, *Pichely* 1712 Morton

'*Peoht*'s clearing or woodland,' *v.* leah.

COX'S LODGE is perhaps to be associated with the family of Thomas *Cox* of Kettering (1635 Wills).

---

[1] Professor Ekwall takes the first element to be OE *wiþþe*, 'willow.'

Scaldwell

SCALDWELL [skɔ·ldwəl] 73 H 12

Sca(l)de(s)welle 1086 DB
Schaudewelle 1199 FF
Scaldewell(e) 12th Survey *et passim* to 1428 FA with variant
  spelling Scaude-, Skalde- 1301 FF, 1313 Ipm
Schaldewell(e) 1241 Cl, 1284 FA, 1285 Ass, 1290, 1325 Cl,
  (Scaldewell al.) 1325 Ipm, Shaldewell 1298 Cl

'Shallow spring,' *v.* sceald, wielle. The initial *sk-* sound is
due to Scandinavian influence, *v.* Introd. xxiii. The place probably takes its name from a spring still to be found in the village
(LG 206).

ROSEHOLM (Kelly) is *Rosholmbroke* 1345 *Finch-Hatton*. This may
be a compound of ON *hross*, 'horse' and holmr, 'island,' etc.

Walgrave

WALGRAVE 73 H 13

Waldgrave, Wold(e)grave 1086 DB
Waldegrauia 1185 BM *et passim* to 1404–10 AD v with
  variant spellings -grave and Waude-
Walgrava 1195 P, Waldgrave 1241 Cl *et freq* to 1428 FA,
  Walgrave al. Waldegrave 1576 AD vi

Walgrave adjoins Old (*supra* 128) and the first element is
doubtless identical with that name. The second element is OE
graf(a), this particular grove pertaining to Old.

XI. SPELHOE HUNDRED

Spelhoh a. 1076 Geld Roll *et passim* to 1316 FA with variant
spellings -ho, -hou, Spelho, Spelehot, Spelehou, Sperehou 1086
DB, Speleho 12th Survey, Spelesho 1185 P, Spello(we) 1337 Ass,
1428 FA. 'Hill of speech,' *v.* hoh and cf. *spelstow* (BCS 129,
882), 'place of speech,' used probably of the site of some moot.
Cf. further Spella and Speller *supra* 33, 78, Spelborw (14th)
and Spello (15th) in Daventry, Spelwell spring in Daventry

(Bridges i, 41), and Spellow Close *infra* 155. The site of the hundred meeting-place was in Weston Favell. According to tradition it was in a field called *Bush field otherwise Spelhoe field* near an extensive quarry of slaty limestone. Careful examination of local tradition, for which we are indebted to Mrs Crick, makes it clear that this is a field in the north of the parish where two Stone Pits are marked on the 6″ map. It is on high ground with old tracks leading to it.

Abington

ABINGTON　83 B 12

Habintune a. 1076 Geld Roll

Abintone 1086 DB *et passim* to 1349 Cl with variant spellings *Abyn-, Abing-, Abyng-, Abbinton'* 1230 P

Abendon 12th Survey, 1201 Cur, *Abyndon* 1231 Cl *et passim* to 1428 FA with variant spelling *Abyn-, (without Northampton)* 1298 Ipm, *-doun* 1389 Cl, *Abyngdon* 1422 AD iii

' *Abba*'s farm,' *v.* ingtun.

ABINGTON MILLS (6″) is *Abyngdon Milnes* 1422 AD iii.

Billing, Great and Little

BILLING, GREAT and LITTLE　83 B 14

Bel(l)inge 1086 DB, *Bellinges* 1179 P, 1252 Cl

Billynges 1156 (1318) Ch, *-inges* 1223 BM, 1305 Ipm, *Byllynges* 13th *NthStA*

Bethlinges 1155–8 (1329) Ch, 13th *NthStA*

Billing(g)e Magna 12th Survey, (*Parva*) ib., *Magna, Parva Byllinge* 1272 Seld 13

(*Majore*) *Billing* 1220 Fees *et freq* to 1253 Ch

Billing Magna al. Much Billing 1674 Recov

Billing Mina (sic) 1710 ParReg

The interpretation of this name depends upon the weight we attach to the twice-repeated form *Bethlinges*. It is difficult not to take this into account. If so, we may take this to be an ingas-derivative of a pers. name **Bȳdel*, a diminutive of *Bȳda*, which is on record. This name is probably found also in Biddlestone (PN NbDu 21). Confusion of *dl* and *thl* is common. Later, assimilation of *dl* to *ll* took place. If we neglect these two forms we must take the name to be an ingas-derivative of *Billa*. Hence, 'people of *Bydel*' or 'of *Billa*.' The spellings with *e* are AN spellings with *e* for *i* (IPN 113).

BILLING BRIDGE (6″) is *Billyngbrige* 1520 *FF*.

BILLING LINGS is *le Lyng* 1585 *Ct*. This is ON lyng, 'heather.'

Boughton

BOUGHTON [bɑutən] 83 A 12

> *Bochetone, Buchenho, Buchetone* 1086 DB
> *Buchetune* 1148–66 NRS iv (p), *-ton* 13th AD ii
> *Bucton* 1175 P (p), 1196 Cur (p), 1199 FF, *Bukton'* 1274 RH
> *Bogton, Bugton* 1196 FF, *Bugeton* 1241 P
> *Boketon* 12th Survey *et freq* to 1349 Cl, *Bokton* 1274 Ipm, (*juxta Norhampton*) 1317 *Ass*, *Bokinton* c. 1265 AD ii
> *Buketon(e)* c. 1200 Dane, 1201 Cur *et passim* to 1343 Ipm
> *Bouhton* t. Hy 3 *NthStA*, *Boughton* 1302 Cl, *Boghton* 1402 Cl
> *Bucketon* 13th AD ii, 1394 AD i
> *Bucton al. Boketon* 1305 Ipm, *Bukton al. Boughton* 1546 FF, *Bucton al. Bowghton* 1597 NRS iii

The early forms make it impossible to carry this Boughton back to OE *bōc-tūn*, 'beech-tree farm.' Rather it must be a compound of OE bucc, 'buck' or bucca, 'he-goat' or the pers. name *Bucca* and tun.

Kingsthorpe

KINGSTHORPE 83 B 12

> *Torp* 1086 DB, 1174, 1175 P, *Trop* 1195 P, *Thorp by North-ampton* 12th Survey, *Throp* 1217 WellsR, *Thorp without Northampton* 1232 Ch
> *Kingestorp* 1190 P, *Kyngesthorp* 1305 Cl, 1316 FA, *Kynges-thorp al. Thorp* 1442 Pat
> *Kinestorp* 1202 Ass, 1203 Abbr

v. þorp. The king held the manor already in DB. For the later manorial addition cf. Abthorpe *supra* 89 and Rothers-thorpe *infra* 151.

KING'S WELL (6") is *Kingeswelle* 14th *NthStJ* and gives a further trace of the royal holding in Kingsthorpe. ST DAVID'S (6") is *Saint Dewys or David or Trinity's Scite* 1767 *EnclA*.

Moulton

MOULTON 83 A 13

Multune a. 1076 Geld Roll, *Multon(e)* 1086 DB *et passim* to 1359 Ipm, (*without Northampton*) 1295 Cl, -*tun'* 1241 Cl, 13th *PeterbA*

Molton(e) 1086 DB, 1302 Ipm, 1375 AD iii

Muleton(e) 1086 DB *et freq* to 1275 RH

Molentun 1205 Pap, *Moleton* 1272 Seld 13, 1275 Pat, 1657 NRS ii

Multon al. Moltone 1266 Ipm, *Molton al. Multon* 1313 Ipm

Moulton 1576 AD vi, *Mowlton* 1599 *FF*

'Mule farm,' *v.* tun and OE *mūl*.

MOULTON LODGE. Cf. *Loggeweye* 14th *NthStA*. Here, as elsewhere in the county, we doubtless have ME *logge* used in the sense, first recorded in the NED *s.a.* 1465, of 'house in a forest serving as a temporary abode in the hunting season.'

HOG HOLE SPINNEY. Cf. *Hogshole* 1773 *EnclA*. MOULTON PARK is *Multon Park* 1359 Ipm, and was probably the home of Simon *de Parco* (1202 Ass). THORPLANDS is *Tharpland* 1657 NRS i, *Thorpelands* 1773 *EnclA*. *v.* þorp.

Overstone

OVERSTONE 83 A 13

Oveston 12th Survey *et passim* to 1428 FA

Uviston' 1220 Fees, *Oviston* 1220 WellsR, 1235 Fees, 1247-55 Ch, *Ovyston* 1316 FA

Wyveston 1242 Fees

Ouston 1275 Ch, *Oweston* 1509 LP

Overston 1284 FA, 1285 Cl, *Overeston* 1482 AD iii

Uveston 1421 Pat

Overston al. Oveston 1468 Pat, *Ovestone al. Overstone* 1610 Recov

'*Ofe*'s farm,' *v.* **tun.** The *r* is apparently due to early folk-etymologising. Cf. Silverstone *supra* 43.

COWPASTURE SPINNEY. Cf. *the Cowpasture* 1613 *Lumley*. GOLDENASH SPINNEY is *Gold Ash* 1779 F. OVERSTONE PARK is *Oveston Park* 1510 LP.

Pitsford

PITSFORD 73 J 12

Pidesford 1086 DB, *Pitesford* ib.

Pittesford 12th Survey, 1203 Cur, 1247 *Ass*, 1269 Ipm

Pitesford 12th AD iii, 1203 *FF*, 1220, 1242 Fees, *Pitisford* 1202 AD ii

Pictesford, Piccessford 1235 Fees

Picheford 1247 *Ass*, 1266 Pat

Pisseford 13th AD ii, 1284, 1316 FA, 1337 AD ii, 1341 Cl, (*al. Spisseford*) 1304 Ipm, *Pysforde* 13th *NthStA*

Pyceford, Pyzeford, Pizeford 1250 Seld 13

Pettiford c. 1260 AD i

Pithisford 1270 Ipm

Pisteford 1290 Cl, 1294 *Ass*

Pisford 1337, 1369 Cl, 1428 FA, 1550 AD v, *Pys-* 1555 AD vi, 1779 F

Probably '*Peoht*'s ford,' as suggested by Professor Ekwall and Dr Smith. Cf. Pytchley *supra* 130.

Spratton

SPRATTON 73 J 11

Spreton(e) 1086 DB, c. 1220 AD ii, *Spretton* 1235 Fees

Sprotone 1086 DB, *Sprotton* 12th Survey *et passim* to 1484 AD iv, *Sprotun* 1205 *FF*, *Sprottun* 1222 ClR, *Sportton*' 1235 Fees

Spratton 1613 FF

This would seem to be a compound of OE *sprēot*, 'pole' and **tun**, hence 'pole-farm,' but the reason for the name it is now impossible to determine. The only other compound of *sprēot* that has been noted is *spreot mere* in BCS 938, a Hampshire charter. *sprēot* is used specially of a punting-pole, so that a compound with *mere* is a probable one.

Broomhill. Cf. *Bromhil well* 13th *NthStJ*. *v.* brom, hyll.

Weston Favell

Weston Favell [wesən feivəl] 83 B 13

> *Weston(e)* 1086 DB *et passim*, (*juxta Parva Billyngg'*) 1317 Ass, (*near Northampton*) 1319 Cl, (*Fauvel*) 1376 Cl, (*Fawell*) 1395 Cl
> *Wesson Favell* 1614 *FF*

'West farm,' *v.* tun. *West* with reference to Little Billing to the east. Hugo *Fauvell* held the manor in 1235 (Fees).

Booth Fm is marked as *Buttocks Booth* (1779 F, 1823 B, c. 1825 O.S.). It is probably the dialectal word *booth*, 'cowhouse,' etc., ultimately from ON boþ, 'temporary shelter.'

XII. HAMFORDSHOE HUNDRED

> *Anduerðeshoh* a. 1076 Geld Roll, *Andferdesho* 1086 DB, *Hanverdesho*, *Anvesdesor* ib.
> *Anfordesho* 12th Survey, 1220 Fees, *Aunf-* 1316 FA
> *Amfordesho* 1202 Ass, 1313 Ipm, *Amph-* 1265 Misc, *Hamfordesh.* 1285 FA, *Hamfordshoe* 1346 FA
> *Alfordes howe* 1541 Statutes

'The hoh or hill of *Andferð*.' The personal name *Andferð* is not on record in OE, but we have *Andhun*, *Antsecg*, which is probably for *Andsecg*, and possibly *Andscoh* in *Andscohes ham*, though this has been interpreted otherwise by Björkman (*Die Eigennamen im Beowulf* 67). Names in *-ferð* or *-frið* are common in OE. The names in *And-* seem all to belong to an early period. Cf. further *Andolfescroft* in Geddington (1251 Misc).

In a Survey (1565) among the Compton MSS at Castle Ashby we have mention under *Meers Ashby* alias *Asheby Low* alias *Alfordes Hoo* of the holding of the hundred-court at 'Low Hill abrode in the feld in the particion between Barton Feld and

Ashebye.' This is clearly the meeting-place of Hamfordshoe Hundred. It is to be identified with the field now called Round Hill, in the corner of which is a small mound which Miss Wake convincingly identifies with the meeting-place of the hundred. This field is on the parish boundary, in a commanding situation, with a view of the whole countryside. Clearly the hill has, at various times, been called *hoe* (*v.* hoh), *low* (*v.* hlaw), and hill.

Mears Ashby

MEARS ASHBY [mɛ·əz æʃbi] 84 A 1

Asbi 1086 DB, *Essebi* 1166 P, *Aissebi* 1176 BM

Northesseby 1220 Fees, 1242 Ch, *Northescheby* 1241 P

Esseby Mares 1281 Ipm, (*Maris*) 1284 Cl, *Ass(c)heby Mars* 1330 Cl, 1415 BM

Mares Assheby 1297 Ipm, *Northasseby juxta Sywelle* 1304 *Ass*
Meeres Asshebye 1578 BM, *Maires Ashby* 1659 StJ, *Ashby Mares* 1791 Bridges

'Ash-tree by,' *v.* æsc. *North*, probably with reference to Castle Ashby to the south. Bridges (ii, 137) notes that it was so called because on the north side of the Nene. Robert de *Mares* held the manor in 1242 (Ch).

WOODLODGE FM. Cf. *Assheby Wode* 1330 *Ass*.

Earls Barton

EARLS BARTON 84 B 1

Barton(e) 1086 DB *et passim*, (*comitis David*) 1187 P, *Erlesbarton* 1261 Ass, *Barton Pynkenye* 1334 Cl, *Barton Yerles* 1545 LP, *Erles Barton al. Barton Comitis* 1574 *Recov*
Berton(a) 1155–8 (1329) Ch, 1166 P, 1200 Cur

v. beretun. The manor was held by David Earl of Huntingdon in the 12th century (Survey). Robert de *Pynkeny* held half a fee in 1290 (Ipm).

BROIL (lost) is *Bartonbruil* 1324 Ipm, *le Broill of Barton* 1331 Pat, *Berton Broyle* 1401 FF. This is the word *broil* (LL *brolium*) used for a park or wood stocked with deer or other beasts of the chase. Cf. Broyle (PN Sx 70) and *Broyl subtus Schortewod* (13th

For) in Whittlewood. 'Here was antiently a wood called *Barton-Broil*' (Bridges ii, 137).

DOWTHORPE END

> *Barton Thorp* 1261, 1317 *Ass, Bartonethorp* 1335 *Ass*
> *Thorp juxta Barton* 1293 *FF, Thorp in parochia de Barton Comitis* 1511 *FF, Dowthorpe townes end, Thorpe hill* 1641 *Terrier*
> *Thorp lane end* 1740 *Terrier*

It has been suggested that this is the DB manor of *Widetorp*, but it is difficult to connect the forms. The addition of *Dow-* is also a difficulty. In a *Terrier* of 1740 we have *Dowlands* in the East Field of Barton. It is clear that we must associate *Dow*thorpe, on the east side of Barton, with *Dow*lands, but the significance of the added element is uncertain.

BERRY MOUNT (6″). Cf. *Berry Close* 1772 *EnclA*. There is an old earthwork here, *v.* burh. BROOKHILL FM (6″). Cf. *Brook field, furlong* 1740 *Terrier*. COPPLEMORE BARN (6″) is *Copplemore slade* 1740 *Terrier*. SYKE WAY (B). Cf. *Sike Gutter* 1740 *Terrier*. *v.* sic. WHITE MILLS (6″) is *White Mills* 1772 *EnclA*.

Great Doddington

GREAT DODDINGTON 84 A 2

> *Dodintone* 1086 DB *et passim* to 1397 Cl with variant spellings -*yn-, -ing-, -yng-, (near Wendleburg)* 1300 Cl, *Great Dodding-ton* 1290 Cl, *Dodington Magna* 1346 FA
> *Dudinton* 1201 *FF*, 1220 Fees, 1249 Cl, (*Maiori*) 1242 Fees, -*ing-* 1313 Cl
> *Dadinton* 1215 ClR
> *Dorrington al. Doddington* t. Eliz *CtWards, Dorrington* 1675 Ogilby

'*Dodda*'s farm,' *v.* ingtun. For the last forms cf. Darracott (PN D 43).

Ecton

ECTON 84 B 1

> *Echentone* 1086 DB, *Ecchenton* t. Hy 2 *D & C Linc* (p)
> *Echeton* 1164 P (p) *et passim* to 1428 FA with variant spellings *Eke-, Ecke-, Ekiton* 1169 P (p)

Hecheton 1168 P (p), *Hekinton* 1182 P (CR), *Heketon* t. Hy 2
D & C *Linc* (p), 1235 Fees
Ekinton 1175, 1181, 1190 P, *Ekenton* 1285 FA, *Ekyngton*
1355 Cl
Neketon 1235 Fees
Ecton al. Egton 1585 *Recov*, *Ecken* 1675 Ogilby

'*Ecca*'s farm,' *v.* ingtun. Cf. Eckworthy (PN D 88).

FLAXLANDS SPINNEY (6") is *Flexlands* 1649 NthNQ v. MORTAR
PITS is *Mortar pitts* ib.

Holcot

HOLCOT [houkət] 73 J 13

Holecote 1086 DB *et passim* to 1305 Cl, *Holicote* 1202 Ass (p)
Halecote 1086 DB, *-ta* 1183 P
Holokote 1250 Seld 13, *-cothe* 1329 Ch
Holcot(e) 1286 Cl, 1316 FA, (*juxta Waldegrave*) 1352 FF,
Hollecot 1368 Cl
Holcott al. Hocott 1590 *Recov*

'cot(e) in the hollow,' *v.* holh. The village lies in a well-marked
hollow.

HOLCOT BRIDGE is *Holcotebrygge* 13th *NthStA*.

Sywell

SYWELL [saiəl] 83 A 14

Snewelle 1086 DB
Siwell(a) 1086 DB, 1155–8 (1329) Ch *et passim* with variant
spellings *Sy-* and *-well(e)*
Seywell 1287 *Ass*

Professor Ekwall takes this name to be identical with Seawell
supra 40, Sewell (PN BedsHu 129, and O). He also notes
Seuewelledale (Db) in the Darley Charters (Derbys. Arch. Soc.
xxii, 24), and takes all to be from OE *seofon willan*, 'seven
springs,' while in Sywell we have OE *syfan* (which is on record)
in place of the normal *seofon*, the DB form for Sywell being presumably an error for *Suewelle*. As parallels he notes further *seofan
wyllan broc* (KCD 450) in Staffordshire and *Sevenewelles* in

Leicestershire (AD ii) and the German *Siebenbrünnen*, of which Förstemann (ON ii, 712) gives three examples.

HAYES LODGE is *Hayes* 1598 *FF*, *v.* (ge)hæg. SYWELL WOOD is *Sywell wode* 1543 LP.

Wellingborough

WELLINGBOROUGH[1]   74 J 2

Wendle(s)berie 1086 DB, *Wendlesburg* 1221 ClR
Wedlingeberie 1086 DB
Wendliburc, Wellingburg 1167 P (p), *Wendliburc* 1203 *FF*
Wendlingburch 1178 P *et passim* to 1389 Cl with variant
  spellings *-burgh, -borwe* 1298 Ipm
Wenlingeburc 1185 P, *-burg(e)* 1199 FF, 1228 WellsR, *-ling-*
  burc 1199 FF, *-burg* 1285 FA
Wendelburg 1205 ClR, 1261 *Ass*
Wendlingwurc 1205 FineR, *Wendlebrig* 1300 Cl
Wendelingburg 1268, 1285 *Ass, Wendelyngburgh* 1343, 1384 Cl
Wellyngburgh 1316 FA, *-burue* 1384 Cl
Whellingburgh 1330 FA, *Whelyngburgh* 1361 Cl
Wyndylburgh 1439 *FF*

'burh of *Wændel*'s people,' *v.* ing. Cf. Wensdon Hill (PN BedsHu 114). To the names there noted may be added Wallington (Herts), *Wallingtone* DB, *Wandelingtona* t. Hy 2 Dugd ii, 228, *Wenlingetone* 1199 *FF, Wandlington* 1235 Fees, *Wendligtone* 1240 *FF, -lyngton* 1269 *FF*.

APPLEBY GATE is probably to be associated with the family of Galfridus de *Apelby* (1241 P) and Henry de *Appelby* (1292 Cl). They may have come from Appleby (Lei).

CROYLAND HALL FM. This represents the manor held by the Abbot of Croyland (cf. 1199 FF, 12th Survey).

RODWELL MILL (B). Cf. *Rodewellemor* 14th *NthStA*. 'Reed spring,' *v.* hreod, wielle.

---

[1] CHEESE LANE is possibly identical with *Gyes lane* 1549 NthNQ vi. CHURCH ST, cf. *le Churchelane* 1541 *Ct.* GOLD ST is *gold strete* 1549 NthNQ vi. HIGH ST is perhaps *le Brodestrete* (1541 *Ct*). MARKET ST is probably *le Chepyngstede* of 1330 (*Ass*), *v.* cieping, stede. WEST ST, cf. *le Westende* 1541 *Ct.*

STANWELL SPRING is *Steynewelle* 14th *NthStA*. The first element is stan. There are old stone-quarries in the immediate neighbourhood. In the ME form it appears in the Scandinavianised form *steyn*, *v*. steinn.

BROAD GREEN (6″). Cf. *Brodeland* 1590 NthNQ vi. BROOK FM (6″) was probably the home of Philip *Attebrok* (1253 *Ass*). DEBDALE HO (6″). Cf. *Depdalewey* 14th *NthStA*, *v*. dæl. There is a well-marked valley here.

Wilby

WILBY 84 A 2

Willabyg c. 1067 (12th) AS Wills
Wilebi 1086 DB *et freq* to 1334 Cl with variant spellings *-by* and *Wyle-*
Willeb(i) 1186 France (p), *-by* 1232 *FF*, *Wylleby* 1268 *Ass* (p), 1343 *FF*, *Willyby* 1382 AD iv
Wyliby 1230 P, *Wylyby* 1285 *Ass*, (*juxta Wenlingburgh*) 1294 *Ass*, *Wylby* 1321 Cl, *Wilbe* 1572 *FF*
Wyluby 1285 *Ass*, 1297 Ipm, *Willuby* 1285 *Ass*, *Wylughby* 1353 Ipm, 1394 Cl, *Wilughbi* t. Ed 3 *For*, *Wylughby* 1394 Cl, *Wyloughby* 1428 FA
Weluby 1316, 1346 FA, *Weleby* 1377 Cl, *Welby* 1383 Cl

This may be 'by by the willows,' *v*. welig, wylig. Cf. Willbury (Herts), *Wiligbyrig* 1007 Crawf 11. The early forms suggest, however, that we should perhaps start rather from a Scand pers. name *Willi* (cf. *Wille*, Lundgren-Brate 300), with later confusion of the first element with the common welig, 'willow.'

WILBY THORP (lost) is *Wylebythorp* 1251 Misc, *Wylughbythorp* 1317 *Ass*. thorp probably has here the meaning of 'outlying or detached hamlet,' *v*. þorp. The site may be identical with that of the present WILBY HALL, which is situated in a remote part of the parish.

XIII. WYMERSLEY HUNDRED

Wimereslea a. 1076 Geld Roll, 1187 P, *Wymeresle* 12th
   Survey
Winemereslea 1086 DB, 1182 P
Wimereslea, Wimeresle, Wimareslea 1086 DB
Wimerleu 1086 DB, *Wymerle* 1275 RH
Wymersle 1284 FA, *Wymbersley* 1541 Statutes

'*Winemǣr*'s clearing or wood,' *v.* leah. Baker (i, 335) notes
that the hundred was probably so named from *Wimer* or *Winemar*
who had been lord of it in Saxon times. He may have thought
that this was actually the *Winemar* who (TRW) held many
manors in Northamptonshire, notably in this hundred, but as
he was a Fleming, it is clear that the hundred could not have
been named after him, for the name is certainly far older. The
site of the hundred meeting-place is Wymersley [wimǝzli] Bush
in Little Houghton, a field on the west side of the railway, ¾ mile
ENE of Great Houghton Lodge. The same spot is probably
referred to in the 13th cent. in the Cartulary of St Andrews,
Northampton, as *Motelowe*, i.e. moot-hill, *v.* hlaw.

In this hundred has been absorbed the hundred of Collingtree which in DB included the vills of Collingtree, Milton,
Rothersthorpe, Blisworth, and Courteenhall. It is called *Colentreu, Colestreu* in DB, cf. Collingtree *infra* 145. It is probably
the same as the hundred of *Coltrewestan* in DB, in which
Hardingstone is said to lie.

Castle Ashby

CASTLE ASHBY 84 C 2

Asebi 1086 DB, *Esseby* 12th Survey, (*David*) 1275 RH
Axeby 1235 Fees, *Assheby Davy* 1325 Ipm
Castel Assheby 1361 Cl, (*Chastel*) 1362 Cl, *Ashby al. Ashby
   Davy al. Castle Ashby* 1611 *Recov*

'Ash-tree by,' *v.* æsc. It formed part of the fee of *David* Earl
of Huntingdon (Fees 494). There was a castle here in earlier
days.

CHADSTONE [tʃædsən]

Cedestone 1086 DB, Cheddeston 1391 Cl

Chaddeston 12th Survey, 1220, 1242 Fees, -den 1275 RH, Chaddiston by Assheby 1349 Ipm

Chadeston 1235 Fees, 1261 Ass (p), 1350 Cl, Chadston 1316 FA

Chadreston 1284 FA

Chadson 1702 Poll

'Ceadd's farm,' v. tun, and cf. Chaddesley (PN Wo 234).

Blisworth

BLISWORTH [blizwəθ] 83 E 11

Blidesworde 1086 DB, 1205 Pap, -wurða 1184 P, -worth 1216 ClR, Blidewurð 1220 ClR

Blieswurda 1162, 1166 P, -wurth 1199 FineR, 1213 ClR

Bliseworthe 1166 RBE et freq to 1400 Cl with variant spelling Blyse-

Blethesworthe 12th Survey, Bledesworth c. 1220 For, Blecches- 1284 FA

Blithesworth 1200 Abbr et freq to 1297 Ipm with variant spelling Blythes-, Bliheswurth 1242 Fees

Blicheworth 1215 PatR

Blysworth 1317 Cl, Blis- 1428 FA, Blysseworth 1388 Cl

Bleseworth 1337 Ipm, 1362, 1398 Cl, Blayseweurthe 1348 Ch, Bluseworthe 1362 Cl

Blissworth 1791 Bridges

The element Blīð- is found in two OE names—Blīðhere, Blīðweald, though the simple name Blīðe is not on record. In OGer we have Blida, Blidilo, Blidin(a), Bliding, and doubtless the name was found in OE itself, hence 'Blīðe's enclosure,' v. worþ.

THE LOUNDES is the Lound, the Lound pitts, Lowne pitts 1672 LRMB, Blisworth Lowns c. 1825 O.S. This is ON lundr, 'grove.' Cf. Long Lown Wood infra 187.

BLISWORTH HILL is Hill 1550 Ct. BUTTERMILK HALL is so named in 1823 (B). A common type of nickname, partly humorous, partly contemptuous in origin.

Brafield on the Green

BRAFIELD ON THE GREEN [breifi·ld] 83 C 14

Brache(s)feld 1086 DB, *Brachafeldie* c. 1150 *NthStA*
Bragefeld(a) 1086 DB, 1155–8 (1329) Ch, 1162, 1166 P,
   Bragfeld c. 1150 *NthStA*, *Brahefeld* 1166 P
Braunfeld 12th Survey, 1284 FA, 1324 Ipm, 1333 Cl
Branfeld(e) c. 1150 *NthStA*, 1200 Cur *et freq* to 1397 Cl
Bramfeud 1209–35 WellsR, 1242 Fees, *-feld* 1348 Ipm
Brawfeld 13th *NthStA*, *Brawefeld* 1220 Fees
Brafeld 1241 Cl, *Braifeld* 1316 FA
Braumfeld 1316 Fine
Brayfield de le Grene 1503 AD iii, *Brafelde of the Grene* 1539
   LP, *Brayfeild super le Greene* 1663 *Recov*, *Bravefield Green*
   1714 ParReg

This name is clearly identical with (Cold) Brayfield (PN Bk 3),
ten miles away on the other side of Yardley Chase. When dealing
with that name, it was suggested that the two names should be
associated, and the element *Bragen-* taken as some old name
for the area later known as Yardley Chase. See further *s.n.*
Bransford (PN Wo 189).

Cogenhoe

COGENHOE [kuknou] 84 C 1

Cugenho 1086 DB *et passim* to 1428 FA with variant forms
   Cughanhoog t. Hy 2 Dane, *Cugeho* 12th Survey, *Cugenhou*
   1235 Fees
Cogeho 12th Survey, *Cogenhou, -inhou* 1274 RH, *Cogenho*
   1313 Ipm, 1319 Fine, 1347 Cl
Cuggenho 1204 Cur, 1251 *AD* C 9807, *Cuggeho* 1275, 1277 Cl,
   -hoo 1287 *Ass*
Kukenho 1247 Cl, *Cuken-* 1280 Ipm
Gukenhou 1275 Ch, *Gugeho, Gukehou* 1275 Cl
Cokenalle al. Cokenoo, Cuknall 1565 Compton, *Cogenhoe al.*
   Cookenoe 1639, (*al. Cooknoe*) 1689, *Cogenhow or Cooknow*
   1749 *Recov*
Codginhoe 1657 NRS i, *Cooknoe or Coggenhoe* 1779 F

'The hoh or hill of one *Cugga*.' The name *Cuga* is found in LVD[1]. Sweet may or may not be right in assuming that the vowel was long, but whether long or short, if the single *g* is correct, and it most probably is, in this early text, then such a name would have given ME *Couwe* and the like. A name from the same root with geminated consonant, or of independent origin, seems however to have existed in OE, for we have *cuggan hyll* in a Worcestershire charter (BCS 1298), and apparently the same name in Cogenhoc. *Cugga* would be a regular pet form for such an OE name as *Cūþgār*.

Collingtree

COLLINGTREE 83 D 12

Colentreu 1086 DB, *-tre* 1216 ClR, 1228 *FF*, 1236 Fees, 1264 AD vi, 1369 AD iv, 1587 BM

Colintrie 1162 P, 1199 FF, *-tre* 1203 *FF et passim* to 1398 Cl with variant spelling *Colyn-, Coluntre* 1250, 1274 Ipm

Colyngetre 1322 Cl, *Colingtre al. Colintre* 1322 Ipm, *Colyngtre* 1349 Ipm

Colyngtrough(e) 1367, 1382 Cl, *-trow(e)* 1350 BM, 1398 Cl, *-trogh* 1410 Cl, *Colentrough* 1675 Ogilby

Collingthright 1541 Statutes, 1542 LP

'*Cola*'s tree,' *v.* treow, with later inorganic *ing* for *in*, from *en*.

Courteenhall

COURTEENHALL [kɔ·t(ə)nɔ·l] 83 E 12

Cortenhale 1086 DB, 12th Survey *et passim* to 1316 Fine

Curtehala t. Hy 1 NRS iv, t. Hy 2 (1316) Ch, *Curtenhal(e)* 1205 Pap, 1235 Cl

Cortehalle 1109–22 (1356) Ch, *Cortahala* t. Hy 2 (1316) Ch, *Corthala* 1181 P (p), *Kortinhale* 1261 *FF, Cortenhalle* 1299 Ass, *Cortonhale* 1341 Cl

Corinhall 1284 FA

Cortnall 1529 *FF*, 1563 *Recov, Cawtnoll al. Curtenhall* 1539 FF, *Corknehale* 1595 NRS iii, *Cotenhall, Coffenhall* 1675 Ogilby, *Courtnall* 1702 Poll

Courtenhall, Courtinhall 1657 NRS i

[1] The further example of this name quoted by Searle from a Wiltshire charter (BCS 595) is a ghost. The name in the charter is *Cufa*.

For this name we may compare Corburn (PN NRY 14), Curtisknowle (PN D 300), *Cortenhul* (c. 1200 *Ashby*) in Moreton Pinkney, *curten stapele* (14th BCS 34), and *Curtenersh* (1255 *Ass* (p)), both in Surrey, which suggest the likelihood of an OE pers. name *Corta* or *Curta*, hence 'Corta's nook of land,' *v.* healh.

Denton

DENTON 84 C 1

Dodintone 1086 DB *et freq* to 1376 Cl
Dodington, -yng- 12th Survey, 1275 RH, 1325 Ipm
Dudintun 1195 FF, *-ton* 1200 Cur, (*Parva*) 1220 Fees, 1229 Cl, *Parva Dudington* 1235 Fees
Little Denynton 1371 AD iv, *Denenton* 1483 *Charter*
Dodington al. Deynton 1563 *FF*, *Doddington parva al. Deynton* 1579 ib., *Denton or Doddington Parva* 1749 *Recov*, *Denton or Little Doddington* 1768 ib.

v. Doddington *supra* 138. *Parva* in contrast to *Great* Doddington. For the modern development cf. Dainton (PN D 513) and Dunton (PN Bk 67).

SHORTGROVE COPSE (6″) is *Shortegrave* t. Ed 3 *For*.

Grendon

GRENDON 84 C 2

Grendon(e) 1086 DB *et passim*, (or *Grenton*) 1349 Ipm
Crenden 1241 P (p)
Gryndon 1313 Ipm, *Grindon* 1622 *FF*
Greendon 1633 *FF*

'Green hill,' *v.* dun.

PARKHILL FM. Cf. *le Park* 1253 *Ass*.

Hackleton

HACKLETON 83 D 14

Hachelintone 1086 DB *et passim* to 1405 AD v with variant spellings *Hakeling-, Hakelyng-, Hakelin-*
Bachelintone (sic) 1086 DB

Haclinton(*a*) 1155–8 (1329) Ch, n.d. AD ii, *Haclyn-* 13th AD i
Hakilton c. 1265 AD ii, *Hakelton* 1368, 1376 Cl

No OE personal name *Haca* is on record, but we have every reason to believe in its existence on the evidence of such a p.n. as Hackness (PN NRY 112), c. 750 Bede *Hacanos*. See also PN D 69, 116. It would be identical with OE *haca*, 'hook, bolt, bar,' and have its exact parallel in the personal name *Hōc*, which is identical with the common OE *hōc*, 'hook.' It has its further parallel in OWScand *Haki*, OSw *Haki*, ODan *Hake*, which is by origin a nickname (ZEN 43). *Hæcel* would be a regular diminutive of this name and is found also in Hacklestone (W), 1367 Ipm *Hackelston*. Hence '*Hæcel*'s farm,' v. ingtun.

Hardingstone

HARDINGSTONE 83 C 12

Hardingestorp 1086 DB, -*trop* c. 1120 ScotCh
Hardingestone 1086 DB, *Herdingeston'* 1235 Fees, *Harding-ston'* 1236 Cl, *Hardynstone* 1316 FA
Hardighestorn c. 1145 NRS iv, *Hardingesthorn*(*a*) 1155–8 (1329) Ch *et freq* to 1428 FA with variant spellings -*yng-* and -*torn*(*e*), -*thorn*(*e*)
Harthingistorne 13th *NthStA*
Hardenston, Hardenstone 1675 Ogilby

'*Hearding*'s thorn bush,' v. þorn, with occasional confusion with the elements þorp and tun. Cf. Slapton *supra* 44.

COTTON END, FAR COTTON

Cotes 1199 FF *et freq* to 1316 FA, (*extra Norħt*) 1289 *FF*, (*juxta Norħton*) 1294 *Ass*
Cotun 13th *NthStA*, *Coten juxta Norħton* 1294 *Ass*, *Cotene* 1297 *FF*, 1337 Cl, *Coten al. Coton* 1325 Ipm, *Coton juxta Norhampton* 1394 *Ass*
Cotten End 1686, 1711, *Cotton-end* 1720, 1747 ParReg
West Cotton or Far Cotton 1779 F, *Far Cotton, Cotton End* 1823 B

'The cottages.' For the variant *Cotes* and *Coten* cf. *s.n.* Claycoton *supra* 68. Cotton End and West or Far Cotton were formerly two distinct hamlets; they are now practically joined.

DELAPRE ABBEY. The earliest reference for the name of the abbey is *Sancte Marie de Prato* (1217, 1220 WellsR), *Sancte Marie de Pratis extra Norhant.* (1232 Cl). The Latin form is used almost universally in early documents. Later we find *de la Preez* (1316 FA), *Delapre* (1328 Cl), *Dalapray* t. Hy 8 Dugd iv, 214, *St Mary de Pratis al. de la Prey* 1536 LP, *Daleprey, Dalaprey* 1540 *LRMB, De la prey* 1610 Camden. It is the Latin *pratum*, OFr *pred*, 'meadow.' Cf. similarly the hospital *Sanctae Mariae de Pratis* (c. 1190 Dugd iii, 335) near St Albans, which has given rise to Prae Wood (*Pray wode* 1487 Dugd) in St Michael's parish. So also we have Pray Heath in Woking (Sr), the home of Peter de *la Preye* (1263 *Ass*) and a field called *pettepre* (1227 FF) in Warwickshire.

HUNSBURY HILL is *Hunsbarow* 1712 Morton, *Hunsborrowe Hill* 1739 Camden (Gough), *Hunsborough Hill* 1791 Bridges. The burh refers to the ancient 'camp' here, as in Rainsborough *supra* 56. The first element is no doubt a pers. name but the forms are too late for any certainty.

NUNN MILLS (6″) is *Quyn Johns al. Quingeons Mills al. Nunne Mills* 1591 *Depositions*, and is named from Delapre Abbey near by. The name *Quyn Johns* or *Quingeons Mills* was explained by Mr R. W. Brown in the *Transactions of the Northamptonshire Natural History Society and Field Club* xxiii, 151–5. The Mills are referred to in Elizabethan times as *the Queenes Mylles* and *Her Majestie's Mills*, and take their name from *Joan* of Navarre, the second wife of Henry IV, part of whose dowry was land in Northamptonshire, and included what are now known as Nunn Mills.

BRIAR HILL FM is *Brerehyll* 13th *NthStA*. RUSH MILLS (6″) is *Rysshemylle, Risshemylne* 13th *NthStA, le Russhmylles* 1540 *LRMB.*

Horton

HORTON 83 E 14

> *Horton(e)* 1086 DB *et passim*, (*outside Northampton*) 1290
> Ipm, *-tun* 1224 ClR, 1236 Cl, (*juxta Haclynton*) 1317 *Ass*
> *Hurton* 1301–4 Ipm

'Muddy farm,' *v.* horh, tun. Distinguished as 'outside' Northampton and 'near' Hackleton.

CHEYNEY FM is possibly to be associated with the family of Ralph de *Cheney*, mentioned in connection with Salcey Forest c. 1220 (*For*). HORTON WOODS is *boscus de Horton* c. 1220 *For*.

Houghton, Great and Little

HOUGHTON, GREAT and LITTLE [houtən] 83 C 13

Hohton(*e*) 1086 DB, 1200 Cur
Hoctona 1131 P (p) *et freq* to 1251 Ipm, *Hoctune* t. Hy 2 BM,
    Hoctona Parva c. 1220 WellsR, *Hocktone* 1230 ib.
Hochton t. Hy 2 BM, *-tun* 1205 Pap
Houctone t. Hy 2 BM, 12th Survey, (*Magna*) 1233 WellsR
Houton(*a*) 1197 FF, (*Magna*) 1199 FF, *Howtone* 1226
    WellsR, *Magna Houhtone* 1234 ib., *Magna, Parva Houghton*
    1316 FA, *Michelhoughton* 1342 *Ass*, *Howghton* 1428 FA,
    (*Moche*) 1553 *Rental*
Hoketon 1201 Cur
(*H*)*oghton* 1291 Cl, (*Little*) 1302 Ipm

'Farm on the spur of land,' *v.* hoh, tun. There are two well-marked hills here.

CLIFFORD HILL is *Klyffordehyll* 13th *NthStA*, *Klyfford* 1303 BM, *Clifforde* 1330 *Ass*. *v.* clif. There is an artificial mound here, which is possibly the *motte* of a Norman castle.

CONEY GREE PLANTATION (6″) is *Conigree* 1782 *Terrier*. Cf. Coney Geer Coppice *infra* 210 and the note on *conyger infra* 272.

PLAXWELL'S BARN (6″). The modern form seems to be corrupt. Cf. *Clackeswelle* 13th *NthStA*, *Claxwell slade* 1672 *LRMB*, *Claxwell Barn* 1823 B. The pers. name here may be either English or Scandinavian. There may have been an OE pers. name *Clacc*, as suggested by *clacces wadlond* (BCS 216) in Oxon, but the boundaries are a late addition to the Charter, and both places alike may take their names from Anglo-Danish settlers bearing the name *Klak*. Cf. Glassthorpehill *supra* 83.

Milton

MILTON 83 D 11

> *Mideltone* 1086 DB *et passim* to 1428 FA with variant spellings
> Middel-, Middle-, Middil-, (*juxta Norhampton*) 1299 *Ass*,
> (*juxta Colyntre*) 1332 *Ass*, (*Malsores*) 1395 Cl
> *Middleton Mallesworth* 1542 LP, *Milton al. Middleton Malsor*
> 1781 *Recov*

'Middle farm,' *v.* tun. It lies between Gayton and Wootton.
The *Malsor* family held land here in the 12th cent. The form
Mallesworth is an inverted spelling due to the belief that the final
er or *or* was a reduction of an early *worth*, as in the pron. [sæpsə]
for Sawbridgeworth (Herts). Cf. Tansor *infra* 208.

LADY BRIDGE (6″) is *the Lady Bridge* 1586 BorRec.

MILTON HAM is so spelt c. 1825 O.S. The site makes it clear that
we have here an example of the dialect word *ham* (from OE
hamm), 'flat low-lying pasture,' 'land near a river.'

Piddington

PIDDINGTON 83 E 13

> *Pidentone* 1086 DB, 12th Survey, *Pidinton* 1204 *FF et passim*
> to 1405 AD v with variant spellings -*yn*-, -*yng*-, -*ing*-, and
> *Pyd*-, *Pytyngton* 1350 Ipm
> *Pedinton* 1166 P, 1203, 1262 *FF*, -*yng*- 1313 Ipm, 1376 Cl,
> t. Hy 7 *MinAcct*
> *Pydelington* 1253 *Ass*
> *Podinton* 1284 FA, -*ing*- 1285 *FF*, *Pudinton* 1296 Ipm

'*Pyda*'s farm,' *v.* ingtun. Cf. Pidley PN BedsHu 211. The 1253
form may be due to the influence of the neighbouring Hackleton.

CRABTREE THICK (6″) is *Crab Tree Thick Copse* 1790 Woods
Rept. For 'thick' *v.* Blackmore Thick *infra* 206.

Preston Deanery

PRESTON DEANERY 83 D 13

> *Preston* 1086 DB *et passim*, (*juxta Norħt*) 1301 *FF*, (*juxta*
> *Pydyngton*) 1381 *Ass*, *Preston Denary* 1720 *FF*, *Preston*
> *Deanry* 1739 Camden (Gough)

'Priests' farm,' *v.* preost, tun. *Deanery* 'from its having given name to the deanery of Preston in the ecclesiastical division of the county' (Bridges i, 379).

WEST HALL. Cf. *le Hale, Haleiate* c. 1300 *For, le Hale* 1330 *Ass, Hallezate* 1346, *Haleiate* 1349 *For, Hallfeelde al. Totehill feelde* t. Eliz *LRMB, Westhail* 1747 *Recov.* If this identification is correct the name is a corruption of earlier *hale* from healh, 'nook, corner.'

PARK FM. Cf. *parci de Preston* 1332 *Ass.* PRESTON WOOD (6″) is *Prestewode* c. 1300 *For.* This is OE *prēosta wudu,* 'priests' wood,' the modern form being corrupt.

Quinton

QUINTON 83 E 13

> *Quintone* 1086 DB, 1200 Cur, *Qunton* 1274 Ipm, *Quynton* 1337, 1376 Cl, 1511 Ch
>
> *Quenton(a)* 1148–66 BM *et passim* to 1428 FA, *Quenynton* 1287 *For*
>
> *Queenton* 1342 Cl, *Queneton* 1439 Ch

The forms of this name resemble those of Quainton (PN Bk 108), Quinton (PN Wo 42), and Quinton (Gl), except for earlier and more persistent forms with *Quin-* rather than *Quen-*. They may come from OE *Cwēningtūn,* 'farm of a woman named **Cwēna*' (cf. Quainton *loc. cit.*). Karlström suggests (ZONF vii, 251) OE *cwenena-tūn,* 'farm of the women,' cf. Whenby (PN NRY 30), which denotes similarly a 'by belonging to women.'

Rothersthorpe

ROTHERSTHORPE [θrʌp] 83 D 11

> *Torp* 1086 DB, 1194 P, *Trop* 12th Survey, 1235 Fees, 1296 Ipm, (*Advocati*) 1220 Fees, *Throp* 1226 WellsR
>
> *Retherestorp* 1231 Ch *et freq* to 1387 Cl with variant spellings -*thorp*, -*throp*, -*throup* 1373 Cl, *Rethirsthrope* 1406 Inq aqd
>
> *Ritheresthorp* 1242 Fees, 1316 FA, *Rithersthorpe* 1346 FA, *Rytherthorpe* 1538 LP

Rutheristorp' 1247 *Ass*, *Rotherestrop* 1333 Cl, *Reotherestrop*
    1359 Ipm, *Rothersthrope* 1456 AD ii
Ruddistrip 1541 Statutes, *Ruddisthrupp* 1542 LP
Thrupp al. Rothers Thrupp 1675 *Recov*, *Rothersthorp* or
    Thorp 1702 Poll

'The *þorp* of one *Rethær*.' Lindkvist (75) shows that here, as
in Raisthorpe (Y), Rotherby (Lei), Rearsby (L), we have a Scand
pers. name, OWScand *Hreiðarr*, ODan *Rethær*, OSw *Redhar*.
Later there seems to have been confusion with the common word
rother, 'cattle,' from OE hryðer. For late addition of the holder's
name cf. Abthorpe *supra* 89. The short form of the name is still
used locally and survives in Thrupp Osier Beds in Milton, while
the bridge connecting Rothersthorpe and Wootton is similarly
commonly called Thrupp Bridge. The 'advocatus' of *Betton*,
i.e. Béthune (France), held the manor in 1194 (P).

ARKSOME (field-name) is *Irkesham* (1240 *FF*, 1540 *LRMB*),
Yrkesham (1540 *LRMB*), *Thorpe Arksholme* (1780 *EnclA*).
Bridges (i, 262) quotes forms *Yrkesholm*, *Irkesham*, from the
Cartulary of St James', Northampton, which cannot now be
traced, and speaks of *Arxam* near Upton Mill. *Arksholme* is also
the name of a field on the other side of the river, in Wootton.
Professor Ekwall notes the possibility of a compound containing
Anglo-Scand. *Yric* (on record in OE) for ON *Eiríkr*. He points
out that such a compound of OE ham and a Scand pers. name is
unlikely, but the situation would suggest the possibility of a
hamm in the bend of a river as the second element.

THE BERRY (6″) refers to some entrenchments here, cf. VCH ii,
417, *v.* burh. BROOK FM was the home of Richard *attebrok*,
i.e. 'at the brook' (1253 *Ass*).

Whiston

WHISTON [wiʃtən] 84 C 1

Hwiccintunæ t. Wm 1 (13th) ChronRams
Wichentonam 974 (13th) ChronRams
Wice(n)tone 1086 DB, *Wichenton(a)* 1114–30 (c. 1350)
    Ramsey, 1175, 1187, 1191 P, 1200 Cur, 1202 Ass (p),
    Wichanton t. Ric 1 Cur, *Wichinton* 1216 ClR, 1229 Cl.

Whiston 12th Survey, *Whyston* 1262 *FF*, 1274 *Ass*, 1316 FA,
   Wyston 1274 *Ass*, 1275 RH, 1284 FA
Wicheton' 1220 Fees
Hwiche-, Hwychetone 1231 WellsR, *Whicheston* 1242 Fees,
   Whicheton 1247 *Ass* (p), *Whichinton* 1253 BM
Whysheton 1294 *Ass*, *Wyshton* 1318, 1362 Cl, *Whissheton*
   1357, 1455 *FF*, *Whiston* 1357 Cl

'The farm of one *Hwicce*,' *v.* ingtun and PN Wo xv. The pers.
name *Hwicce* is not on record, but would be a regular formation
from the folk-name *Hwicce*.

Wootton

WOOTTON 83 D 12
   Witone 1086 DB, *Witton*' 1235 Fees
   Wutton(a) 1162 P (p), 1220 Fees, 1231 Bracton, 1234 Cl, 1271
      FF, Whutton 1313 Ipm
   Weton 1198 Cur
   Wotton 12th Survey *et freq* to 1324 Ipm, (*Wutton al.*) 1304
      Ipm, *Wootton* 1346 FA

'Farm by the wood,' *v.* wudu, tun.

Yardley Hastings

YARDLEY HASTINGS 84 D 2
   Gerdelai 1086 DB, 1155–8 (1329) Ch, *Gerdele* t. Ric 1 BM,
      12th Survey, *-leia* 1314 Ch, *-ley* 1374 Cl
   Jerdele 1220 Fees *et freq* to 1348 Ipm with variant spellings
      Yerde-, Ierde-, (*Est*) 1230 P (CR), (*Hastinges*) 1316 FA,
      Zerdeley Hastinges 1428 FA
   Jordele 1273–6 Ipm, *Yardele* 1314 Ch

v. Yardley Gobion *supra* 108. *East* to distinguish from that
place. The family of *Hasting(es)* is first mentioned in connection with the manor in 1250 (Cl).

ARNISS COPSE may be identical with *Arnho, Arnehou* 1274 Ipm,
with later pseudo-manorial *s* added, *Arniss* being for *Arnho's*. It
is *Allnesse* 1565 Compton. The meaning is 'Eagle's spur of land,
or hill,' *v.* earn, hoh. Cf. Arno's Grove (Mx) for earlier *Arnholt*.

BLENLEY LODGE is *Blyndlye* 1565 *Compton*. We may compare Blindley Heath in Godstone (Sr), *Blyndley Heathe* 1559 Lambert's *Godstone, Blyndlye heathe* 1608 SrAS ix, 175. Possibly 'blind' in both these names has the sense of 'hidden' or 'concealed,' cf. Blindwell (PN D 354).

GRIMPSEY COPSE is *assart de Grimeseth* 1247 *Ass, Grymsee* 1565 *Compton*. This is probably '*Grim*'s wood or enclosure,' *v*. (ge)hæg, the 13th cent. spelling being corrupt.

POTTOSY POND (6″) cf. *Potters solloe close* 1565 *Compton. solloe* may be identical with OE *sulh*, 'furrow, gully,' cf. Solway's Cottages (PN D 631).

RAVENSTONE ROAD COPSE [rɑ·nsən] is *la Rode* 1247 *Ass, Raveneston Rode* 1348 Ipm, *Raunson Roade* 1565 *Compton*. 'Clearing,' *v*. rod. It is on the county boundary by the adjacent parish of Ravenstone (Bk).

ROUNDHAY WOOD (6″) and FM is *boscus de la Roundeheye* 1287 *For, le Roundehai* 1324 Ipm. This is probably a ME name meaning 'round enclosed wood,' *v*. (ge)hæg. Cf. Roundhay in Leeds (Y).

THE WOLD is *le Wold* 1324, *le Wald* 1348 Ipm, *le Old(e)* 1565 *Compton. v*. weald.

YARDLEY CHASE is *the chase of Jordele* 1277 Ipm, *bosco de Jerdele* 1285 *Ass, chace of Yerdeleye* 1302 Ipm.

YOUNG AUSWAY [ɔ·zə] is *Younge Osey, Olde Ozey, Oseyfeld* 1565 *Compton, Ausway Field or Osway Field* 1652 ib. BIGGIN LODGE is *Biggin Lawn* c. 1825 O.S. *v*. bigging. For *Lawn v*. Wakefield Lawn *supra* 105. CHURCH SLADE is so named 1565 *Compton, v*. slæd. COLD OAK COPSE is so named 1823 B. Cf. Coldthorn *supra* 46. COLLIER'S HERNE (6″) is *Colliers Hyerne* 1565 *Compton*. 'The hyrne or corner of land of one *Collier*' or 'charcoal burners' corner'. COWPER'S OAK is named after the poet, who frequented Yardley Chase when living at Olney (Bucks). GOG OAK and MAGOG OAK (both 6″) are the names of two giant oaks larger than Cowper's Oak (Kelly). HAY COPSE is *le over, nether Hey* 1565 *Compton, v*. (ge)hæg. HOWBROOK COPSE (6″) [houbru·k] is

Holbroke 1565 *Compton, Hollow Brook Coppices* 1672 *LRMB*, 'stream in the hollow' or 'with hollow banks,' *v.* holh, broc. HOWCUT LANE (6″) is *Howcott Lane* 1823 B. NEW HAY is *New Haye* 1565 *Compton, v.* (ge)hæg. POUND RIDING (6″), cf. *le pound, Pound close* 1565 *Compton, v.* hryding. 'Pound' means 'cattle pound or enclosure.' SANE COPSE is *Seene* 1565 *Compton.* SPOTLEY [spɔtlə·] CORNER and COTTAGES (both 6″) is *Spottlowe* 1565 *Compton.* The second element is probably hlaw with the later change to 'ley' as in Cockleyhill *supra* 35.

XIV. CORBY HUNDRED

Corebi a. 1076 Geld Roll, *Corbei, Corbi(e)* 1086 DB, *Coreby* 12th Survey. *v.* Corby *infra* 162. Part of the hundred, centring round Stoke Albany (*infra* 171), was known as *Stoce* a. 1076 Geld Roll, *Stoch(e)* 1086 DB. It included Wilbarston, East Carlton, Brampton Ash, Dingley, Sutton, Weston-by-Welland, Ashley, Cottingham, Beanfield Lawns, and Rockingham (Bridges ii, 271). The meeting-place of the Hundred of Stoke was probably, as suggested by Miss Joan Wake, near the field in Wilbarston now called *Speller*, but *Spellow Close* in an early 19th cent. map. For this name, cf. Spelhoe Hundred *supra* 131.

Ashley

ASHLEY 73 B 13

> *Ascele* 1086 DB, *Estelai* 1109 Eynsham, *Estlaia* c. 1160 Reg Antiquiss, *Esselega* 1195 P *et passim* with variant spellings *As(s)he-, Asse-,* and *-le, -lee*

'Ash-tree clearing or wood,' *v.* leah.

Beanfield Lawn

BEANFIELD LAWN 74 C 2

> *landa de Banefeld* c. 1220 For, 1235, 1244 Cl, 1252 Seld 13, 1252 Ch, 1287, t. Ed 3 *For*
> *landa de Banifeud* c. 1220 For, *-feld* 1246 Seld 13, *Banyfeld-launde* 1337 Ass

landam de Benigfeld 1236, *Benifeld* 1238 Cl, 1255 Seld 13,
   Benigfeud 1250 Cl, *Benyfeld* 1255 Seld 13, *Benyfelde Laund*
   1551 Pat
landa de Benefeld 1244 Cl, *laund of Benefield* 1791 Bridges

This was originally an open space in Rockingham Forest
belonging to the manor of Benefield (*infra* 211). In recent times
the names have unhappily been divorced from one another by
a new and artificial spelling and pronunciation of Beanfield.
For *lawn v.* Wakefield Lawn *supra* 105.

Blatherwycke

BLATHERWYCKE 74 A 5

Blarewic(he) 1086 DB, 1166, 1175 P, *-wik'* 1200 *FF*, *Blaerwich*
   1166 P (CR), *Blarwic* c. 1150 (1331) Ch
Blatherwyk 12th Survey *et passim* to 1436 AD i with variant
   spelling *-wik(e)*, *Blatherewich* 1242 Fees, *Blathirwyk* 1248–
   61 BM, *Blayerwyk* 1526 SR
Bladerwiche c. 1210 WellsR, *Bladherwic* 1220 Fees, *Bladrewyc'*
   1230 P, *Bladerwyke al. Blatherwyk* 1464 Pat
Blauerwik 1229 Cl
Blatherwygge 1391 Cl
Bletherwyk(e) 1530 *CtWards*, 1546 LP

This is a difficult name, but from the point of view of form it
looks as if the first element were OE *blæd(d)re*, ME *bladder*,
blather, *blether*, 'bladder.' This is found as a common element
in plant-names, e.g. *bladder-wort*, *bladder-fern*, *bladder-campion*,
and is also used by itself in the plant-name *bleddre*, for *berula*,
'cardamine,' in a 15th cent. vocabulary (*v.* NED *s.v.*). It may
be that just as Bromwich was a **wic** or farm where 'broom' grew
in abundance, Blatherwycke was the farm where one of these
bladder-plants was frequently found.

BRITAIN SALE (6″) is *Bretonnes Dybbyng* 1306 Ipm, *Bretounes-
dybbyng* 1374 Pat, *Bretonesdybbynges* 1391 Cl, *Bryteyn Sale*
c. 1550 *AOMB*, and is to be associated with the family of Ranulf
Brito who was granted a wood here in 1227 (Ch), and is associated
with an assart here in 1275 (RH), the family name being spelt
Breton 1275 RH, *le Bretun* 1306 Ipm. The word *dybbyng* is clearly

a woodland term. It is found in forest areas in Northampton-shire, the earliest reference being *Newe dibbing* (1223 *FF*) and *les Dibbinges* (t. Ed 1 *Finch-Hatton*) and it appears in modern field-names as *Dibbin(s)*. There can be little doubt that it is to be associated with the rare dialectal vb. *dib* (cf. the more common *dibble*), 'to make small holes,' *dib* rather than *dibble* being the common form in Bedfordshire and south Northamptonshire. In these districts the term can be used of setting out young acorns for a new oak plantation, and there can be little doubt that *dibbing* is an old word for such a plantation.

sale is found as a place-name element in various early minor names in Northamptonshire: *boscus vocat. la Sale* (1293 *For*), *Middlesale, Briggisale* (1313), and *Fremansale* (1401) in Higham Ferrers, and *le Salecorner* (1337). It is difficult to know how to interpret this element; topography and context alike make it clear that it is not the word *sale* sometimes found in place-names and derived from OE sealh, 'willow.' The EDD records from Northamptonshire the word *sale* as a name for a "division or 'quarter' of a wood, of which the underwood is cut down and sold." It is exceedingly unlikely that such a meaning of the word could go back to the 13th cent.; one cannot imagine a piece of woodland thus marked for sale in those days. More probably the old word *sale* (of which the sense is now lost) was taken over in comparatively recent times, and, by some mis-understanding, given a new and more comprehensible sense.

CADGE WOOD is *Cagge* 1237 Ch, *Caggestedes* 1367 *For*. This name is obscure. The early forms suggest that the vowel was originally short. There is a noun *cadge*, used in falconry for a frame on which several hawks are carried to be sold, which might have given rise to the name, but the history of that word is uncertain, and it has not before been noted in place-names.

HOSTAGE WOOD is possibly identical with *Haspehege* 1227 Cl, *-hegge* t. Ed 3 *For*. If this identification is correct, we seem to have a compound of OE *hæpse*, 'hasp, fastening,' and hecg, 'hedge,' describing perhaps some locked enclosure.

LYNN WOOD is *Lyndewode* t. Ed 1 *PeterbB*, 14th Dugd vi, 451, *Lynwod* 1324 Ch, *Lynewodde* 1535 VE. 'Lime-tree wood,' *v.* lind.

Brampton Ash

BRAMPTON ASH 73 C 13

Branton(e) 1086 DB *et freq* to 1219 WellsR, *Braun-* 1223 WellsR

Brampton 12th Survey *et passim*, (*juxta Dingelegh*) 1287 FF, (*Dyngle*) 1394 Pat

Bramton 1203 Cur, 1220 Fees, *Netherbramton* 1220 WellsR

v. Brampton *supra* 79. 'The Town on Account of its Pre-heminence for this Sort of Tree has received the name of Brampton in the Ash' (Morton 30).

BRAMPTON WOOD is *in bosco de Brampton* 1239 *FF*. DOB HALL is so named 1739 Camden (Gough), 1791 Bridges. FIELD BARN (6"), cf. *Fildegate* 1231 WellsR, v. feld. THE HERMITAGE, HERMITAGE WOOD. Bridges (ii, 284) mentions *The Hermitage House*, stating that there had formerly been a chapel here, pulled down about 16 years earlier. HIGHGATE WOOD (B). Cf. *Hye-gatestybbyng* 1430 *Finch-Hatton*. For *stybbing v. infra* 270.

Brigstock

BRIGSTOCK 74 D 4

Bricstoc 1086 DB, *-stoke* 1175 P, 1206 ClR, 1207 PatR, 1246 Seld 13

Bricestok 11th (1275) Ch, *Brichestoch* 1095–1100 AC *et passim* to 1312 Cl with variant spellings *Brike-*, *Bricke-*, *Brikke-*, and *-stok(e)*, *Bricchestok'* c. 1165 NRS iv, *Bricastoc* c. 1180 *PipewellA*

Brixstok(e) 12th Survey, 1251 Seld 13, 1290 Pat, *Bristok* 1379 Cl

Brikenestok' 1222 ClR

Birckestoc' 1226 WellsR, *Birggestok* 1235 Cl, *Berkestok'* 1245 Cl, *Byrxstoke* 1370 Pat

Brikel(s)tok 1236 Cl, *Brikelestoke* 1346 Pat

Briggestok(e) 1237 Cl *et passim* to 1343 Cl with variant spellings *Bryge-*, *Brige-*, *Brygge-*, *Brigstoke* 1466 Ch, *Brydgstock* 1614 FF

Brukestok' 1255 Cl, *Brugestok* 1315 *Ass*, *Briggestowe* 1318 Fine

The history of Brick Mere (PN BedsHu 214) probably provides the clue to the interpretation of this difficult name. Most of the early forms of that p.n. show that it is from OE *bierca-mere* or *beorc-mere*, 'mere of the birch trees,' with hesitation between forms derived from **bierce** and **beorc** respectively. This name appears with metathesis of *r* as *Brychmere* in the 14th cent. Ramsey Cartulary. So similarly in that cartulary we have a place called *Brycheholt*, clearly for earlier *Byrcheholt*. We may also note *Brykhyll* (14th *NthStA*) in Brixworth (Nth). In Brigstock we seem to have a compound of **bierce** and **stoc(c)**, 'birch-tree stump,' or possibly '**stoc** marked by birch-trees.' In this name the metathesised form is found earlier than the unmetathesised one; there has been the usual confusion between ME *birche* and *berke*, later *briche* and *brike*, and also a further confusion between ME *briche* and *brigge*.

CHERRY LAP is *Shenelelappe* c. 1300, 1337 *For*, *Schelleylappe* c. 1300 *For*, *Schelleye*, *Schilappe* t. Ed 1 *PeterbB*, *Shilleghlapp* 1374 *For*, *Sherylappe* 1540 LP, *Cherry Lap* 1651 NthNQ ii. *Shenele* is perhaps 'bright clearing or wood,' *v.* leah, and cf. Shenley (PN Bk 23) and (Herts). *lap* must be OE *læppe* used either of the edge of something larger, or, in the more technical sense 'detached portion, district,' *v.* BT *s.v.*

FARMING WOODS

> *boscus de Ferma* c. 1220 *For*, (*la*) *Ferme* 1235, 1242 Cl, *boscus de Fermes* t. Ed 1 *PeterbB*, 1281 Pat, 1290 Ipm, 1382 Cl
> *Ferminwod* 1229 Cl, *Fremyngwodes* 1375 Pat, *Fermyng Wood* 1551 Pat
> (*ballium de*) *Firma de Bricstok* 1248 Seld 13, *in bosco de Firma* 1254 ib.

The original name seems to have been descriptive of a piece of woodland held at a *farm* (ME *ferme*) or rent. How *Ferme-wood* later became *Ferming-wood* or *Farming-wood*, unless it be through some process of folk-etymology, is obscure. Cf. further *Farmyngeshawe* t. Ed 3 *For*. For such a late and hybrid *ing*-compound we may however compare Templeton (Berks), held by the Knights Templars, which is called *Templington templariorum* in 1284 (*Ass*).

HARLEY WAY is *Hareleia* 1223 *FF*, *Harleruding* 1272 Seld 13, *Harleymere* 1337 *For*, *Harleimere* 1340 *Brudenell*, *Harleyfelde* 1469 *Ct*. As Harley Way is just by the boundary alike of Brigstock parish and Rockingham Forest, Harley may be a compound of har and leah, hence 'boundary wood,' though 'hare wood' is also possible. The *mere* will be one of the small ponds in the woodland here or the boundary itself, *v.* (ge)mære and cf. Althorp Meer *supra* 80. See also hryding.

LAUNDIMER WOODS is *Landimere* c. 1220 *For*, 1299 *Ct*, 1330 *Ass*, *Landemerehyl* 1293 *For*, *le Landimere* 1300 *Brudenell*, -*dy*- c. 1400 *Ct*. This is OE *land-gemǣre*, 'boundary.' The wood lies on the parish boundary.

LUSCOTE'S WOOD and LODGE are *Lesecotes* t. Ed 1 *PeterbB*, *Luzecotes* 1327 *Brudenell*, *Lusecotes* 1337, *Luscotes* 1345 *For*, 1805 *EnclA*. This is from OE hlose and cot(e), hence 'pigstye cottages.'

MOUNTERLEY WOOD is *Maunterley* 1480 *Ct*, t. Hy 8 *LRMB*, *Montreley* 1651 NthNQ ii, *Monterley Sale* 1805 *EnclA*. This is a difficult name, but it may be suggested that it is a compound of ME *manteltre* and leah (ME *ley*), *manteltre* being a common term for the big wooden beam which forms the lintel of an old open fireplace. Hence, 'wood where *mantel-trees* are known to have been cut, or where the thickness of the branching timbers suggests *mantel-trees*.'

STEPHEN OAK RIDING (6″) is *Steven Oke* 1642 Woods Rept, and takes its name from what Morton (397) describes as 'the capacious hollow old Tree call'd *Stephens Oak*, or as vulgarly *King Stephen's Oak*, one of the Boundaries of *Rockingham* Forest....From this very Tree, according to Tradition, King *Stephen* once shot at a Deer.'

STUBBY STILES (6″) is *Stubbyngstighele* 1337 *For*, *Stubby Stile* 1651 NthNQ ii, 1805 *EnclA*. 'Path or stile by the place which has been stubbed.' Cf. Ekwall, PN in -*ing* 26, and Stubbing PN NRY 271.

BOCASE FM (6″) is named after *Bow Case Tree* 1642 *Deed*. Cf. *Bocase Riding* 1794 *EnclA*. This was a tree on the boundary of

Rockingham Forest of which the site is now marked by Bocase Stone. BUSHYLAWN LODGE (6″). Cf. *Busshie close* t. Hy 8 *LRMB*. CAUSIN LEYS and WAY (6″) may be associated with *Cosyngesridyng* 1337 *For*, and *Cousin Lane* and *Field* 1805 *EnclA*, *v.* hryding. HARRY'S PARK WOOD. Cf. *Harris Parke Corner* 1642 Woods Rept, *Harry's Park* 1806 *EnclA*. MEADOW LEYS (6″) is *Meadowleys* 1651 NthNQ ii, *v.* læs. OLD DRY HILLS is *Old Dry Hill* 1628 Woods Rept. Cf. *Old Dry Hill Coppice* 1642 *Deed*. ROYAL COPPICE is so named in 1651 (NthNQ ii). SAMBY SYKES is *Sembey Sykes* 1826 G. TRESSHAM COPPICE (6″) is *Treshams Coppice* 1642 *Deed*. The Treshams held the neighbouring manor of Lyveden (VCH iii, 170).

Bulwick

BULWICK [bulik] 74 A 5

Bulewic, -k 1162 P (p) *et freq* to 1301 Ch
Bolewyk, -i- 12th Survey *et freq* to 1406 AD iii
Bulwic 1248 Ipm, *-wyk* 1385 Cl
Bullewyk(e) 1315 *Ass*, 1381 AD ii, *Bullicke* 1622 *FF*
Bollewyk al. Bulwyk 1323 Ipm, *Bollewyk* 1323 Cl

'Bull farm,' *v.* wic. Cf. Cowick (PN D 438).

HENWICK (lost) is *Henewyk, Hynewyk* 12th Survey, *Hanewyc, Hennewychawe* c. 1220 *For*, *Henewic* 1248 Ipm, *-wyk* 1303 Ipm, *Henewichauwe* 1286 *For*, *Henwick Haw* 1642 Woods Rept. Probably 'hens' farm,' *v.* wic.

HOLLOW BOTTOM LODGE is *Hollowe Bot(t)ome* 1538 *Brudenell*, 1584 *Map*, *Hallowe Bottam* 1570 AD iii, 1669 *Clayton*. The last two spellings make it clear that this name should be associated with the neighbouring Hollow Wood in Harringworth *infra* 168, and *hollow* taken as a corruption of earlier *hallow*.

FERRELS WOOD. Possibly we may compare *Fayrhull* 1352 Ipm, *Fayrehill* 1538 *Brudenell*, the *s* being pseudo-manorial. GREAT-SALE WOOD (6″). For *sale v.* Britain Sale *supra* 156.

East Carlton

EAST CARLTON 74 C 1

> (*æt*) *Carlatune* 11th (13th) *PeterbA*
> *Carlintone* 1086 DB, *Carlenton* c. 1115 *Swaffham*
> *Carleton* c. 1115 *Swaffham et passim* to 1349 Ipm with variant
> spelling *Karle-*, *Karelton* 1220 Fees, *Carelton* 1246 Seld,
> *Carylton* 1253 *FF*, *Carleton juxta Rokyngham* 1303 *FF*,
> (*juxta Cotyngham*) 1349 BM
> *Karlton* 1274 Cl

v. **karla-tun**. The addition of 'East' is quite modern, probably
in distinction from Carlton Curlieu (Lei) to the west of it.

BAR COPPICE (6″) is *Bare Copie* 1580 *Map*, *Beare Coppice* 1660
Clayton, *Bar Copse* 1823 B. CARLTON PURLIEUS. Cf. Oakley
Purlieus *infra* 170.

Corby

CORBY 74 C 3

> *Corbei*, *-bi* 1086 DB *et passim* with variant spelling *-by*
> *Corebi* 1166 P, *Coreby* 12th Survey *et freq* to 1252 Cl
> *Carbe* 1538 LP

'The **by** of *Kóri*.' Björkman (ZEN 57) notes the OWScand
name *Kóri* and a similar Swedish name, found in place-names.

BANDY SLADE (6″) is so called in 1831 (*EnclA*). GREAT and
LITTLE EXCELLENT (6″) are *Great, Little Exland* 1580 *Map*, 1831
EnclA, *Excellent* c. 1825 O.S. If the earlier form is the more
correct, as seems probable, the name may contain *exen*, the old
mutated plural of *ox*, hence, 'oxen-land,' but cf. Bullicks Wood
infra 186. OCCUPATION FM. Possibly the sense is 'piece of land
occupied by a tenant,' one of the meanings given in the NED *s.v.*
PENGREEN LODGE (6″) is *Pen Green* 1642 Woods Rept, *v.* penn.
SOUTH WOOD is *Suhtwode* 1286 *For*, *Sowe Woods* 1642 Woods
Rept, *Sow wood al. Southwood* 1631 *Finch-Hatton*. STOCKEY
WOOD (B) is *Stockerwood* 1580 *Map*, 1831 *EnclA*. THOROUGH-
SALE WOOD is *Throughsale* 1580 *Map*. *Thurser* field, which is
adjacent to it, probably shows a colloquial reduction of this name.
For *sale v.* Britain Sale *supra* 156.

Cottingham

COTTINGHAM 74 B 1

Cotingeham 1086 DB *et freq* to 1227 Ch, *Cotingham* 1137 (12th) ASC (E) *et passim* to 1343 Ipm with variant spelling *Cotyng-*, *Cotynham* 1343 Ipm
Cottingeham 1162, 1166 P

'ham(m) of *Cotta*'s people,' *v*. ing.

GREAT CATTAGE WOOD (6″) is *Catteheggis* c. 1400 *Rental*, *Cathege* 1551 Pat, *Cattedg* 1553–8 *Ct*. 'Wild cat hedge,' cf. Wolfidge *supra* 123.

BURY HO (6″). Cf. *Bery dikes* c. 1400 *Rental*. *bury* is here used in its manorial sense, *v*. burh and cf. Berryfields *supra* 15. HILL HO FM (Kelly) is *le Hill* c. 1400 *Rental*.

Deene

DEENE 74 B 4

Den 1065 BM, 1206 Cur (p), 1227 *Ass* (p), 1230 P, 1270 Ch (p), 1285 FA
Dene 1086 DB *et freq* to 1486 Ch, *Dena* 1166 P (p), 1178 P
Deen 12th Survey, c. 1242 AD v, 1313 Cl, 1316 FA
Dien' 1205 Cur (p), *Dyen* 1216 FineR (p)

'Valley,' *v*. denu. It lies in the valley of the Willow Brook.

DIBBIN'S WOOD is *Dybbyngeshirne* 1324 Ch, *Dybbynges* 1538 Brudenell, *Deepings* 17th id. '*Dibbings* corner.' *Dibbins* is here really a plural and not a genitive form as suggested by the modern O.S. spelling. See further *s.n.* Britain Sale *supra* 156.

Deenethorpe

DEENETHORPE 74 B 3

Torp 1086 DB, 13th AD iii, *Trop* 1235 Fees
Deenthorp 1246 FF, 1382 Cl, *Denthorp* 1287 FF, 1316 FA
Dyngthorp 1538 FF, *Dynthorp* 1563 BM, *Denethorpe al. Dingthorpe* 1639 Recov, *Deenethorpe al. Thorpe juxta Deene* 1668 ib.

v. þorp. The sense here is that of 'secondary settlement' (from Deene).

BURN COPPICE is *Burmans copy al. Brent copyes* 1514 *Brudenell*, *Burnte Copice* 1642 Woods Rept. LANGLEY COPPICE (6″) is *landa de Langeleye* 1235 Cl, *Lound of Langeleye* 1288 Cl, *Langleyfeld* 1416 *Brudenell*. 'Long clearing or wood,' *v.* lang, leah. In the ME forms there seems to be confusion between *landa* or 'lawn' (cf. Wakefield Lawn *supra* 105) and *lound*, 'wood' from lundr.

Dingley

DINGLEY 73 C 12

> *Dinglei* 1086 DB, -*leg* 1241 P, *Dyngle* 1428 FA
> *Tinglea* 1086 DB
> *Dingele, -y-, -leye, -lea* 1166 RBE *et passim*, *Dinggele* c. 1214 AD iv, *Dyngyle* 1274 RH
> *Dynelay* 1348 Cl

The ground here is much broken, and this name may be a compound of *dingle* and leah. The word *dingle* is of obscure origin (*v.* NED *s.v.*), but is found elsewhere in place-names (cf. PN Wo 390 *s.n. dingle*). Hence, 'leah marked by one or more valleys.' Dr Smith suggests that this may alternatively be from OE *Dynningleah*, '*Dynne*'s clearing,' with the same loss of a syllable as in Finghall (PN NRY 247).

Fineshade

FINESHADE 64 J 5

> *Eccl. S. Marie de Castrohyniel* c. 1200 BM, *prioratus de Castro Iniel, Inyel* 1226 WellsR, *Castle Himel* 1227 Ch, *Castro Himel* 1228 Pat, *Castle Himel now called priory of Finesheved* 1324 Ch, *Castrum Hymel* 1330 Dugd vi, 449
> *Finnisheved* t. John For, *Finesheved* 1226 WellsR, 1227 Ch, 1246 Cl, -*hed'* 1246 Cl
> *Finnesheved* 1234 Pat *et freq* to 1341 AD ii, -*hevet* 1254 For, *Finnis-* 1323 Ipm, *Fynneshed* 1363 AD ii, *Fynnishead* 1639 Recov, *Finshead* 1702 Poll, *Finshed* 1712 Morton
> *Fenesheved* 1316 FA

The origin of the name of the castle which later became the site of the priory is unknown. If it was (*H*)*iniel* or (*H*)*inyel* rather than *Hymel* or *Himel*, we may hazard the suggestion that it was named after one *Ingeld*, a name which would naturally yield *Inyeld* in ME, and is found in Latin as *Hinieldus*. Loss of final *d* would readily take place. Close at hand, in the parish of Bulwick we have in a fine of 1223, mention of a *crucem Ingaldi*, which may contain this name partially Scandinavianised, and refer to the same person. The priory was founded a little to the north-east of the castle. It would seem to have taken its second name from the hill on which it stands. This would seem to have been named 'Finn's head,' *v.* heafod, but the reason for such a name is obscure. For the pers. name cf. *Finnesthorpe* in the list of Peterborough land-sureties (BCS 1130). For the use of heafod in this county, cf. the field-names *Tostisheuyd* in Twywell (1251 *For*), *Cynestanes heafod* in Kettering (956 BCS 943), *Wyvelesheved* in Armston (1250 *Buccleuch*).

THE GULLET (6″). Cf. The Gullet *supra* 46. MILL WOOD (6″). Cf. *Estmelne* 1330 Dugd vi, 449. OLD SALE (6″). For *sale*, *v.* Britain Sale *supra* 156. ST MARY'S WOOD (6″) is *Marewde* 1330 Dugd vi, 449, *Seyntmariwode* 1345 *For*, *Seynte Mary Wodde* 1535 VE. For St Mary *v.* Fineshade *supra*.

Geddington

GEDDINGTON 74 E 3

Geitenton(e) 1086 DB *et passim* to 1356 Cl with variant spellings *-y-*, *-in-*, *Geytington* 12th Survey, 1252 Seld 13, 1287 Cl, 1337 Ipm, *Geiting-* 1247 *Ass*, 1356 Cl, *-yng* 1296 Cl

Gadinton(e) 1086 DB, 1195 Abbr, *-na* 1131 P (p), *Gaden-* t. Hy 2 (1324) Ch

Geintendone 1154 RBE, *Geintinton* 1235 Ch, *Geyn-* 1225 Bracton

Gaitintun(e) 1156 P *et passim* to 1316 Ch with variant spellings *-y-*, *-en-*, and *-ton(e)*, *Gaytington(am)* 1189 France, t. Ric 1 (1389) Pat, *Gaytingeton* t. Ric 1 (1252) Ch

Gat(t)inton 1158, 1162 P, 1202 Cur, 1204 PatR, c. 1220 AD ii, *Gatyngton* 1354 Cl

Gainton 1174 P (CR), *Geinton* 1241 ib., *Geynton* 1244 Cl

Gaidintun', *-ton* 1189 (1371) Ch, 1196 P, t. Ric 1 (1318) Ch, *Gayd-* 1214 ClR

Getintuna t. Ric 1 (1318) Ch, *-ton* 1199 FF, 1204 PatR,
   Getyngdon 1339 Cl, *Gedyngton* 1397 ib.
Geidinton 1204 ClR *et freq* to 1227 *FF* with variant spellings
   Geyd-, -yng- 1376, 1397 Cl

This name is a hybrid compound of the OWScand pers.
name *Geiti*, ODan *Geti*, and the English ingtun. The circumstances under which such compounds could arise must for the
present be left open. (Cf. Lindkvist 54 and Zachrisson, *English
PN's in -ing of Scandinavian Origin* 115.)

GEDDINGTON CHASE is *foresta regis de Geytinton* 1229 Cl

RISING BRIDGE is *Risenbrige* c. 1220 *For*, *Risene-* 1247 Seld 13,
Rysenebrigge 1272 *For*, *(la)* c. 1300 *For*, *Rysingbridge* 1612
Depositions. 'Bridge or causeway made of brushwood,' from an
unrecorded OE adjective *hrīsen*, a derivative of hris. Cf. further
Rice Bridge (PN Sx 258).

SART WOOD (6") is *Sart Coppes* 1547 Pat, *le Assart* 1642 Woods
Rept. This is the AFr *essart*, 'woodland clearing.' See further
PN D 634.

BRAND, GREAT and LITTLE (6") is *the Brand* 1608 *Depositions*,
Geddington-Bran 1791 Bridges. Evidently 'a place cleared by
burning.' Cf. Braunder (PN D 223). CRAB TREE HILLS (6") is
Crabtre Hyll Coppes 1547 Pat. LANGLEY QUARTER (6") is
Langelesike c. 1300, *Langeleghe* 1337 *For*. 'Long clearing or
wood,' *v.* lang, leah, sic.

Gretton

GRETTON 74 B 4
   Gretone 1086 DB, 1215 ClR
   Grettone, -tun 1163 P *et passim* to 1346 FA, (*super Weland*)
      1297 Pat
   Gratton c. 1220 *For*, 1274 Ipm, (*al. Gretton*) 1670 *Recov*
   Cretton 1285 FA

   'Big farm,' *v.* great, tun.

COTTON (lost) is *Kotes* 1247 *FF*, *Coten(e)* 1274 Ipm *et freq* to
1362 Cl, *Cotone* 1316 FA, *Cotes by Rokyngham* 1350 Ipm, *Coten
near Rokyngham* 1355 Cl. *v.* Claycoton *supra* 66.

HARBOROUGH HILL is *Harberwe* t. Ed 1 *PeterbB*, *Hareberuwe* 1286 *For*. The hill is on the Gretton-Harringworth boundary, and the name may be a compound of **har** and **beorg**.

KIRBY HALL

> *Chercheberie* 1086 DB, *-bia* 1121–9 France
> *Chirchebi* 1162 P, *Kirkeby* 12th Survey *et freq* to 1324 Cl with variant spelling *Kyrke-*
> *Cerkeby* 1196 Cur
> *Kirby* 1568 AD iii, *Kerby* 1623 *Recov*

'by by or with a church.' There is no church (and indeed no village) here now.

THATCHAMS COPSE (6″) is *Thakholm* c. 1400 *Rental*, *Thakholme grene* 1530, *Thackholme Coppice* 1571 AD iii, *Thackham's Wood* 1837 *EnclA*. 'Thatch river-meadow,' *v.* holm. The name must have referred to low-lying marsh-land where reeds were gathered for thatching purposes.

BROCKHOLES (B) is *Brockholes* 1614 *Clayton*, *Brockholds copies* 1669 ib., 'badger holes,' cf. Brockhall *supra* 80. BROOKFIELD LODGE. Cf. *Grettonbrok* t. Ed 1 *PeterbB*, *Gretton Brooke* 1642 Woods Rept. EVENHOE (B) is *Evenhoo Quarter* 1584 *Map*, *Eueno* 1669 *Clayton*, *v.* hoh. The first element is uncertain. It may be the word 'even,' i.e. 'level,' 'smooth.' GRETTON PLAIN. Cf. *campus de Gretton* t. Ed 1 *PeterbB*. GRETTON WOODS is *boscus de Gretton* t. Ed 1 *PeterbB*, *Grettunwod* 1345 *For*. PORTER'S COPPICE (6″) is *Porters Copie* 1669 *Clayton*. PRESGRAVE COPSE (B) is *Prestgrave* c. 1400 *Rental*, *Prisgrave al. Broadoke Copies* 1669 *Clayton*. 'Priests' grove,' *v.* preost, grafa.

Harringworth

HARRINGWORTH 64 J 3

> *Haringwrth* c. 1060 (13th) ChronRams *et passim* to 1332–6 Ipm with variant spellings *Haryng-* and *-worth*
> *Haringeworde* 1086 DB, *Haringewurða* 1166 P *et freq* to 1274 Cl with variant spelling *-worth*, *Harengwrth* 1235 Fees
> *Halingewurda* 1162 P

Heringewurða 1183 P, *Ering(e)worth* 1199, 1206 Cur, *Herynge-worth* 1261 *Ass*
Harryngworth 1323 Ipm

An OE pers. name *Hering* is on record, and we seem to have this name in *Hæringes geat* (KCD 739) and *Heringes leah* (ib. 1062) and *Heryngeswde* (14th *NthStA*). Cf. also Hornsey (Mx) with early forms *Haring-, Hering-,* the former being the most numerous. If the names here given are all ultimately the same name, then Redin's association of them (172) with OE *here* must be wrong. Phonologically it would be easier to associate it with OE *hæring,* 'herring,' but semantically that does not seem possible, and, unfortunately, the etymology of *hæring* is entirely obscure. It should be noted, moreover, that Harringworth seems to be formed from a gen. pl. *Hæringa,* so that the exact significance of the name must remain obscure. It is 'the enclosure (*v.* worþ) of H- or the people of *H-,*' but the exact form of the name must remain uncertain.

HOLLOW WOOD is *wood of Halgh* 1306 Ipm, *boscus de Halugh* 1333 BM. 'Wood in the nook or corner,' *v.* healh, with later confusion with 'hollow' from holh. It is probable that Hollow Wood was originally the name for the whole of the large wood here, now divided into two parts, since the name is clearly to be associated with Hollow Bottom *supra* 161.

TURTLE BRIDGE (6″) is *Thurkelbregge* 1298 Ipm and is probably to be associated with the family of Ralph *Turcle* mentioned in connection with Harringworth in 1247 (*Ass*). This surname is of Scandinavian origin, answering to ON *þórketill.*

DRYLEAS WOOD is *Dry lease* 1647 *Clayton.* LODGE POND is *The Great Lodge pond* 1647 *Clayton.* PARK LODGE. Cf. *Haringworth Parke* 1642 Woods Rept. SHORT WOOD is so called in 1773 (*EnclA*). SHOTLEY is *Shotle* 1430 AD iii.

Laxton

LAXTON 74 A 4
Lastone 1086 DB, *Laxton(a)* 1166 P (p) *et passim*
Laxeton(a) 1131 P, 1198 Fees, 1275 *FF*

Laxinton(a) 12th Survey, 1222 Bracton
Lextone 1226 WellsR, *Lexitone* 1231 WellsR
Laxon al. Laxton 1723 *Recov*

Lax is a Scandinavian nickname from *lax*, 'salmon,' and this p.n. may be for *Laxestun*, hence '*Lax*'s farm,' *v.* tun. For *Laxintone* cf. note on Geddington *supra* 166. Dr Smith notes the parallels of Laxton (Nt) *Laxintune* DB, *Laxton* 1291 Tax and Laxton (ERY), *Laxinton* DB, *Laxton* 1285 FA.

LAXTON WOOD (6″) is *bosco de Laxton* 1330 Dugd vi, 449.

SPANHOE FM and WOOD is *Spanhoe Wood* 1826 G. Possibly it is identical with *Sanhowe bosc. infra forest. de Rokingham* 1316 Inq aqd. If so, the latter form must be corrupt. *Span* may be due to confusion of OE *spōn*, 'chip of wood' and the corresponding ON *spánn*. Such a name in this woodland area is very probable. *v.* hoh.

Middleton

MIDDLETON[1] (74 B 1) is *Middelton* 1197 FF, (*juxta Rokyngham*) 1335 *Ass, Midelton* 1270 Ch, (*in the parish of Cotyngham*) 1391 Cl, *Middilton* 1285 FA. 'Middle farm,' *v.* tun. It lies between Carlton and Cottingham.

SWINAWE WOOD is *Swinehawe* 1203 *FF, Swyne-* t. Ed 1 *PeterbB, Swinehawebroc* c. 1250 *PipewellA, Swyn-* 1345 *For, Swynehawe copie* 1446 Pat. 'Swine enclosure or wood,' *v.* haga.

ASH COPPICE is *Ashe Cop(p)ice* 1580 *Map*, t. Jas 1 Woods Rept. BROAD ANGLE WOOD (6″) is *Brode Angle* 1535 VE, *Brodeangle Copice* 1580 *Map*. GAULBOROUGH SPINNEY (6″). Cf. *Gaulborough Field* 1825 *EnclA*. YOKEWOOD LODGE (6″) is *Yoke wode* 1535 *Compotus, Yokewood* 1580 *Map, Yoake wood coppice* 1660 *Clayton*. For the interpretation of such a name cf. *s.n.* Yokehurst PN Sx 300. The most likely meaning would seem to be 'wood used for making yokes.'

---

[1] Formerly a hamlet of Cottingham.

Newton

NEWTON 74 E 2

Newetone, Neutone 1086 DB *et passim* with variant spellings
  New-, Niwe-, (Parvam) 1229 Cl, 1230 P, *(Magna)* 1285 FA,
  (juxta Geytington) 1294 *Ass*
Niwenton 1162 P, *Neuwenton* c. 1220 *For, Newenton* 1378 Cl,
  (Maiore, Minore) 1220 Fees

'New farm,' *v.* tun.

Oakley, Great and Little

OAKLEY 74 D 2

Aclea 11th (13th) ChronRams *et passim* to 1303 Cl with
  variant spellings *-ley, -lei, -le, Accle* 1175 P, *ii Acleie* 1178 P,
  Little Acle 12th Survey, *(Maiore, Parva)* 1220 Fees, *(Magna)*
  1246 Seld, *Akele* 1242 Fees, *Westacle* 13th *PipewellA,*
  Estackleye 1287 *For*
Achelau 1086 DB, *Achele(ia)* 1166 P, *-lee* 1204 Cur, *Maiori*
  Akele 1242 Fees
Westokle 1275 RH, *Ockele Magna, Parva* 1316 FA, *Ockle*
  1332 Ipm, *Ocle* 1349 Ipm, *Okelee* 1389 Cl, *Mykyll Okeley*
  1478 BM, *Great, Little Ockley* 1675 Ogilby
Hokkelegh 1287 Fine

'Oak clearing or wood,' *v.* ac, leah.

OAKLEY PURLIEUS [pəˈliz]. Cf. *Oclewod* 1374 *For. purlieu* is
found fairly often in forest-names, and denotes a tract on the
border of forest-land (NED *s.v.*). The local pronunciation is illustrated in Morton's phrase (443) "the Earl of Exeter's Purlees." In
modern field-names it takes the form *Purley* and even *Purleigh.*

SNATCHILL LODGE is *Snoteshal* c. 1220 *For, Snoteshal(l)e* 14th
PipewellB, Snatteshall Gate 1642 Woods Rept, *Snatchall* 1831
EnclA. '*Snot*'s healh.' The pers. name *Snot* is found in DB, and
lies behind Nottingham, *Snotengaham* ASC *s.a.* 868.

KINGS WOODS is *Kinges wood copice* 1580 *Map.* LYVEDEN LODGE
is not marked on the earliest edition of the 1″ O.S. (c. 1825) and
is very likely a modern name. Cf. Lyveden in Aldwinkle *infra*
178. SOWER LEYS (6″) is *Sower Leaze* 1616 Woods Rept. *v.* læs.
For a name of opposite meaning cf. Sweetlands (PN D 650).

Rockingham

ROCKINGHAM 74 B 2

Rochingeham 1086 DB, 1125–9 NRS iv, 1131 P, *-ingheham*
1151 BM, *Rokingeham* 1174 P *et passim* to 1223 ClR with
variant spelling *-ynge*

Rogingham 1137 (12th) ASC, 1207, 1216 ClR, *-ingeham* 1197
FF, 1234 Cl

Rokingham 12th Survey *et freq* to 1316 FA with variant
spelling *-yng-*, *Rokengam* 1203 FF, *Rokenham* 1255 Seld 13

Rokkynggham 1519 AD iii

'The ham of the followers of *Hrōc(a)*.' For such a pers. name
cf. MLR xiv, 241. Mansion (29) has an interesting 9th
cent. continental parallel in *Hrokingahem*.

Stanion

STANION 74 C 3

Stanere 1086 DB, *Stannere* 1195 P

Stanern(a), *-e* 1162 P *et passim* to 1314 Ipm

Stanhern(e) 1203 Cur, 1204 FineR, 1220, 1226 WellsR

Stanierne 1362–7 Ipm, *Stanyerne* 1481 AD vi, *Stayneyerne*
1486 Ch

Staunyerne 1607 BM

Stannyon 1631 NRS i, *Stanyan* 1712 Morton

v. stan, ærn. The plural form of ærn is the same as the sing.
form and the village name probably simply denotes (a collection
of) stone-buildings.

CORBY HAW (6″) is *Corby hall leys* 1560 *Finch-Hatton*. This may
show the reverse form of the change found in Weekley Hall
infra 173. HARRY'S WOOD is *Harris woode* 1584 *Map*.

Stoke Albany

STOKE ALBANY 73 C 13

Stoche 1086 DB *et passim* with variant spelling *Stoke*

Stokis 1175 P, *Stokes* 1175 P (CR), 12th Survey *et freq* to
1242 P

Stok(e) Daubeny 1274 Cl, 1275 RH, 1388 Ch, *Stok Daubeney*
    1285 Ipm, *Stok(e) Aubeny* 1301 Ipm, *-ey* 1343 Ipm, *Stoke*
    Awbony 1622 *Recov*
Stoake Albane al. Stoake Dawbney 1626 *Recov*, *Stoke Olbenny*
    1657 NRS i

v. stoc(c). William *de Albinni* held the manor in 1155 (P), the
surname being variously spelt *Daubeny* 12th Survey, *de Albeny*
1208 Fees, *de Albin* 1221 ClR, *de Albiniaco* 1233 Cl.

BOWD LANE WOOD. Cf. *Bowdes or South Field* 1632 *Glebe
Terriers*. STOKE PARK FM is *Stoke Parke* 1612 *FF*.

Sutton Bassett

SUTTON BASSETT 73 B 12

Sutone 1086 DB, *Sutton* 1185 RotDom *et passim*, (*Basset*)
    1309 Cl, (*juxta Dyngele*) 1317 *Ass*, (*by Weston upon Wylond*)
    1394 Cl

'South farm,' *v.* tun. It is south of Weston. Richard *Basset*
held the manor in the 12th cent. (Survey).

Wakerley

WAKERLEY [weikəli] 64 J 4

Wacherlei 1086 DB, *-lai* 1162 P, *Wakerlea* 1184 P *et passim*
    with variant spellings *-lega, -ley, -le*, *Wacer-* 1166 P (CR),
    Water- 1168 P
Wakeleg 1215, 1216 ClR
Wakirle 1274, 1385 Cl, *-ley* 1414 AD vi
Waukerle 1282 Cl

This is a difficult name. Wakerley has a commanding situation
above the valley of the Welland, and it is difficult not to believe
that the name should in one way or another be associated with
OE *wacor*, 'watchful.' We can hardly suppose that that adj. was
used in direct description of the leah, for we have no parallel for
such a name-type. More probably, the name was originally
wacra-leah, 'leah of the watchful ones.' The most natural compound would have been an OE *wæccera-leah*, 'watchers' leah,'
but this should give later *Watcherley*. Possibly that was the

original form and it was modified under the influence of the common adj. *wacor*, of similar meaning but different pronunciation.

GREENWOOD SALE (6″). For *sale v.* Britain Sale *supra* 156. WAKERLEY BRIDGE (6″) is *Wakerle Brigge* 1298 Ipm. WAKERLEY GREAT WOOD is *boscus de Wakerleg'* 1287 *For.*

Weekley

WEEKLEY 74 E 2

(*to*) *wiclea* (*forde*) 956 (c. 1250) BCS 943, *Wiclei* 1086 DB *et passim* to 1382 Cl with variant spellings *Wyk-, Wik-,* and -*le*(*e*), -*ley*

Wichelai 1166, *Wikelea* 1172 P *et freq* to 1526 SR with variant spellings *Wyke-,* and -*legh,* -*ley,* -*le*(*e*), *Wichchelea* 1175 P

Wicklea 1194 P, *Wickly* 1655 StJ

Wekelee 1395 Cl

'Clearing or wood by the wic,' *v.* wic, leah.

BOUGHTON Ho [bɑutən]

Boctone 1086 DB, *Boketon* 12th Survey

Bohtun 1162 P, *Bochtun* 1162 P (CR)

Buketon 1201 Cur (p), *Buchton* 1220 Fees, *Buhton* 1230 P (p), *Buton* 1255 Seld 13, *Button* 1255 ib., *Bughton* 1280 *FF,* *Buthton* 1313 Ipm

Bouhton 1246 Seld 13, *Bouton* 1253, 1255 ib. (p), 1285 FA, *Bhouton* 1313 Ipm

Boughton 1316 FA, 1353 Ipm, (*by Geytington*) 1325 Ipm

This is probably from OE *bōc-tūn,* 'beech-farm,' though some of the forms suggest the same history as that put forward for Boughton *supra* 133. The probability is that in both names alike there has been a good deal of confusion between like-sounding possibilities.

WEEKLEY HALL WOOD is *Wikelehawe* 1332, 1337 *Ass,* 1345 Ipm. *v.* haga. The modern form is corrupt. (Cf. Priors Hall *infra* 174.) *haga* normally denotes an enclosure, but its modern descendant *haw* is, according to EDD, used of a small wood or coppice.

Weldon, Great and Little

Weldon, Great and Little 73 C 4

Walesdone, Waledone, Weledene 1086 DB
Weledone 1086 DB *et freq* to 1300 Ipm, *-dune* 1255 Seld 13
Welledon 1166 P *et passim* to 1324 Ch, (*Magna*) 1184 P,
   (*Parva*) 1213 ClR, (*Maiore, Minore*) 1220 Fees, *-den* 1293
   Cl, *-doun* 1385 Cl
Wellendon 1201 PatR, 1253 *Ass, Welendon* 1217 ClR
Waledon 1234 Cl, *-den* 1241 P
Wheledon 1330 *Ass*
Weldon Basset 1355 Ipm, *Myche Weldon* 1523–7 BM,
   Parva al. Petit Weldon 1573 *FF, Parva al. Peat Weldon*
   1610 *FF*

'Hill with the spring,' *v.* wielle, dun. Weldon was the head of
the Honour of *Basset.*

Bangrave Wood is *Barnegrave* c. 1220 *For, Barnegraue* 1247
Seld 13, *Barnegraves* 1293 *For, Bangraves* 1625 *Deed.* 'Grove
by the barn(s).' *v.* bern, graf(a).

Cowthick Lodge is *Midlecouthik, Coothike, Coethik* 1580, 1584
Map, wood called Co(e)thick 1625 *Deed, boscus voc. Cothicke* 1642
Woods Rept, *Coethick* 1794 *EnclA.* For *thick v.* Blackmore
Thick *infra* 206. The first element may be the word 'cow' (OE
cu), but the forms are too late for any certainty. Cf. Coe Fen or
Cow Fen in Cambridge.

Hunterswood Lodge. This is *Huntes woode copie* 1584 *Map,
Huntswod* in 1636 (Bridges ii, 358), and is to be traced to one
Hamon *le Venor*, i.e. the hunter, t. Hy 4 (Bridges *loc. cit.*).

Priors Hall is *Priors Hawe al. Finshead Wood* 1628 *Brudenell,
Priors Hawe* 1642 Woods Rept, 1794 *EnclA*, with the same
corrupt modern form as in Weekley Hall *supra* 173. Fineshade
Priory held land in the parish (Bridges ii, 358).

Weldon Park is *Weldonparke* 1416 *Brudenell.*

Weston by Welland

WESTON BY WELLAND 73 B 12

Weston(e) 1086 DB *et passim*, (*by Asshele*) 1341 Ipm, (*super Wylond*) 1377 BM

Weston Bassett al. Weston by Wolland 1609 *Recov*, (*Super Wool(l)and*) 1739, 1748 Poll

'West farm,' *v.* tun. It must have been so named by the people of Ashley. The *Basset* family held the manor in 1191 (P).

Wilbarston

WILBARSTON [wibəstən] 73 C 14

Wilberteston(e) 1086 DB, 1175, 1192 P, *-tun* 1155 P

Wilberdeston(e) 1086 DB *et passim* to 1285 FA with variant spellings *-dis-*, and *Wyl-*, *Wlb-* 1200 FF, *Wilberdestre* 1235 Ch

Wilberdestoch 1160 P, *-stoke* 1196 P, 1220 Fees, *Wilbertestoch'* 1198 P, *Wilbernstok'* c. 1220 WellsR

Wilebeldeston 1189 P

Wylleberston 1285 *Ass*, *Wilberston* 1301 Ipm, *Wybbarston* 1602 *FF*, *Wilbaston* 1675 Ogilby

'*Wilbeorht*'s farm,' *v.* tun, with some confusion in the second element with stocc, perhaps owing to the neighbourhood of *Stoke* Albany.

ASKERSHAW WOOD (6") is *Asketeshawe* 1143 (1323) Dugd iv, 434, *Asketeleshaie* c. 1255 *PipewellA*, *Askeeceleshawe* (sic) 1343 Ipm, *Asketshawe* 1642 Woods Rept. '*Asketill*'s enclosure,' *v.* haga or hagi and (ge)hæg. *Asketill* is a well-known OScand name; in the form *Aschil* it is found elsewhere in the county in DB.

BARROWDYKES WOOD (6") is *Barodyke* c. 1400 *Rental*, *Barrow-dyckes*, *le Barrow Close* 1547 Pat. This is probably a compound of OE bearu and dic, hence '*dikes* or *ditches* in the woodland.'

PIPEWELL [pipwəl]

Pipewelle 1086 DB *et passim* to 1551 AD v

Pipwell(e)(a) 1166 P (CR) *et freq* to 1428 FA with variant spelling *Pyp(p)-*

Pippewell(e) 1177 P, 12th Survey *et passim* to 1391 Cl,
  Pippenwell 1331 *AD*
Peppewella 1231 Bracton

As Pipewell Abbey is on Harpers Brook (*supra* 2), it must be named from a spring rather than a stream. The first part is probably a pers. name *Pippa* (cf. *Pippanleah* BCS 1235 and *Pipe* a p. n. in DB). Hence, '*Pippa*'s spring,' *v.* wielle. The original name of the Abbey was *Sancta Maria de Divisis*. It was so called because the Abbey demesne lands lay on both sides of Harpers Brook, which here divides Corby and Rothwell Hundreds. Similarly the precincts of the castle of Devizes (W) lay on the boundary of two hundreds. Cf. PN D 128.

RAWHAW WOOD (6″) is *Rahage, Rohawe, Rohawedick* 1143 (1323) Dugd v 434–5, *Rohal'* 1198 P, *Rohawe* c. 1220 For, *Rahaige* 1235 Ch, *Rohaye* t. Ed 1 *PeterbB*, *Rawhawe, Rawhawfelde* 1547 Pat. 'Roe enclosure' or 'enclosed wood,' *v.* ra, haga or hagi. Cf. Roehoe Wood (Nt), *Rahage* 1156 Holtzman, *Pabsturkunden*, 1185 P. The charter of 1143 says with reference to Rawhaw 'et sciendum quod monachi boriales scripserunt in cartis nostris Rahage pro Rohawe.' It is difficult to say how far this difference between northern and local usage depended purely on a difference of dialect, OE long *a* being preserved in Northern English, or how far it may represent a Midland form reflecting Scandinavian influence, and going back to ON *rá-hagi*.

LITTLE HAWS WOOD (6″) is *Litelhawe* c. 1180 *PipewellA*, *Lytle Hawe Coppes* 1547 Pat. *v.* haga. MONK'S ARBOUR WOOD is *Monkes Woodes* 1547 Pat, *Monks Arbor Coppice* 1670 *Clayton*, with reference to the monks of Pipewell.

XV. HUXLOE HUNDRED

Hoches hlawa a. 1076 Geld Roll, *Hocheslau* 1086 DB, *Hokes lawe* 12th Survey *et freq* to 1275 RH, *-lowe* 1280 Ipm, 1316 FA, *Hockeslawe* 1185 RotDom, *Hoggeslawe* 1247 *Ass*
Part of the hundred bore the name of
Navereslund a. 1076 Geld Roll, *Neveslund* 1086 DB

North-, Suthnaveslunt 12th Survey, *Sudnaweslond* 1202 Ass, *Nornaueslond* ib., *Nordnaveslund* 1220 Fees, *Sudnaveslund* ib.

The name of the hundred is '*Hōc*'s hlaw,' i.e. his barrow or hill. Bridges (ii, 246) states that *Huxlow Furlong* and *Huxlow Cross* half-a-mile south-east of Lowick church, were the meeting-place of the hundred. There is still a field called *Huxlow* on the Drayton estate (*ex inf.* Miss J. Wake), and cf. *Huxloe Field* in Islip (1801 *EnclA*). For *Naveslund v.* Navisford *infra* 216.

Addington, Great and Little

ADDINGTON, GREAT and LITTLE 74 G 5

Edintone 1086 DB, *-a* 1131 P (p), *Edintune* 1348 Ch
Addintona 1185–1209 NRS iv, *Netheraddington* 1617 *FF*
Adinton 1189 (1332) Ch *et passim* to 1428 FA with variant spellings *Aden-, Adyn-, Ading-, Adentona* 1197 FF, (*Maiore, Minore*) 1220 Fees, (*Suht*) 1247 *Ass*, (*Major, Parva*) 1284 FA
Adynton Waterville 1287 *Ass*

'*Eadda*'s farm,' *v.* ingtun. Little Addington is *south* of Great Addington, which in turn is *nether* to Little Addington, in that it is lower down the Nene valley. Hugh de *Waterville* held the manor of Little Addington in 1199 (FF).

SHOOTERS HILL is *Scitershul* 1232 WellsR. This name probably means what it says, and the more correct ME form would be *schetereshul*. Presumably the hill was so called because used for archery practice. Cf. Shooters Hill (K), earlier *Shetereshelde* 1331 *Ass, Sheteresselde* 1374, *Shetereshill* 1394 Pat, in which the second element is OE h(i)elde, 'slope,' and *Schytereshulle* in Easton Neston (1281 AD ii).

Aldwinkle, All Saints and St Peter

ALDWINKLE [ɑ·nikəl] 74 E 6

Aldewincla 11th (13th) PeterbA *et passim* to 1401 Cl with variant spellings *-wyncle, -wincle,* and *Aude-, Aldevincle* 1086 DB
Eldewincle 1086 DB

Aldewingel c. 1150 (1137 E) ASC
Alewinca 1162 P, *Alwynkell* 1539 LP, *Alwinkle* 1664 StJ
Aldewencle 1178 P, 1294 *Ass*
Aldwyncle 1317 Cl, *-wincle* 1346 FA
Oldwincle 1614 *FF*

The second element is OE wincel, 'corner,' with reference to the big bend in the course of the Nene here. The first must be the OE pers. name *Ealda*, the name of its one-time owner.

BRADSHAW WOOD (6″) is *Bradehauw* 1293 *For*, *Bradyhawe* 1540 LP. 'Broad enclosure,' *v.* brad, haga.

BRANCEY BRIDGE (6″) is *Brantsey* 1488 Pat, *Brantsy* 1513 LP. This is '*Brant*'s island' (*v.* eg), cf. Braunston *supra* 15. The island is formed by the twofold course of the Nene here.

LYVEDEN, OLD and NEW

Louenden 1175 P (p), *Luueden(e)* 1178 P (p), 1230 P
Lieueden' 1179 P (p), *Leueden(e)* 1181 P (p), 1285 *Ass*, 1287
   For, *Leyndone* 1326 Cl
Liveden(e) 1220 Fees *et passim* with variant spelling *Lyve-*,
   (*Over, Nether*) 1398 Cl, *-denne* 1347 Cl, *Lyvedene Pottere*
   1285 *Ass*, *Pottereslivedene* 1312 FF, *-lyvedene* 1344 BM,
   Lifden 1622 *Recov*
Lyvendene 1253 *Ass*, 1255 Seld 13, 1261 *Ass* (p)

'*Lēofa*'s valley,' *v.* denu. For *Pottereslyveden* we may perhaps compare Potterspury *supra* 105.

SOUTHER WOOD is *Suthauwe* 1286 *For*, *Southawe, Sowthhay* 1491, 1506 Ipm. *v.* haga.

LADY WOOD is *Ladywood* 1540 LP. LANG HILL LODGE is *Langehull* t. Ed 1 PeterbB, *Langhul* 1286, *-hil* 1337 *For*. 'Long hill.' GREAT SALE WOOD. For *sale v.* Britain Sale *supra* 156.

Barnwell All Saints

BARNWELL ALL SAINTS[1] 74 D 7

(*æt*) *Byrnewilla(n)* c. 980 (12th) BCS 1130
Bernewell(e) 1060 (1350) KCD 809, 1086 DB *et passim* to
   1424 AD iii

---

[1] Barnwell St Andrew is in the hundred of Polebrook.

Beornwelle 1077 (13th) ChronRams
Bernwell 1322 Ipm
Kyngesbernewell(e) 1344 Pat, 1353 Ipm

The spelling in the first form shows the same substitution of *y* for *e* that we find in Helpston *infra* 236, and we must take the correct form of the name to be *Beornewelle*, later *Bernewelle*. The interpretation may be 'warriors' spring' from OE *beorna-wielle*. *beorn* is only used in poetic texts in OE, but since this is an important settlement in the Nene valley, we may take it to be of early origin, made at a time when the word *beorn* may well have been still in ordinary use. We may note other compounds of *beorn* in Barnhill in the East Riding of Yorkshire, *Beornhyll* (BCS 1052), and Barnham (Sf), *Byornham* c. 1000 AS Wills. See further Barnack *infra* 230. Skeat (PN C 36 *s.n.* Barnwell) would prefer to assume a pers. name *Beorna*, from the same stem, a pet-form of one or other of the OE names in *Beorn-*. This might suit Barnwell, but will not suit Barnhill or Barnham. Bridges (ii, 392) writes 'About the town are seven or eight wells, from which, and the custom of dipping *Bernes* or children in them, the town is supposed to be denominated.' The form of the OE word for 'child' is, however, *bearn*, and would have given *Barn-* and not *Bern-* in ME. The manor was held by the king in 1086.

BARNWELL WOLD. Cf. *le Woldfeld* c. 1230 *Buccleuch, le Waldfeld, Waldesdale* 14th *Deed, Barnwell Wold* c. 1825 O.S. *v.* weald.

Barton Seagrave

BARTON SEAGRAVE 74 F 2

> *Berton(e)* 1086 DB, 1166, 1194 P, 1200 Cur
> *Barton(e)* 1179 P *et passim, Northbarton'* 1242 Fees, 1303 AD i, *Barton Haurad* (sic) 1307 Ipm, (*Segrave*) 1321 Ipm, (*by Keteringe*) 1322 Ipm, (*Hanred*) 1372 Cl, 1462 AD iv

v. beretun. William de *Henred* held the manor in 1201 (Cur) and it had passed to Stephen de *Segrave* by 1220 (*FF*). *North* in relation to Earls Barton *supra* 137.

HAYFIELD LODGE is *Hayfeild* 1624 *Clayton*. SOUTHFIELD FM is *the Southfeild* ib.

Burton Latimer

BURTON LATIMER 74 G 3

> *Burton(e)* 1086 DB *et passim*, *-tun'* 1257 Cl, (*juxta Thingden*)
> 1285 *FF*, (*Latymer*) 1482 AD iv, 1512 LP, *Burton Latymer*
> *al. Pryors Manor* t. Hy 8 AD iii
> *Birton'* 1230 P

v. burhtun. William *le Latimer* held the manor in 1280 (Ipm).
The *Prior* of Bradenstoke also held a manor here (VCH iii, 182).

BUCCLEUCH FM (6″). In 1803 the Duke of Buccleuch claimed to
own a manor in Burton Latimer (VCH iii, 183). HARPUR'S
LODGE (6″). The manor of Burton Latimer was purchased by
John *Harpur* in 1760 (VCH iii, 181). BURTON WOLD is referred
to as *super Waldam* 1222 *FF*, *Burton Old* 1631 NRS i, *The
Wolds* 1804 *EnclA*. *v.* weald. For the second form cf. Old
supra 128.

Cranford St Andrew and St John

CRANFORD 74 F 4

> *Craneford* 1086 DB *et passim* to 1332 Ipm, *Cranne-* 1208 Fees
> *Cranford(a)* c. 1150 (1267) Ch *et passim* with occasional
> spelling *Craun-*, *Esseby Cranford* 1242 Fees
> *Cramford* 1205 Cur, 1214 ClR
> *Graneford* 1314 Cl
> *Cranesford* 1328 Cl

'Crane(s') or herons' ford.' Cf. Cranford (Mx). *Esseby* from
the holding of Wm de *Esseby* (1248 Cl).

FREER WOOD is *Freierwood* 1648 BM. KIRTLEY BARN (6″). Cf.
Curtley Field in Slipton (1771 *EnclA*), and *Carkley Lane* 1823 B.
SALE HILL WOOD (6″) is so named in 1823 B. For *sale v.* Britain
Sale *supra* 156.

Denford

DENFORD 74 G 6

> *Deneford(e)* 1086 DB *et passim* to 1428 FA
> *Danefort* c. 1150 St Werb
> *Denford* 1241 Cl, 1346 FA
> *Derneford* 1241 P (p), 1249 Cl (p)
> *Doneford* 1275 RH

'Ford in the valley,' *v.* denu. Denford lies in a small valley. The forms with *derne*, as if from ME *derne*, 'hidden,' are probably errors.

DENFORD ASH. This estate probably covers the area known as *le Wolde* 1325 Ipm and as *Denford Wold* as late as 1791 (Bridges ii, 185). Cf. Barnwell Wold *supra* 179 and Ashton Wold *infra* 210.

Finedon

FINEDON [findǝn] 74 H 3

> *Tingden(e)* 1086 DB *et freq* to 1274 RH with variant spelling *Tyng-*
> *Tindena, -e* 1167 P (p) *et freq* to 1241 Cl, *Thynden* 1281 Cl
> *Thingden(e)* 12th Survey *et passim* to 1363 Cl with variant spelling *Thyng-*
> *Tingdon* 1247 *Ass, Thingdon* 1302 Ipm, 1318 Ipm, 1702 Poll, *-doun* 1396 Cl
> *Fyndon* t. Jas 1 ECP, (*Thingdon al.*) 1606 *Recov, Thindon al. Thingdon al. Finedon* 1685 ib., *Finedon al. Thingden* 1719 ib.

'Valley where the "thing" assembled,' *v.* þing, denu. The earlier form of the name survives in THINGDON MINES. Bridges (ii, 250) tells us that the place is in common pronunciation *Findon*, showing that the vowel should be short.

DEBDALE GROVE (6″) is *pastura de Depdale* 1423 *AddCh.* 'Deep valley.' Cf. Debdale *supra* 119. FINEDON BRIDGE (6″) is *pontem de Tyngdene* 1275 RH, *Findinge Bridge* 1657 NRS i. FINEDONHILL FM was perhaps the home of Matilda *super montem* (t. Ed 3 *SR*). RYEBURY HILL is *Reberg* 1222 *FF, Ryeborough* 1808 *EnclA. v.* beorg and cf. Ryehill Fm *supra* 66. WESTFIELD LODGE is *Westfeld* 14th *NthStA.*

Grafton Underwood

GRAFTON UNDERWOOD 74 E 3

> *Grastone* 1086 DB
> *Grafton(e)* 1166 P *et passim,* (*juxta Craneford*) 1335 *Ass,* (*juxta Keteryng*) 1342 *FF,* (*Underwode*) 1367 *Ass,* (*by*

Geydyngton) 1398 Cl, (*by Warton*, i.e. Warkton) 1449 Ch, *Grafton al. Grafton Underwood* 1708 *Recov*

Crofton 1205 ClR

'Grove farm,' *v.* grafa, tun. It lies near Rockingham Forest.

GRAFTON PARK WOOD and PARK FM (6"). Cf. *Grafton Park* 1449 Ch, *Graftonwodys* ib. Simon Symeon was granted licence to impark his wood of Grafton in 1348 (Pat). OLD HEAD WOOD is so named in 1823 B, and nearby are also marked *Wold Coppice* and *Warkton Wold*. The meaning may have been 'wood at the head or end of the "wold,"' *v.* Old *supra* 128.

Irthlingborough

IRTHLINGBOROUGH[1] [ɑˑtəlbərə], [jɑˑtəlbərə] 74 H 4

Yrtlingaburg 780 BCS 1334, *Yrtling Burch* 1125–8 Chron Petro

Erdi(n)burne 1086 DB

Irtlingburg 12th Survey, *Irtelingburg'* 1221 *FF et passim* to 1428 FA with variant spellings *Irtling-, -lyng-, -burgh*, *Yrthlingburc* 1212 Cur, *Irklingburg'* 1253 FF, *Iretelingburgh'* 1330 QW, *Irtlinge-* 1341 Ipm

Hirtlingaburch 1125–8 ChronPetro, 13th *PeterbA*, *Hyrtling-beri* 1137 (12th) ASC (E), *Hirdlingburc* 1241 P (p), *Hirtling-buri* 1274 Ipm, *Hertlingburge* 1285 FA

Ur(t)ling(e)burc(h) 1175, 1180 P, *Urtliburc* 1200 Cur, *Hurt-ling(e)burc* 1203, 1204 Cur, *Urtlingburg* 1214 FineR

Ertlinburg' 1205 Cur, *Ertelingburg* 1275 Cl, *Ertlingeburgh* 1287 *FF*

Irthyngborough 1428 FA

Artilburgh 1469 Pat, 1500 ECP, *Artleborowe al. Arteling-brough* 1583 *Recov*, *Irtlingborough al. Artleborough* 1616 ib., *Artleborough* 1651 StJ

Arthelborow, Athlingborough 1612 *FF*

This is a difficult name. It is clearly a name of an early type, and it would seem that *Yrtlinga-* must go back to earlier Ger-

---

[1] In a *Rental* of c. 1400 we have mention of *le Kirklane*, i.e. 'the church lane,' the form showing Scandinavian influence as in Peakirk *infra* 241. Other street-names mentioned in the same document are *le Personeslane*, i.e. 'the parson's lane' and *Flexmongerisplace* where the sellers of flax congregated.

manic *Urtilinga-. No name stem Urt- is known, but it may be
noted that in Sussex (v. PN Sx 483 s.n. Wartling) we have in
three or four place-names evidence of a pers. name Wyrtel,
which would seem to be a derivative of wyrt, 'root.' Corresponding to this *wurti stem, there seems to have been a Germanic side-form *urti, which gave rise to Gothic aurtigards,
OE ortgeard. It may be suggested that from this form arose a
pers. name *Urtila or Yrtla. Hence, 'burh of the sons of
Yrtla.'[1]

DITCHFORD MILL is Dichesford 1235 Fees, Digeford ib., Dich(e)-
ford 1242 Fees, 1327 Ipm, 1330 FA, molendinum de Dycheford
1253 Ass, Dickford Mulnes 1282 Abbr, Dikfordebrigg 1292 Compotus. 'Ford by the dic,' possibly one of the subsidiary courses
of the Nene at this point.

IRTHLINGBOROUGH BRIDGE (6″) is Artelburrough bridge 1591
DuLaMiscBks.

Islip

ISLIP [aizlip] 74 F 5

> Is slepe, Hyslepe c. 980 (c. 1200) BCS 1130
> Islep, Slepe 1086 DB
> Islep(e) 1175 P (p) et passim to 1316 FA with variant spelling
> Ys-
> Hystlapa 1190 P (p), Ystlapa 1191 P (p), Istlepe 1247 Ass,
> Ystlepe 1273 Swaffham
> Islape 1205 Cur, 1242 Fees, Isalop 1205 Cur
> Isselep(e) c. 1220 WellsR, (juxta Thrapston) 1317 Ass
> Itheslepe c. 1220 WellsR, Itteslep' 1253 Ipm
> Hislep 1241 P, Islip 1275 RH, 1346 FA
> Eslep 1284 FA, Iselep 1294 Ass, 1331 Cl

The second element in this name is clearly OE slæpe, 'slippery
place,' referring to the hill which slopes down sharply to the
Nene. It is difficult to suggest any solution of the name if we
take the initial sound to be Is-. If it is His-, as some of the
earliest forms suggest, we may take it that the first element is

[1] Karlström (99) suggests possible association with Orlingbury, but the
phonetic difficulties, which he himself mentions, are insuperable. He also
suggests the possibility of an alternative name for the Nene as explaining the
name, but one can hardly get round the difficulty in that way.

OE *hys(s)e*, 'young man, warrior,' again a word which like the *beorn* of Barnwell *supra* 178 is only found in poetic texts, but which at an early date may have been in common prose use. Hence 'slippery hill of the young men or warriors.' For other possible occurrences of this term in place-names *v.* Husborne Crawley (PN BedsHu 118).

Professor Ekwall would take the *Is*-forms to be the correct ones, and suggests that at some time in its history the Nene may have been known at this point by the name of its important tributary the Ise (*v. supra* 3) which joins it a few miles farther north. Cf. the history of Leicester (RN xlii), which probably takes its name from the tributary *Legra* (on which stands Leire), whose name was transferred to the main river Soar on which Leicester itself stands. In that case the name would mean 'slippery bank of the Ise river.'

Kettering

KETTERING[1] 74 F 2

to, æt Cytringan 956 (c. 1200) BCS 943, *Kyteringas* 972 (c. 1200) BCS 1280

Keteiringan c. 965 (c. 1200) BCS 1128

Ketering 963 (12th) BCS 1281 *et passim* to 1347 Cl with variant spellings -*yng*, -*ynge*, -*inge*, -*ingge*

Keteringes 11th (13th) *PeterbA*, 1125–8 ChronPetro, 1227 Ch

Cateringe 1086 DB, *Kateringes* 1125–8 ChronPetro, 13th *PeterbA*

Ketterynge 1557 AD vi

Ketreyng, Ketren 1657 NRS i[2]

---

[1] BCS 943 is a grant by King Edwy of land at Kettering. The boundary runs from 'Cransley bridge,' i.e. presumably the point where the Northampton road crosses the brook which divides Kettering from Cransley. It then goes along the *burna* to *Hunan bricg*, i.e. the next bridge upstream, where the boundary leaves the stream and goes north-east to Warren Hill, where perhaps stood the next boundary mark, viz. the *galhtreow* or gallows tree, to Debdale *supra* 119. From Debdale to *Cynestanes heafod*, which is probably the northernmost point of the parish. Thence to the long *dic* and from the *dic* to Weekley ford, i.e. by Weekley Mill, thence along the Ise to Pytchley ford, i.e. by Pytchley Lodge, thence along the brook, i.e. the tributary stream here, to Cransley Bridge.

[2] NEWLAND ST. Cf. *le Newelond* in 1292 (*Compotus*) and Newland in Northampton *supra* 7.

No explanation of this name can be offered. It would seem to contain the same word or name as the first element in Ketteringham (Nf).

LINKS LODGE (6″) is *The Lynches* 1587 *Map*, *the Linkes, the Lyncks* 1603 DKR 38. *v.* hlinc. NORTHALL (6″) is *Northolde* 1577, *Northall* 1610 NthNQ ii. Possibly 'north wold,' *v.* weald. WADCROFT (6″). Cf. *Wadcroft lane* 1680 NthNQ v. 'croft where woad was grown,' cf. Wadground *supra* 52 and *v. infra* 273. WARREN HILL FM (6″). Cf. *Kettering Warren* 1603 DKR xxxviii.

Lilford-cum-Wigsthorpe

LILFORD 74 D 7

> *Lilleford(e)* 1086 DB *et passim* to 1428 FA, *Lyllford* 1430 AD iv
> *Lillingford* 1205 Cur (p)
> *Lillesford* 1284 FA

> 'Lilla's ford,' *v.* ing.

WIGSTHORPE is *Wykingethorp* 1232 *FF*, *Wykingestorp* 1247 *Ass*, *FF*, -*thorp* 1253 *FF*, 1330 *Ass*, *Wygingestorp* 1278 Cl (p), *Wikingisthorp* c. 1300 *PeterbA*, *Wykinsthorp* 1337 *Ass*, *Wigisthorp* 1428 *FF*, *Wigstroppe* 1624 *Recov*. The first element is the ON *Víkingr*, 'Viking,' here probably used as a pers. name. Cf. Great Wigston (Lei) *Wichingestone* DB and Wiganthorpe (PN NRY 35).

Lowick

LOWICK [louik], [lʌfik] 74 E 5

> *Ludewic, Luhwic* 1086 DB
> *Lufuuich* c. 1137 NRS iv *et passim* to 1376 Cl with variant spellings -*wik*, -*wyk*, *Luffwyc* 1248 WellsR
> *Luffewyk* c. 1148 (1348) Ch *et freq* to 1401 Cl with variant spellings -*wich*, -*wik*, -*hic* 1275 RH
> *Hluwic* 1163 P (p), *Luwic* ib. (CR)
> *Lofwyc* 12th Survey *et freq* to 1385 Ch with variant spelling -*wik*
> *Lowike* 1262 Ipm, *Louwyke* 1284 FA, 1307 Ipm

Luffik, -ic 1275 RH
Loufwyk, Lughwyk 1305 *Ass, Lughwyk* 1344 *Ass*
Luffweke 1517 DBE, *Luffwick al. Lowick* 1604 *Recov*
Luffwick 1702 Poll, 1779 F, (*or Lowick*) 1823 B, *Luffwick,
  commonly called Lowick* 1791 Bridges

This is a difficult name, but comparison with the forms of
Loughton (PN Bk 20) suggests that we have the personal name
Luha, recorded from the 10th cent. The forms of Loughton
show that an original *Luhingtun* might, already in the 12th
cent., appear as *Lufton*. The spellings with *Luffe-* are probably
due to the influence of the names like Luffenham (R) containing the personal name *Luffa*. Hence '*Luh(h)a*'s wic or
farm.'

BULLICKS WOOD (6″)

Bulex c. 1220 *For*, 1252 Seld 13, *Bolex* 1286 *For*, 1315 *Fine*,
  1345 *For*
Bolax 1245, 1247 Seld 13, 1258, 1283 Cl, 1314 Ipm, *Bulax*
  1249 Seld 13, 1254 *For*, 1272 Seld 13, 1337 *For*
Boleax c. 1300 *For*, t. Ed 1 *PeterbA*, *-hax* 1290 Ipm
Bolleax 1326 Cl, *Bollax* 1347 Ipm
Bullwick's Wood 1771 *EnclA*

There can be little doubt that the second element in this name
is the OE word **etsce, *ætsce*, discussed under Cleeve Axe
(PN Sx 511). One sense of that word (ME *axe, exe*) seems to be
'pasture.' The first element is OE *bula*, 'bull,' and the whole
name would mean 'bull pasture.' The second element may repeat
itself in *Exhawe* (1249 *For*) which was immediately adjacent, and
perhaps in Excellent *supra* 162. Further examples of this element have now been noted in Surrey, viz. Mapledrake in
Ewhurst, *Mapeldresshe* 1241 *Ass* (p), *Holdemabiltrix, Olde
Mapuldriks* 1436, 1524 (SrRecSoc xxxii, 59–60), in which it is
compounded with the tree-name mapuldor, and possibly in
Longrethenex (1370 AD ii), a field-name in Camberwell.

DRAYTON HO is *Drayton* 12th Survey *et passim* with variant
spelling *Drai-*, (*by Lufwyk*) 1363 AD iii, *Dreyton* 1273 Fine,
1352 Cl, *Draton* 1346 FA. *v.* dræg, tun, and cf. Drayton *supra* 20
and Addenda lii.

LONG LOWN WOOD is *la Lund* 1232 *FF*, *(le)* 1261 *FF*, *The Long Lawne* c. 1650 *Clayton*, *Long Lounds* c. 1825 O.S. This is ON lundr, 'grove, small wood.' *Long* to distinguish from Round Lown *infra* 188. In early times the two copses doubtless formed one wood.

TITCHMARSH WOOD is so called c. 1650 (*Clayton*). John Lovel of *Tychemersh* (Titchmarsh *infra* 221) held the manor in 1314 (Ipm).

Slipton

SLIPTON 74 F 4

> *Slipton(e)* 1086 DB *et passim* with variant spelling *Slyp-Sclipton'* 1166 P (CR), 1237 Cl, *Scilpton* 1348 Cl, *Clipton* 1428 FA
> *Sliptun* 1199 FF

The first element here may be the word *slip* used of mud or slime in the *Promptorium* (c. 1440), and have reference to the soil here. Cf. also Slipe Fm *infra* 239. Another alternative is to take it as containing the same word *slipe* found in Slipe Fm (PN Sx 280), and denoting strip of land. Cf. *slipe infra* 273. v. tun.

BARROW HILL COPSE (6″) is *Barrow Hill Coppice* 1771 *EnclA*. EKENS'S COPSE (6″) is *Ekin's Coppice* ib.

Sudborough

SUDBOROUGH 74 E 5

> *Suthburhc* 1065 BM, *-burg(a)* 1209–18 WellsR, 1236, 1275 Cl, *Suthburi* 1284 FA
> *Sutburg* 1086 DB, *Suht-* 1247 *Ass*
> *Sudburc* 1168 P, *-burgh* 1293 Cl, 1317 Ch *et freq*
> *Subroc* 1200 Cur, *Subburg'* 1249 Cl

'The south burh.' *South* perhaps with reference to Brigstock to the north.

CAT'S HEAD LODGE is *Cattesheuyd'* 1251 Seld 13, *-heved* c. 1300 *For*, *Chattesheved* t. Ed 1 *PeterbA*, *Cat(t)eshed* 1345, 1374 *For*. The reason for the name is unknown.

Assart's Coppice (6"). Cf. Assart Fm *supra* 106. Oxen Wood. Cf. *Oxenhawe* t. Ed 1 *PeterbA*. *v*. haga. Round Lown Wood (6") is *Round Lounds* c. 1825 O.S. This is ON lundr, 'grove,' *v*. Long Lown *supra* 187. Snapes Wood. Cf. *le Snape* t. Ed 1 *PeterbB*, 1293 *For, Snape's Close* 1684 *Terrier*, and Snaplands (PN Sx 28), the reference probably being to the marshy character of the ground. Sudborough Green Lodges is *Sudburgh grene* 1540 LP.

Twywell

Twywell[1] 74 F 4

> *Twiwel* 1013 (14th) KCD 1308, *Twiwell(e)* 1017–25 (14th) *Thorney et passim* with variant spelling *Twy-, Tuiwella* 1086 DB, *Twywell* 1235 Cl, *Tuwywell* 1384 Cl
>
> *Tevwelle* 1086 DB
>
> *Toewella* 1094–1100 NRS iv, *Thiwell* 1198 P, *Tywell* 1230 P, 1275 RH, *Tyuewell* 1235 Fees, *Tweywell* 1438 *FF*
>
> *Tuwella* 1163 P, *Tiwella* ib. (CR)

'Double spring' or 'double stream.' There are several springs here and there is also a double stream to the east of the village. *v*. twi, wielle. Cf. *Twowelles* in Islip (1203 *FF*).

Warkton

Warkton [wɔ·ktən] 74 F 3

> *Werchintone* 1086 DB, *-kin-* 1176 P, *-kene-* 1228 Cl
>
> *Wercheton* 1166 P (p), *-ke-* 12th Survey *et passim* to 1386 Cl, *Werkestone* 1233 WellsR, *Verketon* 1248 Seld 15
>
> *Warton* 1449 Ch

There is ample evidence for OE pers. names *Weorc, Weorce*,

---

[1] KCD 1308 is a grant by Æthelred of land at Twywell. The text is a bad one. There is another text in the *Red Book of Thorney* (f. 15) which reads *nafrys* for *nafrist*, *ðrawoldeswelle* for *-wel*. The boundaries run along *nafrysbroc* to *ðrawoldeswelle*, then up the *slæd* or valley to the *garan* (i.e. the gores) and from the gores to the *mere* and from the *mere* up to *ealles* (? *ealde*) *herestræte*. *nafrysbroc* must be the nameless stream forming the southern boundary of Twywell. *ðrawoldeswelle* is presumably the tiny stream which joins *nafrys broc* at the point where the Twywell boundary leaves it. The boundary follows this tiny stream, up a shallow valley to a triangular projection (i.e. the gore), and goes round it. The *mere* may be the pool by BM 266, 3. The *herestræt* is the Thrapston Road.

and *Weorca*. Cf. Warkworth (PN NbDu 207) and Walkwood (PN Wo 321). Hence, '*Weorc(a)*'s farm,' *v.* ingtun.

ACRELAND FM is perhaps identical with *Hakermanislond* 1299, *Akermanyslond*, *Akermanlond* 1480 *Ct*. The first element is the ME occupational surname *Acreman*, *Akerman*.

WARKTON BRIDGE (6″) is *Warktonbridge* t. Eliz *Ct*. The medieval bridge was a few yards to the east.

Woodford

WOODFORD 74 G 5

Wodeford 1086 DB *et passim* to 1353 Cl with variant spelling
   W(u)de-, (*juxta Trapston*) 1294 *Ass*, *Woddeford* 1403 AD v

Self-explanatory.

HILL HO (6″) was the home of Henry *atte Hil* (t. Ed 3 *SR*).

XVI. HIGHAM FERRERS HUNDRED

Hehham a. 1076 Geld Roll, *Hecham* 1086 DB, *v. infra* 191.

Bozeat

BOZEAT [bouʒət] 84 C 3

Bosiet(e) 1086 DB, 1216 ClR, 1284 FA
Bosegete c. 1155 BM, *Bosgieta* c. 1180 BM
Bosiate 1162 P, 1200 FineR, 1294 Cl, *Bosiath* 1201 Scot,
   Bosehate 1235 Fees
Basegata 1194 P, *Bosegate* 1209–35 WellsR, 1211 Scot, 1285
   Fine, 1298 Ipm, *Bosigate* 1220 Fees
Bosesete 12th Survey, *Boseyete* 1216 ClR
Boseyate 12th Survey *et freq* to 1397 Cl with variant spelling
   -iate
Bosyat(e) 1246 Ch *et freq* to 1389 Cl with variant spelling
   -iat(e), *Boceyate* 1346 Pat
Bosezate 1325 Ipm, *Boszate* 1428 FA
Bosgate 1526 SR, *Bozeatt al. Bosgate* 1632 *Recov*

This is '*Bosa*'s gate' with the same pers. name noted in Bozenham *supra* 100. *v.* geat. There seems to have been considerable hesitation between *yate* and *gate* in the second element. Cf. Pilsgate *infra* 231.

DUNGEE BARN is *Dytchfeild al. Dungiefeild* 1602 *Spencer*. This takes its name from the adjacent Dungee Fm (PN BedsHu 33). STOCKING HOLLOW (6″) is *Bosyate Stoking* 1550 Pat. *v.* stocking.

Chelveston-cum-Caldecott

CHELVESTON [tʃelsən] 74 J 6

> *Celuestone* 1086 DB
> *Chelveston(e)* 1206 Cur *et passim* with variant spelling -*vis*-
> *Chelfiston* 1262 Ipm
> *Cheston(e)* 1461 Pat, 1675 Ogilby
> *Chelston al. Chelneston* (sic) t. Jas 1 ECP, *Chelston* 1779 F,
>   1823 B
> *Chelveston al. Chelston* 1689 *Recov*

'Farm of *Cēolf* or *Cēolwulf*,' *v.* tun and cf. Chelston (So), KCD 816 *Ceolfestun*.

CALDECOTT is *Caldecote* 1086 DB *et passim*, *Caude-* 1234 Cl, -*cotes* 1269 *FF*, *Calcote* 1461 Pat, *Caucot* 1675 Ogilby, *Caldecott al. Calcott* 1689 *Recov*. 'Cold cottages,' *v.* ceald, cot(e).

Easton Maudit

EASTON MAUDIT 84 C 2

> *Estun* 656 (12th) ASC (E), 1239 Ch
> *Eston(e)* 1086 DB *et passim* to 1389 Cl
> *Estonemaudeut* 1298 *FF*, *Estonmauduyt* 1377 Cl
> *Estone juxta Boseyate* 1305 *Ass*
> *Esson Mawdett* 1611 *Rental*

'East farm,' *v.* tun. *East* perhaps with reference to Denton and Whiston. John *Maled* (Latin *Maledoctus*) held the manor in 1166 (P), the family-name being also spelt *Mauduit* (1242 Fees), *Maudut* (1268 Ipm).

HORN WOOD is *Hurnewod(e)* c. 1220, 1287 *For*, -*wud* 1228, 1246 Cl, *Hirnewode* 1253 Pat, *Hernewod(e)* 1255 BM, 1287 *For*, *Hornewod* 1287 *For*, *le Abbottes Hornewood* 1550 Pat. It lies in a corner (*v.* **hyrne**) of the parish, hence probably the name. The Abbey of St James, Northampton, held land in Easton Maudit (1316 FA). Bridges (ii, 163) speaks of "Abbat's *Hall-Wood,* now corruptly *Hornwood,*" but the corruption is clearly the other way round.

Hargrave

HARGRAVE [ha·greiv] 74 H 7

> *Haregrave* 1086 DB *et passim* to 1330 FA, *-graf* 1282 Fine
> *Heregrave* 1086 DB, 1282 Ipm
> *Haragrava* 1125–8 ChronPetro, 1229 WellsR, *-ve* 1227 *FF*
> *Hargrave* 1242 Fees
> *Hordegrave* 1526 SR, *Hardgrave* 1535 VE

Possibly 'hare grove,' *v.* grafa, though as the parish is on the Beds-Hunts border it is more likely to be 'boundary grove,' *v.* har. Cf. Harragrove PN D 233, Hargrave in Bockenhill (Wa) where three parishes meet, and Hargrave Barn in Sapperton (Gl), by the parish boundary.

Higham Ferrers

HIGHAM FERRERS 74 J 5

> *Hecham* 1086 DB with the same run of forms as for Cold
>   Higham *supra* 91 except for:
> *Hekham* 1247 *Ass, Heccham Ferrar'* 1279 Cl, *Heccam Fereres*
>   late 13th BM, *Hegham Ferrers* 1300 Ch
> *Higham Ferys* 1517 DBE, *Higham Ferries* or *Higham Ferrers*
>   1675 Ogilby, *Higham Ferries* 1702 Poll

'High ham.' The town stands high above the Nene valley. The family of *Ferrers* are first mentioned in connection with the place in 1166 (RBE), when the Comes de *Ferariis* held the manor. For the history of the manorial addition *v. Complete Peerage* iv, 195.

BUSCOTT'S MEADOW (field) is *Britwinescote* late 13th BM, *Brywynscott* 1611 *Recov, Brytwynscott* 1618 *FF.* 'cot(e) of *Brihtwine* (*Beorhtwine*).' For the modern form cf. Buscombe (PN D 61).

HIGHAM PARK. This was a detached part of the manor some miles to the south. It is earliest referred to as *parco de Hecham* in 1167 P.

DUCHY FM (6″). The manor of Higham Ferrers belongs to the Duchy of Lancaster. NORTH END is *le North Ende* 1543 LP. SAFFRON MOAT (6″). Cf. *Saffron Yard* 1564 VCH iii, 269. WARMONDS HILL is *Warmanshill* 1549 VCH iii, 266.

Irchester

IRCHESTER [ɑ·tʃestə] 84 A 4

Yranceaster 973 (c. 1250) BCS 1297

Hirecestre 1086 DB, *Hirencestre* 1205 Pap

Irencestre 1086 DB, 1109–22 (1356) Ch *et passim* to 1428 FA with variant spellings *Yren-*, *Yrin-* 1200 Cur, 1248 Ch, *Irin-* 1227 *FF*, 1289 Cl

Irecestre 1167 P (p), 1203 Cur, 1242 Fees, 1316 Ch, 1339 *FF*

Irnecestre 1261 *Ass*, *Irncestre* 1270 *Ass*, 1327 Ipm

Irrencestre 1290 Cl, 1306 *FF*

Irchestre 1291 *Ass*, *Irchester al. Irenchester* 1565 *Recov*

Ircestre 1330 FA, 1346 Pat

Archestre 1503 Ipm, *Archester* 1510 *FF*, 1712 Morton

Erchester 1657 NRS i

Axchester 1675 Ogilby

The only suggestion which can be made for this name is that put forward in the VCH (i, 180), viz. that the first element is the pers. name *Ira*, the name of a sometime owner of the site. The name is not on record in OE except as that of a moneyer of Ethelred II, and there it may well be an Anglo-Scandinavian name denoting a Viking from Ireland.

CHESTER HO is *Cestre* 1236 Fees *et freq* to 1428 FA, (*at Irencestre*) 1247 *Ass*, (*Parva*) 1284 FA, *Littlecestre* 1327 Ipm, *Cestre juxta aquam* 1339 *FF*, *Cestresourleyewe* 1378 AD vi. *ch*-forms appear as follows: *Chestre juxta Higham Ferrers* 1316 Inq aqd, *Chestrebethewatre* 1357 Cl, *Chestre-on-the-water* 1369 AD iv, *Chesterbythewater* 1494 *FF*. This is the Roman settlement which gave name to Irchester itself (*v*. ceaster). The place lies by the Nene and *sourleyewe* answers to Modern French *sur l'eau*.

KNUSTON [nʌstən]

Cnutestone 1086 DB

Knoston 12th Survey *et freq* to 1517 DBE with variant spelling *Cnos-*, *Gnoston* 1274 Cl

Cnoteston 1220 Fees, *Cnotston, Knotteston* 1247 FineR
Nuston 1730 Poll

This is '*Cnut*'s farm,' *v.* tun. Cf. Knowstone (PN D 340).

WYMINGTON SPINNEY (6"). Cf. *Wymmington hedg corner* 1591
DuLaMiscBks. It is on the county boundary, taking its name
from Wymington in Beds.

Newton Bromswold

NEWTON BROMSWOLD 84 A 6

Niwetone 1086 DB *et passim* with variant spellings *New(e)-,*
Neu-, Newton Bromsholde 1605 *Buccleuch*
Neuuenton(e) 1086 DB *et freq* to 1333 *FF* with variant
spellings *Niwen-, Newen-, Newin- (juxta Hegh(h)am*
Ferer(e)s) 1309 *Ass*, 1333 *FF*, *Neunton* 1329 Ch, 1428 FA
Newenton al. Newton Bromswolde al. Newnton juxta Higham
Parke 1639 *Recov*

'New farm,' *v.* tun. Bridges (ii, 183) remarks with regard to
the addition *Bromswold* that for that appellation we can give no
certain reason. That may be true so far as its late appearance is
concerned, but the history of the name itself can to some extent
be cleared up. There is a Bromswold eight to ten miles to the
N.E., in Huntingdonshire, in the parish of Leighton Bromswold
(PN BedsHu 245, 250). We may note further that Lutton in
Northamptonshire (*infra* 204) is spoken of as on and as near
Brouneswold. This place is some eight miles north of Leighton
Bromswold, and this distribution of the three references to
Bromswold suggests that it covered a wide area. This is confirmed
by the only other records of the name that have been noted.
Gaimar in his *Lestorie des Engles*, ll. 5548–54, tells us that when
Hereward left Huntingdonshire, seven hundred men followed
him to *Bruneswald*, and, soon after, he assaulted Peterborough.
In the *Gesta Herewardi* as printed in the Rolls edition of Gaimar
(i, 392), we read that Hereward escaped to the *Bruneswald* and
into the great forests of Northampton. These last passages indicate clearly that *Bromswold* or *Brownswold* was originally a
large area, probably of woodland, on the borders of Huntingdonshire and Northamptonshire. It seems to have included

Leighton, Lutton and Newton within its borders. The name means the 'weald of a man named *Brūn*,' with that gradual transition of sense in the word weald from woodland to open country, which is discussed in EPN *s.v.*

Raunds

RAUNDS [rɑ·ns] 74 H 6

(*æt*) *randan* c. 980 (1200) BCS 1130

Rande 1086 DB *et freq* to 1316 FA with variant spellings *Raund(e)*, *Randa*

Raundes 12th Survey *et passim* with variant spellings *Randes*, *Raunds*

Rawns 1442 Pat, *Rawnes* 1570 Recov, *Raundes al. Rawnes* 1651 ib., *Rance* 1712 Morton

This is OE (*æt þæm*) *randum*, 'at the borders or edges,' *v.* rand. Presumably the place was so called because it lay on the eastern edge of the county. The name of the local marble, *Rance Rag*, preserves the old pronunciation of the name.

COTTON CAMP[1] (6″). This is the last trace on the map of more than one manor called *Cotes* or *Cotton* in Raunds and the neighbouring parish of Ringstead. In the 12th century Survey we have mention of *Cotes* and *alia Cotes*, but there were already three distinct holdings. So also in 1275 (RH) we have mention of *Parva Cotes, Media Cotes* and *Cotes*. *Media Cotes* appears as *Middelcot'* (1253 *Ass*), *Middelcotes by Raundes* (1303 Pat), *Middle Cotton* 1571 *FF*. In 1330 (QW) we have mention of *Wylinecotys, Mullecotes* and *Litlecotes*. The last is the *Parva Cotes* of 1275. *Mullecotes* is first mentioned as *Milnecotes* (1312 *FF*), later *Milnecoten* (1317 *Ass*), *Mulne Cotes al. Chamberleincotes* (1408 IpmR), *Mill Cotton grene* (1591 *DuLaMiscBks*). It was clearly by a mill (*v.* myln), and it had once belonged to the *Chamberlein* family (cf. 1291 Ipm). *Wylewynecotes* is first mentioned in 1307 Ipm, *Wylewenecotes* 1314 Ipm, *Wellewenecotes* 1330 *PeterbA*, *Wilwencotes* 1373 IpmR, *Wyllyngcotes* 1423 *FF*, *Wylyenecotes*

---

[1] The camp is not a camp military or otherwise. Excavation has revealed a series of round cottages or dwelling places, rather like medieval dovecotes, the remains apparently of a lost village (*ex inf.* Mr G. V. Charlton and Mr J. A. Gotch).

1434 *FF*, *Willowcotes* 1530 *FF*. This was a holding of Gilbert de Clare, who also held *Middelcotes* (1307 Ipm). It would seem to be 'cottages by the willows,' *v.* **welig**. We have mention also of a *Westcotes juxta Raundes* (1317 *Ass*) and *Cotes juxta Ryngstede* (1330 *Ass*) and a *Cotis Bidun* (1284 FA), so called from the holding of the *Bidun* family (1191 P). Bridges (ii, 190) distinguishes *West Cotton* in Raunds, *Mill Cotton* in Ringstead, and another manor which he calls *Mallows Cotton*.

DARSDALE FM was the home of Gilbert *de Deresdale* (1315 *Ass*). This may be '*Dēor*'s valley,' *v.* **dæl, dalr**, with the same pers. name as in Desborough *supra* 112.

KNIGHTON'S ROW (6″) takes its name from the family of Thomas and George *Knighton* (1650 *ParlSurv*). SCALEY FM. Cf. *Scaley Field* 1800 *EnclA*.

Ringstead

RINGSTEAD 74 G 5

> *Ringsted(e)* 12th Survey *et passim*, -*stude* 1428 Ch
> *Rinsted'* 1202 Ass, 1203 Cur, *Rincsted'* 1242 Fees
> *Ringestede* 1203 Cur *et freq* to 1348 Cl with variant spellings *Ringge-, Rynge-*
> *Renggested* 1337 Cl

'Circular place,' *v.* **hring, stede**. The significance of the name as applied locally is uncertain. Cf. Ringsted (Nf). The latter lies in a large depression but such a depression is not particularly apparent at Ringstead.

Rushden

RUSHDEN [rʌʒdən] 84 A 4

> *Risdene, Risedene* 1086 DB
> *Rissend(en)* 1109–22 (1356) Ch *et freq* to 1316 Ch, *Rysindenne* 1298 Cl
> *Ressenden(e)* 1200 *FF*, 1229 WellsR
> *Russenden* 1205 Cur, 1251 Ch, -*in*- 1248 Ch
> *Rischedeñ* 1222 *FF*, *Rischyndon* 1285 *Ass*, *Rishendon near Hegham* 1288 Cl, *Ryschdeyne* 1391 AD iii
> *Russedene, Ruschinden* early 13th Dunstable
> *Rushedon* 1316 FA, *Russhenden* 1337 Ipm, *Russheden* 1428 FA
> *Rushdowne* 1675 Ogilby

'Rushy valley,' *v.* denu, the first element being an adjective *ryscen* formed from OE rysc. Cf. Rushden (Herts) with a similar run of early spellings.

BENCROFT FM is *Banecroft* 1218 ClR, *Bancroft* 1370 IpmR, *Bencroft* 1779 *EnclA*. 'Bean field,' *v.* croft. A common place-name.

Stanwick

STANWICK [stænik] 74 H 5

Stan wigga 10th (c. 1200) *PeterbA*
Stanwige, Stanewica 1086 DB
Stanwigga 1125–8 ChronPetro *et freq* to 1428 FA with variant spellings *-wigg, -wygg, -wigge, -wygge, Stanwighe* 1140 Sparke
Stanewig 1137 (12th) ASC, *-wigge* 12th Survey *et freq* to 1344 Cl with variant spellings *-wygge, -wigg, -wygg*
Stanewica 1209–18 WellsR, *-wyk* 1285 *Ass*, *-wic cum Newenton* 1316 FA, *-wyk(e)* 1347, 1375, 1400 Cl, 1536 *Recov*
Stanwik 1232 Cl

It may be that this is from OE **stan** and **wic**, hence 'stone farm or village.' From early times the place must have been noted for its quarries, and the houses built of stone rather than any other material. The *wig(g)*- forms are difficult to account for. The only parallels that have been noted are two forms of Winwick *supra* 77, which have *-wyg* for *-wyc* in 1288 (*PeterbA*) and 1428 (FA), and *Blatherwygge* for Blatherwycke in 1391 (Cl), but these forms are comparatively late and sporadic. In Stanwick (PN NRY 296) and Stanwix (Cu) we have a compound of ON steinn and veggr, 'wall,' but these names show persistent *sten-*, *stein-*, *stain-* and *-wegges* in their early forms, showing that they are genuine Scandinavian names, and *-wyk* spellings do not come in before the 15th century. It may be noted, however, that for Stanwick we have forms in *-wigges* from the 13th and 14th centuries. It may be that a genuine OE *stan-wic* was early contaminated by the influence of Scandinavian *veggr*, but it should be noted that the area is not one in which Scandinavian influence was particularly strong.

Strixton

STRIXTON [striksən] 84 B 3

> Strixton(e) 12th Survey *et passim*, *Stricston'* 1202 Ass (p),
> 1275 RH, 1287 *Ass*, *Stricxstone* 1230 WellsR
> *Trikeston* 1247 Misc, *Straxton* 1316 FA, *Strextone* 1323 Ipm
> *Strickson* 1658 StJ

'*Strīc*'s farm,' *v.* tun. For this Anglo-Scandinavian pers. name (ON *Strikr*), cf. *Wulnoth Stricessune* (BCS 1130) from the same district. Bridges (ii, 196) notes that *Stric* was the 'Saxon' holder (TRE) of land in the neighbouring village of Wollaston, and there can be no serious doubt that it was this man who gave his name to Strixton. *Stric* also held land in Bozeat.

Wollaston

WOLLASTON 84 B 3

> *Wilavestone* 1086 DB, *Willeveston* 1219 WellsR
> *Wullauestonia* c. 1150 BM, *Wullaueston* 1190 P *et passim* to
> 1274 RH with variant spellings *Woll-, -av-, Wul-, Wol-,*
> *Wl-, Wulauston* 1226 ClR
> *Wurdlaueston* 1190 P
> *Wolaston* 12th Survey, 1274 RH, 1284 FA, *Wollaston* 1279 Cl

'*Wulflāf*'s farm,' *v.* tun.

HARDWATER MILL (6″) is *molend. de Herdewath'* 1330 *Ass, pons de Hardewath'* c. 1377 Seld 40, *Hardwater mill* 1826 G. The second element in the first two forms looks like OScand vað, 'ford,' but it is difficult to see how *wath* could have developed to *water*, and in the absence of further forms the name must remain unexplained. We may perhaps compare Broxwater (Co), earlier *Froxwade* (1263 FF) where there has clearly been confusion between OE wæd, 'ford' and *water*.

RYEHOLMES BRIDGE is *Ryeholm* 1337 *Ass, Rye holme* 1591 *DuLaMiscBks*. Probably 'the holmr or marshy island where rye grew.'

WOLLASTON MILL (6″) is *molendino de Wulaueston* 1219 *FF*.

XVII. WILLYBROOK HUNDRED

Wilebroc(e) a. 1076 Geld Roll, 1086 DB, 1185 RotDom,
  Willebroc(h) 1179, 1180 P, *Wylebrok* 12th Survey, 1275 RH,
  1330 Ipm
Wilibroc 1086 DB, 1202 Ass, 1224 ClR, *Wilybroc* 1220 Fees,
  Wilibrok 1247 Fees, 1349 Ipm, *Willebybrok* 1330 *Ass*,
  Willibroke 1346 FA
Welybrok 1294 *Ass*, 1316 FA, *Wellebrok* 1322 Ipm

v. Willow Brook *supra* 4. The hundred court was held at
King's Cliffe, by the Willow Brook (VCH ii, 542).

Apethorpe

APETHORPE [æpθɔ·p] 74 H 7

Patorp 1086 DB
Apetorp 1162 P *et passim* with variant spelling *-thorp*
Apeltorp 1166 P, *Appelthorp* 1222 ClR, *Ap(p)eltrop* 1294
  Ass
Appetorp 1166 P (CR) *et freq* to 1442 *FF* with variant
  spelling *-thorp*
Abbetoft 1250 Fees
Apthorp 1281 Fine, 1326 Cl

The first element is probably the ODan, OSw pers. name *Api*
(cf. Nielsen 5, ZEN 13), hence '*Api*'s village,' *v.* þorp. There is
an *Apperup* in Denmark. Cf. also Abterp (*Sønderjyske Stednavne* 408). Some forms have been influenced by the common
word *apple*.

HALEFIELD LODGE is *Hala* 1086 DB, 1178 P, *Hale* 1185 RotDom
et passim, *Suthale* 1275 RH, *Halefeld* 1367 *For*, *Hale or Hale fee*
1760 *Recov*. 'Nook or corner of land,' *v.* healh, feld.

BLUE FIELD LODGE. Cf. *Blue Ffield* 1773 *EnclA*, *Blue Field
Coppice* 1787 Woods Rept. BUSHRUBS WOOD (6″) is *Buchscrub*
c. 1220 *For*, *Bushrobs* 1614, *Bush Shrubs* 1642 Woods Rept, a
compound of 'bush' and 'shrub.' TOMLIN WOOD is *Tomlyns-
wood* 1557 Woods Rept.

King's Cliffe

KING'S CLIFFE 64 J 6

> *Clive* 1086 DB *et passim* to 1328 Ipm, with variant spellings
> *Clyve, Cleve* 1343, *Clif* 1349, *Clyf* 1393 Cl
> *Kyngesclive* 1305 Cl, *-clyve* 1306 Cl, 1344 Ipm, *-cleve* 1462
> Ch, *Clyve Regis* 1347 Cl
> *Clyvepark* 1301 Cl

v. clif. The village is on a hill slope above the Willow Brook. The manor was held by the king as early as DB, and was often visited by the Norman kings.

BUXTON WOOD is *Buckston Sale* t. Jas 1 Woods Rept, and is possibly to be associated with the family of Roger *Bucstan* found in Paston in 1247 (*Ass*). For *sale v. supra* 157.

CALVEY WOOD (6″) is *Caleweheye* c. 1300 *For*, *Calwheye* ib., *Caluheye* 1318 Pat, *Calneheye* (sic) 1319 Inq aqd, *Kaluhey* 1336 Orig, *Calouheye* 1343 Cl, *Calfhay* 1813 EnclA. This must be 'bare enclosure,' *v.* (ge)hæg, the first element being OE *calu*, 'bare, bald,' with later folk-etymologising.

SETEHILL (lost) is *essart of Sechelle* (sic) 1227 Ch, *Setehul* t. Ed 1 PeterbA, *Sethelle* 1330 Dugd vi, 449, *Setehill Gate* 1642 Woods Rept. This must be a compound of OE *set*, 'seat, camp, entrenchment,' and hyll.

WESTHAY LODGE and WOOD is *Westhey(e)* c. 1220 *For*, 1251 Misc, 1272 *For*, *Vesthey* 1254 Seld 13, *Westhey Woods* 1642 Woods Rept. 'The west (ge)hæg or forest enclosure.' *West* with reference to Morehay *infra* 207.

CORNFORTH HOLMES (6″) is the name of almshouses endowed by Mrs Cornforth in 1891 (VCH ii, 584). THE FAIR TREE (6″) is *Fair Tree* 1642 Woods Rept. HAZLEWOOD (6″) is *Haselwood Sale* t. Jas 1 Woods Rept. For *sale v.* Britain Sale *supra* 156. HOLLOW WOOD (6″) is *Hollowood Coppice* 1718 Woods Rept. LAW'S LAWN is *the Laund* t. Jas 1 Woods Rept, and is to be associated with the family of William *Lawe* (1605 HMC Buccleuch iii), an ancestor of William Law, the author of *A Serious Call to a Devout and Holy Life*. For 'laund' *v.* Wakefield *supra* 105. HITHER and

FAR MIERS (6″) may be identical with *Myrey Sale* t. Jas 1, *Myre Sale* 1718 Woods Rept. ROUGHILL (lost) is *le Roughul* 1321 Ipm, *Great Roughill Coppice* 1718 Woods Rept. 'Rough hill,' i.e. overgrown with brushwood etc., *v.* ruh. STOCKINGS (6″) is *Stocking Sale* t. Jas 1 Woods Rept. *v.* stocking. GREAT and LITTLE WATKINSON (6″) is *Watkinson Sale* t. Jas 1 Woods Rept.

Collyweston

COLLYWESTON [kɔli'wesən] 64 G 6

> *Weston(e)* 1086 DB *et freq* to 1330 *Ass*, *-tun'* 1203 Cur, (*by Keten*) 1322 Ipm, (*juxta Staunford*) 1330 *Ass*
>
> *Colynweston* 1309 Pat, 1323 *Ass*, 1328 Ch, 1347 Cl, *Colines Weston* 1332 *FF*
>
> *Colyweston* 1374 Cl, *Collyweston* 1575 AD vi, *Collywesson* 1611 Belv

'West farm,' *v.* tun, with reference to Easton-on-the-Hill *infra* 201. It is near Ketton (R) and Stamford. *Colin* is said to be a pet-form of the name of *Nicholas*, who held the manor in the 13th century (VCH ii, 551).

COLLYWESTON GREAT WOOD is *boscus de Weston* 1287 *For*.

Cotterstock

COTTERSTOCK 74 B 7

> *Codestoche* 1086 DB, *Codestoc* 1100–20 (c. 1200) *PeterbA*, 1189 (1332) Ch, *-stoke* t. John BM, c. 1220 WellsR, 1227 Ch, 1229 Cl, 1232 WellsR
>
> *Coþestoche* c. 1175 Middleton (p), *Cothestok'* 1225 ClR
>
> *Cotherstok(e)* 12th Survey *et passim* to 1428 FA, *Cothere-* 1285 *Ass*, 1286 FF, *Cothirstoke* n.d. AD iii, *Cothyrstok* 1276–89 Ipm
>
> *Godestok'* 1200 Cur, 1280 Cl, *Gade-* 1200 Cur
>
> *Cottestoc'* 1241 P
>
> *Coderestoke* 1253 *Ass*, 1302–7 Ipm, *Coder-* 1275 RH, 1302 Fine, *Codery-* 1285 *Ass*, *Codyr-* 1380 Cl
>
> *Cot(t)erstok(e)* 1316, 1346 FA
>
> *Cotterstocke al. Cotherstock* 1615 *Recov*, *Cotherstock* 1791 Bridges

This is a difficult name. The suggestion may be hazarded that it is from OE *corþer-stoc(c)*, with dissimilatory loss of the first *r*, owing to Anglo-Norman influence (cf. Zachrisson, *AN Influence* 136, and Fotheringhay *infra* 202). The word *corþer* is only found in poetry in OE, where it denotes 'troop, band, multitude, assembly.' Cotterstock would then denote the stoc or place where such a band gathered. If this interpretation is correct, we have a further example of the use of an archaic word in the Nene valley.

Duddington

DUDDINGTON 64 H 5

> *Dodinton(e)* 1029 (c. 1350) Ramsey, 1086 DB *et passim* to 1391 Cl with variant spellings *Doding-, -yng-, -yn-, -tun, (juxta Staunford)* 1285 *Ass*
>
> *Duditun* 1155 P, *Dudinton(a)* 1174 P *et passim* with variant spellings *-ing-, -yng-, -ton, Duddington* 1246 Cl
>
> *Dutintonam* 13th ChronRams
>
> *Dadinton* 1231 Ch
>
> *Dorington* 1713 ParReg
>
> '*Dudda*'s farm,' *v.* ingtun.

ASSART FM is *essart de Dudinton* 1226 ClR, *close called lez Sert* 1551 Pat, *Assert Farm* 1826 G. *v.* Sart Wood *supra* 166.

DALES WOOD (6″) is *Dale* c. 1220 *For*. 'Valley,' *v.* dæl, dalr.

Easton-on-the-Hill

EASTON-ON-THE-HILL 64 G 6

> *Eston(e)* 1086 DB *et passim, (juxta Staunford)* 1309 *FF*

'East farm,' *v.* tun. It is north-east of Collyweston and near Stamford. It is situated on the brow of a hill and hence "sometimes named Easton on the Hill" (Bridges ii, 443).

EASTON HORNSTOCKS is *Hornedestok* t. Ed 1 *PeterbB, Hornestock* 1642 Woods Rept, *Hornstock's Wood* 1820 *EnclA*. The wood presumably took its name from some peculiar shaped stump, *v.* stocc.

VIGO LODGE is *Vigo House* 1826 G. This is probably a name given in honour of the naval victory at Vigo (Spain) in 1702. Cf. the farm-names Portobello and Waterloo, the former found in Mx and Herts, and the latter in several counties.

WOTHORPE GROVES (6″) is *bosc. voc. Graues* 1261 *FF*, *v*. grafa. It adjoins Wothorpe parish *infra* 247.

Fotheringhay

FOTHERINGHAY [fɔðəriŋgei] 74 A 8

Fodringeya c. 1060 (13th) ChronRams, -*eia* 1086 DB *et passim* to 1457 Ch with variant spellings -*eie*, -*eye*, -*ay* and -*yng*-, *Fodrengeye* 12th Survey
Frodigeya 1075 (13th) *NthStA*, *Frodrigéé* c. 1195 *Add*
Foderingeya (*Regis Scottie*) 1168 P *et passim* to 1428 FA with variant spellings -*yng*- and -*eye*, *Foderingham* 1241 P
Foddringeia 1174 P, 1176 BM, -*heye* 1261 *Ass*
Fotheringeia 1212 ClR, c. 1250 MP, *Fotringeye* 1252 Fine
Foderingheie 1232 *FF*, *Fodringhey*(*e*) 1235 Cl, 1316 FA, -*yng*- 1308 Ch
Fautheringhay 1652 ParReg (Castor)

The earliest form of this name was probably *Forðheringa-eg*, 'island of the people of *Forðhere*,' *v*. ing, eg. Fotheringhay lies on low ground between the Nene and Willow Brook. *r* was early lost by Anglo-Norman dissimilation of *r* (cf. Cotterstock *supra* 200), though, if that form be not a blunder, it may have left its trace in the forms, *Frodigeya*, *Frodrigee*, which at the same time show metathesis of the *r*. It is worthy of note that *Forðhere* is an early OE name, not found later than the middle of the 8th century.

The manor was held by the king of Scotland in the 12th century.

PARK LODGE. Cf. *parcum de Foderingeya* 1230 Cl.

WALCOT LODGE is *Walecote* 1261 *Ass*, *pons de Walcotforth* 1330 *Ass*. 'cot(e) of the serfs or Britons,' cf. Walcot *infra* 242.

Glapthorn

GLAPTHORN[1] 74 B 7

Glapt(h)orn 1185 RotDom *et freq*

Glapet(h)orn 1189 (1332) Ch *et freq* to 1277 Ipm

Clapethorn(e) t. John BM, 1248 Cl, *Clap-* c. 1220 *For*, 1268 *Ass*, 1522 LP

Glaptorp 1200 Cur

Glapthorn al. Clapthorn 1396 Pat

In considering this name we should take note also of *gleppan felda, glæppan felda* (BCS 1295, KCD 657) which Wallenberg (KPN 215) identifies with a present-day Clatfields (K), Glapwell (Db), with forms *Glapewelle* and the like from DB onwards, and Glaphowe (PN NRY 145). Middendorff (60) suggested an unrecorded OE adj. *glæp*, 'sloping,' allied to a German stem *glapp-, glepp-*, 'to glide, be open,' for the first name, but as such an adjective could hardly be applied to a thorn or a spring or stream, we may probably dismiss it from consideration. Bosworth-Toller connects the name with *glæppe*, an OE plant-name denoting possibly the buck-bean, but a genitival compound of a plant-name and feld is impossible, as is also a compound of such a word with þorn. Wallenberg notes that the three places are by streams—a dangerously weak line of argument—and suggests the possibility of a stream-name, but a compound *glæppan feld* with the river-name in the genitive is most unlikely, and a compound of þorn with a river-name equally improbable, so perhaps we may after all best take the first element to be the OE pers. name *Glappa*, which is actually on record. It may be noted that this name belongs to the early days of the Anglian settlement, being given by Bede as the name of one of the earliest kings of Northumbria.

PROVOST LODGE. Cf. *Provestes Closes* 1549 Pat, *Provost Closes* 1642 Woods Rept, *Provey Lodge* 1739 Camden (Gough), 1823 B. This is a relic of the 'Provost's Manor' (VCH ii, 555) which endowed a provost and twelve chaplains in the church of

---

[1] This place is mentioned as *Glapthorn'* (BCS 22), *Glaphton* (ib., 409), *Glapthorn(e)* (ib., 461, 521, 872, 1178) in a series of worthless Croyland charters.

St Andrew at Cotterstock. The form *Provey* seems to preserve the pronunciation elsewhere shown by the spelling *provo* (*v.* NED *s.v.*).

Lutton

LUTTON 74 C 9

Lundingtun c. 970 (c. 1200) BCS 1130
Ludyngtone 1052–65 (13th) ChronRams *et freq* to 1430 *FF* with variant spellings -*ing*, -*in*-, -*yn*-, -*tun*
Luditone, Lidintone, Lidentone 1086 DB
Lodington 12th Survey *et freq* to 1428 FA with variant spellings -*in*-, -*yn*-, -*yng*-
Loudington 1329 Ipm
Ludyngton-on-Brouneswold 1339 Ipm, Cl, (*juxta Brouneswold*) 1430 *FF*
Luddyngton 1394 Cl
Lutton al. Ludington 1428 IpmR, (*al. Luddington*) 1601 Recov

'*Luda*'s farm,' *v.* ingtun. For the addition 'on Brouneswold,' 'juxta Brouneswold,' cf. Newton Bromswold *supra* 193. The first form is clearly due to an error of transcription.

Nassington

NASSINGTON 74 A 8

Nassingtona 1017–34 (13th) ChronRams *et passim* with variant spellings -*yng*-, -*yn*-, -*in*-, *Nassintone* 1086 DB, *Nassenton* 1190 P
Nessinton(e) c. 1152 *D & C Linc* D ii, 88/1 *et freq* to 1241 P, *Nesin-* 1166 RBE
Naseinton' 1237 Cl, *Nassayngton* 1318 Ch, *Nasshyngton* 1517 BM
Nossington 1415 BM

Nassington stands on a broad headland above the Nene, and the probable interpretation of the name is that it is from OE *næssingatun*, 'farm of the dwellers on the ness,' *v.* næss, ing, tun. Cf. Nazeing (Ess) in PN in -*ing* 47. Another possibility is that this is an outlying settlement of persons from the 'ness' of Peterborough, *v.* Nassaborough Hundred *infra* 223.

G<small>REAT</small> B<small>YARDS</small> S<small>ALE</small> is *Bayard Sale* 1726 *Recov* and is to be associated with the family of William Avenel de *Biart* (1161 P). For *sale v.* Britain Sale *supra* 156.

R<small>ING</small> H<small>AW</small> is *Dringhawe* c. 1220, *Drynghawe* c. 1300 *For*, *Dryngehawe* 1333 Ipm, *Drinkhawe al. Ringoe* t. Jas 1, *Ringhaw al. Dringhawe* 1642 Woods Rept. This is a compound of the Scandinavian **dreng** and **hagi**, hence 'enclosure held or occupied by a group of drengs, holding by their particular form of tenure.' Cf. Drinsey Nook (Nt), containing the same elements. For the loss of initial *d*, cf. the somewhat similar loss of initial *th* in the word *riding* (PN NRY 1).

S<small>ULEHAY</small>, O<small>LD</small> and N<small>EW</small>

> *Sywleg'* 1219 *FF*
> *Syule, Syuele* c. 1220 *For, Syuele* 1254 *For, Siuele* 1268 Ipm, *Seule* 1329 *Ct*
> *Suleye* 1286 *For, -lee* 1310 *For, -ley(e)* 1333 Ipm, 1420 Pat
> *Seule* 1329 *Ct, Sewele fermes* 1416 IpmR, *Seweley* 1463 Pat
> *Old Suley Haye* t. Jas 1 Woods Rept, *Sewlhay* 1665 *Recov*

This is probably from OE *Seofan-leage*, 'leah of one *Seofa*.' For this pers. name cf. *Seofus* (LVH) and *Seofocanwyrð* (BCS 1002). The *hay* is a piece of folk-etymology due to the influence of such names as Morehay *infra* 207.

F<small>AIR</small> O<small>AK</small> S<small>ALE</small> is *Faire Oak Sale* t. Jas 1 Woods Rept. For *sale v.* Britain Sale *supra* 156. L<small>YVEDEN</small> F<small>M</small>. There was a William de *Lyveden* mentioned in connection with Nassington in 1330 (*Ass*), probably taking his name from Lyveden *supra* 178. M<small>ORTON</small> S<small>ALE</small> is so spelt t. Jas 1 Woods Rept, 1726 *Recov*. M<small>OUNTJOY</small> S<small>ALE</small> (6″) is *Mountioy Sale* t. Jas 1, *Lord Montjoy's Sale* 1718 Woods Rept. S<small>HORT</small> W<small>OOD</small> (6″) is *curto bosco de Nassington* c. 1220 *For, Nassyngtonschorte* 1345 *For*. S<small>PIRES</small> W<small>OOD</small> (6″) is *Spyres Copice* t. Jas 1, *Nassington Spiers* 1704 Woods Rept. S<small>WAN</small>'<small>S</small> N<small>EST</small> (6″). Cf. *Swannisnest* (1299 *Ct*) in Brigstock and *Swannesnest* (13th *NthStA*) in Pitsford.

Southwick

SOUTHWICK [sɑuðik] 74 B 6

> (æt) *Suthwycan* c. 980 (c. 1200) BCS 1130
> *Sudwic* 1131 P, 1147 BM, -*wich'* 1206 Cur
> *Sothewyk* 12th Survey, 1275 Ch, 1307 Ipm
> *Suwic'* 1204 Cur, 1209 Seld 13, *Suthwyk* 1235 Fees *et freq*
>   to 1316 FA with variant spellings -*wyke*, -*wic*(*k*), *Suthewik*
>   1273 Cl
> *Southwyk* 1298 Ipm, *Sowick* 1657 NRS i

'South dairy farm(s),' *v.* wic, possibly in relation to Ape-thorpe. The first form seems to be dat. pl. in form.

BLACKMORE THICK FM is *Blakemerethycke* 1345, *Blakemerehegh*, *Blamerethyke* t. Ed 3 *For*, *Merethyck* 1551 Pat, *Blackmore Thick* 1704 Woods Rept. There is a small mere close at hand. Already in the Vespasian Psalter we have OE *þiccan* (pl.) denoting 'thickets,' and it is this word *thick* which we have here and else-where in Northamptonshire.

PARK COLSTERS is *Colestertis* 1286, *bosc. de Colstretes* t. Ed 3, *Colstertes* 1345, 1367 *For*, *Colesteres* 1642 Woods Rept. The ground is much broken here, and we have OE steort, 'tail of land,' in the plural. Cf. *Stertes* in Greatworth (1271 *FF*) and in Welton (t. Ed 3 *Rental*) and *supra* 12 n. In this forest area the first element is perhaps OE *col*, 'charcoal,' hence 'pieces of land where charcoal was burned.'

CRAYLEY WOOD (6″) is *Graylee* 1367 *For*, *Crayley* 1551 Pat. We have very little to go on here. The first part of the name may show common confusion of initial *c* and *g*, cf. Glendon and Glapthorne *supra* 113, 203. If so, the name means 'grey wood or clearing,' *v.* leah. It is on a tiny stream, so that a river-name Cray (cf. RN 103) is possible.

HORSESHOES (lost) is *Horishawe* 1319 Inq aqd, *Horyngeshawe* 1345 *For*, *Horyshawe* 1370 *For*, *Horeshawes* (*Wood*) 1523 LP, 1551 Pat, *Great*, *Little Horseshoes Coppice* 1718 Woods Rept, 1823 B. This is probably a compound of OE *horig*, 'foul, dirty,' and sceaga, 'shaw, wood.'

Morehay Lawn is *Morhey* 1249, 1254 Seld 13, 1262 Ipm, *-hay* 1283 Pat, 1329 *Ct, Morheyhegges* t. Ed 1 *PeterbB, Morhayweld, Mourhay* 1367 *For, laund of Morehay* 1551 Pat, *Moorhey Lawne* 1665 *Recov.* 'Enclosure on marsh ground,' *v.* mor. For *lawn* cf. Wakefield Lawn *supra* 105. For *weld*, see Introd. xxxi.

New Hall is *Newehawe* 1345 *For,* 1469 Pat, *Newhawe* 1551 Pat, 1642 Woods Rept. *v.* haga. For the modern form cf. Weekley Hall *supra* 173.

Perio [periou] Barn and Mill (both 6″) is *Piriho* c. 1220 *For et freq* to 1383 Cl with variant spelling *Pyri-, Pirehou* 1275 RH, *-ho* 1280 AD iv, *Puriho* 1277 Ipm, *Pyreho* 1282 FF, *Peryho* 1316 FA, *Perry Lane Mill* 1779 F. 'Spur of land marked by a pear tree,' *v.* pyrige, hoh.

The Spa is a medicinal spring first mentioned by name as *the Spaw* in 1713 (Morton 274), though known earlier. For the history of *spa* as a name for a medicinal spring, *v.* NED *s.v.*

Tottenhoe Lodge

    Totenho 1205 BM, *Toteho* 1229 Cl, *Totinho* 1286 *For, Toten-*
       howe 1316 Fine, 1342 Cl, *Totnowe* 1551 Pat
    Tothou 1254 Seld 13
    Totenhobrok, Totenhoridinge t. Ed 1 *PeterbB, Totenhowe*
      Hacche 1319 Pat, *Totenhowhacche* 1338 Ch

'*Totta*'s spur of land.' *v.* hoh, hryding. The *hacche* (*v.* hæcc) will be one of the gates into the forest area.

Boar's Head Fm is *Boars Head* 1823 B. Cross Way Hand Lodge is *Cross-a-hand Walk* 1704 Woods Rept, *Cross with Hand* 1779 F. Frere Hill Wood is *Fryers Hill Sale* t. Jas 1 Woods Rept. For *sale v.* Britain Sale *supra* 156. The manor of South-wick belonged to the priory of St Mary of Huntingdon. Holey Brookes (6″) is *Hollowbrookes* t. Jas 1 Woods Rept. Howe Wood (6″) is *Howewode, Howgate* 1642 Woods Rept. New Wood (6″) is *Neuwood* 1642 Woods Rept. Old Sale (6″) is *Olde Sale* t. Ed 1 *PeterbB, le Holdesale* 1337 *Ass, Eldesale* 1338 *For, Oldsale* 1642 Woods Rept. For *sale v.* Britain Sale *supra* 156. Shire Hill Lodge is *Shirehill, Shire Hill* t. Jas 1 Woods Rept. Short Wood is *le Schortwode* t. Ed 1 *PeterbB, Shorewode by*

Suthwik 1462 Ch, *Shortwode* 1515 LP, *Shortewood* 1551 Pat. SOUTHWICK WOOD is *Suthwik Copies* 1462 Ch, *Southwicke Coppice* 1642 Woods Rept. STONE HILL. Cf. *Stonhillfelde* 1563 *Terrier*. STONE PIT LODGE (6″). Cf. *Stony pitt feild* 1633 *Terrier*.

Tansor

TANSOR 74 B 8

> *Tanesovre* 1086 DB, *Tanesouera* c. 1152 *D & C Linc* D ii 88/1, 8 *et freq* to 1307 Ipm with variant spellings -*overe*, -*ouere*, -*owere* 1275 RH, *Thanes*- 1224 WellsR
>
> *Tanesores* 1205 Cur, *Tanesour* 1206 Cur, *Taneshore* 1314 Cl
> *Tanneshore* 1314 Ipm
> *Tanshore* 1320 Ch, *Tansore* 1346 FA, 1392 Cl, 1428 FA
> *Taunesore* 1386 Cl, *Taunesover* 1401 Cl
> *Tansworth* 16th *Brudenell*

This name should probably be taken in conjunction with Tansley (Db), DB *Taneslege*[1], and *tanes bæce* in Herefordshire (BCS 1040). As suggested by Dr Ritter, these names point to an OE pers. name *Tān*, which would be a parallel to OHG *Zeino* (Förstemann PN 1387). Hence, '*Tān*'s bank.' For the form *Tansworth* cf. Milton *supra* 150.

Woodnewton

WOODNEWTON 74 A 7

> *Niwetone* 1086 DB, *Neweton* 12th Survey, 1209 Seld 13
> *Newinton* 1166 P (CR), *Newenton* 1196 FF, 1220 Fees, 1384 Cl
> *Wodeneuton* 1255 Seld 13 *et freq* to 1324 Ch, *Wode Neuton juxta Apthorp* 1298 FF, *Wodenewenton* 1305 FF
> *Newton al. Wood Newton* 1599 *Recov*

'New farm,' *v.* tun. Distinguished from the other Northamptonshire Newtons by its situation within the Forest of Cliffe.

NEWTON SPINNEY is so called 1642 Woods Rept.

PRIORS HAW (6″) is *Hawe* t. Ed 1 *PeterbB*, *boscus prioris de Finshed qui vocatur Hall al. the Priors Hall* 1642 Woods Rept. *v.* haga. For the modern form cf. Weekley Hall *supra* 173.

---

[1] DB has also *Teneslege* but there is no other form with an *e*.

Yarwell

YARWELL [jærəl] 64 J 8

Jarewelle 1166 RBE *et freq* to 1289 Ipm, *Yarewelle* 12th
  Survey, *Jarwell* 1247 Fees, *Iare-* 1252 Cl, 1255 Seld 13,
  Yarwelle 1318 Ch
Gerwella 1176 P, *Garewell'* 1244 Fees
Iaruwelle c. 1220 *For*
Jerewell 1220 ClR
Yardewell 1316 FA

Yarwell is half-a-mile from the Nene, but the original settlement may have been by Yarwell Mill on the Nene itself. Here
there is a spring marked on the O.S. map, and the **gear** may be
a fishing pool or pools on the Nene, thus 'spring of (or by) the
yair(*s*) or fishing-pools.' OE *gearuwe*, 'yarrow-grass,' is also a
possibility, hence 'spring by which yarrow grows.'

MORTAR PITS (6″) is *le Morterpytt* t. Eliz *Ct*.

XVIII. POLEBROOK HUNDRED

Pocabroc a. 1076 Geld Roll, *Pochebroc* 1086 DB
Polebroke 1316, 1346 FA
v. Polebrook *infra* 215.

Armston

ARMSTON 74 D 8

Mermeston 1086 DB, *Ermeston* 1227 Ch
Armestun 1140 Sparke *et passim* to 1428 FA with variant
  spelling *-ton*(*e*)

This would seem to be '*Eorm*'s farm,' *v.* tun. For such a pers.
name cf. Arngrove PN Bk 115–16 and PN D Pt i, Addenda l.

BURRAY SPINNEY (6″) takes its name from *Burweye* (1404
Fraunc). Cf. *Burrays Field* 1716 *Map*. This is clearly a compound
of burh and weg, descriptive of the track which here leads up to
a moated site in the village, or possibly of the same track as it
comes up from the castle at Barnwell.

ARMSTON GROVE (6"). Cf. *Grove Corner* 1602 *DuLaSpecCom.*
CONEY GEER COPPICE (6"). This is a corruption of ME *conyger,*
'rabbit warren.' Cf. *infra* 273. COW SHACKLE COPPICE (6") is
Cowshakell slade, Cowshakell bushes 1602 *DuLaSpecCom.*

Ashton

ASHTON 83 F 12

>*Ascetone* 1086 DB, *Acheston* 1248 WellsR
>*Ayston* 12th Survey, *Aiston* 1227 Ch
>*Aston* 1284 FA, *Ashton juxta Undele* 1299 *Ass*

'Ash farm,' *v.* æsc, tun.

ELMINGTON LODGE

>*Elminton(e)* 1086 DB, 12th Ord, 1219 *FF,* -*myn*- 1275 RH,
>   *Elmyngton* 1316 FA
>*Elmenton* 1189 (1332) Ch, 12th Survey, 1227 Ch, 1299 *Ass,*
>   *Elmetone* t. Ed 3 *SR*

No satisfactory explanation of this name can be offered. There
is an OE place-name *Elmanstede* found in an original charter of
811, now Elmstead (K). This name is equally difficult of interpretation. *v.* KPN (118–19).

ASHTON WOLD is so named c. 1825 O.S. CHAPEL FM (6").
Ashton was formerly a chapelry of Oundle.

Barnwell St Andrew

v. Barnwell All Saints *supra* 178.

EMPTY SPINNEY (6") may be the place called *le Hympeheye* 1285
Buccleuch, Ass, le Imphey 1450 *Deed.* This is clearly the same as
the *Imphaghe* which lies behind Limbo (PN Sx 117), except that
we have (ge)hæg rather than haga as the second element. The
meaning is 'enclosure made of *imps,* i.e. saplings or shoots.'

BROADWAY CORNER (6"). Cf. *Bradeweye* 1337 *For.* CASTLE FM
was perhaps the home of William *atte Castel* (1308 Pat). The
remains of Barnwell Castle still stand (6").

Benefield

BENEFIELD [benifi·ld]¹ 74 C 6

Beringafeld 10th (c. 1200) BCS 1129, 1130, *Berifeld* 1201 P
Benefeld 1086 DB, 1213 ClR, 1346 FA, *-feud* 1255 Seld 13
Bennifeld 1130 P (p)
Banefeld c. 1150 (1252) Ch, 1230 P (CR), 1252 *AD* C 9856,
    1293 *For*, 1356 Cl
Benifeld 1189 (1332) Ch, 12th Survey *et passim* to 1481 AD i
    with variant forms and transcription *Bein-, Beny-, -feud*
Beningfeld 1213 PatR, c. 1220 WellsR, 1269 *FF*, 1285 *Ass*,
    1321 Ch, 1349 Ipm, Cl, 1357 Cl *et freq* with variant
    spelling *-yng-, Beningfeud* 1273 Cl, 1275 Ch, RH
Benfeld 1227 Ch
Banifeld 1230 P (CR), 1246 Seld 13, *-feud* 1255 Seld 13
Bamigfeld (sic) 1230 P
Benigfeld 1268 *Ass*, c. 1270 Gerv
Benyfeld Netherthorp 1481 AD i

The survival of two independent forms *Beringafeld* (with
medial *r*) from the Peterborough Cartulary, supported by the
form *Berifeld* in the Pipe Roll of 1201, makes it clear that the
n of all the other forms is most probably due to Anglo-Norman
assimilation (cf. IPN 106). One cannot explain the forms with
r as due to Anglo-Norman dissimilation, for there is no trace of
Anglo-Norman influence in this part of the Peterborough Cartulary. On the other hand, complete AN assimilation is natural
in a ME name in a district so highly feudalised as the one in
question². This name must be a derivative of the pers. name
*Bera discussed under Barford (PN BedsHu 51). Hence, 'open
land of *Bera*'s people,' *v.* feld³. *Netherthorp*, i.e. 'lower village'
in contrast to *Upthorpe* now Upper Benefield *infra* 212.

¹ The trisyllabic pronunciation of the name in the 17th century is shown
by its use in Drayton's *Polyolbion* (1623).
² For a similar complete change of consonant cf. Bellingham (K), which
has *r* in *Beringahamm* (973 BCS 1295) and *l* in all later forms, cf. KPN
300.
³ Karlström (105) would associate this name with Banhaw Wood, Bangrave and Beanfield Lawn *infra* 212 and *supra* 174, 155. The early forms of
Banhaw and Bangrave now at our disposal make association with Benefield
impossible, while Beanfield is only a repetition of *Benefield*, not an independent name.

BANHAW WOOD [bænə] is *bosco de Banho* 1253 *Ass*, 1280, 1298 Ipm, 1292 *Compotus*, *Banneho* t. Ed 1 *PeterbB*, *Banhouwe* 1286 *For*, *le Estbanhowe* 1330 *Ass*, *Bannow wood* 1662 *Clayton*. This is probably from OE *bēanhō(h)e*, 'hoh or hill where beans grow.'

BIGGIN HALL[1] is *la Bigginge* c. 1250 *Swaffham*, *la Byggynge*, *la Buggynge*, *la Byggenge* 1285 *Ass*, (*by Undele*) 1304 Ch, *Byggynges in Oundell* 1550 Pat. 'Building,' v. bigging.

CHURCHFIELD FM[1] is *ciricfeld* c. 964 (1200) BCS 1129, *Circafeld* 1125–8 ChronPetro, *Chirchefeld* 1189 (1332) Ch *et freq* to 1428 FA with variant spelling *-feud*, *Kirkefeld* 1202 Ass (p), c. 1250 *Swaffham*, *Curchefeld* c. 1220 *For*, *Churchfeld* 1346 FA, *Chirchefeldewode* 1395 Pat. 'Open land by the church,' v. cirice, feld, the reference being to a chapel which formed the subject of a grant to the Abbey of Peterborough in 1189 (Ch).

UPPER BENEFIELD is *Upthorp* c. 1220 *For et freq* to 1376 Cl, *Huptorpriding* 1286 *For*, *Upthrop al. Upthorp* 1325 Ipm, *Uptorp* t. Ed 3 *SR*, *Benefeild Overthorpe* 1641 *FF*. 'Upper village,' v. þorp, hryding. It lies above Benefield.

BLACKTHORNS is *wood called Blackthornes* 1675 DKR xl. BROOK FM (6″) was the home of Wm *a le Broke de Benifeld* c. 1250 *Swaffham*. COCKENDALE WOOD (6″) is *wood called Co(c)kendale* 1662 *Clayton*, 1675 DKR xl. FRINDSHAW (Kelly) is *Frendeshawe* t. Ed 1 *PeterbB*, *Frindshaw* 1820 *EnclA*. LAMMAS FM (6″) is *Lammasclose* 1677 *Brudenell*. Cf. *infra* 273. SILLEY COPPICE (6″) is *Sallowe Coppice* 1570 AD v, 1723 *Brudenell*, i.e. willow coppice. SPRING WOOD. Cf. *Great Spring, Ladye Spring* 1662 *Clayton*, *Springwood* 1825 *EnclA*. SWALLOW HOLES (6″) are nine holes where the land-floods occasionally flow and disappear (VCH iii, 77). YOKEHILL FM is possibly *Hochil* 1254 *For*; it is *Yoke Hill* 1825 *EnclA*.

Hemington

HEMINGTON   74 D 9

Hemmingtune 1077 (13th) ChronRams, *Hemmingetonam* 12th (13th) ChronRams, *Hemmictona* 1176, *Hemmincton* 1177–81 NRS iv, *Hemmingethon* 1186–7 NRS iv, *Hemmington*' 1219 *FF*, *-yng-* 1278 Cl, 1301 Ipm, 1346 Cl

[1] Formerly in Oundle parish.

Heminton(e) 1086 DB *et freq* to 1428 FA with variant spelling
-*yng*-, *Heminctona* 1149 NRS iv, *Hemingeton* 1205 Cur
Hinintone 1086 DB, *Heninton* 1275 RH
Haminton(e) 1184–9 (c. 1350) Ramsey, 1200 Cur, 1283 Cl

'Farm of *Hemma* or of his people,' *v.* ingtun. Cf. Hemingford
(PN BedsHu 260).

ELLANDS FM may be identical with *le Heylond* 1285 *Ass*, a place
mentioned in connection with Barnwell and Armston. This may
contain OE heg, 'hay' or (ge)hæg, 'enclosure.'

Luddington-in-the-Brook

LUDDINGTON 74 D 9

(*æt*) *lullingtune* c. 970 (c. 1200) BCS 1130
Lullinton(e) 1086 DB *et freq* to 1348 Ch with variant spellings
-*yn*-, -*ing*-, -*yng*-, *Loulyngton* 13th *PeterbA*
Lillington 12th Survey, *Lylington* 1316 FA
Lollinton 1253 (1327) Ch, -*ing*- 1264 Ipm, -*yng*- 1348 Ch
Lodyngton in the Brooke 1424 Pat
Luddyngton al. Lullyngton 1556 *FF*

'*Lulla*'s farm,' *v.* ingtun. The later spellings have been influenced by those for Lutton (*supra* 204) near by. Bridges (ii,
402–4) describes the situation of the village as "low and dirty"
from the over-flow of Alconbury Brook, and attributes its title
to this cause.

Oundle

OUNDLE[1] [ɑundəl] 74 G 7

(*in*) *Undolum* c. 725 (11th) Eddius, *Undola* c. 1000 Saints
in provincia Undalum c. 750 Bede, *in Undalum* 12th ASC (E)
    s.a. 709

---

[1] BCS 1129 is a list of boundaries of land belonging to Oundle. The task
of following them is a very difficult one. It is complicated by modern changes
in the boundaries of Oundle, but even if we correct them, it remains uncertain
how much land is covered by the document, and, more particularly, what
part of Benefield is included in the phrase at the end of the document, 'and
the land at Benefield, so far as it is included in the boundaries, belongs to
Oundle'.
Through the kindness of Mr Walker the opening point of the boundaries
has become clear, for *Cylleseg* survives as *Kilsey* or *Kelsey* meadow, a few
yards from the South Bridge. After that we can only be certain about Churchfield *supra* 212 and Benefield *supra* 211.

(*to*) *Undelan, Vndelum* 963 (c. 1200) BCS 1128, 1129

Undele 1086 DB *et passim* to 1316 FA

(*on*) *Undalana mægþe, an þære mægþe seo is gecyged Inundalum*
c. 1100 AS Bede

Vndle 1183 P, *Undle* 1189 (1332) Ch, 1260 *FF*, 1268 Ch, 1375
Pat

Undel 1189 (1332) Ch, 1227 Ch, 1231 Bracton, *Hundel* 1270
Ch

Oundel 1301 Seld 9, *Oundele* 1339, *Oundell* 1381, *Owndele*
1382, *-delle* 1392 Cl, *Owendell* 1430 Pat

Owndale 1675 Ogilby[1]

Oundle is clearly an old regional name. Like many such names
it presents great difficulty, and no solution can be offered here.
It may be noted that the older etymologies, which suggested that
the second element was 'dale,' are rendered impossible by the
OE forms, and they make it even more obvious that 16th cent.
topographers, such as Camden, had no justification for suggesting
that the name was really *Avon-dale*.

BERRYSTEAD (6″) is *Buristeede* 1559 Law. The present house is
not on the original site (VCH iii, 86). That was to the north-west
of the church. *bury* is here probably used in its manorial sense,
v. burh, stede.

CROWTHORP (lost) is *Crowethorpe* 12th Ramsey (p), 1285 *Ass*,
1305 Pat, (*juxta Undele*) c. 1310 *PeterbB, Crouthorpe* 1267
ChronRams, *-torp* t. Ed 3 *SR* (p), *Crawethorp'* 1274, 1285 *Ass*,
Crowethorpbrigge 1312 Seld 9, *pontem de Crowethorp* 1330
Ass, Cruthorp juxta Undele 1330 *Ass, Crowthorp* 1336 BM.
'Crow-village,' *v.* þorp. It was near to Oundle South Bridge
(1312 Seld 9).

---

[1] BLACK POT LANE is on the site of *Dowell wong* 1565 Law, *v.* vangr.
CHAPEL END is *Chapell End* ib. This was the name of the district where the
roads from Benefield and Stoke Doyle unite. It was so called from a medieval
chapel of St Thomas of Canterbury which stood here (VCH iii, 85). CHURCH
LANE is so called in 1565 (Law). DUCK LANE is *Ducke Lane* (1565 Law) and
is possibly a corruption of *le Dikelane* (c. 1400 *Rental*), *v.* dic. MILL LANE
is so named in 1565 (Law). NEW ST was formerly *Berry Streete, Bury Streete*
1565 Law, cf. Berrystead *supra*. ST OSYTH'S LANE is *St Sithes Lane otherwise called Lark Lane* 1565 Law. Cf. Size Lane (London), *Seint Sythes
lane* 1401, *Seintsitheslane* 1438 Calendar of Wills in Hustings Court. SHIP
LANE was called *Parva Venella*, i.e. 'Little Lane' in 1565 (Law). WEST ST and
NORTH ST were formerly *High Street* 1565 Law.

HERNE LODGE. Cf. *Hern Meadow* 1811 *EnclA*. It is in a loop
formed by the river Nene and contains OE hyrne, 'corner.'
PARK WOOD is *les Parke* c. 1400 *Rental, Oundell pke* 1535 VE.

Polebrook

POLEBROOK 74 C 8

Pochebroc 1086 DB, *Pokebroc* 1207 *FF et passim* to 1428 FA
with variant spelling *-brok(e)*, *Pokesbrok* 1314 Ipm
Pockebroc 1203 Ass, *Pokbrok* 1229 Cl, *Pakebrok* 1428 FA
Polebroc 1254 Seld 13, *-broke* 1428 FA, *Polbrok* 1316 FA
Polebroke al. Pokebroke 1608 *Recov*

'Goblin-brook,' *v.* puca, broc.

KINGSTHORPE LODGE is *Chingestorp* 1086 DB, 1223 ClR,
Kynges-, Kyngisthorp 1428 FA, *Kynesthorp* 12th Survey, 1270
FF, 1275 RH, 1348 Ch, *Kines-* 1330 *Ass*, *Kenes-* 1348 Ch, *Torp*
1209–35 WellsR, *Trop* 1275 RH. 'Village belonging to the
King,' *v.* þorp. In DB the manor belonged already to Peterborough Abbey so that the association of the place with a *king*
must belong to some early period of Anglo-Saxon history.

Warmington

WARMINGTON 74 B 8

Wyrmingtun, Wermingtun c. 980 (c. 1200) BCS 1130
Warmintone 1086 DB, *Warmyngton* 1392 Cl
Wermintone 1086 DB *et passim* to 1428 FA with variant
spellings *-ing-, -yng-, Wermenton* 1202 Ass
Wirmint' 1175 P, *Wirmi(ng)ton* 1208, 1210 Cur, *Wyrmitton*
1255 Seld 13
Wurmintone 1206 *FF*, *Worminton* 1285 Cl

'*Wyrma*'s farm,' *v.* ingtun. Cf. Worminghall (PN Bk 129),
Warminghurst (PN Sx 182), Wornditch (PN BedsHu 245), and
Wormegay (Nf), DB *Wermegeia*. The persistent early forms in
Werm-, Warm- are a little surprising, but have their parallel in
a smaller degree in the other names quoted.

EAGLETHORPE is *Ekelthorpgrene* 1297 AD ii, *Eggilthorp* 1373 *FF*,
Egyl- c. 1400 *Rental, Egelthorp, Egylthorp* 1404 *Fraunc, Egle-*
thorp(e) 1517 BM, 1528 *Recov, Egilthorp* 1535 VE. Professor

Ekwall calls attention to the parallel of Egleton (R), *Egoluestun* in 1218 (*For*), *Egeliston* in 1242 (Fees), and suggests that this name denotes the þorp of a man named *Ecgwulf*.

PAPLEY is *Pappele* 12th Survey *et freq* to 1428 FA, *Pappelle* 1242 AD iii. '*Pap(p)a*'s clearing,' *v.* leah. Cf. *Pappelode* in Titchmarsh (1347 Ipm), Papworth (C) and *papan holt* BCS 596.

DAVEY'S FM (6″) is to be associated with the family of Richard *Davie* (1537–40 Wills). BIG and LITTLE GREEN (6″). Cf. *le grene* c. 1400 *Rental*. STOCK HILL. Cf. *Stocwong* c. 1250 *Swaffham, Stokwong* c. 1400 *Rental*. The hill and the vangr or field were perhaps near the same stocc or stump.

XIX. NAVISFORD HUNDRED

Neresforda a. 1076 Geld Roll
Nar(r)esford 1086 DB
Nauesford 12th Survey, 1202 Ass, -*vis*- 1242 Fees
Nauenesford 1179 P
Naveresford 1220 Fees

The hundred meeting-place must have been by the Nene at the point where Aldwinkle, Thorpe Achurch and Titchmarsh meet, for the name survives in two fields in Titchmarsh just to the west of Thorpe station. The name would seem to have been originally *Naveresford*. It is clear that the first element of this name also appears in *nafrysbroc*, the name of the brook which bounds Twywell on the south side (*v. supra* 188 n.) and joins the Nene some three miles south of Navisford. It would seem almost certain that *nafrysbroc* must, in its turn, be associated with *Nauereslund*, an alternative name for part of Huxloe Hundred, which includes Twywell. The site of *Nauereslund* is unknown. *Nafarr* is a Scandinavian personal name recorded from the Viking period (Lind *s.n.*) and it can only be suggested that it was the name of some powerful Viking settler who gave his name alike to the ford, the brook and the lundr or grove. Most significant is his giving his name to the hundred. Similar names of early meeting-places in the Danelaw are Toseland (PN BedsHu 251) and Framland (Lei), DB *Franelund*.

Clapton

CLAPTON 74 E 8

Cloptun c. 960 (13th) BCS 1061
Clotone 1086 DB, 1201 Cur, *Clotton(a)* 1174 P, 1182 NRS iv,
 1201 Cur
Clopton 1175 P *et freq* to 1316 FA, *Sclopton* 1184 P
Clepton, Cletton 1200 Cur
Clapton 1227 Ch, (*al. Clopton*) 1683 *Recov*

Probably 'farm marked by a stub or stump.' *v.* tun and cf.
Clapham (PN BedsHu 23).

LONG THONG FM is *Langetuang* c. 1250 *Swaffham, Longeyonge*
t. Ric 2 *Rental.* This is clearly a compound of the common word
thong (OE *þwang*), used of a narrow strip of hide or leather, here
probably applied to a piece of ground of a particular shape. The
y of the second form given above is due to the common confusion in ME between *y* and the OE *þ*, as in the well-known *ye*
for *the.*

BROOK LODGE. Cf. *Brocfurlong* c. 1250 *Swaffham.* CROW'S
NEST FM is *Crows Nest* c. 1825 O.S. Cf. Swan's Nest *supra* 205.
FAYWAY is so named c. 1825 O.S. RINGDALES WOOD (6″). Cf.
Ryngdone, Reyngdoune t. Ric 2 *Rental.* Locally it is still called
Ringsdon Wood. SIX ACRE COPPICE (6″) is *Six acres* t. Ric 2
Rental. SKULKING DUDLEY COPPICE (6″) is to be associated with
some member of the Dudley family, who held a manor here in
the 14th cent. (VCH iii, 125–6). According to local tradition
the family was hunchbacked.

Pilton

PILTON 74 D 7

Pilchetone 1086 DB, *Pilketon* 1227 Ch *et freq* to 1428 FA with
 variant spelling *Pylke-*
Pilkenton 1189 (1332) Ch, 1225 ClR, 1253 *Ass*, t. Ed 1 AD ii,
 -kin- 1230, 1241 P, *Pylkyn-* t. Ed 1 AD ii
Pilton 1313 Cl, *Pylketon al. Pylton* 1582 *Recov, Pilkinton al.
 Pilton* 1675 Ogilby

'*Pīleca*'s farm,' *v.* tun, and for the pers. name cf. PN La 49 *s.n.* Pilkington and Pilt Down (PN Sx 346).

BEARSHANK WOOD is *wood...called Bareshanke* 1488 Pat, 1513 LP, *Bareshanke wood* 1540 LP. Robert *Bareschanke* of Castor paid dues for his land in Pilton in the 13th cent., so that the name is here clearly derived from the sometime holder of the land (VCH iii, 129). He seems also to have given his name to a lost *Bareshankhill* in Castor (c. 1400 *Rental*). Strangely enough, we find the field-name *Bareshanks* in Wilby (1778 Mears Ashby *EnclA*) and *Bearshanks* in Floore and in Thorpe Malsor (1777 *EnclA*). It can hardly be personal in origin in all these names. Was it a nickname for a 'barren field' with 'no ham on the shank,' so to speak?

WINNING FOOT HILL

(*via regia de*) *Wininge* 1255 Seld 13
(*wood called*) *Whynnyng* 1326 Cl, *Great Whinning Close* c. 1660 *Clayton*
Whynney grene 1540 LP

Winning seems originally to have been the name of a wood. Ekwall (PN in -*ing* 89) is probably right in associating this with the vb. *win.* *win* is commonly used in the NCy in the sense 'to get, obtain,' and *winning* is used of a new mine. The NED *s.v. win* vb. 5 c, notes that the vb. was used t. Hy 8, and again by Tusser, of the reclaiming of marshland for cultivation, and it may be that the word could similarly be used for the taking into cultivation of old woodland. The alternative possibility would be to take it as a collective compound of *whin*, 'gorse, furze,' cf. Bramble Bottom, earlier *Bremling*, and Hazeldean, earlier *Haseling* (PN Sx 418, 263), and Thurning *infra* 221, but the ultimate history of the word *whin* is obscure. In this part of the country change from *wh* to *w* is more probable than one from *w* to *wh*.

Stoke Doyle

STOKE DOYLE 74 D 7

Stoche 1086 DB *et freq* with variant spelling *Stoke, Stokes* 1175 P, 1189 (1332) Ch, 1199 FF, (*extra Undel'* 1210 Cur), *Stokys juxta Pylketon* 1285 *Ass, Stokes by Undele* 1301 Ipm

Stoke Doyly 1344 *Ass*, 1431 *Cl*, *Stoke Doyle* 1621 *FF*, *Stoke Doily* 1791 Bridges

v. stoc(c). John de *Oyly* held the manor in 1286 (Cl).

HATCHDOYLE LANE (6"). Cf. *Hatchdole* 1618 *Terrier*, *Hatchdole meadow* 1640 *Clayton*. dole, 'portion of the common field' (*v.* dal), has here been corrupted to *Doyle*. How HILL FM (6") may have been the home of Henry and Bartholomew *ad le Ho* of Lilford, an adjacent parish (t. Ed 3 *SR*), *v.* hoh. Cf. *Howhill feild* 1618 *Terrier*. RIDGE LEYS PLANTATION (6"). Cf. *pasture called Rigg leaze* 1660 *Clayton*. STOKE WOOD is *Stokewode* c. 1300 *For*.

Thorpe Achurch

ACHURCH 74 E 7

Asencircan, Asecyrcan c. 980 (c. 1200) BCS 1130
Asechirce 1086 DB, -*cherche* 1164 P (p), -*chirche* 1166 P (p),
   -*kirche* 12th (c. 1350) Ramsey (p), -*chyrche* 13th *PeterbA*,
   -*kirke* 1209–18 WellsR, *Aschyrche* 13th *PeterbA*
Achirche 12th Survey *et freq* to 1372 Cl
Accherche 1285 *Ass*
Thorp Hacchurch 1316 FA, *Thorp Achirch* 1428 FA

There are in OScand a man's name *Ási* (ODan *Ase*, OSwed *Asi, Ase*) and a woman's name *Asa*. Both alike are on record as used in England in the Danelaw, and we may have either of these names in Achurch, which would seem to be an example of an owned church. If so, it is an interesting late example of this practice (cf. Mawer, *PN and History* 26–7). The parish-name seems to have been formed by the union of *Achurch* and *Thorpe* (*v. infra*). Cf. Bridges (ii, 364), "Achurch, usually called *Thorp-Achurch* or *Achurch cum Thorp*."

THORPE WATERVILLE is *Torp(e)* 12th Survey, 1199, 1206 Cur, *Thorp(e)* 1220 Bracton, 1227 Ch, (*Watervile*) 1300 Ch, (*Watrefeld*) 1485 AD iii, (*Waterfeld*) 1509 LP. *v.* þorp. Ascelin de *Waterville* held the manor in the 12th cent. Survey.

THE LINCHES may be identical with *Linches* 1227 *FF*, *Lynch* c. 1400 *Rental*, *v.* hlinc. There is a steep wooded hillside here. The first of the above references deals with the neighbouring parish of Titchmarsh, so that the identification is not certain.

Thrapston

THRAPSTON [θræpsən] 74 F 6

Trapeston(e) 1086 DB *et freq* to 1247 WellsR, *-tona* 1138 NRS iv, *-tun* 1160–5 NRS iv, 1235 Cl, *Trappeston* 1299 *Ass*, 1359 Cl

Strapetona 1130 P (p), *Strapton* 1204 ClR, *Strapeston* 1262 Ipm, 1275 Cl

Thrapston 12th Survey, 1253 FF, 1346 FA, *-ne* 1314 Ipm

Traspton 1202 Ass (p), *Thraspton* 1353 Ipm

Trapston(e) 1219 WellsR *et freq* to 1307 Ipm

Thrapeston 1225 ClR, 1253 *Ass, FF*, 1317 Ch, 1319 Cl

Threpston 1289 Cl, *Thropston* 1605 HMC Buccleuch iii

Tharpston 1553 *Rental*, 1610 Camden

Thrapson 1631 NRS i

This is a very difficult name, and, like other names in the Nene valley, may contain elements of great antiquity. There are traces of a pers. name which may be found in the first element. Förstemann (PN 1461) gives *Trapsta* as the name of a Burgundian, and we have *Trafstila* (*v.l. Thraufistila, Trapstila*) as the name of a 6th cent. Gepid king mentioned by Jordanes, who appears elsewhere as *Trap(e)stila, Strapestila*. The stem from which this name is derived is probably the *thrafst-* of Gothic þrafstjan, 'to comfort,' but there would seem to have been a tendency to change *fst* to *pst* from the earliest times. It may be that we have in this p.n. a very early pers. name *Ðræfst* or the like, from the same stem. For the sound change cf. OE *wæfs*, *wæps*, 'wasp,' from a Teutonic stem *wabiso-*, and OE *ræfsan*, *ræpsan*, 'to blame,' MHG *refsen, respen*, 'to punish.' Hence, 'farm of *Ðræfst* or *Ðræpst*,' with early loss of consonants from the difficult compound *Ðræfstestun, Ðræpstestun*.

GALE'S LODGE (6″) preserves the name of the manor held by John *Gale* in 1574 (VCH iii, 141). THRAPSTON BRIDGE (6″) is *pontem de Trapstone* 1224 WellsR, *pontem de Tharpston* 1285 *Ass*.

Thurning[1]

THURNING 74 E 9

Torninge 1086 DB, *Thornyng* 1348 Ipm, 1542 *FF*

Thirninge c. 1150 (14th) *Thorney*, 12th (13th) ChronRams
et freq to 1428 FA with variant spellings *-yng(e)* and
Thyrn-[2]

Thurning' 1175 P (p), *Turnīg* 1207 FineR, *Turninges* 1207
Cur, *Turming* 1220 Fees, *Thurnīge* 1227 *Ass*, *Thurning* 1303
FA

Therninge 12th Survey *et freq* to 1330 QW with variant
spellings *-yng* and *Tern-*, *Trerning* 1262 Ipm

Thurnyng al. Thyrnyng 1565 *FF*

This is clearly a name of the collective type noted under
Winning Foot Hill *supra* 218. It denotes a place overgrown with
thorn-bushes. See further Ekwall, PN in *-ing* 15–16, who notes
the same name in Thurning (Nf).

Titchmarsh

TITCHMARSH 74 F 7

Tut(e)anmersc 973 (late copy) BCS 1297

Ticanmersc, Ticanmersce, Ticceanmersce c. 975 (14th) *Thorney*

Tircemesse 1086 DB

Ticemerse 1086 DB, *Tichemers* 1175 P (p) *et passim* to 1428
FA with variant spellings *Tyche-* and *-mershe*

Tikemers 1176 P

Titemerse 1206 Cur

Tichesmerse 1235 Fees

Thychemers' 1255 Seld 13

Techemers 1285 *Ass*, *Thechemers(he)* 1382 Cl, 1428 FA

Titchemersh 1428 FA

Tyschemerchse 1430 AD iv, *Tysshemershe* 1485 AD iii

The forms from the Thorney Cartulary make it clear that this
is 'Ticcea's marsh,' *v.* mersc, with the pers. name found in the
signature *signum manus Ticcean* to a grant of Ine (BCS 108).

---

[1] Formerly in Hu. Transferred to Nth in 1888.

[2] Forms *Thirning(e)*, *Thiring* are found in the worthless Croyland Charters
(BCS 521, 872, 1178).

BIDWELL FM (6″)[1] is *Bidewell* 1227 *FF*, *Bydwell meade* t. Eliz *Rental*. This would seem to be identical with *Bydewil* (1043 KCD 767) in Wiltshire, Bidwell (PN BedsHu 128), Biddles Fm (PN Bk 216), Bedlar's Green in Hallingbury (Ess), earlier *Bedewelle*, Beddell in Stanway, Bedwell in Aldham, *Bedewelle* in Widford (1280 *Ct*), *Bedwell* in Ashton (1548 *Pat*) all in Essex, *Bedewell* in Willesden (Mx) (1304, 1420 AD iv), Bedwell in Essendon (Herts) (*Bedewell* 1248 *Ass*) and in Stevenage (Herts) (*Bedewell* 1307 *SR* (p)) and two Bidwells in Devon and one in Somerset (PN D 410, 573). We may note also *Bydemulle* (1331 Ipm) in Hammoon (Do), and Bibbern Brook (Do), *bydeburna* BCS 696. This series of names makes it clear that the first element is a significant word. It is probably an OE **byde* (discussed in PN D 410), meaning 'hollow, depression,' found in such a personal name as Joseph *Attebyde* of Ardleigh (Ess) (1248 *Ass*). He probably lived near such a hollow[2].

CHEQUER HILL COPPICE (6″) is *Cheker garden* 1523 LP. Cf. *le Chekerestede* in Wittering (1357 Cl), a meadow called *le Cheker* in Brackley (1415 *Magd*), *Chekereshalle* (1330 *Ass*) in Nassaburgh Hundred, and *lez Chekiracre* (1501 *Compotus*) in Peterborough. Elsewhere we have *le Cheker* (1468 AD i), a field in Camberwell (Sr), *Chekermede* (1548 *LRMB*) in Cobham (Sr), and *the Chequer* (1522 SrAS xx) in Merstham. Fields so named probably took their name from their appearance with their varied crops.

COALES'S LODGE is perhaps to be associated with the family of Thomas and William *Coles* (1702 Poll). FOXHOLES FM is *Foxholles* 1227 *FF*. POLOPIT is probably to be identified with *Puddle Pit* 1779 *EnclA*.

Wadenhoe

WADENHOE [wɔdnou] 74 D 6

> *Wadenho* 1086 DB *et passim* to 1428 FA, -*hou* 1166 P (CR), 1241 P, -*howe* 12th Survey, 1330 *Ass*, 1373 Cl, -*hoo* 1343 Cl
> *Waudenho* 1184 P

---

[1] Bridges (ii, 162) mentions a spring in Higham Ferrers giving rise to a brook called Bidwell-water.

[2] For the Essex forms we are indebted to Dr P. H. Reaney.

Wadeho 1236 Cl, 1249 Ch, 1255 Seld 13, *-hou* 1295 Pat
Watenho 1254 *AD* B 6221
Waddeho 1275 RH, *Waddenhoo* 1675 Ogilby
Wadnoe t. Jas 1 ECP, 1730 Poll

'*Wada*'s spur of land,' *v.* hoh.

XX. NASSABOROUGH HUNDRED

This double hundred, which coincides with the Soke of Peterborough, was earliest known as *Uptune* a. 1076 Geld Roll, *Optone, Optonegren, Optonegrave wapent.*, *Optongren* 1086 DB, *þas twa hundred to Uptune grene* 11th (c. 1200) *PeterbA*.

The later name appears as (*of*) *þam twam hundredum ute on þam nesse þe Medeshamstede onstent* c. 970 (c. 1200) BCS 1120, *two Hundreds de Nasso* 12th Survey, *two hundreds de Wapentach de Burch* ChronPetro, *ij hundredis de Nesse de Burc* 1181 P, *Nassum Burgi* 1215 Cl, *Nasso Burgi* 1216 PatR, *Nesto burgi* 1218 ClR, *Nassus Burgi* 1220, 1242 Fees, 1275 RH, *Nasto de Burg'* 1221 ClR, *Nassaburgh* 1227 Ch, *Nest' de Burgo* 1237 Cl, *Hundred de Nasso* 1301 Cl, *Nassaburgo* 1346 FA, *Hundred de Nasso Burgi al. the Nesse of Borough* 1541 LP.

The earliest reference to this hundred is in BCS 1130 where we hear that the abbot of Peterborough bought 20 acres of wood and *feld* from Osgod of Bainton 'in the presence of two hundreds *æt Dicon*.' The traditional meeting-place of the hundred was at Langdyke Bush in Ufford *infra* 244, at the junction of the parishes of Ufford, Upton and Helpston; hence it is spoken of as the 'Abbot's hundred of Langedyk' in 1305 (Ipm), and as 'Upton' or 'Upton Green hundred[1].' The 'long dyke' is the Roman road, commonly known as King Street, a branch of Ermine Street, which comes up here from the Nene and makes its way due north to Bourne (L). The other 'dyke' of the dat. pl. *Dicon* was probably the ridge-road from Peterborough to Barnack, which intersects King Street at Langdyke Bush.

The hundred was later called the 'hundred of Ness' or the

---

[1] The use of *gren*, 'green' in DB is noteworthy. It is far earlier than any hitherto recorded example of that noun.

'hundred of the Ness of Peterborough,' since it occupied the bold næss or promontory pushing out into the fens between the Welland and the Nene (Bridges ii, 443). Round (VCH i, 268 n. 3) notes that the adjacent wapentake of Lincolnshire, forming the south-western angle of that county, is similarly known as *Nesse* in DB.

The term *hundred* was sometimes replaced by the Scandinavian *wapentake*, *v*. Introd. xxvi.

Peterborough

PETERBOROUGH 64 H 12

According to Bede the site of the original monastery here was known as *Medeshamstedi* (c. 750). *Medeshamstede* is the form in the numerous forged OE charters from 680 onwards (BCS 48, 271, 464, 1128).

On the rebuilding of the monastery after the Danish invasions (*v*. Introd. xiii) the place came to be known as *Burg* or *Burgh*, probably in the sense of 'fortified town.' Early ME forms are *Burg* 1086 DB, *Burh* c. 1115 Dugd i, 390, *Burc* 1155, *Burch* 1167 P, *Medeshamstede qui modo Burg dicitur* 12th Ord. The usual official spelling in medieval documents is *villa* or *Abbas de Burgo* or *de Burgo Sancti Petri* or *Sancti Petri de Burg*(o) from the dedication of the Abbey. The modern form has been noted first as *Petreburgh* 1333 Cl, 1385 Pat, *Peterburgh* 1397 Cl, *Petirburgh* 1401 Cl. Later spellings of interest are: *Borowe Seynt Per'* 1378 AD vi, *Borough Seynt Peter* 1571 AD v, *Petreborow* 1512 LP, *Peterborough al. Borough Saynt Peter* 1588 Recov, *Peeterborrow* 1657 NRS i.

For the older name Professor Ekwall notes that in ASC (*s.a.* 654) we are told that *Medeshamstede* was named from *Medeswæl*. In this name *wæl* is OE *wæl*, 'pool,' probably a pool in the Nene. He suggests that the first element in both names is an OE **Mēde*, a derivative of the element *Mōd-*, common in OE names, and equivalent to the OHG *Muotine* (Förstemann, PN 1128).

PETERBOROUGH STREET-NAMES

NOTE. The following are the chief street-names: BOROUGHBURY is *Burubyry* c. 1320 *CartN*, *Burghbery* 1334 *Compotus*, *Burg(h)byry* 1346 *PeterbB*, c. 1350 *CartN*, *Burghbery Gapp* 1512 *Compotus*, *Burghbury al. Boroughbery* 1541 LP. The street takes its name from the old manor of Burghbury, i.e. Peterborough Bury, *bury* having the later manorial sense, *v.* burh and cf. Berryfields *supra* 15. BRIDGE ST is *Hithegate* c. 1250 *Swaffham*, (*le*) c. 1375 *Compotus*, c. 1400 *Rental*, (*le*) *Hydegate* 1296, 1348 *CartN*, *Hyegate* 1478 AD iii, *Hyghgate* 1502 *Compotus*, *High Gate Street* 1539 LP, *Brigstrete* 1572 *Rental*, *Highgate or Narrow Bridge Street* 1811 *EnclA*, so called because it led to a hithe or landing place by the Nene (*v.* hyð), and later to the bridge near the same spot. BUTCHERS ROW is *le Bocherow* 1521 *Compotus*, *Butcherowe*, *Batchers Rowe* 1639 *Minute Bk*, *Butcher-row* 1811 *EnclA*. This was the name for the west end of the present Market Street. CHAPEL ST is *Chapelrowe* 1521 *Compotus*. COWGATE is *Cougate* 1362, (*le*) *Cow(e)gate* 1404 *Fraunc*, 1417 *Compotus*, presumably the street where cows were bought and sold. CUMBERGATE c. 1250 *Swaffham*, *le Comberegate* 1337 *CartN*, *Comber(e)sgate* 1362, 1375 *Compotus*, *Combrisgate* 1488 *Rental*, and was the street of the wool-combers of the city. DEACON ST takes its name from one Thomas *Deacon*, a Peterborough feoffee of the early 18th century who founded Deacon's School here. ST JOHN ST. This name is quite modern. It was earlier known as (*le*) *Bondegate* 13th *PeterbA*, 1330 *Ass*, 1375 *Compotus*, 1382 *Rental*, 1390 *Compotus*, (*le*) *Band(e)gate* c. 1400 *Rental*, *Bund(e)gate* 1512 *Compotus*, 1539 LP, *Bungayte* 1636, *Boonegate* 1639 *Minute Bk*, containing ON *bóndi*, possibly from its having been the home of the 'bonds' or peasants or churls, as opposed to the burgesses and others of higher social rank. LONG CAUSEWAY is *The Long Causeway* 1811 *EnclA*. MARKET ST is probably identical with (*le*) *Marketstede* 1246 *Pytchley*, 1247 *PeterbB*, 1390 *Compotus*, *v.* stede. MIDGATE is identical with *Howegate* c. 1250 *Swaffham*, (*the*) 1341 *Rental*, *le Howgate* 1390 *Compotus*, *le Haweʒate* c. 1320 *CartN*, *Hawegate* 1375 *Compotus*, *Hawgate* c. 1400 *Rental*, *Hougate* (ib.), and must take its name from some now forgotten tumulus or burial mound here, *v.* haugr. PADHOLME ROAD is on the site of fields formerly known as *Padinholm* 13th *PeterbA*, *Padeholm* 13th *PeterbA*, 1346 *PeterbB*, c. 1400 *Rental*, *Padholme* 1542 *Rental*, probably a compound of OE *pade*, 'toad,' and holmr. PRIESTGATE is *Prestgate* 1214–22 *PeterbB*, c. 1400 *Rental*, *Prestegate* 1362 *Compotus*, 1404 *Fraunc*, *Presgate* 1539 LP, *Prisgate lane* 1642 *Minute Bk*, 'priests' street.' WESTGATE is *le West(e)gate* c. 1320 *CartN*, 1362 *Compotus*, *Wesgayte* 1636 *Minute Bk*, 'west street.'

Of lost street-names we may note *Bradegate* 1245 *PeterbB*, 'broad or wide street,' *le Cokerowe* 1390 *Compotus*, *Dedmanslane* 1417 ib., *Dedemanslane* 1512 ib., *Gropelane* 1500 ib., perhaps a very dark thoroughfare, *Ratonrowe* 1362 *Compotus*, *lez Ratonrowe* 1495 ib., *Rotonrow* ib., a common street-name in old towns, probably a term of contempt, *in Veteri Scaccario* 1390 *Compotus*, *Vetus Scaccarium* 1512 ib., i.e. the (ex)chequer, cf. *the Checker* in Northampton *supra* 8, *Schowe(s)lane* 1273 *Swaffham*, c. 1280 *Pytchley*, *Showlane* 1500 *Compotus*, to be associated with one Robert *Schow* who was living there in 1273, and *Sowterrowe* 1390 *Compotus*, where the *sowters* or shoemakers must have congregated. *Gate* in the Peterborough street-names is from ON *gata*, 'road.'

ALWALTON GULL ROAD (6″). Cf. *Allerton Gull* 1753 Fenland NQ ii. It is probably to be associated with the family of Geoffrey de *Alewalton* who bought land at Peterborough in 1234 (Cl), and must have come from Alwalton (Hu). In 1315 (*Ass*) there is mention also of William Lyntot de *Alwolton* in connection with the parish. *gull* is the same word which is found in Gull Field (PN BedsHu 205), a variant of *goule*, 'watercourse.' The EDD gives the sense 'a deep gutter where water runs,' and notes that it is used in Northamptonshire.

DOGSTHORPE *olim* [dɔstrəp]

Dodest(h)orp(e) 12th (963 E) ASC *et freq* to 1308 Sparke with variant spelling *Dodis-*, *Dodestorp* 1241 P (p)

Doddestorp c. 1115 Dugd ii, 390, -*thorp* t. Ed 3 *SR*

Dud(d)estorp 1247 *Ass*

Dodingthorp 1285 *Ass*

Dosthorp(e) 1428 FA, 1540 Dugd i, 367, 1632 *Recov*, *Dostrop* 1517 DBE

Dastropp 1541 LP, *Dusthorpe* 1556 *FF*, *Doggesthropp* 1578 *FF*

'*Dodd*'s village,' *v.* þorp.

EASTFIELD is *Æstfeld* 12th (963 E) ASC, *Estfeld* 1189 (1332) Ch, 1227 Ch, -*feud* 1253 *Ass*, -*feelde* 1578 BM. *v.* feld. It lies just east of Peterborough.

EDGERLEY (DRAIN) (6″) is *Eggerdesle* c. 1250 *Swaffham*, c. 1350 *CartN*, 14th NthNQ iv, *Eggersle* 14th *PeterbB*, c. 1400 *Rental*, *Egerdele* c. 1400 *Rental*, *Edgerly meadow* 1540 Dugd i, 367, *Egerley medowe* 1542 *Rental*. '*Ecgheard*'s clearing,' *v.* leah.

FLAG FEN is *Flagg(e) Fen(n)* 1666 *Rental*, 1677 *Depositions*. It was also known as *Borrow Little Fenn* 1642 *Rental* in distinction from Borough (Great) Fen *infra* 231.

FULHAM ROAD (6″) is a new thoroughfare, preserving the name of the district formerly known as *Falholm* c. 1280 *Pytchley*, 1404 *Fraunc*, *Faleholm* 1302 *CartN*, *Falholmhyrne* 1484 *Compotus*. Probably 'fallow island' or 'marshland,' *v.* fealh, holmr.

GARTON END is *Carton* 1248 *PeterbA et passim* to 1383 *FF*, *Cartonhowes* 1329 *CartN*. No explanation of this name can be offered. It may well be only a coincidence that it is near Car Dike *supra* 5. For *howes* cf. Howe Drain *infra* 237.

LONGTHORPE and THORPE HALL are *Torp*, *þorp* 972 (c. 1200) BCS 1130, *Torp* 1086 DB, (*juxta Burc*) 1176 P, *Thorp(e)* 1189 (1332) Ch, *Langethorpe* 1285 *Ass* (p), *Longethorp(e)* 1285 *Ass*, *Longthorp juxta Peterburgh* 1503 *FF*. *v.* þorp. The descriptive adjective must first have been applied to the village along the main road from Peterborough to Castor, the manor house retaining the original uncompounded form of the name.

LOW FM is *le Lowe* c. 1400 *Rental*, 1500 *Compotus*, *the Low* 1811 *EnclA*. *v.* hlaw. This farm was recently demolished, the Corporation Isolation hospital now occupying the site (W. T. M.).

NEWARK is *Nieuyrk* 1189 (1332) Ch, *Newerc* 1227 Ch, *-werk* 1308 Sparke, *Neuwerk* 1323 *FF*, t. Ed 3 *SR*, *Newewerk* 1330 *Ass*, *Newerk Gate* c. 1400 *Rental*. 'The new fort or defence,' *v.* (ge)weorc and Addenda lii.

OXNEY HO is (*on*) *Oxanige*, *Oxanege* c. 970 (c. 1200) BCS 1130, *Oxanig* c. 975 (14th) *Thorney*, *Oxeneylode* 1247 *PeterbB*, *Oxeney(e)* 1249 Ch, 1253 *Ass*, 1314 BM. 'Oxen island' or 'land in the marsh,' *v.* eg, (ge)lad.

SNOSSELLS (lost) is *Snorishil* 1404 *Fraunc*, *Snoryshylls* 1500 *Compotus*, *Snorehill(s)* 1542 *Rental*, *Snoshills*, *Snossells* 1811 *EnclA*. This p.n. seems to involve the same pers. name which is found in Snoring and Snarehill (Nf). On this name cf. Ekwall, PN in *-ing* 81. Ekwall suggests that it is a lost OE name **Snār(a)*, allied to *snearh*, 'swift.' That adjective may be found in *Snarebroc* in Brixworth (13th AD iii).

SPITAL BRIDGE (6″). Cf. *Spitelfeld* 1375 *Compotus*, *Spittilfeld* c. 1400 *Rental*, *farm of the Spittle* 1540 Dugd i, 367, *Spyttle* 1542

Rental. This marks the site of St Leonard's hospital, an old hospital for lepers, afterwards a small priory and grange under the care of the Abbey almoner, who held Spital Grange as part of his fee (W. T. M.).

ADDERLEY DRAIN (6″). This probably takes its name from a Mr Adderley who reclaimed marshes in the district in the early 19th cent. (W. T. M.). Cf. *Mr Adderley's private road* (1812 Fenland NQ ii). HONEY HILL is *Hony-hill* 1753 Fenland NQ ii. MILLFIELD is *Milnefeld* 1375 *Compotus, le Mylnefeld* 1500 (ib.), *Milfeild* 1665 *Clayton.* NEW ENGLAND is a modern district which grew up round the railway works here *post* 1850 (W. T. M.). PARK MEADOW FM (6″) is *Parkemedew* 1512 *Compotus.* WESTWOOD is *Westwude* 13th *PeterbA*, *-wode* c. 1220 *For.* It lies to the west of Peterborough.

Ailsworth

AILSWORTH[1] 64 J 9/10

> *Ægeleswurð, to ægeleswurðe* 948 (c. 1200) BCS 871, *Aegeleswurð* 10th (c. 1200) BCS 1131, *-wyrð* ib.
> *Eglesworde* 1086 DB
> *Eleswurda* 1166 P, *Elleswurda* (CR)
> *Ayleswrth* 1189 (1332) Ch, *Aileswurth* 1227 Ch

---

[1] BCS 871 gives us the bounds of Ailsworth. They start at the south-west corner at the Nene and go to the old *dic* on the boundaries of Sutton. The *dic* must be the old Ailsworth-Sutton road. Thence they go to the old *stræt*, the boundary here making a short right-angled turn to Sutton Cross on Ermine Street. Thence it goes to *maman þorn*, thence to *marmedue* and ever straight on to the wood and so within the wood along the bounds of Upton to the bounds of Ufford. From Sutton Cross the present boundary makes its way with a certain number of zig-zags to the south end of Moore Wood, whence it makes its way due north (forming the boundary of Upton) to Langdyke Bush in Ufford (*maman þorn* is probably an error for *mænan þorn*, 'common thorn,' i.e. on the common boundary, the *mar* in *marmedue* is the pool just south-east of Upton Manor House, on the parish boundary, *mære* being a variant form of *mere* occasionally found in OE, and giving rise to dialectal *mar(e)*). Thence it goes to the boundary of Helpston, i.e. the straight west-to-east stretch to the south-east corner of Helpston parish, thence to the Castor boundary and so out of the wood, and from the wood by the Castor boundary to the road and over the road (which runs) along the old *dic*, and from the *dic* back to the Nene. The first point where it touches Castor parish is clearly its extreme north-west corner. Thence the boundary went through woodland (referred to earlier in the Charter—there are still patches of woodland here). Thence we make our way to the Castor-Ailsworth-Sutton road, which runs along the 'old *dic*' referred to above, and so to the Nene.

Eilewrd 1198 Cur, *Eilesworth'* 1202 Ass, *Eylesworthe* 1214–22
PeterbB, *Eylisworth* 1284 FA
Eylleswurth 1305 Ipm

'*Ægel*'s farm,' *v.* worþ, cf. Aylesbury (PN Bk 145) and Ayles-
beare (PN D 580).

CASTOR HANGLANDS is *bosc. voc. Castrehanggand* c. 1400 *Rental*,
Castor Hangins 1569 *Rental*. The name clearly refers to the
wooded slope here. The EDD notes this use of *hanging* in
Northants in the phrase 'it lies on the hangings,' i.e. on the side
of a hill. Cf. *Hangginde* in Eydon (13th AD i) and *le Hanggyng*
in Yelvertoft (1406 AD iii). The ME form is that of the Northern
ME pres. participle rather than that of the verbal noun.

MOORE WOOD is *bosc. voc. le Moore* c. 1400 *Rental, Moore wood*
1631 *Rental*. Cf. also *Morhauwe, Eylisuuorthe Mor* c. 1250
Swaffham. v. mor, haga. The ground is marshy here.

WILDBOARS COPPICE (6″) is probably to be associated with the
family of *Wildbore* who held land in various villages in the Soke
of Peterborough in the 16th and 17th cent. (cf. VCH ii, 494).

Bainton

BAINTON 64 F 9

Badingtun c. 980 (c. 1200) BCS 1130 *et freq* to 1428 FA with
   variant spellings *-yng-, -in-, -yn-, Badintune* 1198 FF,
   Badenton 1201 Cur
Baynton 1369 Cl, *Badyngton al. Baynton* 1536 *FF*, 1604
   Recov

'*Bada*'s farm,' *v.* ingtun. Cf. *Aelfnoð badan sune* among the
Peterborough sureties in BCS 1130 and Bainton (O), DB
Baditone.

ASHTON is *Æsctun* c. 960 (c. 1200) BCS 1128, *Ascetone* 1086 DB,
Esctona 1125–8 ChronPetro, *Eisetuna* 1140 Sparke, *Aiston* 1189
(1332) Ch, *Ayston* 12th Survey, *Axton* 1253 *Ass, Asshton juxta
Badyngton* 1330 *Ass, Assheton* 1386 Cl. 'Ash-tree farm,' *v.* æsc,
tun.

HILLY WOOD is *Hylhawe* 1293 Misc, (*le*) *Hilhawe* 1298 WellsR,
1330 Ipm, *Hillawe* 1350 Ipm, *Hillow Knowle* 1642 DKR 39.

'Hill-enclosure,' *v.* haga. There was a *boscus de Hage* close at hand in 1198 (P).

LAWN WOOD (6″) is so named 1825 O.S. This is probably a further case of confusion of ON lundr and ME *launde,* for this wood is perhaps to be identified with the *Raveneslund* of 1198 (P).

Barnack

BARNACK 64 J 8

>   (*on*) *Beornican* c. 980 (c. 1200) BCS 1130
>   *Bernak*(*e*) 1052–65 (c. 1350) Ramsey, 1053 (13th) ChronRams,
>   (*la*) 1210 Cur (p), *Bernakes* 1151–4 France, 1196 Cur
>   *Bernech*(*a*) 1053 (13th) ChronRams, 1166 P (p), 1176 BM,
>   12th Ord, 1210 Cur
>   *Bernac* 1086 DB, 1200 Cur, Seld 3
>   *Bernec*(*a*) 1162, 1184 P (p), 1200 Cur (p)
>   *Bernek* 1189 (1332) Ch, 1209 Seld 13, 1227 Ch, 1259 Seld 13
>   *Bernack*(*e*) 1205 FineR, 1209 WellsR, n.d. AD iii
>   *Barneck* 1284 FA, *Barnicke* 1582 Cai, *Barnoak* 1779 F

The forms in BCS 1130 are not sufficiently good for us to lay great stress on them, but it is impossible to believe that an OE *beornic* (possibly for *beornwic*) could have been so early and so persistently folk-etymologised to a form in *ac,* 'oak,' especially in view of the fact that wic is a common p.n. suffix, and ac is a rare one. More probably we must take it that the original form of the name was *beorna-āc,* 'warriors' oak,' with alternative form (in the dat. sg.) *beorna-ǣce,* which would account for the early forms in *-ech, -ek.* It is possible also that the *ech, ek* forms are due to the nom. pl. *ǣc,* rather than the dat. sg. That would perhaps explain better the fact that the OE form is apparently in the dat. pl. (? for *beorn-ācum* or *-ǣcum*) with occasional later *-akes.* For the form *eche* cf. the field called *benethen ye eches* in Barnwell (1316 *Buccleuch*).

HILLS AND HOLES is a tract of broken ground, the site of former large quarries of 'Barnack rag' which provided most of the building material for the abbeys of Peterborough, Croyland, Thorney, Ramsey and most of the churches of Holland in Lincolnshire and the Marshland in Norfolk (Bridges ii, 489).

PILSGATE

Pilesgat(e) c. 965 (c. 1200) BCS 1128, 1221 WellsR, 1189 (1332) Ch, 1198 FF, 1227 Ch, 1284 FA, *-gatha* c. 1210 WellsR (p)

pilesgeat c. 980 (c. 1200) BCS 1130, *Pilesgete* 1125–8 Chron Petro

Pillesgete 1086 DB, *Pillesgate* 1203 *FF*, 1253 *Ass*, *Pyllesyate* 1364 *FF*, 1478 AD iii, *Pyllysate* 1517 DBE

Pyliate 1558 *Recov*

'The gate of a man named *Pīl*,' *v.* geat. We have a diminutive of this pers. name in Pilton *supra* 217. For hesitation between *yate* and *gate* cf. Bozeat *supra* 190.

THE SYNHAMS (6″) is *Synholms* 1570, *Synholm leas* 1635 VCH ii, 461.

Borough Fen

BOROUGH FEN (6″) is *Burgfen* 1307 *Pytchley*, *Burghfen* 1331 Ramsey, 1380 *Compotus*, 14th *PeterbA*, c. 1400 *Rental*, *Boroughe Fenne* 1557 *FF*, *Peterborowe Fen* 1614 *Recov*, *Burrough Great Fenn* 1683 ib., *Boro' Fen or High Boro' Fen or Peterboro' Great Fen* 1718 DKR xl. Borough or Peterborough Fen was an extra-parochial district comprising the area of fenland to the north of Peterborough lying within Northamptonshire. In 1822 the parish of Newborough (*infra* 239) was formed from it, the remainder of the area being consequently known as *Oldborough*, as in Greenwood's map and the earliest editions of the 1″ O.S.

GRAY'S FM, PANK'S FM and SPEECHLY'S DROVE (6″) are to be associated with the families of Thomas *Gray* (1623 *Minute Bk*), William and Paul *Panke* (1620, 1629 ib.) and Thomas *Speachly* and Richard *Speechlye* (1631, 1636 ib.). For *drove, v. infra*.

CROWTREE FM is *Crowtre* 1561 *Compotus*. DECOY FM takes its name from a duck 'decoy' here, one of the best known in the fen district (W. T. M.). EARDLEY GRANGE. The Eardley Wilmot family owned most of the parish of Borough Fen until recently (VCH ii, 472). HORSESHOE FM. Cf. *Horse Shoe Drove* 1823 B. 'Drove' is a term used in the fens for a road along which cattle are driven, and for a water-way (PN BedsHu 294).

Castor

CASTOR [kɑ·stə] 64 J 10

> (*to*) *Kyneburga cæstre*, (*be*) *Cyneburge cæstre* 948 (c. 1200) BCS 871
> *Castre* 1086 DB *et passim* to 1428 FA, (*near Peterborough*) 1325 Cl, *Castra* 1174 P (p), *Caster al. Castre* 1456 Pat
> *Castor* 1189 (1332), 1227 Ch, 1316 Cl
> *Cestre* 1327 Ipm

v. **ceaster**. The Roman camp here is the station of Duro-brivae on Ermine St, a compound of British *duro-*, 'fortress,' and *briva*, 'bridge,' cf. *Durobrivae* as the old name for Rochester. The church is dedicated to *St Kyneburga*, daughter of Penda, king of Mercia, who according to tradition founded a monastery here in the 7th cent. Her name is preserved in a ridge locally known as Lady Conyburrow's Way (Bridges ii, 499). According to Henry of Huntingdon (c. 1115), the place was at one time called *Kair Dorm, id est Dormeceastre*, while two centuries later John of Tynemouth in his *Historia Aurea* tells us that the place was called *Dormundescastre* and afterwards named *Kine-burga castrum*. It would seem therefore that the site of Castor was at one time in the possession of an Englishman named *Dēormund*. *Dormeceastre* is a reduction of the earlier name, while *Kair Dorm* is a pseudo-British form. Cf. VCH ii, 472.

BELSIZE FM is *Belas(s)ise* 1214–22 *PeterbB*, c. 1250 *Swaffham*, 14th *PeterbA*, c. 1400 *Rental, Belseys Wood* 1535 VE. This place-name, found also in Du, Mx, Nb, and Y, is of AFr origin, meaning 'beautiful site, or spot.' The place is situated in the wooded district to the west of Peterborough and may have seemed a pleasant spot by comparison with the flat featureless fenland to the north and east. In 1214 Abbot Robert of Lindsey built houses here, and planted hedges and drained it (VCH ii, 474).

FERRY HO corresponds in site to *Gonewade* c. 1150 *Thorney*, *Gunnewade in Castre* 1330 QW, *aqua de Gonwade* 1503 *FF*, *Gunworth Ferry* 1702 Poll, *Gunwade Ferry* 1791 Bridges, 1826 G. '*Gunni*'s ferry or ford,' *v.* **wæd**. *Gunna* is found as a pers. name among the Peterborough sureties (BCS 1130). It is of Scandi-navian origin, *v.* Björkman, NP 56.

MILTON PARK is (*on*) *mylatune*, (*on*) *Myletune* 972 (c. 1200) BCS
1130, *Meleton*(*e*) 1086 DB, 1189 (1332) Ch, 1205 Cur, *Miletuna*
1140 Sparke, *Meltona* 13th *PeterbA*, 1227 Ch, *Multon* 1284 FA,
Milton(*e*) 1304 Ch *et passim*. 'Mill farm,' *v*. myln, tun.

NORMANGATE FIELD (6″) is *Normangate* c. 1350 *CartN*, c. 1400
Rental. It is difficult to say whether *Norman* here is for *North-
man*, i.e. Norseman, or for *Norman*. 'Gate' is probably Scandinavian gata, 'road.'

ROBIN HOOD and LITTLE JOHN are the names of two stones in
Castor Field near Gunwade Ferry, now covered with thorn-
bushes. Morton (551) writes as follows: "Erroneous tradition has
given them out to be Two Draughts of Arrows from *Alwalton*
Church-Yard thither, the one of *Robin Hood*, and the other of
Little *John*. But the Truth is they were set up for Witnesses,
that the carriages of Stone from *Bernack* to *Gunwade-Ferry*, to
be conveyed to *St Edmund's-Bury*, might pass that way without
paying Toll. And in some old *Terriars*, they are called *St Edmund's* Stones. These Stones are nicked in their Tops after the
manner of Arrows, probably enough in Memory of St Edmund,
who was shot to Death with Arrows by the *Danes*. The Balk they
stand upon is still call'd *St Edmund's* Balk. They are supposed
to be the *petrify'd* Arrows of those Two Famous Archers."
Morton's history of these stones, based in part on Gunton's
History of Peterborough, has good early authority. Mr Mellows
calls our attention to a passage in Henry of Pytchley's *Book of
Fees* (100) and a charter surviving in a copy of the lost original
in the Registers of the Precentor which make this clear. There
we have recorded grants by the abbot of Peterborough to the
abbot of Bury of a rood of land in the field of Castor, with free
carriage on the public road from Barnack through that land
down to the Nene and across the Nene between Peterborough
and Alwalton, for the conveyance of marble and other stone for
the use of the monks of Bury.

CASTOR LINCH (6″) is *le Lynche* 1512 *Compotus*. *v*. hlinc. CLAY
LANE (6″). Cf. *Clayfurlong* c. 1400 *Rental*. LOVE'S HILL is to be
associated with the family of *Love* (1592 etc. ParReg). OLD-
FIELD POND (6″) is *Oldfeld* c. 1400 *Rental*. *v*. feld. SALTER'S

Wood and Tree (6″). Cf. *Saltersgate* c. 1400 *Rental*. They lie by a road, presumably an old salter's road (*v.* gata and PN Wo 4 ff.).

Deeping Gate

Deeping Gate (64 E 10/11) is *Depynggate* 1390 Cl, 1422 *Ct*. This is the 'gate' or road to Deeping (L). *v.* gata.

Etton

Etton 64 F 10

    Etton(a) 1125–8 ChronPetro *et passim*
    Ecton 1189 (1332) Ch, 1301 Ipm

There is very little to go on here. The *c* in the second series of forms is probably an error for *t*. The name may be from earlier *Ēatan-tūn*, hence 'Eata's farm.'

Simon's Wood (6″) is *Symundeswode* 1245 *PeterbB*, *Simmons Wood* 1823 B. '*Sigemund*'s wood.'

Woodcroft Castle is *Wodecroft* 1140 Sparke *et passim* with variant spelling *Wude-*. 'Croft by the wood.'

Eye

Eye 64 G 13

    Ege 12th (963 E) ASC, c. 1115 Dugd i, 390
    Eia 1125–8 ChronPetro, *Eya* 1189 (1332), 1227 Ch
    Eye 1284 FA, 1305 Pat, 1306, 1348 Ch

'Island,' *v.* eg. Bridges (ii, 513) says it is "situate on a rising ground, and, before the draining of the fen, in winter time (was) surrounded by water."

Northolme Ho is *Northolm* 1247 *FF*, 1305 BM, 1313 *PeterbB*, (*by Eye*) 1306 Ch, (*juxta Eye*) 1330 QW, *Northolmgrove* c. 1400 *Rental*, *Northamwood* 1535 VE. 'North holmr or island.' It lies in the fenland north of Eye.

The Reaches is *le Reche* 1375 *Compotus*, c. 1400 *Rental*, *lez Reche* 1512 *Compotus*. This is the name of the fenland road from Eye to Powder Blue House. It would seem to be the same word *reach* discussed in PN BedsHu 125 *s.n.* Reach, and found also in Reach (C) in the fen district. It denotes a narrow strip of road.

SINGLESOLE FM (6")

> *Senglesholt* 1189 (1332) Ch, t. Hy 3 *PeterbA*, *-halt* 1227 Ch,
> *-lis-* 1503 *Compotus*
> *Singlysholt* 1503 *Compotus*, *Singleholt* 1541 LP, *Synglesholt*
> 1542 *Rental*, *Singlesole* 1666 *Rental*

Dr Ritter suggests that we may here have to do with a pers.
name *Singulf*, which might perhaps best be explained as a Scand
loan-name from OGer. Cf. *Singulph* (Förstemann, PN 1338),
and for early loss of *f* in this Scand name cf. Rygh, GP 217, *s.n.*
Singull, *Singulf*. Hence '*Singull*'s wood,' *v.* holt.

TANHOLT HO

> *Talnholt* 1247 *PeterbB*, c. 1250 *Swaffham*, *Talnostfen* (sic)
> 1331 Ramsey
> *Talneholt* 14th *PeterbA*
> *Tanholte Herne* 1576 NthNQ vi, *Tonholt* 1645 *FF*

Professor Ekwall and Dr Smith agree in suggesting an original
compound of OE *tǣnel*, 'basket,' and holt, hence, '(osier) holt
in which baskets are made.' For metathesis of *nl* to *ln*, cf. Onley
and Olney *supra* 14, 44 and Binley (PN Wa 25) DB *Bilner*.
Herne is OE hyrne. The place lies in the S.E. corner of the
parish.

CAUSEWAY END COTTAGES (6"). This is on the causeway leading
to Thorney and Wisbech. Cf. *Oxneycause* c. 1400 *Rental*.
CRANMORE (6") is *Cranemore* 1512 *Compotus*. 'Crane or heron
mor.' EASTWOOD FM is *Estwude* 13th *PeterbA*. EYEBURY FM is
Ibury 1386 IpmR, *Eybury Parke al. Ibury Parke* 1541 LP,
Eybury, Iburye, Iverye 1609 BM, *Eybury al. Ibury* 1732 *Recov.*
bury is here used probably in the manorial sense, *v.* burh. EYE
GREEN is so named in 1826 G. POWDER BLUE FM is so named
in 1823 B. The NED defines 'powder-blue' as 'powdered smalt,
especially for use in the laundry.' The reason for the application
of the name is unknown.

Glinton

GLINTON 64 F 11

> *Clinton* 1060 (c. 1350) KCD 809, 13th AD ii, 1285 *Ass*
> *Glinton(e)* 1086 DB *et freq* to 1227 Ch
> *Clemton* 1194 Cur (p)

Glintonhowe 1209 *FF*
Glenton 1285 *Ass*

This is a difficult name. It is on the dead level, and so cannot contain ODan *klint*, 'hill.' It is on a stream, and it is possible that this is another example of the river-name *Glym(e)* found in Oxfordshire (*Glim* in BCS 1043). *Clemton* may preserve a further trace of the *m*[1]. For confusion of *c* and *g*, cf. Glendon and Glapthorn *supra* 113, 203.

BROOK DRAIN (6″). Cf. *le Brok* c. 1340 *CartN*.

Gunthorpe

GUNTHORPE[2] 64 G 11

Gunetorp 1130 P (p) *et freq* to 1206 Cur, *-thorp* 1189 (1332) Ch, 1227 Ch, *Glunetorp* 1198 Cur
Gunestorp 1176 P, 1227 Ch
Gunnetorp' 1182 NRS iv (p)
Gunthorp 12th Survey, *-torp* 1208 PatR, *-thorpe* 1284 FA
Gonethorp 1277 ChronPetro

'*Gunni*'s village,' *v.* þorp and Ferry Ho *supra* 232. The same place-name occurs in L, Nf and R.

Helpston

HELPSTON 64 G 10

hylpestun ge mære 948 (c. 1200) BCS 871, *Hylpestun* c. 980 (c. 1200) BCS 1130
Helpestun(e) 1125–8 ChronPetro (p), 1148–66 NRS iv (p), *-ton* 1162 P (p) *et passim* with occasional spelling *-pis-*
Eelpeston 1284 FA
Elpston 1322–7 Ipm, *Helpston* 1390 Cl
Helperston 1517 DBE, *Helpson al. Helpston* 1571 FF

The forms from the Peterborough Cartulary show the confusion of *e* and *y* (*i*) noted under Barnwell *supra* 179; the correct vowel is doubtless *e*. The stem *help* is found in the OE pers. names *Helpric* and *Helpwine*. From this stem also we have an

---

[1] There is a form *Gluinton* in the printed edition of the Charter Rolls (vol. i, 19). This is, however, an error for *Glinton*.
[2] Formerly a hamlet of Paston.

ON woman's name *Hialp* (v. Lind), found in Helperby, Helper-thorpe (ZEN 45). In this name we probably have an unrecorded OE *Help*. Hence '*Help*'s farm,' v. tun. It is possible that the same pers. name is found in Helsthorpe, PN Bk 88.

HOWE DRAIN (6″). Cf. *le Howe* c. 1340 *CartN*, *le Howefeld, le Heyhowe* c. 1400 *Rental*. This probably is ON haugr, '*how*, hill.'

OXEY WOOD (6″) is so named c. 1825 O.S., 1826 G. 'Ox en-closure,' v. (ge)hæg. Cf. Oxhey (Herts).

RICE WOOD is *wood called le Rys* 13th *Deeds Enrolled*. This is OE hris, 'brushwood.'

WOODGATE END (6″) is probably near the place called *Wodehalle* 1280 ChronPetro (p), *la Wodehall* 1294 *Ass* (p), *Wodehull in Helpstone* 1443–50 ECP, *Woodhall* 1576 FF.

Marholm

MARHOLM [mærəm] 64 H 10

Marham 1052–65 (c. 1350) Ramsey *et passim* to 1525 AD iii, *Marhamwode, Marhamhirne* 1398 *Rental*
Marreham 1166 P (CR) (p), *Marram* 1428 FA
Marenham 1236 WellsR
Morham 1308 Cl
Marome 1526 SR, *Marholme* 1739 *Recov*

There are pools by the manor house, and this may be 'ham(m) by the mere,' v. mere. For the form *mar(e)*, cf. the form *marmedue supra* 228 n, which must denote 'pool-meadow.' *Marhamhirne* must refer to a corner or angle of the parish, v. hyrne.

MUCKLANDS WOOD is *boscus vocatus Muklund* 1270 Abbr. The second element is ON lundr, 'grove, copse.' The first element may be early ME *muk*, 'manure,' a word of Scandinavian origin.

Maxey

MAXEY 64 F 10

Macuseige c. 965 (c. 1200) BCS 1128
Macusie, Macesige, Macusige c. 970 (c. 1200) BCS 1130

Makesia 1184 P (p) *et passim* to 1428 FA with variant
    spellings *-eya, -eia, -eye, -e, -ey, Machesia* 1327 Ch
Maxey 1515 AD iv

'*Maccus*' island,' *v.* eg. *Maccus* is first recorded as the name
of a Western earl who shared in the defeat of Eric Bloodaxe at
Stainmoor in 950 (*v.* Roger of Wendover *s.a.*). It is next found
as the name of a warrior fighting on the side of the English at
the Battle of Maldon in 991. Cf. Maxwellheugh in Roxburgh-
shire, for which Johnston, *PN Scotland s.n.* gives 12th cent.
forms *Macchuswel, Maccuswell* from the book of Kelso. This was
named from one *Maccus*.

LOLHAM HALL, BRIDGE and MILL

Lehalm(*e*)   c. 1150 *Thorney*, t. Hy 3 *PeterbA, Lealme* 1253,
    Leaume 1257 *FF*
Loholm   c. 1160 NRS iv, c. 1250 *Swaffham*, 1272 *FF et freq*
    to 1353 Cl
Lehame   13th *PeterbA*
la *Haum*(*e*)   1202 Ass (p), 1221 WellsR, *Lehaume* 1212 Cur,
    1232 Pat, *Le Haume* 1257 *FF*
Leiham   1229 Cl (p)
Leham (*molendinum de*) 1243, 1285 *FF*, 1316, 1428 FA,
    Lehom 13th AD i
Lelham   1284 FA
Leum   1289 *FF*
Leholm   1306 *FF*, 1330 *Ass*, t. Ed 3 SR, *le Holme, the Holme*
    1389 Cl
Lolleham   1529 *FF, Loleham al. Leham* 1551 *FF*
Lolleham Myll, Mylleholme 1551 Pat
Lolham Brydge 1552 Pat
Lawlone al. Lowlam 1553 Pat

Professor Ekwall suggests that this is a compound of OE hleo,
'protection,' and helm, 'cattle-shed,' hence, 'sheltering shed.'
Possibly *healm*, 'straw, thatch,' would suit the forms of the
second element better, though the sense, 'sheltering thatch,'
would be much the same. Lolham Bridge is on Ermine Street,
at the point where that road, running north from Castor, crosses
the Welland. Such a shelter might well be found in this position.

Nunton Lodge

> Nunnetun c. 963 (c. 1200) BCS 1128, Nunneton 1285 Ass
> Nunton(a) 1226 Bracton et freq, Nunton Holme 1621 DKR 38

'Nunna's farm,' v. tun. Cf. Nunningham (PN Sx 481).

Newborough

Newborough 64 F/G 12. This was a part of Borough Fen (supra 231) which was formed into a new parish in 1822. It is Newborough in 1823 (Recov).

Kennulph's Drain (6″). This preserves the name of Kenulf, abbot of Peterborough in 1005 (VCH ii, 85).

Werrington End Fm is Werrington Ends 1753 Fenland NQ ii, and was perhaps the home of Thomas attetonesende (i.e. 'at the town's end') de Wytheryngton (1330 Ass). It adjoins Werrington parish.

Baxter's Bridge (6″) and Turves Fm are probably to be associated with the families of Leonard Baxter (1666 Rental) and John and William Turvey (1488, 1501 Compotus).

Hill Fm was the home of John de le Hille (t. Ed 3 SR). Hurn Fm was the home of Walter in le Hurne (t. Ed 3 SR) and William in the Hirne (c. 1400 Rental). v. hyrne. Long Meadow Fm (6″) is Langemedwe 13th PeterbA, Longemede c. 1400 Rental. Milking Nook is Milking Nook Tunnel 1753 Fenland NQ ii. Norwood Ho is Northwude 13th PeterbA, Northwode aliquando vocabatur Totteswode c. 1400 Rental. North with reference to Eastwood and Westwood supra 228, 235. Slipe Fm (6″) is the Slipe 1753 Fenland NQ ii, The Slipe Fen 1826 G. The name is descriptive of the projecting arm of the parish here. Cf. slipe infra 273. The Wash is molend. de Wasse 1198 FF. v. (ge)wæsc. Woolfell-hill Road (6″) is Woolffenhills 1753 Fenland NQ ii. Perhaps 'wolf fen,' the modern form being corrupt.

Northborough

Northborough 64 F 11

> Norðburh 12th (656 E) ASC.

Northburg 12th Survey *et freq* to 1338 Cl, *-bourgh* 1295 Ch,
　　Norburc 1200 Cur (p), 1217 ClR (p), *-burgh* 1227 Ch
(*in*) *Norburgo* 1189 (1332) Ch, *Noreburg* 1219 *FF*, *Norberewe*
　　1525 AD iii
Northborough al. Norborough 1541 LP, *Norborow* 1704 *Recov*
Narborow al. Norburghe 1549 BM, *Narborow* 1702 Poll

'The north burh,' perhaps with reference to Peterborough.

NORTH FEN is *mariscus de le Northfen* 13th *PeterbA*.

WALDERHAM HALL (6″) is *aulam Walraund* 1275 RH, *Wal-romdeshalle* 1330 *Ass*, *Waldramhalle, Peykirkchaere al. Waldram-halle* 1538 LP, *Waldroom Hall* 1753 Fenland NQ ii. This clearly takes its name from the family of *Waleran*, son of Ralf, in Help-ston, of whom we have record in 1177–89 (NRS iv), and *Waleran* of Ufford (c. 1205 ib.). *Peykirkchaere* points to its adjacency to the parish of Peakirk *infra*. Professor Bruce Dickins suggests that in *chaere* we may have OFr *chaere* for which Littré (*s.v. chaise*) gives the explanation 'terme de fief,' 'en partage de fief noble, nom des quatre arpents de terre qui environnent de plus près le chateau.' This suggestion is con-firmed by the fact that *chaere* is here applied to land around the hall of an important military tenant.

GIDDON'S DROVE and RIPPON'S DROVE (both 6″) are probably to be associated with the families of Benjamin *Gidding* and Anne and Sarah *Rippin* (1671, 1672, 1675 ParReg).

Paston

PASTON [pɑˈstən]　64 H 12
　　Pastun 12th (963 E) ASC, *Paston* 1166 P (p) *et passim*
　　Paxtona 1199 FF[1], *Pastune hawe* t. Ed 1 BM

This is probably ' *Pæcci*'s tun.' Note the 1199 form for the only trace of the earlier consonantal group and cf. Pattishall *supra* 92. *Pastune hawe* may be for PASTON HALL. Cf. *supra* 173.

CATHWAITE (perhaps surviving in *Thwaites* 1826 G)
　　Cadweit 1212 Cur, *Cathweit, Cathueit* c. 1220 *For*, *-weyt* c.
　　　1250 Swaffham, *Catheweyt*(*h*) 1300 *PeterbB*, c. 1300 *CartN*,
　　Cathweyt in Paston 1338 Pat

---
[1] Checked from MS.

Catweyth c. 1280 *PeterbB*, *Cathweyth* 14th *PeterbA*
Cathwat 1288 *PeterbA*
Catthweyt 1330 *Ass*, *Cahtwheyt* c. 1400 *Rental*, *Cathwayts*
   1505 *Compotus*
Thwaites 1728 *Deed*

This is probably a compound of a lost ON **ká, kó*, 'chough, jackdaw,' and *þveit*, hence 'corner of land frequented by jackdaws,' cf. Cawood (La, Y) in Lindkvist (184) and PN La 180. *Thwaites* may be a different place, as we have mention c. 1400 (NRS ii) of *le Twheytes*.

NAB LANE (6″) is *Nabbe* 1247 *PeterbB*, c. 1400 *Rental*, *le Nab* c. 1400 *Rental*, *Nabbewode* c. 1400 *Rental*, *the Nobbs*, *Paston Nabbs* 1764 *Deed*, *Nob Wood* 1823 B. This is clearly ON *nabbr*, *nabbi*, 'projecting peak' or 'knoll.' Cf. *le nabbe* in Brampton Ash (1231 WellsR). The application here is uncertain as we no longer know where the *nab* was.

GRENFELL HO is a modern name (W. T. M.). PAYNE'S NOOK (6″). Cf. *Paynesholm* c. 1250 *Swaffham*, 1280 *Pytchley*, v. holmr. *Payn* (*Paganus*) was probably a 12th or 13th cent. holder of land here.

Peakirk

PEAKIRK 64 F 11

Pegekyrk 871 (c. 1200) *ChronPetro*, *Peykyrke* 1048 ib.
æt Pegecyrcan 1042–66 (c. 1200) *KCD* 726
Peichirch(e) 1140 *Sparke et freq* to 1247 *Ass* with variant
   spelling *Pey-*
Peikirke 1198 FF, 1284 FA, *Peykerk* 1336 Cl, *-kirk(e)* 1339,
   1347, 1390 Cl
Peiechirch 1206 *FF*, *Peyechurche* 1226 WellsR
Paycherch 1249 Pat, *Paykyrk* 1526 SR
Peyekirk 1253 *Ass*
Poykyrke 1525 AD iii, *Pykerk* 1525 *FF*, *Pekkyrke* 1554
   Recov

The church (*v.* cirice) takes its name from St Pega, sister of St Guthlac, who is reputed to have established a cell here. The *kirk*-forms show Scandinavianising of ME *chirche*.

FOLLY RIVER (6″). In *PeterbA* we have mention in the 13th century of *locum quem vocant Folies*. Cf. *Folly bank* in 1753 (Fenland NQ ii).

PEAKIRK MOOR (6″). Cf. *Peykyrkefen* 13th *PeterbA*, *Peychyrchfen* 1307 *Pytchley*.

Southorpe

SOUTHORPE 64 G 8

> *Sudtorp* 1086 DB, 1198 Cur, 1199 Abbr, 1200 Cur, *-trop'*
> 1201 Cur, *-thorp* 1227 Ch, 1241 P
> *Sutthorp* 1189 (1332) Ch, *Suthorp(e)* 1227 Ch *et freq* to 1346
> FA, *Sutrop* 1202 Cur
> *Suthtrop* 1236 WellsR, *-torp* 1275 Cl, *Suththorp* 1306 Cl,
> *Southorp* 1340 Cl, 1353 Ipm, *Sowthorpe* 1541 LP

'South village,' v. þorp. Probably so called because south of Barnack.

MILL FM. Cf. *le Holdmilne* 1302 *PeterbB*, *Newemelne wonk* 14th *PeterbA*. *Wonk* is for *wong*, v. *infra* 270–1.

WALCOT HALL is *Walecot(e)* 1125–8 ChronPetro, 1189 (1332) Ch, 1227 Ch, 1239 *FF*, *-kote* 1247 *Ass*, *Walecotholm* 1189 (1332) Ch, *-cote-* 1227 Ch, *-chote-* t. Hy 3 *PeterbA*, *Walcott* 1284 FA, *-cote* 1327 Cl, 1330 Ipm. 'Cottage of the serfs or Britons,' v. wealh, cot(e).

St Martins Without (Stamford)

ST MARTINS WITHOUT 64 F 7

> *Stanfort* 1125–8 ChronPetro, *Stanford*, *Stanforton'* c. 1220
> WellsR, *Staunford in com Norhampton* 1294 *Ass*, *Staunford*
> *ultra pontem* c. 1300 *PeterbA*
> *Stamforde Barne* 1558 FF

'Stone ford,' v. stan, ford. This is the part of the town of Stamford (L) which lies to the south of the Welland in Northants. *Barne* is for *Baron*, this part of Stamford being known as Stamford Baron. Peck's *Annals of Stamford* (261) suggests that "the reason for this name might be from its being part of those lands which the abbot of Peterborough held *per Baroniam*, to distinguish it from Stamford, which was always called the King's Borough."

BURGHLEY HO is *Burchle* 10th (13th) *PeterbA*, *Burglea* 1086 DB, *Burgelai* 1177 P (p), *-le* 1189 (1332) Ch, 1206 Cur, 1227 Ch, *Burhclei* 13th *PeterbA*, *Burghele* 1247 *Ass*, *Bourle* 1285 *Ass*, *Burle(e)* 1301 Cl, (*by Staunford*) 1309 Ch, *Little Burlee near Staunford* 1355 Cl, *Burghle* 1363 AD iii, *Berughly* 1484 AD iii. This is probably 'the woodland or woodland clearing' (*v.* leah) by the burh of Stamford. Cf. Burleigh (Herts), Burley (R) with a similar run of early spellings.

Sutton

SUTTON 74 J 9 is *suðtun* 948 (c. 1200) BCS 871, *Sutton(a)* 1189 (1332) Ch *et passim.* 'South farm,' *v.* suð, tun. *South* with reference to Upton to the north.

SUTTON WOOD is *Suttonwoode* 1535 *Compotus.* Cf. *Suttone frith* c. 1250 *Swaffham v.* fyrhðe.

Thornhaugh

THORNHAUGH 64 H 8
  Thornhawe 1189 (1332) Ch *et freq* to 1346 FA, *Thornawe* 1227
    Ch, *Tornhauwe* n.d. AD iii, *Thornhagh* 1275 RH
  Tornau 1205 Cur, *Tornawe* 1211 Cur, *Tornehae'* ib.
  Thorney 1526 SR, (*al. Thornhawe*) 1572 *FF*

'Thorn enclosure,' i.e. defended by a thorn hedge, *v.* haga. Cf. *Thornhawe* in Oakley (13th *PipewellB*).

SIBBERTON LODGE is *Siberton* 1189 (1332) Ch *et freq* to 1428 FA with variant spelling *Syb-*, *Sibbeton* 1203 *FF*, *Sibirton* 1254 *For*, *Syburton* 1345 *For.* '*Sigeberht*'s farm,' *v.* ingtun. The earliest form is probably a reduction of *Sigeberhtingtun.* Cf. Sibbertoft *supra* 121.

ABBOT'S WOOD (6"). The manor belonged to the abbot of Peterborough. BEDFORD PURLIEUS is *my lorde of Bedfordes woodes* 1611 *Brudenell.* The manor belonged to the Duke of Bedford from the 15th cent. down to 1904 (VCH ii, 530–1). For *purlieu v. supra* 170. COCKER WOOD (6") is *Cockley Wood* 1823 B. COOK'S HOLE is so named c. 1825 O.S. and is probably to be associated with the family of Robert *Cocus* (t. Ed 3 *SR*).

PEBBLEGATE SALE (6″) is *Pebble Gate* 1823 B. For *sale v.* Britain Sale *supra* 156. ST JOHN'S WOOD FM is *Johns Wood* 1823 B. The *St* is probably a modern addition since there is no record that the Knights of St John ever held land in the parish. WEST WOOD (6″) is *boscus de Westwode* 13th *PeterbA*.

Ufford

UFFORD 64 G 9

> (*to*) *uffawyrða* (*gemære*) 948 (c. 1200) BCS 871
> *Uffewurda* 1178 P (p) *et freq* to 1227 Ch with variant spellings -*wurth*, -*wrth* and *Vffe*-
> *Upford* 1202 Ass, 1206 Cur, *Hufworth'* 1206 Cur
> *Ufford*(e) 1209 Seld 13 *et freq* to 1525 AD iii, (*by Staunforde*) 1389 Cl
> *Offord* 1272 *FF*, 1301 Ipm, Cl

This was originally 'Uffa's farm,' *v.* worþ, but the second element was early assimilated to *ford*.

DOWN HALLS (6″) is *Downhall in Ufford* 1443–50 ECP, *Downhall* 1572 *FF*. According to the VCH (ii, 535) this was originally a small manor, but the name is now preserved only in that of a wood.

LANGDYKE BUSH (6″) is *Langedyk* 1305 Ipm, 1330 *Ass*, *Langdyk-grene*, *Landykbush* c. 1400 *Rental*, *Langdykbush* 1512 *Compotus*. For this name *v. supra* 223.

SOUTHEY WOOD is *Suthawe* 13th *PeterbA*, *bosco de Suthhawe* 1330 *Ass*, *Souhthawe* c. 1400 *Rental*. 'South enclosure,' *v.* haga.

TORPEL (not on map)

> *Torpelt* 1131 P (p) *et passim* to 1515 AD iv with variant spelling -*pel*
> *Thorpel* 1189 (1332) Ch *et freq* to 1353 Ipm, -*pelle* 1226 Bracton (p), *Thorpele* 1243 *FF*
> *Torpeyl* 1280 Cl, -*peil* 1281 Cl
> *Torphill* 1509 LP, 1560 *ChDecRoll*, *Torpell al. Thorpell al. Ashton* 1687 Recov, *Torpell al. Thorpell* 1759 ib.

The name of this manor is clearly an Anglo-Norman diminutive of the common þorp. This place was the seat of one of the

Norman barons of Peterborough Abbey and remains of his castle still survive.

Upton

UPTON 74 H 9

uptun 948 (c. 1200) BCS 871, (on) uptune, (on) Optune 972 (c. 1200) BCS 1130

Huppetune late 12th NRS iv, Vppetona 1174 P, Uppeton 1175 P, 1189 (1332) Ch, 1197 FF, Upeton 1191 P, 1227 Ch

Upton 1179 P, (juxta Castre) 1294 Ass, (juxta Walmesford) 1312 Ass

'Higher farm,' v. uppe, tun and Sutton supra 243.

HAYESWOOD SPINNEY (6″). Cf. les Hayes 1512 Compotus. 'Enclosures,' v. (ge)hæg. UPTON WOOD. Cf. Uptunefrith c. 1250 Swaffham. v. fyrhðe.

Walton

WALTON 64 H 11

Waltun 972 (12th) BCS 1281, Wealtun 1016 (c. 1200) KCD 726

Waleton(e) 1086 DB

Walton(e) 1086 DB et passim

This is probably a compound of weall and tun, hence, 'walled enclosure.' For the possibility of weall we may perhaps compare the field-name Walleswong (1440 Compotus) in this parish.

GRIMESHAW WOOD (6″) is Grymeshawe 1246 Pytchley, Grimeshawe 1247 PeterbB, 13th PeterbA, Grimshaw 1805 EnclA. 'Grim's enclosure or wood,' v. hagi. Cf. Grymmeswro 1302 (CartN) in the same parish. v. vra.

Wansford

WANSFORD[1] 64 J 8

(æt) Wylmesforda 972 (c. 1200) BCS 1130

Walmesford(e) late Hy 2 NRS iv et passim to 1428 FA, Waumeford 1210 Cur

Welmeford 1213 PatR (p), Welmesford 1233 FF

[1] Wansford lies partly in Hu and partly in Nth.

Wamesford 13th *PeterbA*, *Waumesford* 1253 *Ass*, *Wanesford* 1346 FA, *Waunceford* 1464 Pat, *Wantsworth* 1675 Ogilby

'Ford of or by the spring,' the first element being OE *wielm*, *wælm*, 'spring.' See PN BedsHu 198. For the phonology *v.* Introd. xxxii.

WANSFORD BRIDGE (6″) is *pontis de Walmesford* 1221 WellsR.

Werrington

WERRINGTON 64 G 11

Witheringtun, *Wiðringtun* 972 (c. 1200) BCS 1280, 1281, *Witherington* 1202 Ass, 1284 FA, *-tune* c. 1250 *Swaffham*, *Wyth-* 13th AD iii
Widerinton(e) 1086 DB, 1178 P, 1189 (1332) Ch, 1227 Ch, *Wide Rīton* t. Ric 1 Cur, *Widerington* 1227 Ch
Wirrintona 1125–8 ChronPetro, *Wirrington* 1712 Morton
Widerinton 1162 P, *Witherinton* 1199 FF, 1209 *FF*
Wit(e)rintoñ 1166 P, *Wittirinton* 1199 FF
Widringeton 1198 Cur
Weteryngton 1285 *Ass*, *Weryngton* 1428 FA (p), 1525 AD iii
Wyrryngton al. Wytheryngton 1563 *Recov*

In Werrington and Wittering *infra* 247, we seem to have the same pers. name *Wiðer*, probably a shortened form of such a name as OE *Wiðergyld*, cf. Ekwall, PN in *-ing* 89. Hence, '*Wiðer*'s farm,' *v.* ingtun. As Werrington and Wittering are only seven miles apart, they may be named from the same person.

HAMFIELD FM (6″) is *Hamfeld* c. 1300 *CartN*, c. 1400 *Rental*, (*le*) 1400 *Compotus*. Cf. also *Hambalke* 1440 *Compotus*. This is probably a compound of hamm, 'flat low-lying pasture,' and feld. Cf. Inhams *infra*, which is close at hand, and ham in EDD, which gives 'enclosed level pasture' as the meaning of this word in Northants.

THE INHAMS is *Imhambrygge* c. 1400 *Rental*, *le Inham*, *le Inham extra Wytherington* ib., *Inhams* 1805 *EnclA*. The 'in' or 'home-pasture.' Cf. Hamfield *supra*.

Wittering

WITTERING 64 H 7

(*æt*) *Wiðering ige*, (*on*) *Wiðeringa eige* 972 (c. 1200) BCS 1130,
  Widringaiʒ, Wiðringaig c. 975 (14th) *Thorney*
Witheringham 1086 DB, *Wythering* 1227 Ch
Witering(*a*) 1166 P (p), 1178, 1190–1195 P, 1189 (1332) Ch,
  1275 ChronPetro *et passim* to 1428 FA, *Wyteringg* 1275 Cl
Winteringes 1201 P
Wuitteringͣ (sic) 1201 FineR, *Wittering* 1284 FA, 1346 FA
Weteryng 1349 Cl, 1517 DBE
Whitring alias Wittering 1675 Ogilby, *Whitering* 1709 Poll

'Settlement of the people of *Wiðer*,' *v.* Werrington *supra* 246.

LOUND WOOD is *the Lounde* c. 1400 *Rental*. This is ON lundr,
'grove, small wood.' Cf. also *Burgelelund* 13th *PeterbA* which
must have been not far distant, near Burghley *supra* 243.

BONEMILLS FM. A 'bonemill' is defined by the NED as a 'mill
for grinding or crushing bones or bone-black.' The place-name
occurs also in Surrey. CHURCH FM was probably the home of
Walter *atte Cherche* (1315 *Ass*).

Wothorpe

WOTHORPE [wʌðəp] 64 G 7

Writhorp 11th (13th) *PeterbA*, 1209–35 WellsR, -*torp* 1086
  DB, *Wrythorp' jux' Stanford* 1275 RH
Wridtorp(*e*) 1086 DB, 1224 WellsR, c. 1250 *Swaffham*
Wertorp 1181 P (p)
Wirthorp(*e*) 12th Survey, 1247 *Ass*, 1257 AD iii, 1261 *FF*,
  1354 RegAntiquiss, -*thorpt* (sic) c. 1250 AD iii
Wrthorp c. 1257 AD ii
Withrope c. 1270 Gerv, *Withorpe* 1662 Fuller
Wyrethorp̄ 1285 *Ass*, 1327 Ch, -*tort* (sic) 1327 Ch
Worthorp 1354 RegAntiquiss, 1440 AD ii, *Wortherop* 1539 LP
Wathrop Hall 1675 Ogilby, *Wottrop* 1712 Morton

This is a compound of OE wriþ, 'thicket' and þorp, hence,
'village by the thicket.' Cf. Wordwell (Sf), BCS 1018 *Wride-
wellan*.

THE ELEMENTS, APART FROM PERSONAL NAMES, FOUND IN NORTHAMPTONSHIRE PLACE-NAMES

This list confines itself for the most part to elements used in uncompounded place-names or in the second part of compounded place-names. Under each element the examples are arranged in three categories, (*a*) those in which the first element is a significant word and not a pers. name, (*b*) those in which the first element is a pers. name, (*c*) those in which the character of the first element is uncertain. Where no statement is made it may be assumed that the examples belong to type (*a*). Elements which are not dealt with in the *Chief Elements used in English Place-Names* are distinguished by an (n) after them. The list omits a few of the minor names which appear to be of late origin.

ærn Stanion. **æsc** Ashton (Cleyley Hundred).
*ætsce (n) Excellent (?), Bullicks Wood.
ac Barnack. **bæc** ('hill') Haselbech.
beorg Gawburrow, Har-, Hazel-, Ho-, Lang- (2), Litch-, No-borough, Ryebury, Studborough, Thornburrow, (b) Orlingbury (?).
beretun Barton (2). **bigging** Biggin (2).
bold, botl Newbold, Newbottle (2), Nobold, Nobottle.
brand (ME) (n) Brand.
broc Brook (7), Braybrooke, Holey Brookes, How-, Kingbrook, Polebrook, Sholebroke, Wash-, Willy-brook, (b) Cottesbrooke, (c) Bugbrooke, Harpers Brook.
brocc-hol Brockhall, *Brockholes*.
brycg Dow Bridge, Rising Bridge.
burh Berry, Berrydale, Berryfields, Bury (3), Borough Hill, Peterborough, Arbury (2), Eyebury, Northborough, Sudborough, (b) Desborough, Grimsbury, Guilsborough, Irthlingborough, Stuchbury, Wellingborough, Whittlebury, (c) Hunsbury, Kislingbury, Rainsborough.
burhtun Burton. **burna** Lilbourne.
by Ashby (5), Barby, Kirby, Thornby, (b) Badby, Buckby, Catesby, Corby, Holdenby, Kilsby, Kirby Grounds, Naseby, Sulby, (c) Wilby.
cætt Cathanger, Cattage, Cattlehill, Catwell.
cagge (ME) (n) Cadge Wood.
ceald Caldecote, Caldecott, Cold Ashby.
ceaster Castor, Chester, Towcester, (b) Irchester.

ceorl Charlton   chace (ME) (n) Yardley Chase.
chapel(le) (ME) (n) Chapel.   cild *Chilcotes*.
cirice Church Fm, Churchfield, Churchill, Kirby, (b) Achurch,
   Peakirk.
clif *Fawcliff*, King's Cliffe.
conygre (ME) (n) Coney Geer, Coney Gree.
coppis (ME) (n) Ash and Bar Coppice, Lodge Copse, Porters
   Coppice, Prentice, Silley, and Thorny Copse.
cot(e) Costow, *Cotes*, Coton, Cotton (4), Burcote (2), Caldecote,
   Caldecott, *Chilcotes*, Claycoton, Falcutt, Foscote, Holcot,
   Hulcote, Luscote's, Murcott, Muscott, Nethercote, Potcote,
   Walcot (2), (b) Astcote, *Buscott*, Dalscote, Duncote, Eastcote,
   Grimscote, Heathencote, Huscote, (c) Edgcote.
croft Bencroft, Woodcroft.
cumb Coombehill, Westcomb, (b) Chalcombe, (c) Snorscomb.
dæl Dale, Dales, Berrydale, Debdale (4), Mazedale, Merrydale,
   (b) Darsdale, (c) Clippendale, Cockendale.
dal Hatchdoyle.   (ge)delf Delf Spinney.
denu Dane Hole, Deene, Bradden, Finedon, Rushden, Smalladine, (b) Helmdon, Lyveden, Ramsden, (c) Hellidon.
dibbing (ME) (n) Dibbin's Wood.
dic Barrowdykes, Langdyke, Sowditch, (b) Car Dike.
dreng Ring Haw.
dun Bugbrooke Downs, Downtown, Blackdown, Everdon,
   Farndon (2), Glendon, *Graundon*, Grendon, Haddon (2),
   Harrowden, Langden, Oxendon, Ringdales, Rytonhill, Steppington, Warden, Weedon (2), Weldon, (b) Boddington,
   Bowden, Elkington, Eydon.
eg Eye, Oxney, Surney, (b) Brancey, Fotheringhay, Maxey.
ende Blackwell and Cotton End, *Gravesend*, Hartwell, Moor, and
   North End, Woodend, (b) Tew's End.
eofor Everdon.
fealh (n) *Falham*, *Fawcliff*.
feld Field Barn (2), Berryfields, Bray-, By-, Church-, Crow-,
   East-, Hall-, Ham-, Hay,- High-field, Mill-, North-field,
   North Field, Northfields, Old- (3), South-, Tif-, West-,
   Whit-field, (b) Attlefield, Benefield, Wakefield.
fenn Borough, Flag and North Fen, Woolfellhill (?).
feorðung Farthing (2).
ferme (ME) (n) Farming Woods.   flor Floore.
ford Bar-, Clif-, Cran-, Den-, Ditch-, Hey-, Maid-, Stam-,
   Stan-, Strat-, Then-, Traf-, Twy-, Wans-, Wat-, Wel-,
   Wood-ford (2), (b) Dodford, Lilford, Pitsford.
fox-hol Foxhall, Fox Hall, Foxhole, Foxholes (2).
fyrhðe Thrift.

gata Deeping Gate, Normangate.

geat (b) Bozeat, Pilsgate.

græf Sulgrave (?).

graf(a) Grove, Bangrove, Hargrave, Nobottle Grove, Short-grove (2), Sulgrave (?), Walgrave, Wothorpe Groves, (b) Cosgrove.

grange (ME) (n) Grange Fm, Warden Grange.

grene (ME) The Green (3), Big and Little Green, Pengreen, Sudborough Green, *Upton Green*.

hæcc Brackley Hatch (?).

(ge)hæg Hay, Hayes (4), Calvey, Empty, Morehay, New Hay, Oxey, Priesthay, Roundhay, Westhay, (b) Grimpsey (?).

hæsel (n) Badsaddle. **hæþ** Heath Fm, Harlestone Heath.

haga Bradshaw, Hilly Wood, Little Haw, New Hall, Oxen Wood, Priors Hall, Priors Haw, Rawhaw, Souther Wood, Southey, Swinawe, Thornhaugh, Weekley Hall, (c) Frindshaw.

hagi Ring Haw, (b) Askershaw, Grimeshaw.

ham(m) *Falham*, Higham (2), Inhams, Isham, Marholm, Newnham, (b) Passenham, Syresham, Wappenham.

hamstede (b) *Medeshamstede*.

hangra Hanger, Cathanger, Shutlanger, (b) Denshanger.

haugr Howe Drain (?), Ostor.

heafod Cats Head, (b) Fineshade.

healh Halefield, Hollow Wood, West Hall (?), (b) Courteenhall, Dagnall, Snatchill, (c) Rignall.

heall Hall Fm, Down Hall, *Woodhall*.

healm (n) or **helm** (n) Lolham. **hearg** Harrowden.

hecg (n) Black Hedges, Cattage, Hostage (?), Longhedge, *Wolfage*.

heordewic Hardwick. **hid** Hyde.

hlaw *Low*, Cockleyhill, Mitley, Rowler, (b) Franklow, *Huxloe*, (c) Spotley.

hlinc Castor Linch, Linches, Links.

hoh Hoe, How, Arniss (?), Banhaw, *Evenhoe*, Farthinghoe, Furtho, Halse, Lindow, Perio, *Spelhoe*, Spella, Speller, Wallow (?), (b) Aynho, *Birchenho*, Bozenham, Cogenhoe, *Hamfordshoe*, Tottenhoe, Wadenhoe, (c) Spanhoe.

holmr (a) Fulham, Northholme, Roseholm, Ryeholmes, Thatch-ams, (c) Synholms.

holt The Holt, Tanholt, (b) Singlesole. **hris** Rice Wood.

hyll Hill (7), Blowhill, Briar Hill, Broomhill, Bucknell, Churchill, Corn, Cot and Dust Hill, Ferrels (?), Flinthill, Fox Hill, Foxhill, Greenhill, Grub Hill, Hobberill, Honey Hill (2), Hoppin(g) Hill (2), Kingshill, Lang Hill, Marstonhill, *Roughill*, Ryehill, Rye Hills, *Setehill*, Shooters Hill, Smanhill,

Stepnell, White Hill, (b) Pattishall, *Snossells*, (c) Yoke Hill.

hyrne Herne (?), Hurn, Collier's Hern. **hyrst** Sandyhurst (?).

ing Thurning, Winning.

ing(a) Farthinghoe, Kislingbury, (b) Arthingworth, Benefield, Elkington, Fotheringhay, Irthlingborough, Wellingborough.

ingaham (b) Cottingham, Rockingham.

ingas (b) Billing, Wittering, (c) Kettering.

ing(a)tun (a) Nassington, (b) Abington, Addington, Alderton, Bainton, Brington, Dallington, Denton, Doddington, Duddington, Ecton, Geddington, Hackleton, Hannington, Harrington, Hemington, Loddington, Luddington, Lutton, Piddington, Warkton, Warmington, Werrington, Whiston, (c) Elmington.

karlatun Carlton. **klint** Clint Hill, Gaultney.

læppe (n) Cherry Lap.

læs Dryleas, Moorwell Leys, Ridge Leys, Sower Leys.

lacu Charlock, Litchlake.

land Acreland, Ellands, Excellent, Flexlands, *Flitland*, Langlands, Thorplands.

la(u)nde (ME) (n) Beanfield Lawn, Law's Lawn, Lawnhill (?), Wakefield Lawn.

leactun Leighton.

leah Ash-, Blen-, Burgh-ley, Cherry Lap, Cle-, Crans-, Crayley, Ding-, Even-ley, Fawsley, *Fernily*, Fox-, Hand-, Har-, Lang-(3), Maws-, Mounter-, Oak- (2), Ol-, Pux-, Row-, Ship-, Shot-, Waker-, Week-ley, Wetley's, Whistley, Yardley (2), (b) *Ailwardeslea*, Blakes-, Edger-, Pap-, Pytch-, Sewards-ley, Sulehay, Wymersley, (c) Brackley, Brankley, Onley.

logge (ME) (n) Lodge Copse, Moulton Lodge.

lundr Lawn Wood (?), Lound Wood, The Loundes, Long and Round Lown, Eckland, Loatland, Muckland.

lyng Billing Lings (?).

mæd Long Meadow, Park Meadow.

(ge)mære Althorpe Meer, Laundimer.

*mealo (n) Mawsley, Wythemail.

mere Blackmire's, Blackmore.

mersc (b) Titchmarsh, (c) Kelmarsh.

mor Moor, Moor End, Moore Wood, Cranmore, Middlemore, Radmore (2), Redmore, Rodmore, (c) Danes Moor.

myrr Rough Moor.

næss Nassaburgh, Nassington. **nabbr** (n) Nab Lane.

ofer (b) Tansor.

pearroc (OE) or **parke** (ME) Park (7), Parkhill, Plumpark.

plega Hemplow. **pol** Harpole.

port Lamport. **puca** Polebrook.

pyrige Paulerspury, Perio, Potterspury.

pytt Blackpits (2), Mortar Pits, Sandpit, Stonepit.

ra Rawhaw. **rand** Raunds. **reche** (ME) (n) The Reaches (?).

riðig Coleready. **rod** Roade, Ravenstone Road. **roð** (n) Rothwell.

sale (ME) (n) Britain, Byards, Chambers and Fair Oak Sale, Greatsale, Morton, Mountjoy, New and Old Sale, Thoroughsale.

sceaga *Shaw, Horseshoes.* **scrybb** (n) Shrob, Bushrubs.

slæd Slade, Church Slade. **slæp** Slapton, Islip.

snæp (n) Snapes Wood. **snoc** (n) Snorscomb (?).

spitel (ME) Spital (2). ***stæne** (n) Steane (?).

stan Steane (?), Radstone. **stede** Berrystead, Ringstead.

steort Colsters. **stigel** Stubby Stiles.

stoc(c) Stock Hill, Stoke (3), Brigstock, Cotterstock, Hornstocks.

stocking Stocking(s) (3). **storð** Storefield.

stow Stowe, Costow, (b) *Albodestow.* **stubb** Elderstubbs.

tacn (n) or ***tæcne** (n) Teeton.

thicke (ME) (n) Blackmore and Buckingham Thick, Cowthick, Laythick.

þing Finedon.

þorn Coldthorn, Kingthorn, (b) Glapthorn, Hardingstone.

þorp Thorpe (5), Thorpewood, Thorplands, Thrupp, *Torpel*, Astrop, *Crowthorpe*, Deene-, Kings- (2), Long-, Mil-, Over-, *Up-thorpe*, Westhorp (2), Wilby *Thorp*, Wothorpe, (b) Abthorpe, Althorp, Ape-, Dogs-, Eagle-thorpe, Glassthorpehill, Gun-, Ravens-, Rothers-, Wigs-thorpe, (c) Dowthorpe, Hothorpe.

þveit *Cathwaite.* **þwang** (n) Long Thong.

topt Nortoft (2), (b) Sibbertoft, Yelvertoft.

treow Appletree, Crowtree, Twantry, (b) Collingtree, Daventry.

tun Town Fm, Ash- (2), As-, Bough-, Bramp- (2), Brough-, Charl-, Charwel-, Clap-, Collywes-, Crea-, Crough-, Draugh-, Dray- (2), Dus-, Eas- (2), Gay-, Graf- (2), Gret-, Hin- (2), Hor-, Hough (2), Leigh-, Mars- (2), Middle- (2), Mil- (2), More-, Moul-, New- (2), Nor-ton (2), Old Town, Or-, Plump- (2), Pres- (2), Purs-, Rush-, Slap-, Slip-, Sprat-, Staver-, Sut- (3), Up- (2), Wal- (2), Wel-, Wes- (3), Whil-, Woodnew-, Woot-ton, (b) Adstone, Arms-, Brauns-ton, Chadstone, Chelves-, Clips-, Easton Nes-, Et-ton, Farthingstone, Faxton, Harlestone, Helps-, Knus-, Lax-, Nun-ton, Overstone, Pas-, Pil-, Sibber-ton, Silverstone, Strix-, Thraps-, Wilbars-, Wollas-ton, (c) Boughton, Garton, Glinton, Quinton.

varða Wharf (?).

wad Wadground (?).

wæd (b) *Gunwade*. (ge)wæsc The Wash (?), Washbrook.

weald Old, Wild, Wold (2), Ashton, Barnwell and Burton Wold, Longhold, Northall (?), (b) Bromswold.

wealh Walcot (2). **weall** Burntwalls.

weg Broadway, Burray, Portly (?). (ge)weorc Newark.

wic Wicken, *Wike*, Weekley, Astwick, Blatherwycke, Bul-, *Hen*-, South-, Stan-wick (?), (b) Lowick, Winwick.

wielle Ashalls, Ast-, Bid-, Black-, Bur-, Cas-well, Cattlehill, Cat-, Cost-well, Fousill, *Gold*-, Hart- (2), Hollo-well (2), Kings Well, Ley-, Lud-, Maid-well, Mickle Well, Paddle, Puckwell, Rockhall, Rod- (2), Roth-, Scald-, Sea-well, Sewell's, Shot-, Stan-well, Stockall, Sy-, Twy-, Yar-well, (b) Barnwell, Pipewell, Plaxwell's, (c) Chinkwell, Pitwell.

wincel (b) Aldwinkle.

worþ Greatworth, (b) Ails-, Arthing-, Blis-, Brix-worth, Brownswood, Cul-, Harring-, Is-, Sils-worth, Ufford, (c) Warkworth.

wudu Wood (2), Alder Wood, Ashwood, Barn Wood, Earls Wood, Eastwood, Farming, Freer and Gayton Wood, Hackwood, Harry's Wood, Hazlewood, Hen Wood, Horn Wood, Hunterswood, Kings Woods, Knotwood, Lady, Lynn, Mary, St Mary's, Mawsley, Monks and Nobottle Wood, Norwood, Nun Wood, *Outwood*, Preston Wood, Short Wood (2), South Wood, Westwood, West Wood, Wicken Wood, Yokewood, (b) Simon's Wood.

wulf *Wolfage*.

CELTIC AND FRENCH NAMES

CELTIC. Certain river-names, Crick, Creaton (hybrid). See also Gorse Close *infra* 281.

FRENCH. Assart (2) and Sart Wood, Belsize, *Broil*, Delapre, the Gullet (2), Salcey.

NOTES ON THE DISTRIBUTION OF THESE ELEMENTS

A few notes on the distribution of certain place-name elements may be given, but as the comparative material for other counties is, apart from those counties already dealt with by the Survey, complete in only a few cases, the remarks can in some measure only be tentative.

bold, botl. Northamptonshire belongs to the Mercian area in its use of this element. Twice it uses it in the form *bold*, which is found elsewhere in Wa, Wo, Lei, St, Db, Ch, Sa, La, twice (or possibly three times, if Newbottle Bridge in Harrington is not manorial in origin) in the form *botl*, elsewhere only found in Nb, Du and La and commonly regarded as Northumbrian rather than Mercian in origin. All the examples of the two forms are found on the western side of the county, and that agrees with its general distribution as hitherto observed, for it has never been noted in East Anglia. It is always compounded with *new* and the name seems readily to have lent itself to a jest whereby *new* became *no*.

burh is used in various senses in Northamptonshire. It is used of an ancient fort or camp as in more than one *Arbury*, or of some fortified stronghold as in Desborough. It probably has the later burghal connotation in Peterborough and the manorial one in Eyebury. It is noteworthy that in this county, as distinct from the neighbouring counties of Bucks, Beds and Hunts, we have several examples of the nominative *borough* as distinct from the dative *bury*.

by. There are some eighteen examples of by in the county. Sixteen of these are parish names, recorded as manors in DB, one is a DB manor but not a parish name, and one is first recorded in 1316.

cot(e) is specially common in this county, the counties which most resemble it in this respect being Warwickshire and Oxfordshire and, to a smaller degree, Buckinghamshire. Of the thirty odd examples of it in the county it is not surprising, therefore, to find some sixteen examples of cot(e) and one *cotstow* in the parishes in the south-west of the county which lie between Easton Neston (by Towcester) and the Oxfordshire and Buckinghamshire borders. Twelve examples occur within a radius of four or five miles from Towcester. Further north, but not far from the Warwickshire border, we have Coton and Claycoton with Cothill in Elkington and *Chilcote* in Cold Ashby, Cotton End and Murcott in Long Buckby, Muscott in Norton and a lost *Cotton* in Gretton on the Leicestershire border. In all there are twenty-three examples not far from the western border of the county. There remain only some eight examples on the eastern side of the county, and it is noteworthy that, with the exception of a lost *Britwinscott*, preserved in a field-name *Buscott*, in Higham Ferrers, none of these is of the type in which a personal name is compounded with cot(e), a type which is very common in the south-west of the county. Only eight of the thirty cot(e) names are recorded in Domesday.

dæl, dalr. *dale* is not found in the south and south-west of the county, and this is what we should expect, seeing that this element is either Anglian or Scandinavian. Since it is never found compounded with Scandinavian personal names or significant words, it is probably as a rule Anglian rather than Scandinavian in this county, though there is one clear exception, viz. Debdale in Rothwell *supra* 119. The distribution of this element in field and other minor names tends to confirm this, *v. infra* 262. The *dale* names include four 'deep' dales, now known as Debdale.

feld is fairly common and often describes open land in old forest areas.

haga, hagi. ME *hawe* is found exclusively in the north of the county and is clearly used as a woodland term, for it is found, with one or two possible exceptions, only in the area covered by the ancient forests of Rockingham and Cliffe. We never find it in Whittlewood and Salcey forests. A few compounds, such as Ring Haw and Askershaw, with Scandinavian first elements, suggest ON hagi rather than OE haga, as the source of ME *hawe*. The distribution agrees with that found in field and minor names *infra* 263.

hamstede. The only example of this element is to be found in *Medeshamstede*, the ancient name of Peterborough.

healh is rare in this county, which in this respect goes with Bedfordshire and Huntingdonshire. We have a rare survival of the nominative form in Hollow Bottom *supra* 161.

hoh is a common term for a hill in Northamptonshire and is used for hills of various shapes. The distribution of this element over the county is fairly even, but it is by no means so common as in Bedfordshire.

hyrst. In spite of the wooded character of much of the county this element is only found in one quite late place-name and it is equally rare among minor unidentified names (*infra* 265).

inga-names are certain only in the case of Benefield, Farthinghoe, Irthlingborough, Kislingbury, Wellingborough, and the ingaham-names *infra*.

ingaham. The two examples are close together, on the Leicestershire border.

ingas. There are only three examples, and these are on the east side of the county.

ingtun. The great majority of these are to be found in the valley of the Nene and its tributaries. There are none west of Watling Street, and the only ones outside the Nene basin are Alderton (on the Ouse), Bainton and Duddington (on the Welland), and Werrington.

leah is fairly common, especially in the old Rockingham, Salcey and Whittlewood forests.

lundr, except for an isolated Loundes in Blisworth, is confined, as one might expect, to the north and north-west of the county. See further *infra* 267.

þorp. It is difficult to distinguish the English and Scandinavian examples of this element. We may note, however, that Apethorpe, Glassthorpe, Gunthorpe, Ravensthorpe, Rothersthorpe and Wigsthorpe are compounded with Scandinavian personal names and are therefore presumably Scandinavian throughout. Further in Deenethorpe, *Wilby Thorpe* and *Barton Thorpe* (later Dowthorpe) we clearly have examples of þorp used of a secondary settlement, a usage which, so far as we are aware, did not attach to the English word. As none of these names show forms in *throp(e)* or *trop(e)* except in quite modern times, we have further confirmation of the view set forth in EPN *s.v.* that Scandinavian þorp seldom appears in ME as *throp*. The great home of ME forms in *throp(e)*, *trop(e)* is, as we might expect, in the south-west part of the county, on the borders of Warwickshire, Oxfordshire, and Buckinghamshire. We may note Thrupp in Norton, Westhorpe in Byfield, Milthorpe in Weedon Lois, Overthorpe in Middleton Cheney, Westhorp in Marston St Lawrence, Astrop in King's Sutton, Thorpe Mandeville and Abthorpe. The only names in the west and south-west of the county with *thorpe*-forms only are Thorpe Lubenham and Thorpe Malsor (one *throp*-form), Hothorpe, and Thorpe in Harrington, which is sufficiently far eastwards to be a border-line case. On the other hand we are probably right in assuming that Kingsthorpe by Northampton, Kingsthorpe in Polebrook, Thorpe Waterville, the lost *Crowthorpe* in Oundle, Longthorpe and Thorpe in Peterborough, which are in the east of the county, belong to a time when the Scandinavian *thorp* had come into common use in English speech. The same is probably true of Wothorpe near Stamford. Southorpe is more difficult as it shows one or two early examples of the *throp*-form of the suffix.

topt is found four times in major names, two of them being parish names.

tun is, as usual, very common.

worþ is distributed thinly but evenly throughout the county.

PERSONAL NAMES COMPOUNDED IN NORTHAMPTONSHIRE PLACE-NAMES

Names not found in independent use are marked with a single asterisk if they can be inferred from evidence other than that of the place-name in question. Such names may be regarded as hardly less certain than those which have no asterisk. Those for which no such evidence can be found are marked with a double asterisk.

(A) OLD ENGLISH.

Abba (Abington, Abthorpe), *Ǽfic* (Astcote), **Ǽga* (Aynho, Eydon), **Ǽgel* (Ailsworth), *Ǽtla* (Attlefield), **Ǽttīn* (Adstone), *Ǽþelstān* (Easton Neston), *Ǽþelweard*, *Ǽgelweard* (*Ailwardeslea*), **Andferð* (*Hamfordshoe*), *Bada* (Bainton), *Badda* (Badby), **Bætti* (Badsaddle), **Beorhtel* (Brixworth?), *Beorhtwine* (Buscott), **Bera* (Benefield), *Bicca* (*Birchenhoe*), **Billa* (Billing?), **Blæcwulf* (Blakesley), **Blīðe* (Blisworth), *Bosa* (Bozeat, Bozenham), *Bōta* (Boddington), **Bracca* (Brackley?), **Brant* (Brancey, Braunston, Brownswood), **Bricel* (Brixworth?), *Brūn* (Bromswold), *Brȳni* (Brington), *Bucca* (Bugbrooke), *Buga* (Bowden), **Bȳdel* (Billing?), ***Cǽgla* (Kelmarsh), **Ceadd* (Chadstone), **Ceawa* (Chalcombe), *Cēolwulf* (Chelveston), **Codd*, **Cott* (Cottesbrooke), *Cola* (Collingtree), **Corta*, **Curta* (Courteenhall), *Cotta* (Cottingham), **Cufel* (Cosgrove), **Cugga* (Cogenhoe), **Cula* (Culworth), **Cwēna* (f) (Quinton), **Cȳsel* (Kislingbury?), **Dægel* (Dallington), **Dafa* (Daventry), **Dagga* (Dagnall), *Dēor* (Darsdale, Desborough), *Dēorlāf*, *Dēorstān* (Dalscote), *Dodd(a)* (Denton, Doddington, Dodford, Dogsthorpe, Duddington), *Dunna* (Duncote), *Dynne* (Denshanger), *Eadda* (Addington), *Eadwine* (Eastcote), *Ealda* (Aldwinkle), *Ealdbeald* (*Albodestow*), *Ealdhere* (Alderton), **Earn(a)* (Arthingworth), *Ēata* (Etton), *Ecca* (Ecton), *Ecgheard* (Edgerley), *Ecgwulf* (Eaglethorpe?), **Elta* (Elkington), **Eorm* (Armston), *Finn* (Fineshade), *Forðhere* (Fotheringhay), *Franca* (Franklow), ***Gǽga* (Gayton), **Geldfrið*, **Geldferð* (Yelvertoft), *Glappa*, (Glapthorn), *Grim* (Grimpsey, Grimsbury, Grimscote), **Gyldi* (Guilsborough), **Hǽcel* (Hackleton), **Hǽgla* (Hellidon), **Hǽðhere* (Harrington), *Hana* (Hannington), *Hēahmund* (Heathencote), **Hearding* (Hardingstone), **Helma* (Helmdon), **Help* (Helpston), *Hemma* (Hemington), *Heoruwulf* (Harlestone), *Hnæf* (Naseby), *Hōc* (Huxloe), **Hrōc(a)* (Rockingham), *Hus(s)a* (Huscote), **Hwicce* (Whiston), **Hycgi* (Isworth?), *Lēofa* (Lyveden), *Lilla* (Lilbourne, Lilford), **Lodda* (Loddington),

Luda (Lutton), *Luha* (Lowick), *Lulla* (Luddington), **Mēde* (*Medeshamstede*), *Nunna* (Nunton), *Ofe* (Overstone), **Olla* (Althorp), *Ona* (Onley?), **Ordla* (Orlingbury), *Pæcci* (Paston), **Pætti* (Pattishall), **Pap(p)a* (Papley), *Passa* (Passenham), **Peoht* (Pitsford, Pytchley), **Pīl* (Pilsgate), **Pīleca* (Pilton), **Pippa* (Pipewell), **Pyda* (Piddington), *Rægenbeald* (Ramsden), **Seofa* (Sulehay), **Sifel* (Silsworth), *Sigebeorht* (Sibbertoft, Sibberton), *Sigehere* (Syresham), *Sigemund* (Simon's Wood), *Sigeweard* (Sewardsley), *Sigewulf* (Silverstone), ***Snāra* (Snossells), **Snoc* (Snorscomb?), *Snot* (Snatchill), **Stūt* (Stuchbury), **Tān* (Tansor), *Ticcea* (Titchmarsh), *Totta* (Tottenhoe), **Ðræfst*, **Ðræpst* (Thrapston), *Uffa* (Ufford), *Waca* (Wakefield), *Wada* (Wadenhoe), **Wændel* (Wellingborough), **Wæppa* (Wappenham), **Weorca* (Warkton), *Wilbeorht* (Wilbarston), *Wina* (Winwick), *Winemǣr* (*Wymersley*), **Witela* (Whittlebury, Whittlewood), *Wiðer* (Werrington, Wittering), *Wulflāf* (Wollaston), **Wyrma* (Warmington), *Yra* (Irchester?), ***Yrtla* (Irthlingborough).

(B) SCANDINAVIAN.

Api (ODan) (Apethorpe), *Ási* (m), *Ása* (f) (Achurch), *Ásketill* (Askershaw), *Bukkr* (Buckby), *Fákr* (ODan) (Faxton), *Farþegn* (Farthingstone), *Geiti* (Geddington), *Grímr* (Grimeshaw), *Gunni* (Gunthorpe, *Gunwade*), *Hálfdan* (Holdenby), *Hrafn* (Ravensthorpe), *Kæri* (Kirby), *Kárr* (Car Dike), *Káti*, *Kátr* (Catesby), *Klak* (ODan) (Glassthorpe, Plaxwell's), *Klyppr* (Clipstone), *Knútr* (Knuston), *Kóri* (Corby), *Lax* (Laxton), *Maccus* (Maxey), *Nafarr* (Navisford, *Navereslund*, *Nafrysbroc*), *Reðær* (ODan) (Rothersthorpe), *Singulf* (Singlesole?), *Strikr* (Strixton), *Sula, -e* (Sulby), *Víkingr* (Wigsthorpe), *Willi* (Wilby?), *Yric* (*Arksome*).

FEUDAL AND MANORIAL NAMES

Manorial owner's name added: Barton Seagrave, Burton Latimer, Easton Maudit, Higham Ferrers, Marston Trussell, Middleton Cheney, Moreton Pinkney, Preston Capes, Stoke Albany, Bruerne, and Doyle, Sutton Bassett, Thorpe Lubenham, Malsor, Mandeville, and Waterville, Weedon Beck, Weston Favell, Yardley Gobion and Hastings.

Manorial holder's name prefixed: Collyweston, Green's Norton, Mears Ashby, Paulerspury, Potterspury.

Other feudal additions are used sporadically, e.g. Milton Malsor, Wick Hamond.

Other manorial or attributive additions: Stamford Baron, Canons Ashby, Preston Deanery, Earls Barton, King's Cliffe, Kingsthorpe (2), King's Sutton, Grafton Regis.

Miscellaneous additions: Aston-le-Walls, Brafield on the Green, Brampton Ash, Castle and Cold Ashby, Chipping Warden, Cold Higham, Easton on the Hill, Field and Wood Burcote, Grafton Underwood, Hinton in the Hedges, Long Buckby, Luddington in the Brook, Newton Bromswold, Stowe Nine Churches, Thorpe Underwood, Weedon Lois, Woodnewton and numerous cases where parishes of similar name are distinguished by the dedication of the church, e.g. Ashby St Ledgers, Marston St Lawrence.

FIELD AND MINOR NAMES

The field and minor names of Northamptonshire have in this volume, owing to the fortunate circumstances set forth in the Preface (*supra* vi–vii), received much fuller treatment than those of any county hitherto dealt with by the Survey. Following previous precedent we have dealt first with those field-names (excluding those which can be identified with modern field-names) which are mentioned in early documents, treating them under the heading of their most significant element. These are followed by a new section dealing with some common elements found in the field-names of Northamptonshire as recorded in enclosure-awards, estate-maps and other modern documents and as used locally at the present day, but not usually recorded from medieval times. Then follows a small section dealing with miscellaneous field-names, ancient and modern alike. The fourth and last section is an entirely new one and consists of modern field-names arranged under parishes and hundreds in the same order as in the rest of the book, in so far as it has proved possible with the early documents at our disposal, to attempt in any way to interpret them or at least to indicate their history. Here there are inevitably bad gaps, compensated to some extent, however, by occasional exceptional fullness: e.g. for Welton, Yelvertoft, Harlestone, Weedon Lois. The deficiencies arise occasionally because there may be complete absence of information alike on the medieval and on the modern side. More often there are deficiencies on the medieval side and occasionally while we may have a full list of medieval names, they stand in no relation to the present-day names. There has been a very extensive re-naming of fields in modern times and a new creation of field-names since the days of the early Enclosure Acts in the middle of the 18th cent.

(a) *Field and minor names arranged in alphabetical order under the Old (and Middle) English forms of their chief elements, as recorded in EPN.*

æcer is common, the field being sometimes named after its owner as in *Lefsiesaker* (13th), sometimes from the number of acres as in *Tenacre* (1315), sometimes from what grew on or by it as in *Brembelacre* (1270), *Medaker* (1227), sometimes from its shape as in *Nailacre* (1214), *le Hokede aker* (13th), or its age as in *Eldaker* (1275). *Seinte Marie halfacre* (1240) must have been dedicated to the service of that saint, while *Sokemannes acre* (1512) must have been the field of one of the *sochemanni* of whom we hear so frequently in Domesday.

ME balke (n) is fairly common, and is used of the ridge between two cultivated strips. We hear of a *broad, long, east, old* and a *hollow* balk. The earliest one recorded is *Lawemannes balke* (1237) in Whitfield, probably so named from its owner who must ultimately have had Scandinavian connections. *Claverbalke* (1437) was presumably so named from clæfre or clover. Occasionally it has been recorded in modern times as *Bork* or *Boark*.

bedd (n). We have several rush-beds, the earliest being *Russebed* (1226), and a *Withibed* (14th). *Osierbed* is common. *Ernoldesbed* (1415), containing a personal name, is curious.

bekkr is curiously rare in a county where there is a good deal of Scandinavian influence. There was a *Fulbek* (1400) in Irthlingborough, a *Holbek* (1435) in Draughton, also a *Brakebec* (t. Hy 3) and a *Sandbec* (13th). See also Walbeck *infra* 284.

beorg (OE) and berg (ON) are difficult to differentiate. *Scaleberg* (1199) in Braybrooke is purely Scandinavian (*v.* skali, 'hut') and so are *Brakenberuwe* (13th) in Brixworth and *Brakeberge* (c. 1300) in Draughton (*v.* braken). *Slahteberewe* (1200) in Arthingworth and *Sleytteberewe* (13th) in Brixworth seem to commemorate forgotten battles (OE *sleaht, slieht*), *Spelborw* (14th) in Daventry was some lost 'hill of speech' and we have a *Broken berg* (1199) in Braybrooke.

ME breche (n), 'land broken up for tillage,' is fairly common in the county, often in the simple form *la Breche* (c. 1200), but also compounded with 'wheat' and 'pease' as in *Wetebreche* (1255), *Pesebreche* (1274), 'meadow' and 'thorn' as in *Medowbreche* (1400), *Thornbreche* (13th), *Overe-* and *Nethere-* (1260, 1370), 'short' and 'long' and 'mickle' as in *Sortebreche* (1227), *Longebreche* (1310), *Mikelebreche* (1223), crundel (quarry) as in

Crondelbreche (14th) and 'callow,' i.e. 'bare' as in *Caleubreche*
(1199). In *Akremannebreche* (13th) we have reference to its
cultivators. In modern times it appears as *Bratch, Bretch, Britch,
Breach, Breech, Braitch* and even *Bretts* and *Britz.*

brinke. Four early examples of this distinctively East
Scandinavian element have been noted, two examples of *Rede-
brynke* (1343 and 14th), a *Hybrynk* (14th) and a *Wellesladebrinke*
(t. Ric 2). It is found occasionally in modern field-names.

broc is as usual very common, sharing that frequency with sic.
ME brode (n) is found by itself in *le Brode* (c. 1200), in *Swerte-
brode* (15th), *Cowebrode* (1231) and in *Soflebrode* (1195), the last
being perhaps a field which produced some form of *sowl.* Very
common is *Gorebrod* or *Garebrod* (13th), denoting apparently a
broad strip which tapers to a *gore* or point (*v.* gara). In modern
times it takes the form *Garboard, Garberd,* etc.

brycg. Bridges were often named from their owners as in
Botolfesbrigge (1220), *Huberdisbrigge* (1230), sometimes from the
traffic which they took as in *Waynebrigge* (t. Ed 3), *Swynebrygge*
(1333), sometimes from their material or their condition as in
Stanbricgge (10th), *Fulebrigge* (1302). *Childrebrigge* (1272) from
OE *cildra* (gen. pl.), 'youths',' is noteworthy.

burna is very rare in the county.

buskr is fairly common as in *Wythibuskes* (1240), *Thernebusk*
(1398), *Gunnebusc* (1286). The anglicised *busshe* is rare and
late.

ME butte is fairly common. Doubtless it usually has the sense
'strip of land abutting on a boundary,' 'short ridge of unequal
length at right angles to the other ridges in the field,' as in *Buttes*
(1223), *Sortebuttes* (1330), *Seven buttes* (1250), *Oldebutt* (1469),
Halfe aker butt (t. Eliz). In *Robyn hoodes buttes* (1591) it probably denotes an archery ground.

cnoll is found occasionally. *Hamthonescnol* (1280) in Litchborough is curious, used of land abutting on the road to
Northampton. Cf. *Hamtuneford* (c. 1160 *AddCh*) used of a ford
in Welford.

cot(e). A few more examples, in addition to those found in
ordinary place-names, may be noted. *Lambecotes, -coten* is found
seven times, including a *Lambrechotes* (1242) from the OE
genitive plural *lambra. Lambcotes* now often appears as *Lambcuts*, once as *Lamb Courts.* We have also *Schypcote* (14th) and
Hoggescote (14th).

croft is very common. Sometimes it is compounded with a
personal name as in *Brihtgeuescroft* and *Kinewinescroft* (c. 1155).
Often it occurs with some tree or crop name as in *Whetecroft*
(1320), *Corncroft* (1300), *Riecroft* (1223), *Lyncroft* (1408), *Gers-*

croft (1329), *v.* gærs, *Puricroft* (1300), *v.* pyrige, or with a bird or animal name as in *Gosecroft* (1314), *Horscroft* (1371), *Kydecroft* (1302), *Hundecroft* (1250), *Buckescroft* (1224). We have reference to its method of enclosure in *le Walledecroft* (1317), *Hacchecroft* (1300), *Lokcroft* (1204), to its rent in *Penycroft* (1400) and to its users in *Cnihtecroft* (1198), *Cotsetlecroft* (1291). *Bancroft* is a fairly common modern name, a compound of bean.

cros. We have reference to several crosses, including *le Stopindecros* (1254) in Hinton, *le Stoupendecros* in Chelveston (1330), a *Borowcros*, i.e. town cross (14th) in Wellingborough, and a *Twicros* (? some form of double cross) in 1203, identical with Twycross (Lei).

cumb is found some seventeen times and that in the western half of the county, as the topography would lead us to expect. It can be used of something quite tiny.

dæl OE, **dalr** ON is as common as **denu** is rare, and the reason may be that in a good many cases an English *dene* has been replaced by an Anglo-Scandinavian *dale* as in Debdale *supra* 119. *Depedale* is specially frequent. A few of the compounds are entirely Scandinavian, such as *Kirkedale* (1250), *Brakendale* (1199), *Thranedale* (14th), *v.* **trani**, 'crane,' but in most cases it is impossible to say whether the source of this word is English or Scandinavian.

dal, in the form *dole*, is very common. The portions of the common field are often distinguished as long, short, broad, small, east, west or the like. Occasionally we have other names as *le Weldole* (1371), *le Thakedole* (1292), whence *thak* or thatching material came, *Thisteldole* (14th).

(ge)delf, in the compound *stan(ge)delf*, giving ME *stanidelf*, *stonidelf*, is very common in Northamptonshire as was to be expected in a county so rich in quarries. In modern field-names it often takes the form *Standle, Standhill* and the like.

denu. *v. supra s.v.* **dæl.**

dic is very common either in the form *dich(e)* or *dik(e)*. We have also *Cruldych* (1403), 'curling ditch,' and *Meredich* (14th), 'boundary ditch.'

dun is found but rarely. We may note *Ruidun* (c. 1180), i.e. rye-hill.

eng is very rare. We have a *Westeng* (c. 1245) in Maxey, a field called *super henges* (1209) in Warmington, a *Mikelyng* (1300) in Draughton, a *Bernardesheng* (1227), *Goshenges* (c. 1195) and that is about all. This is somewhat surprising in view of the abundance of marshy land in the east of the county.

fal(o)d is very rare except in the compound **stodfald** *infra* 270. We have only *Pindingfold* (1320), in Harleston, a form of the word *pinfold* not recorded in the NED, and a *Middle-*, *Olde-*, and *Wolde-fold*.

feld is common. *Dolefeld* in Harrowden (14th) is a parallel to the name of the Wiltshire Hundred (EPN *s.v.* dal) of that name.

flat is not recorded in ME forms and is almost unknown in modern names.

ford is common. We have a *Stenenford* (1326) or 'stony ford,' two or three *Stakefords*, a *Wildeforde* 1275 (cf. Wildbridge PN Sx 145), several *Fulfords* and one of the common *Dernefords* or 'hidden fords.' *Salteresford* (13th) must have carried a 'salters' road.'

furlang, primarily a strip of ploughed land, is perhaps the commonest of all field-name elements. Commonest is the description of the furlong by what is found on it: *Bere-* (i.e. corn), *Barli-*, *Pese-*, *Nep-* (i.e. turnip), *Ben-*, *Brere-*, *Thack-* (i.e. thatching material), *Clavere-* (i.e. clover), *Hethe-*, *Ling-*, *Med-*, *Note-* (nuts). Next is description by the soil: *Cley-*, *Sten-*, *Water-*, *Mers-*, *Mor-*; or by the shape: *Wowe-* (crooked), *Twyfalde-*, *Tunge-*, *Hole-* (hollow). Occasionally we have reference to the creature which frequents it as in *Emete-* (ant) and *Wesyll-furlang*. In the south-west of the county it often appears in the form *furland*.

ME **galle** (n) is found in *Janekynesgalle* (1403) in Newnham and in two examples of *Watergalle(s)* in Moreton Pinkney (1200) and Yelvertoft (1416), cf. Watergall (Wa). *gall* is recorded in the EDD as a dialect term used of a barren or unfertile spot in a field and also of spongy ground. *watergall* would seem to express the latter idea more fully. Gall and Water Gall alike are fairly common in modern field-names.

gara or 'gore' is, as usual, fairly common.

garðr is not recorded in ME and is very rare in modern names. We may note *Coggarth* in Stoke Albany.

geard is fairly common. *Berneyerd* (1230) in Brackley carries back the word *barnyard* some 300 years earlier than the first quotation in the NED and there are several other early examples of it. *Sclatedȝerdes* (1409), referring to some slated paving, is noteworthy.

grene is used occasionally, as in *le Kirkegrene* (1250) in Armston.

(ge)hæg is fairly common, as one would expect in this well-forested county. There is more than one *Wulfhaia* (1222), a *Swynehey* (1287) and an *Oxehay* (1200).

haga OE, **hagi** ON, is very common and is clearly often used, as it still is in the local dialect, for a small wood or coppice. It is specially common in the old Rockingham Forest area and in Nassaborough Hundred, which was once much more wooded than it is now. In some cases, as in *Scrathawe* in Dogsthorpe (1400) containing ON *skratti*, 'goblin,' it is clear that we have ON **hagi** rather than **haga**. *Lochawe* (1244) would seem to refer to some particular type of enclosure, *Tindhawe* (1247) is one enclosed by some kind of hedge (cf. OE *tȳnan*, 'to enclose with a hedge').

haining, 'enclosed land,' is found once, in *Heyninges* (c. 1400) in Castor.

hamm is fairly common in this county and the form with double *m* is often preserved in ME even in compounded forms. Compounds like *Morhamme* (1250), *le Dikedehamme* (1260), *Flexhamme* (t. Ric 2), *Axmulnehamme* (ib.) are specially suggestive of the sense commonly given for this element, viz. 'flat, low-lying pasture land near a stream or river.' It is occasionally found in modern field-names.

hangra has been noted twice.

hassuc (n), 'tuft of coarse grass,' generally in the plural form *Hassocks*, is specially common in this county as a field-name. It is compounded with ling in *Lingehassokes* (13th).

healh is not common. It is worthy of note that we occasionally have examples derived from the nominative rather than from the much more common dative. Thus *Halch* in Desborough (1207), *Aylwardeshalugh* in Doddington (1262), *la Halegh* in Cranford (1261), *Pottereshalewe* in Yardley Hastings (1348) and *les Halewes* in Floore (13th).

hecg is occasionally found as in *Chircheheges* (13th) in Bulwick, *Stanyhegge* in Glapthorn (1334). We have reference to a broken hedge in *Brustheggewong* (1400) in Oundle.

hlaw is fairly common. *Twamlowe* (1310) in Brackley must be a double hill or barrow and is a parallel to Twemlow (Ch). In contrast we have a single one in *Anlowe* (14th), cf. *infra* 280. We have a *Draclowe* (c. 1199) and a *Drakelowe* (1500), 'dragon hills' or 'barrows' and a *Wakelowe* (1366) in Welton which may have been a 'watch' or look-out hill.

hlinc is occasionally found in field-names in this county, alike in the forms *link* and *linch*.

hliþ is found two or three times, as in *Grenelitheweye* (1343).

hoc is also found occasionally, as in *the Thicke Hok* (1320), *Merehoc* (1143), *Bushyhoc* (1250), *le Wronghok* (1330), i.e. the twisted **hoc**. It is occasionally found in modern field-names.

hoh is fairly common but cannot always be distinguished from **haugr**. We have in addition to the examples noted *supra* 131 two further speech-hills, *Spelhou* (1250) in Paston and *Spello* (15th) in Daventry, a *Galhou* (1320), 'gallows-hill' in Harlestone. *Onehowe* (1400) in Easton and *Tweienhouwes* (1222) are probably compounds of **haugr**.

holmr is still in use in the form *holm* in Northamptonshire, and has much the same sense as **hamm** *supra* 264. Characteristic compounds are *Segholm* (1242), *Thackholm* (13th), from the growing of reeds there, *Flowendeholm* (1203), *Milneholm* (13th). The word, though ultimately of Scandinavian origin, was used so widely in ME that we find it in all parts of the county. See further Cringleholm *infra* 280.

holt is found occasionally as in *Okeholt* (1400), *Assholt* (1347), *Stocholt* (1229), *Willougholte* (1523). *holt* is also occasionally found in modern names.

hrycg has been noted once in ME names and is very rare later.

hryding, 'clearing,' is not as common in early documents as one would have expected in this well-wooded county. We may note *Cuttederidyng* (1200), *Olderudyngg* (1319), and *The Ridings* (Deene) and *Grass Ryden* in Farthinghoe.

hulc (n), 'hovel, shed,' which lingers on in the dialectal *hulk* and was used by the Northamptonshire poet Clare in the phrase 'wattled hulk,' is found in three or four names such as *le Hulkefurlong* (1295), *Hulkestedes* (1404).

hyll is very common indeed. Sometimes we have reference to its surface, shape or soil as in *le Wouhill* (1275), *v.* **woh**, *Sandhulle* (1240), *Klaihil* (13th), *Hardhull* (13th), *Rouhull* (13th), *v.* **ruh**, *Druenhull* (t. Ric 2), *v.* **dryge**, *Calou Hul* (1320), i.e. 'bald hill,' *Hepehil* (1154), *Dusthul* (13th), *Sindrehilles* (13th), *le Brendehull* (1250), i.e. 'burned hill,' *Copthull* (1250), 'peaked hill.' At others we have reference to the crops as in *Cornhulle* (1410), *Ryenhull* (1300), *Clevrehul* (1512), i.e. 'clover hill,' *Benhylle* (1400), *Flaxhull* (1401), *Berhul* (1215), i.e. 'barley (or corn) hill,' *Pesehill* (1200), *Barlichhul* (1200), *Othul* (c. 1279), or to the vegetation generally, as in *Boxhull* (1307), *Brakenhull* (1200), *Gostihull* (13th), i.e. 'gorsey,' *Farnehull* (1312), *Brerehull* (1210), *Thornhul* (1200), *Erthnotehull* (1240), to the creatures that frequent it, as in *Cranehul* (13th), *Nadrehull* (1250), i.e. 'adder hill,' *Stothill* (t. Hy 3), *Rethyrhyll* (14th), i.e. 'cattle hill,' *Haverhil* (1270), i.e. 'goat hill,' to its use, as in *Totehil* (1226) and *Wardehyll* (13th), which must have been look-out hills. In modern times this sometimes appears as *Tuttle* or *Tootle*. *Berrel, Beryl, Barhill, Barehill* are some of the forms which *bere-hyll*, 'barley (or corn) hill,' assumes in modern times.

hyrne, 'corner,' is found occasionally, as in *Nomanslondhirne* (1300), *Sadilbowhirne* (1400).

hyrst has only been noted in *The Hurst* in Wicken in the extreme west of the county.

kiarr has only been found once in ME Northamptonshire field-names, but the word was used in this district, for in a 13th cent. charter relating to Geddington, we have a grant of land *cum kerre et prato*, i.e. with marsh and meadow land. Once or twice we find the word in the form *car(r)* in modern field-names.

lacu is fairly common as a name for a tiny stream or pool. In *Cruddelake* in Evenley (1248), with variant forms *Cro(d)delake*, we seem to have a compound of ME *crudde*, 'curded, congealed,' referring perhaps to the colour of the water, a good deal earlier than the earliest form recorded in the NED *s.v.* curd.

lad, 'watercourse, lode,' is found occasionally, as in *Trendlade* (1233), 'circular watercourse.'

læs, 'pasture, meadow,' is used especially with the names of domestic animals, as in *Oxelese* (1224), *Scabydhorsles* (14th), *Oxeleswe* (1325), *Calvysleswe* (1300). Occasionally we have the form *leasoe* or *leasowe* in modern field-names.

land is very common indeed and is doubtless often used in its technical sense of 'strip of land in an open field.' We have reference to (*a*) its size or shape in *Scortelonde* (1250), *Langlond* (1471), *Wohlond* (1250) from woh, 'crooked,' *Wronglond* (1242), from **wrang**, 'twisted,' *Bradelond* (13th), *Scharplond* (1402), (*b*) its crop in *Flexlondes* (1199), *Banlond* (1230) and *Benlond* (t. Ric 2), *Cornlond* (1314), *Linlond* (1244), *Peselond* (1250), *Ryelond* (1343), *Watelond* (1222) from **hwæte**, 'wheat,' (*c*) the soil and the like in *Radelond* or *Redelond* (1200), *Blakelond* (1290), *Swetelond* (13th), *Hardelondes* (1249), *Smithlond* (1225), *Dedelond* (1451), *Cleilongelandes* (1222), (*d*) the creatures found on it in *Goselond* (1255), *Mulelond* (1226), *Haverlond* (1292), from OE *hæfer*, 'goat,' unless this is a hybrid formation from ME *haver*, ON *hafri*, 'oats.' *Mawelond* (1314) is 'mown land,' *Brandelondes* (14th) describes ground cleared by burning, *Stongelond* (1300) was marked by a *stang* or pole, *le Mokedelond* (1290) was well *mucked* or manured, *Echebenlond* (1200) seems permanently to have been devoted to the cultivation of beans (OE *ēce*, 'eternal') and *Schertebanlond* (1311) was a short bean-strip. What particular form of *superbia* troubled *Prudehavedlond* (13th) we do not know. *Inland* (1220) as opposed to *Utlond* (1250) was probably the lord's demesne land, as distinct from that of his tenants, or possibly enclosed and cultivated land as distinct from common or waste land.

The commonest of all compounds with land is probably 'bean-land,' which in modern times appears in a variety of forms, including *Banlands*, *Bandlands*, *Bantlands*, *Bandilands*, *Ballands*, *Balance*[1]. Next most common is probably '*wrang*-land,' which

---

[1] The reverse form of this phonological development is found in Scottish *ballands*, *ballants* for *balance* (v. Craigie, *Dict. of Older Scottish Tongue*, *s.v.*).

gives *Wranglands* and *Ranglands*. Fairly frequent is '*woh*-land,' which gives *Wollands*, *Woolands*, *Woolens*. The common use of the plural form shows that the usual sense of *land* in these compounds is 'strip of land.'

ME longe (n) is fairly frequent and must have been used of a specially long strip, as in *le Longe* (1250), *Estlong* (1242), *West Longes* (1394). *Schortesouthlonges* (1416) must have had reference to the direction in which the strip ran.

lundr is confined to the north of the county. It is specially common in Nassaburgh Hundred and in the old Rockingham Forest area. It would seem that the word must have been in common use, for hybrids are frequently found as in *Suthlund* (1250), *Estlund* (13th), *Oldelound* (t. Ed 1), *Hethelund* (13th). Only occasionally is it found with a distinctively Scandinavian personal name as in *Thurferdislund* (13th), or with a distinctively Scandinavian word as in *Lundgate* (1330). In modern times it appears as *lound*, *lownd* and occasionally as *lawn*.

mæd is common alike in the form *mede* and *med(o)we*. *Dolemede* (1370) from OE dal, 'share,' has reference to the dividing up of the meadow land. In *Cotmannemede* (14th), *Cotemannemedwe* (1200), *Shirevesmede* (1221), *le Heywardesmede* (1280) we have reference to the users of the particular pieces of meadow land, while *le Menemed* (14th) (from OE (*ge*)*mǣne*, 'common') seems to have been held in common. *Smethemede* (1281) is the antithesis of *le Brokenemede* (1261), *Horemede* (1226) from OE horh, 'filth,' and *Fulmede* (1406) must both have been muddy. *Redemede* (1207) and *Thachingmede* (14th) both alike supplied thatching material. The *Coruenmede* (t. Ed 3) must have been so called from some particular 'carving' or cutting of the grass. *Five Man Meade* (1553) perhaps took five men to mow it while *Boimede* (1226) may have taken but a single boy. Why *Cripsemede* (1265) was distinguished as 'curly' we do not know—possibly from the shape of the meadow-strip. *Penymedouwe* (1300) was so named from its rent, while *Blodehangyrmede* (14th) seems to have been a sloping meadow, once the scene of some bloody fray.

(ge)mære, 'boundary,' 'meare,' is very common. It appears now as *Meer*, *Mere*, *Meare* and the like. In compounds it often appears in the form *Mar-*, as in *Margrave*.

mere is fairly common.

mor is as common as mersc is rare. One of the commonest compounds of mor is *Coppedemor* (1240). It is difficult to say what the meaning can be. The sense can hardly be that of 'peaked.' It may be from *cop*, 'ridge of earth,' noted from Cheshire and Lancashire in the EDD, hence low-lying land protected by an embankment, or we may have an extension of *cop*, 'to poll or pollard,' so that *coppedmor* denoted one in which the reed-thickets had been cut. It is found in the form Cop(p)y-moor and Coppice Moor in modern field-names.

OE mylde (n), a variant of the common *molde*, 'earth,' is fairly common in Northamptonshire, especially when compounded with the adjective blæc, as in *Blakemilde* in Yelvertoft (13th). We have also the compound *Radmylde* in Floore (13th). See further Rodmell (PN Sx 325).

myrr is surprisingly rare in a county where Scandinavian influence is so strong and marshy ground fairly common. Only two early examples have been noted and it is very rare in modern names.

nest. We have three examples of *le Suannesnest* (1150), a *Storkesnest* (13th), a *Crownest* (1200) and a *Crakenest* (1300), 'crow' or 'raven' nest, from ON *kraki*, 'crow.' This hybrid compound is found in Draughton, a parish which shows marked Scandinavian influence.

pæð. We may note *le Clerkespathe* (1346), *Cattespæth* (c. 1225), *le Thuertpath* (1404), i.e. 'thwart or cross path,' *Wormpath* (1437), and *Thistlipath* (c. 1150), with the common *cyric pæð* and *grenan pæð* (1022), 'church' and 'green' path.

pightel (ME) is very rare in early names but very common later. We have *Boyespythel* (1272) in Barnwell and the curious nasalised form *pingle* (NED *s.v.*) in *Swynespyngel* (1404) near Peterborough. In modern times it appears variously as *Pightle*, *Pikle*, *Pikewell*, *Pidell*, *Pittell*, *Pikeall*, *Piecull*, *Pingle*.

plek (ME) (n) is found in *Whytebarn pleck* in Sulgrave (1200). It denotes a small plot of ground.

pytt. We have two 'goblin' pits, e.g. *Pokepyt* (14th), *v.* puca, five or six 'giant' pits, e.g. *Thursput* (1280), *v.* þyrs, *Wlfputtes* (1250), *Blakeput* (13th), *Colpittes* (14th), *Marlepytte* (14th), *Sondepyttes* (14th), *Lympitt* (1400), *le Stonepytt* (t. Hy 8).

queche (ME), 'thicket,' already noted in PN Wo 392 and PN Sx 366 is found in *Quechebrok* (1444), *Quechefen* (1330), *Quecheford* (1401) and *Thirsqueche* (1292), the last being apparently a compound of OE þyrs, 'giant.'

rod, 'clearing,' is fairly common, but cannot always be distinguished with certainty from rōd, 'cross.' We may note *le Cleyrode* (1320), *bradanrode* (11th), *Langrodes* (1400), *ealdanrode* (11th), *le Newerode* (1337), *le Deperode* (1200) and *Apeltrowrode* (1375).

sceaga is rare. It is found in *Thykkeshawe* (1226) twice and may also be found in *Hundeberdeshauue* (13th), though this might also be a compound of haga.

sceard (n) is found in *Redscherd* (1200), *Estsherd* (1240), *Bradischerd* (1404), *Kentelowescherd* (14th). In these names it probably denotes a clearing in a forest, though it might have the more common meaning 'gap or broken place in a hedge, wall,' *v.* NED, EDD, *s.v. shard*.

sceat, 'nook, corner,' is rare as in *Chercheschot* (c. 1200) and *le Shote* (1411).

sic OE, **sik** ON, is common. In the form *-siche*, *-sik* it is very commonly compounded with *well*-names as in *Acwellsyke* (1505), *Ringwelsik* (1299), *Ludewellesiche* (14th). Other compounds having reference to the presence of water are *Fletsyke* (1300), *v.* fleot, and *Rennendesike* (1251). Adjectival compounds are *Radesiche, Redesiche* (1226), *Fulesic* (1022), *Blakesik* (13th), *Fennisiche* (c. 1195). For *Gorsiche* (1371), *v.* gor.

skali. One example of this characteristically Scandinavian element seems to be found in *Cattescalis* (t. Hy 3) in Brockhall. For another, *v.* berg *supra* 260.

skogr, 'wood,' seems to be unknown except for *Scogate* in Harringworth.

slæd is very common and probably has as a rule the sense 'valley, hollow, grassy plain between hills,' though the EDD quotes a further special Northamptonshire use, viz. 'a strip of greensward through a wood, a green road,' hence perhaps three or four examples of *Greneslade* (1242). Other adjectival compounds are *Depeslade* (t. Hy 3), *Sharpslade* (t. Ric 2), *Blakeslade* (1400), *Langeslade* (1300), *le Naruslade* (1311), *Brodslade* (1410). Animals are associated with it in *Haverslade* (1435), *v.* hæfer, *Kattesslade* (1244), *Lampisslade* (1299) (i.e. lamb), *Wlueslade* (1203), plant-names in *Bromyslade* (1320), *Withislade* (1210), *Cleuerslade* (1345), *v.* clæfre, 'clover.' In *Hulsterslade* we have a compound of OE *heolstor*, 'hiding-place,' cf. Hylters (PN Sx 49). As was to be expected there are many compounds of slæd and wielle as in *Willeslade* (t. Ric 2) and *Hukwelleslade* (1240).

stan. There are several examples of the common *Horeston, Harestone* (1317), 'boundary stone,' *v.* har. *Le Gangestones* (1226) probably has reference to some passage across water or marsh. We also have *Plumstones* (1394), *Penistones* (1404), *Schirston* (1344), *Cuttedston* (1501).

steall is found compounded with tun in two examples of *Tunsteall* (c. 1150).

stede is compounded with cot(e) in two or three examples of *Costede* (1200), with burh in two examples of *Byrystede* (t. Hy 2), with *hulc*, 'hovel,' in *Hulkestedes* (1404), with *guildhall* in *Gildhaldsted* in Werrington (1209). There are one or two examples of *Newstede* (1190), a *Stonestede* (t. Hy 8), a *Roughstede* (1681) and a *Checkerestede* (1357). *v.* Mickstead *infra* 283. One example of *Hemsteads* has been noted.

stodfald and **stotfald**. These elements are very difficult to distinguish but are found in several minor names in the county. Cf. *stodfald* (1022) and *Stotfolde* (1242).

strod has been noted once, in *Balstrod* (1315 *Ass*) in Gedding-ton which may be in error for the common *bulstrode*, 'bull marsh,' and in the modern *Stroud Hill* in Woodford Halse.

stubb is fairly common, especially in the compound *Elrenestubb* (1255), 'elder-tree stump.'

*stybbing (n). Side by side with ME *stubbing* from OE stubb, 'stump,' there must have been another form from OE stybb, denoting similarly a clearing in which stumps have been left. Such a form is necessary to explain *le Stibbynges* (1354), *New-stibbing* (13th), *Bullestibbinges* (1198), *Berngerestibbing* (1330), *Warinstibbing* (13th). In later names it occasionally appears as *stepping*.

swæþ (n), ME *swathe*, still used locally in the sense 'measure of grassland,' is found in *Swathes* (1400), *une Swath* (13th), *le Longeswathes* (1353).

ME **thing** (n), presumably denoting 'possession' is found in a group of field-names *Dykenesthing, Serjeantthing, Beaumys-thing, Wakesthing, Vincentisthing, Lionesthing* (1419) in Rothwell, in *Seyntlowesthyng* (1404) in Brampton Ash, in *Colesthynge* (1340) in Walton and perhaps in *Oldeding* (1226). Cf. *Fowleres-thyng* (1435 AD v) in Lapworth (Wa), *Aynolfesthyng* (1356 AD iii) in Ash (Sr).

þorn. We have *Onezorn* (sic) (13th), *Tweynthornes* (14th) and *Twythorne* (c. 1400) and *Fourthornwong* (1400), *Smalyorn* (1348), *Langethorn* (1250), *Gretethorne* (1260), *le Coppedethorn* (1280), i.e. 'the pollarded thorn.' What *shroud* or garment is to be associated with *Schrudthorn* (1386) or how *Restingthorn* (14th) got its name, it is difficult to say. The common use of thorn-trees or bushes as boundary marks is suggested in *mærþorn* (1022), *v.* (ge)mære.

þveit is found occasionally in the Peterborough district and also in two or three field-names in Deene. We may note *Someretweyt* (1415).

topt is fairly common in the Scandinavianised parts of the county.

trenche, ME (n) is found in *les Trenches* (t. Ed 1) in Rocking-ham Forest and *Middeltrenche* (1375) in Whittlewood Forest. It is of interest to note that the earliest sense of *trench* in the NED is 'path or track cut through a wood or forest.'

vangr is very common in field-names and is found even in parishes where there is little other evidence of Scandinavian influence. From this and from the fact that the first element in these field-names is nearly always English rather than Scandinavian we may infer that the word had become a common dialect term in ME, as it still is in the Northamptonshire *wong*, *wang*, and that it is no evidence for Scandinavian settlement. Often it is compounded with a crop-name as in *Banewong* (1250), *Watewong* (1292) (*v.* bean, hwæte), or with a plant-name as in *Brymblewong* (1540), *Thurnewong* (14th), *Fourthornewong* (1346). Adjectival compounds are *Watriwong* (1199), *Blakewong* (1207), *Whitewong* (1403), *Coppidwong*, i.e. 'peaked' (1400), *Scortwong*, *Longewong* (1245), *Bradwong* (1245). We may note also *Childeswang* (c. 1180), *Sherreveswong* (1400), *Marscalleswong* (1371). The only purely Scandinavian compound is *Toftwong* (13th). In modern times it appears as *Wong*, *Wung* and even *Wound(s)*.

vra, 'nook, corner,' is found by itself as in *le Wro* (1313) in Maxey, compounded with myrr in *Myrewra* (14th) and with hlose in *Losewro* (1320). See also The Rows *infra* 288. It has only been noted in the east of the county and in Rockingham Forest.

wæd, 'ford,' is found in a few minor names, as in *Croswade* (1250), *Stanewade* (t. Hy 3) and *Stonwade* (1340). The latter is in contrast to a neighbouring *Greswade* (1209) or *Garswade* (1330), 'grass ford.' In *Qwarnewath* in Glapthorn (1334) we seem to have the cognate Scandinavian vað, compounded with cweorn or Scandinavian *kvern*.

weald, 'forest,' is fairly common. In the south-west of the county it appears in the form *wild*, and in this form has been noted in Brackley, Bradden, Charwelton, Gayton, Green's Norton, Radstone, Syresham, Wappenham, Weedon, only one example being found east of Watling St. Elsewhere it commonly assumes the form *Wold*, but occasionally *Old* and even *Hold* and *Whold*. *v.* Introd. xxxi.

weg. We have many references to roads and tracks of various kinds. *Grenewey* (1232), *Rigewey* (1232), *le Holeweye* (1330), *le Drovewey* (1347), *Carteweye* (1404) are self-explanatory. Often the name has reference to the place to which it leads as in *Chirchewei* (1250), *Mulnewei* (1250), *Fordeweie* (13th), *Coteweie* (1404), *Stondelweye* (14th), from *stan(ge)delf*, 'quarry,' *Madweie* (1226), from mæd, 'mead,' or to the load which it carries as in *Hayway* (1482), *Bereweie* (1250), from bere, 'barley,' used here perhaps in the general sense of corn (cf. PN BedsHu 50-1 *s.n.* Barford). *Maneweye* (1242) is a common road (OE *(ge)mǣne*), *Merewey* (13th) and *Markeweye* (1200) are boundary roads or paths (*v.* (ge)mære, mearc). *Pottereswey* (1228), *Cartereswey* (t. Ric 2), *Mengerweye* (1320), *Thevesway* (1150) have reference

to the users of the roads. *Dernewey* (1400), *Horewey* (1403) and
Twyscledewey (1330) were respectively 'hidden,' 'dirty' and
'forked' (*v.* dierne, horh, twisla).

wielle. Northamptonshire is a county of many springs and
there are very many minor *well*-names. Occasionally these may
refer to streams rather than springs but this is probably true of
comparatively few. We have reference to the character of the
water in *Caldwelle* (1200), *Chaldewelle* (1313), *Warmwelle* (13th),
Colewelle (1320), *Blakewelle* (1219), *Radwelle* (1240), *Whitewell*
(1320), *Fauwell* (1200), *v.* fah, 'stained,' *Freskewelle* (1340),
Clenewelle (1250), *Fulwell* (t. Ed 3), *Swetwelle* (1200), *Milkwelle*
(1200), *Saltwelle* (1320), *Smerewelle* (1199), *v.* smeoru, 'fat'; to
the creatures that frequent it in *Hertwelle* (t. Ric 2), *Hyndewelle*
(t. Ed 3), *Houndewelle* (1469), *Shepwelle* (1403), *Duuewelle* (1199),
Culverewelle (1500) (from OE culfre, 'pigeon, dove'), *Cocwelles*
(1203), *Tranwelle* (15th) (from ON trani, 'crane'), *Snakewelle*
(1250), *Froskewelle* (1222), from forsc, 'frog,' *Shotenewell* (t. Hy 3)
from OE *scēote*, 'trout'; to the things that grow by it as in *Furs-
welle* (1199), *wiðigwylle* (1022), *Osierwelle* (1347), *Rushewell*
(t. Eliz), *Hassokewell* (1501) from hassuc, 'coarse grass,' *Thurne-
welle* (1250), *Carsewelle* (t. Hy 8) from cærse, 'cress,' *Peswelle*
(1199), *Banewelle* (1320) from bean, *Barlichwel* (c. 1219),
Riewelle (1200), *Perewelle* (1330), *Plumwelle* (t. Ed 1), *Srobwelle*
(1223), *Acwelle* (1305); to those who frequent it as in *Beggeres-
well* (1367), *Wrecchewelle* (1250), *Nuneswell* (14th), *Clerkwell*
(14th), *Shytereswelle* (13th) from OE *scīetere*, 'shooter,' and
Boiwell (1201) (probably from ME *boye*, 'boy'). *Michelwelle*
(1232), *Bradwelle* (1318), *Tholdewell* (1250), *Maniwelle* (1250)
are self-explanatory. *Dernewell* (1250) is 'hidden spring,' *le
Blyndewelle* (1270) is one which has no outlet, and there are
three or four examples of *Ringwelle*—why so called it is difficult
to say. Note also *Crumpewelle* (1300), 'curly spring or stream,'
and *Candlemaswelle* (14th). *Rennendewelle* (1332) and *Dripwelle*
(1408) are self-explanatory. *Stayntwell* (1457) from OE *stæniht*,
'stony,' describes the bottom of the stream or spring.

wudu is as usual common. Of adjectival compounds we may
note *Youngwode* (1150), *Thikwod* (1400), *Menewud* (1227) from
OE (*ge*)*mǣne*, 'common,' *Brendwode* (1250) from ME brende,
Miclewod (14th). The meaning of *Friday boscus* (1250) is obscure.
Yerdewode (c. 1200) is a parallel to Yardley (PN D i, p. liii),
a wood whence yards or spars might be taken.

(b) Some of the more common types of field-names, not so recorded.

The word **conyger**, 'rabbit-warren,' with the word **conygarth**,
of similar meaning, with which it has been so freely confused in

English, is very common as a field-name, and assumes a wide variety of forms. The commonest is *Coneygree*, but we may note also *Coneygear*, *Coney Grey*, *Cunny Gray*, *Cun-a-gree*, *Cunningree*, *Cuninger*, *Conyearth*, *Coney Garth*, *Coney Grove*, *Cunney Grift*.

freeboard is fairly common. No early example of its use has been noted. It describes (*a*) a strip of land lying beyond the boundaries of an estate, over which the owner possesses certain rights, (*b*) the pasture edges of an arable field, (*c*) a right of way (*v. EDD s.v. free*).

ground is now very common indeed, but is very rare in documents earlier than the 16th century. See further *s.n.* Newbold Grounds *supra* 17.

hades is fairly common. This term, always found in the plural, denotes first a strip of land left unploughed between two portions of a field, and then a piece of greensward left at the head of arable land, on which the plough can turn (NED *s.v. hade*).

Professors Ekwall and Tolkien have pointed out independently that *hades* has apparently the same sense-usage as the OE pl. *hēafdu*, *andhēafdu*, and that phonologically we have the same development, through ME *haved*, as in ModEng *lady* < ME *lavedy* < OE *hlæfdige*.

hanging(s) is common as a field-name. See further *s.n.* Castor Hanglands *supra* 229.

hop-yard, i.e. hop-garden, is fairly common. No early example has been noted.

lammas is very common as an element in field-names, such as *Lammas Piece*, *Lammas Close*, *Lammas Mead*. Such field-names take their origin from the custom whereby certain lands under particular cultivation till the harvest, conventionally fixed at Lammas-tide (Aug. 1st), became on that day common pasturage, and remained such till the following spring.

ley, specially common in the plural form *leys*, also spelled *lays*, is used of grass-land, untilled land, cultivated land under grass or clover. It is a specialised development of OE leah.

slang is occasionally found. It denotes a narrow strip of land. The diminutive *slanket* has been noted once. No early example of *slang* has been found.

slipe is common. It denotes a long narrow strip. No early example has been noted.

stanch, staunch is occasionally found as a name for a dam.

water-furrows is fairly common as the name of a field in which the water is apt to stand in the furrows. It is now often pronounced and spelled *water-thoroughs*.

Extensive traces of the cultivation of woad (OE wad) are found in field-names. In some cases, as in Wadcroft, Wadground *supra* 52, 185, Wad Cabin, Wadborough, Wadhill, the forms are unambiguous, and clearly contain this element. In other cases, where we now have *Wod* or *Wood*, we probably have, in a large number of examples, a corruption of earlier *wad* or *wod*, as in *Woodhill, Wod Ground*. Morton (17) says, "Of all the Midland counties, this is, or has been, woaded most," and notes that it is specially common round Kettering (375).

In addition to these, we may note:

wandoles. This is found three times in Northamptonshire. It is a modern field-name in Desborough. In an Isham deed of 1503 we have mention of *Wandolis* in Lamport, while in a Stoke Albany Terrier of 1632 we have mention of 3 *Wandells* of land. This is doubtless the word *wandale* discussed in PN NRY 59. It is an obsolete dialect word denoting a share of the large open arable land of a township. Its general distribution, and the early forms, suggest that it is of Scandinavian origin, and its particular distribution in Northamptonshire accords with this view.

(c) Miscellaneous.

Curious isolated names are *Reinbowe* (1250), *Shopys* (t. Ed 4), *boscus voc. Pillowe* (1330), half acre called *Stonimoder* (1243), *Longesmale* (13th), i.e. long-narrow, *Westbithebroc* (c. 1275), *Underwood called Quykfalle* (1426). It is perhaps significant that in Brixworth, so full of ancient remains, we have *Sunkenechyrche* (t. Hy 3) and *Dedmansbyryellys* (14th). *Scitereshovene* (1260) in Whitfield is probably a 'shooter's *oven* or shelter' in this old woodland area. *Morezeue Halle* (1364) is another example of OE *morgen-giefu*, 'morning-gift' from bridegroom to bride (cf. Morgay Fm, PN Sx 519). *Boverie* (1293 BM) in Culworth is a French name, the counterpart of Vetchery (PN Sx 350) and Vachery (Sr). *le Mogwrosene* (1287), *Mugrozen* (1571) in Cosgrove clearly contains the OE *wrāsn*, 'nodus,' discussed in PN Wo 290 *s.n.* Wrens Nest. We have also *le Stenyng* (1306), *Stenyng* (1334) in Furtho. Scandinavian influence is very unlikely here, and we must have another example of the lost OE *stǣning*, 'stony place,' discussed under Steyning (PN Sx 234–6).

There are also numerous modern field-names of the nickname type: Hunger Hill and Hungry Hill *passim* (*Hungerhil* is frequent in ME documents), of which it is often recorded that 'no grass will grow here,' 'the field needs much manure,' and the like, Barren Meadow, Starveall, Starve Devil, Little Gains, Hungerland, Pinch Penny. More complimentary are Fill Barns, Throwswell (noted as very productive). Widows Mite may actually be an old endowment. See also Bellropes *infra* 281. The Parlour is fairly common, but its significance is obscure.

Curiously common are the references to the finding of dead men, and the like—some eight examples of Deadman Furlong, Close, etc., have been noted, as also a *Dedechurl* (13th), and a *Dedquenesike* (13th) containing ME *quene*, 'woman.' *Flithills* is fairly common, and we have also a *Flitwells*, and one or two examples of *Flitnell(s)*. All these are near the parish boundary, and are clearly 'hills (or wells) of dispute' (from OE *(ge)flit*, 'dispute,' or OE *(ge)fliten*, 'disputed '). See also Fleet and Flitnell *supra* 84, 85.

(*d*) *Field-names of which the history can be traced, arranged under hundreds and parishes.*

I. Fawsley Hundred

ASHBY ST LEDGERS. Ballards (*Ballands* 1764 *EnclA*, *v. supra* 266). Chalkpits (*Chalcputtes* 1322 AD iv). Deadmore (*Dedemore* 1366 AD iv). Lambcuts (*Lambecotes* n.d. AD iv). Stadfield (*Statfold* 1690 *ChDecRoll*, 'cattle-enclosure,' *v.* stotfold. Stockwell and Stockle Ground (*Stocwelle* 1326 AD iii). Woolspit is probably 'wolf's pit' or 'snare.'

BADBY. Eaning Close (1820 *Terrier*) is 'lambing close' from vb. *ean*, 'to lamb,' elsewhere found in the form *Yeaning* Close. Squitch is a variant of *quitch* or *couch*-grass.

BARBY. Long Slang is a long narrow field, cf. *supra* 273.

BRAUNSTON. Fish Weir (*Fiswere* 1305 Ipm), cf. *le Fishwere* in Brackley (1494 *Magd*). Oxey (*Oxehay* 1255 FF), 'ox-enclosure,' *v.* (ge)hæg. Mardale is on the parish boundary and is from OE (ge)mære.

CATESBY. Biggin (*Niwebigginge* 1307 AD i, *Biggin Spring* 1791 Bridges), *v.* bigging. Bodcome (*Botcombe* 1471 AD i), *v.* cumb. Bunch Croft (*Boriches croft* n.d. AD i, *Bunchecrofte* 17th cent. map), possibly 'Beorhtric's croft.' Church Hill (*Kirkehill* 1272 Dugd). Windmill Hill (probably *Milnhill* ib.).

CHARWELTON. Gosterlow is probably for *Gorstylow*, 'gorse-covered hill.' Harrods is *Harwoods* (1820 *Terrier*).

DAVENTRY. Inlands (*Inlond* 1383 *MinAcct*). In the Enclosure Award of 1804 we also have Long Low (cf. *le Low* 1357 XtCh), Old Gore (*Oldegore* 1314 XtCh, *Haldegore* 1383 *MinAcct*), Oxhay (*Oxehay* 1255 FF), Pit Furlong (*Putforlong* c. 1300 XtCh), Sowbrooke (*Suthbroc* 1255 FF), Water Furrows (*Waterforowys* 14th *Daventry*).

EVERDON. Clay Furlong (*Claifurlong* 1240 FF). Flaxlands (*Flexlond* 1240 FF), pronounced locally *Flexlonds*. Grass Hill (*le*

18-2

Croshil 1490 *Knightley*), pronounced locally *Crass* or *Cross* Hill. Hangings (*Hangkinde lond* t. Hy 3 *Knightley*). Oak Hill (*Othul* 1240 *FF*), i.e. oat-hill. Woolrush (*Ulfriches* 1316 *Knightley*) from the pers. name *Wulfric*.

HELLIDON. Cislips (*Syslapes* 1402 AD v, *Syslips* 1892 *Map*), is probably from *sideslapes*, 'broad slippery places,' *v.* sid, slæpe. Sharpland (*Scharplond* ib.).

KILSBY. Margate is on the boundary and contains OE (ge)mære, 'boundary.'

LITCHBOROUGH. Starch or Stirch is a corruption of *Sterts*, 'tails of land,' *v.* steort and cf. *infra* 279. For The Purlieu (pronounced *Purley*), *v.* Oakley Purlieus *supra* 170.

NEWNHAM. Hard Meadows (1764 *EnclA*) is *Hardemede* c. 1275 Bodl.

PRESTON CAPES. Fivewells (*Fiwelles* 1377 *Knightley*), cf. *Fivewell Pool* (1759 *EnclA*) in Woodford Halse. Oat Hill (*Othul* 1240 *FF*). Phipps Barn Ground (cf. *Phelypes lane* 1433 *Knightley*). Sharbra (*Shardeborow* 1433 *Knightley*), from OE *scearda beorg*, i.e. broken-hill, cf. *supra* 269. In a terrier of 1820 we have Hollow Combs (*Holoucoumbes* 1377 *Knightley*), and Wheywell (*Weywelle* ib.).

STAVERTON. Blackamore (*Blakemore* t. Ric 2 *Rental*), Cawdle's (*Caldewellehul* 1320 XtCh). Combe's Hill (*Cumbes* t. Ric 2 *Rental*), really a plural of cumb. Hangings (*Hangende furlong* ib.). Henford Hill (*Hegenfordehul* n.d. AD iii). Mereach is a boundary field, *v.* (ge)mære. Narbrook (*Northbrok* t. Ric 2 *Rental*). Showell (*le Schouele* 1320 XtCh). Goodmans Burdge shows dialectal *burge* for *bridge* (*v.* Introd. xxxii).

WELTON. Clay Furlong (*Cleyfurlong* 1390 AD iv). Coleman Lake (*Colemanneslake* 1336 *Spencer*), *v.* lacu, 'small stream.' Cobbed Wells (*Coppedewell* 1336 *Spencer*), the spring perhaps having some *copped* or peaked covering. Crocker Hill (*Crokke Hoo* 1390 AD iv), perhaps the hoh or hill where pots were made or found. Dead Shells (*Dedechurl* 13th AD ii), clearly a field where a churl once lay dead. Debdale (*Depedale* 1365 AD iv). Laycroft (*Leycroft* 13th AD iv). Mill Holme (*le Milleholme* 1422 AD v), i.e. 'mill meadow.' Radmoor Close (*Rodemor* 1365 AD iv, *Redmore* 1755 *EnclA*), probably 'reed swamp,' *v.* hreod, mor. Thornhill (*Thirnehil* 1303 AD iv). Wherrysill Way (*le Weytwysel* 1304 AD iv, *Wedesall Way* 1755 *EnclA*), 'road-fork,' *v.* weg, twisla. Bridges (i, 96) mentions Smith-meadow (*Smethemede* 1409 AD iv), 'smooth-meadow.'

II. Chipping Warden Hundred

BODDINGTON. Buckle (*Buckwell* 1759 *EnclA*).

EYDON. Barchimore (*Barlihwellemor* 13th AD i), 'barley-spring marsh.' Bretch (*la Brech* c. 1200 Wardon), *v. supra* 260. Ful-brook (*Fulbrok* 1281 AD ii). March and The Mere are on the parish boundary. In the Enclosure Award of 1762 we have East and West Fields (*campo del West, Est* c. 1200 Wardon), Bearmon Furlong (*Bealmunt* c. 1200 Wardon, *Belemound* 1313 *Knightley*, 'fine hill'), Blackpool (*Blakepolehul* c. 1200 Wardon), Oathill (*Otehil* ib.), Ruwell (*Riewelle* ib.), Stanchill (*Stanithulles* AD i, 'stony hills'), from *stæniht*, 'stony' and *hyll*, Whethill (*Whitehull* c. 1200 Wardon).

GREATWORTH. Naddocks (*Nattokes* 1271 *FF*, *Nattocks* 1845 *TA*), cf. *Schort Nattokkis* (t. Hy 7 *Isham*) in Lamport, *Nattoc* (1207 *FF*) in Cowley (O), *tenem. atte Nattoke* (c. 1350 *Rental*) in Tolworth (Sr) and *le Naccok* (sic) in Walton on Thames (Sr), (1342 AD iii). Stutch Close is from OE *stycce*, 'piece.'

SULGRAVE. Briar Hill (*Brerehull* c. 1200 *Ashby*). Lambey (*Lambyshill* 13th *NthStA*). Acremase Hill must be for *Acremans Hill*. Winett Hill must be for *wind-yat* hill, where the wind passes through a *geat* or gap.

WOODFORD HALSE. Strangland (*Strangelond* c. 1200 *Ashby*). Berrel is probably *bere-hill*, 'barley-hill,' while Tuttle, on a hill rising to 589 ft., must be *toot-hill*, 'look-out hill.'

III. Green's Norton Hundred

CANONS ASHBY. Grass Close, Preston Field, Water Mill Field, Yew Close are *le Grasse Close, le Prestonfeld, Watermyll feld, le Owe Close* (1537 LP).

BLAKESLEY. Lambcuts is for *Lambcotes*.

BRADDEN. Long Spong (early 19th cent. map) is a long narrow field, and contains the dialectal *spong* (recorded from Nth and Lei), used of a narrow piece of land. It is recorded as a field-name in *Spongfurlong* in Holcot (13th *NthStA*), and *le Spong* in Floore in 1345 (*Finch-Hatton*). This carries the word back some 300 years earlier than the first recorded use of *spang* or *spong* in the NED.

MAIDFORD. Cat's Brain (*Kattesbreyn* c. 1200 *Ashby*) is a very common field-name, the term being used in dialect to describe a soil consisting of rough clay mixed with stones (*v.* PN Bk 127,

PN D Vol. i, p. l). Beryl (*Beril* 1779 *EnclA*) is doubtless *bere-hill*, i.e. 'barley-hill.' Featherbed is moist and spongy ground.

MORETON PINKNEY. In a terrier of 1602 we have Bagmilles (*Baggemulne* 1344 *Rental*), doubtless so called from some peculiarity of shape, The Broode (*le Brode* c. 1200 *Ashby*), Deepe Sladd (*Depslade* ib.). Michelholme (*Mucheleholme* ib.), 'great water meadow,' Swaynes Meadow (cf. *Swenesbrigg* 1281 AD ii). Waterfall Way (cf. *Waterfalmede* 1343 *MinAcct*).

GREEN'S NORTON. Modley Gate, *v. supra* 38.

WEEDON LOIS. Bannel (*Banwell* 1593 *Map*). Beeliege (*Berledge* ib.) is probably for *bere-linch*, 'barley-hill,' cf. *s.v.* hlinc in PN D 665. Bretch (*Breache* ib.), *v. breche supra* 260. Coppice Moor (*Copped More* ib.), *v. mor supra* 267. Face Lane (*Fayer Slade* ib.). Fernel (*Fernehill* ib.). Fowlerdy (*Fowle Riddinge* ib.), i.e. 'dirty clearing,' *v.* hryding. Fox-hill (*Foxon Hill* ib.). Gatridge (*Ga(r)tridge* ib.), probably 'goats' ridge.' Gullimere (*Gunney Meade* ib.). Latables (*Lotable* ib.), i.e. 'land in which the shares are assigned by lot.' Rowler (*Rowlow* ib.), 'rough hill.' Smithnell (*Smithenhill* ib.), 'smooth hill,' from the dative case form. Stanthills (*Stantehilles* ib.), 'stony hills,' from OE *stæniht*; there is an old quarry here. Whitmoor (*Whitemale* ib., *Whitmell* 1875 *Valuation*), perhaps containing the word *male* discussed under Wythemail *supra* 129. Wofurlong (*Waefurlong* ib.), 'crooked furlong,' *v.* woh.

IV. King's Sutton Hundred

AYNHO. In 1792 (*EnclA*) we have Sands Furlong (*le Sonde* 1318 *Magd*), Wolland Field (*le Wouelond* ib.), i.e. 'crooked land,' *v.* woh. Bugler (*Buglow* 1792 *EnclA*).

BRACKLEY. Worledge or Whirledge Lane (*Hwerveldic* c. 1185 *Magd, Werveldiche* c. 1195 ib.), 'curving dyke,' *v.* hwyrfel, dic. In 1839 (*EnclA*) we have Bandlands (*Benlond* 1259 *Magd, le Banlonde* 1262 ib.), 'bean land,' Lincroft (*Lyncroft* 1408 ib.), 'flax croft,' Lynch (*le Linche* c. 1265 *Magd*), *v.* hlinc.

CROUGHTON. Blinell (*le Blyndewelle* c. 1270 *Magd*), 'hidden spring.' The neighbouring Blind Hill is probably a corrupt expansion of *Blindell* from *Blindwell*. Bretch (*le Breche* ib.), *v.* breche *supra* 260. In 1808 (*EnclA*) we have Grinthills Common, possibly containing *Grundhole* c. 1255 *Magd*, The Heath Hethmers c. 1305 ib.), Hollow Moors (*Hollemor* c. 1270 ib.), Horsemoor (*Horsemor* c. 1255 ib.), Whitmoor (*Witemor* c. 1305 ib.).

EVENLEY. Horsley Hill (*Horselawe* c. 1220 *Magd*), 'horse hill.'
Lady Bridge (*Lauedi Bruge* c. 1300 *Magd*) is the bridge over the
small stream under the Brackley-Oxford road. Scotland (*Scotte
furlong* c. 1210 *Magd*), is probably land subject to some *scot* or
payment, cf. Scotland *supra* 117. Firmity was perhaps so called
because it produced the wheat from which 'firmity' was made.
Cf. Furmenty Slade in Brafield (1824 *EnclA*).

HELMDON. Dairy Ground may perhaps be associated with *le
Deyfurlong* c. 1420 *Ct*, from ME *deye*, 'dairy-maid.' Long
Hartwell (*Hertwellelongge* 1381 *Magd*). Marrowell (*Marewelle-
hull* 1317 ib.), perhaps 'mare spring.' Redlands (*le Redelond* ib.).
Stockford (cf. *Stokebroke* 1459 ib., i.e. Weston Brook).

SYRESHAM. The Squitch Field (*v. supra* 275). Bakers Burge
Bridge is said to be named from a word *burge* meaning 'brook,'
but doubtless *burge* is the south midland form of *bridge*, discussed in Introd. xxxii, and the name is really that of the bridge
across the brook. So similarly there is a brook called Burge in
Helmdon, doubtless for the same reason.

WAPPENHAM. Red and White Starch, cf. *Stertes* (c. 1200 *Ashby*)
and Colsters *supra* 206. For Dole Meadow (1762 *EnclA*), cf.
Smaledole c. 1200 *Ashby*.

V. Guilsborough Hundred

LONG BUCKBY. Breakneys (*Brakenhoo* 1446 *Ct*), 'bracken hill,'
v. hoh.

COTON. Big and Little Brant (*Brant* 1764 *EnclA*) are on a sharp
hill and contain the adj. *brant*, 'steep.'

COTTESBROOKE. Rutherhook is probably 'cattle-hook (of land),'
v. hryðer. For Flithills, which is on the parish boundary, cf.
Fleet Fm and Flitnell *supra* 84, 85.

WEST HADDON. Roddle (*Redewellehul* c. 1260 *Pipewell*, *Roddall*
1805 *Valuation*), 'reed-well,' *v.* hreod, wielle. Debdale and Rye
Hill from the *EnclA* (1765) are *Depedale* and *Ryehul* (c. 1200
Pipewell). Marker's Wong and Catchill from the Valuation
List (1805) are *Markeres Wong* (c. 1260 *Pipewell*), *v.* vangr, and
Catteswellehul (ib.). Coppiemore (*Coppet Moor* 1805 *Valuation*),
v. mor *supra* 267.

HOLLOWELL. Twitch Common probably contains dialectal
twitch, 'couch-grass.'

WINWICK. Flimborough (*Flinteboru* t. Hy 3, *Flyntborugh* 1433 *Spencer*), 'flint-hill,' *v.* beorg.

YELVERTOFT. Bancroft (*Bancroft* 1416 AD iii), 'bean croft.' Broadslade (*Brodeslade* 1321 AD iii). Corlung (*Col(l)ewong* 1416 and n.d. AD iii, *Colwong* 1448 AD iv), possibly 'meadow by a stream called *Cole*,' cf. Ekwall RN 85. Flitland (*Flyhtlond* 1390 AD iv). Handler (*Anlowe* 13th AD iv, 1416 AD i, *Anlowpyt* 1406 AD iii), probably 'one hill,' for there is an isolated hill here, *v.* hlaw. Hangings (*le Hangyng* 1406 AD iii). Hollow Mere (*Holowmere* 1416 AD iii) is on the boundary. Long Land (*Langelond* 1353 AD iii). Long Mollow (*le Longemalewe* 13th AD iv), cf. Wythemail *supra* 129, and Long Mallows, a field-name in Clipston. Thistle Dyke (*Thurkeles dik* 1318 AD iv), i.e. '*Thurketill*'s dyke.'

VI. Nobottle Grove Hundred

CHURCH and CHAPEL BRAMPTON. Cringleholme or Cringolone (*Cringleholme* 1584 *Map*) lies by a curving stream, and is a compound of ON kringla and holmr, hence 'circular meadow.' Cf. Kringlum in Denmark (*Sønderjyske Stednavne* 336).

BRINGTON. Banlands (cf. *Hungry Banlond* 1422 *Spencer*), 'bean-land.' Bannel (*Banewelle* 1326 *Spencer*); there is a spring here. It is difficult to say whether the first element is *bān*, 'bone,' or *bana*, 'slayer.' Barch Hill (*Barlichul* 1346 ib.), 'barley hill.' Hook Hill, cf. *Hokemor* t. Ed 1 *Ct*; both must take their name from the projecting hill here. Mill Hill (*Milnehill* 1424 AD i). Stagdell (*Stakedale* 1297 *Spencer*, *Stagdale* 1587 ib.), probably 'valley marked by a *stake* or pole.' Harrow Hill is on high ground by Nobottle, and it is tempting to think that this is from OE *hearg*, 'sacred grove,' and that near here (with many tracks leading to it) was the site of the hundred meeting-place.

BROCKHALL. We have mention in a 16th cent. terrier of *Schouyll way*, cf. *le Schovele* t. Hy 3 *Spencer* and *Barne yerde* (*Berneyert* c. 1230 ib.).

BUGBROOKE. Holme (*Holm* 1294 Ipm), 'water-meadow.' Lockcroft (*Lokcroft* ib.), i.e. 'enclosed croft.' West Meadow (*Westmede* ib.). Switchley Gutter is *Squittley Gutter* (1781 *EnclA*), the first element being the dialectal *squitch*, *v.* Squitch *supra* 275.

DALLINGTON. Starch Hill in a map of 1763 is probably for *starts*, ME *stertes*, 'tails of land,' cf. *supra* 276, 279.

DUSTON. In the Enclosure Award of 1777 we have Bulley

Closes (*Bulehou* 13th *NthStf*), Langdole Field (*le Langdole* ib.), Street Furlong (*Stratfurlong* ib.).

EAST HADDON. Mere Sitch is 'boundary water-course,' *v.* (ge)mære, sic.

HARLESTONE[1]. Ash (*Assfurlong* c. 1320 H de B). Archwell (*Herteswelle* ib.), 'hart's spring.' Bellropes (*Belleropes* ib.) was so called because it provided the endowment for the church bell-ropes; cf. similar field-names in Clipston, Cranford, Gayton and Grafton Underwood. Brackle (*Bracwelle* ib.), cf. Brackley *supra* 49. Brington Way (*Brinton Weye* ib.). Buckham (*Bokham* ib.), 'beech-enclosure,' *v.* boc, hamm. Copy More (*Coppedemor* ib.), *v.* mor *supra* 267. Deepdale (*Depedale* ib.). Foxendale (*Foxendale* ib.). Fulwell (*Folewell* ib.). Gorse Close (*Cors* ib., *Coss Close* 1826), would seem to be from the British equivalent of Welsh *cors*, 'marsh,' cf. PN Wo 197–8, PN Sx 371, PN D 285). Greendale (*Grindale* ib.). Mill Holm (*le Holm* ib.). Horse-moor (*Austemor* ib., *Oustmor* t. Ed 3 *Ct.*), a hybrid compound of austr, 'east,' and mor. Linghall (*Linghou* c. 1320 H de B, *Lynghough* t. Ed 3 *Ct.*), a compound of lyng and hoh, 'hill,' though haugr is also possible. Mere (*Mere at Holes* c. 1320 H de B). Normead (*Normede* ib.). Redland (*Redeland* ib.). Saltwell (*Saltewelle* ib.). Sharrow (*Scharhou* ib.) lies on the bounds of the east and west common fields, and is a compound of OE *scearu*, 'division,' and hoh, 'hill.' Cf. Sharrow near Ripon (Y) on the boundary of the West and North Ridings and Sharrow in Sheffield (Y), near the Derbyshire county boundary. Thornton-dale (*Thorpendale* ib.). Toothill (*Tofthul* ib.), 'hill marked by a topt.' Westmead (*Westmede* ib.). Wheathill (*Whetehul* ib.). Windmill Hill (*ad molendinum ventriticum* ib.). The Wong (1740 *Tithe Accounts*) is *le Wong* (c. 1320 H de B). Dives Heath (1932) preserves the name of the *Dyve* family who had lands here (H de B *passim* and cf. Wicken *supra* 107).

HARPOLE. Row Dykes (probably *Rowedik* c. 1320 H de B), 'rough dic.' Callowell is a field with a rounded hill in it, and is probably *callow* or 'bare' hill (cf. *Calouhul* c. 1320 H de B, in Harlestone). Wung (*The Wong* 1778 *EnclA*). Of Hunger Hill it is reported that it is 'very hungry and needs much manure.'

HEYFORD. The Spung (*v.* Spong *supra* 277). Worston Ford (1758 Sale Catalogue) is by *Horston Brook* on the Bugbrooke

---

[1] This very full list is made possible by the survival of the Estate Book of Henry de Bray, and the labours of Miss E. W. Hughes upon this and other early documents. The map compiled by the school children has also been very useful.

boundary, and is from OE har and stan, 'grey' or 'boundary' stone. Thurspit is 'giant pit' from OE *þyrs*, 'giant.' Cf. pytt *supra* 268.

KISLINGBURY. Elder Stump (*Elderstobbe* 14th *NthStA*). Lakes (*le Lakes* ib.), *v.* lacu, 'stream.'

VII. Towcester Hundred

ABTHORPE. Rowborough (*Rouburgh* 1367 *For*, 'rough hill'), *v.* ruh, beorg.

TIFFIELD. The Bollands (*Banlond* 1232 *FF*).

TOWCESTER. Dockwell or Dockhill Mill (cf. *Dockewellhay*, 'dock-spring,' *Dockwell Mill* 1713 *Terrier*). Hayward's Balks (cf. *Haywardesthorn* 1437 *Easton Neston*). Old Gore (*Eldegore* 1419 ib.). Red Hill (*Reddehell* 1227 *FF*). Wormpath (*Wormpath* 1437 *Easton Neston*).

VIII. Cleyley Hundred

ASHTON. Barhill (*Berehul* 14th *NthStJ*), 'barley-hill.'

COSGROVE. Barley Hill (*Barlichull* 1364 *Furtho*). Sandylands (*Sandilond* ib.). In the Enclosure Award of 1767 we have Bidwell Meadow (*Bydewell* 1283 *Furtho*), cf. Bidwell *supra* 222, Cresses Furlong (*Cresies f.* 1368 ib.), Hillmoor (*Hullemore* 1306 ib.).

EASTON NESTON. Deep Slade (*Depeslade* c. 1220 AD iii). Dust Hill (*Dusthul* 13th AD ii). Fridays Close (cf. *Fridayisstoking* Easton Neston, *v.* stocking). Hanging Hill (*Hangynde Lond* 1371 AD ii).

HARTWELL. The Assarts (*Sart* t. Eliz *AOMB*), OFr *assart*, 'clearing.' Nuttidge (*Nuttedge* t. Eliz *AOMB*). Stocking (*Stockyng* 14th *NthStJ*), *v.* stocking.

PASSENHAM. Ham Meadow (*le Hamme* 1327 Ipm). The Hayes (*le Hammes Hay* ib.), *v.* hamm, (ge)hæg.

PAULERSPURY. Tootle (*Tote Hill* 1650 *ParlSurv*), 'look-out hill.'

SHUTLANGER. The Thrif is a form of *frith*, 'woodland,' *v.* fyrhðe.

IX. Rothwell Hundred

ARTHINGWORTH. Wellboro' (*Welleberwe* 1203 *FF*), 'spring-hill.'

BRAYBROOKE. Flithill (*Flithul* c. 1250 *PipewellA*), 'dispute-hill,' *v. supra* 275; it lies on the parish boundary. Hassocks (*Hassokes*

c. 1250 ib.), *v.* hassuc *supra* 264. Rowham (*Ruholm* ib.), probably 'rough marsh.'

CLIPSTON. Bell Ropes (cf. *supra* 281). Britchell is for Bretch Hill (*v.* breche *supra* 260). Flitwell is on the parish boundary and probably denotes 'spring of dispute' (cf. *supra* 275). Lewshill is by a barn and probably contains OE hlose, 'pig-stye.' Long Mallows (*v. supra* 129, 280).

DESBOROUGH. West Apple Tree (*Westapeltre* 1207 *FF*). Breeches (*Brechewong* 1207 *FF*), *v.* breche *supra* 260 and vangr. Copeland is ON kaupa-land, 'purchased land,' *v.* EPN. Garbutts (*Gorebrodefurlong* 1207 *FF*, *Garbroad* 17th *Map*), 'gore-broad,' *v.* gara. Hesland (*Heselund* c. 1250 *PipewellA*), 'hazel grove,' *v.* hesli, lundr. Mickstead (*Mixenested* 1207 *FF*), 'dung-heap place,' *v.* mixen. Fell Barns (*Filbarns* 17th *Map*). On a 17th cent. map of Desborough (kindly copied by Mr J. E. Plane) we have Ravenlands (*Raveneslund* c. 1250 *PipewellA*), 'raven's grove,' *v.* lundr, Small Glass Furlong (*Smalgras juxta Deseburgh* c. 1320 *For*), Whorestone Furlong (*Horestan* 1227 *FF*) on the boundary, *v.* har, stan, Young Wood (*Jungwode* 1246 Cl). Rowfex Furlong probably contains OE *feax*, 'hair,' 'coarse grass,' hence 'rough grass,' cf. Flexborough Hundred PN Sx 362, and *Fexlond* in Brockhall (16th *Spencer*).

EAST FARNDON. The hill which gives name to fields variously called *Cogboro* and *Cobra* is probably the *Calkeberwe* of 1285 (*Ass*), i.e. 'chalk-hill,' from OScand *kalk* and berg.

HASELBECH. Ballands (*Banlond* t. Ed 1 *Isham*). Five Acres (*Fiueacris* 1324 ib.). Haybrinks (*Heybrinctot* 13th cent. ib.), *v.* brinke, topt. Meadles (*Medhille* ib.).

KELMARSH. Black Hill (*Blakenhull* 14th *NthStJ*, oblique case form). Cobdell (*Coppithul* ib.), 'peaked hill,' *v.* coppede.

ROTHWELL. Littlewood (*Littlewode* 1307 Ipm). There was also a *Miclewode* (1251 Selden 13).

X. Orlingbury Hundred

BRIXWORTH. Grandborough (*Greneberwe* t. Hy 3 AD iii), 'green hill,' cf. Grandborough PN Bk 134. In the Enclosure Award (1780) we have Demsell (*Demeswell* t. Hy 3 AD iii, *Demmeswelle* n.d. ib., *Demmyswelle* 14th *NthStA*), Kingsmill (*Kingesmill* t. Hy 3 AD iii), North Dale (*le Northdale* 1315 Ipm), Waddon Field (*Whaddone* n.d. AD iii), 'wheat hill,' cf. Whaddon PN Bk 74. On a map (1688) we have also Great Breach (*le Breche* 14th *NthStA*), *v.* breche *supra* 260.

CRANSLEY. Ivy Close (*Highway Close* 17th *Map*). Wounds (*The Wonges* 17th *Map*), v. vangr.

HANNINGTON. Trinder is probably 'circular hill,' for *Trindhow*, from OE trynde and hoh.

HARROWDEN. Armitage (*The Hermitage* 1782 *EnclA*).

HANGING HOUGHTON and LAMPORT. Beanhills (*Banehill* 1503 *Isham*). Berrydale (*Berydale* ib.), by Blueberry *supra* 127. Callow Meadow (*Cal(l)omeade* 1465 ib.), 'bare mead' (*v.* calu). Cawkutts (*Calkottis* 1503 ib.), 'cold cottages.' Crabtree (*crabtre pece* 1465 ib.). Langham (*Longham* ib.). Great Hill Pricks (*le Prickes* ib.). Westhill (*Westhill ley* ib.). Windhouse (*Wyndsarse* 1503 ib., *Windesarse* 1635 ib.), i.e. wind's arse. We may note also Hobeck furlong (1635 *Isham*), cf. *Holebeke diche* 1216–72 AD ii.

OLD. Empole (*Enedepol* 13th *Knightley*), 'duck-pool,' from OE ened, 'duck,' cf. Andwell (Ha), *Anedewell* 1248 *Ass* and *Anedemersce* 1219 *FF* (Ha). Mich Field corresponds to land which is said to be *subtus Mic* (13th *Knightley*). There is a Mick Close on the other side of the boundary-stream, in Walgrave, but the meaning of *mic* is obscure.

PYTCHLEY. Sow Moor (*South Moor* 1728 *Deed*).

WALGRAVE. Mareleys is on the parish *meare* or boundary.

XI. Spelhoe Hundred

BOUGHTON. Adam Field (*Adhem* c. 1250 AD iii). Burrows (*Berugh* c. 1242 AD ii), v. beorg. Dam Furlong (*Damfurlong* 1394 AD i), by the dam of Boughton Mill, Greenway (*Grenewei* t. Hy 3 AD ii), Osier Beds (cf. *Osierwelle* 1397 *Spencer*).

KINGSTHORPE. Pitchwell is *Pishwell* (1766 *EnclA*) and is perhaps identical with *Pywell* (t. Ric 2 Kingsthorpiana). Swarbruck is *Swarlbrigge* (t. Hy 7 ib.), 'bridge by a *swirl* or eddy.' Semilong (*Southmyllewong* t. Hy 4 ib.), v. vangr; it is by the South or St Andrews Mill. Sowrelands (*Sourland* t. Ric 2 ib.). Wallbacke, Walbeck (*Walbek*, 1301 Ipm, *Walbecke* 14th *NthStA*), apparently 'wall-stream'; this flowed down Kingsthorpe Hollow, but it is far from the wall of Old Northampton and the reason for the name is unknown, v. bekkr. In the Enclosure Award (1766) we have Manhill Field, going back to *Maniwellefeld* 1368, *Mannellfeld* c. 1500 Kingsthorpiana.

MOULTON. Muzzle (*Mosewelle* 14th *NthStA*), 'moss-spring.'

OVERSTONE. Worley (*Wherledyks* 13th *NthStA*, *Wharledyk* 14th ib.), 'circular' or 'winding' dic, cf. Worledge *supra* 278.

PITSFORD. Bridge Hill (*Burge Hill* 18th *Map*), locally *Birds* shows dialectal *burge* for *bridge*, cf. Introd. xxxii.

SPRATTON. Landamore is a boundary field (OE *land-(ge)mǣre*, 'boundary'). Standells (OE *stān-(ge)delf*, 'stone-digging'), is by an old quarry. Wodells is *Wadhill* (1717 *Constable's Accounts*), 'woad-hill,' *v.* wad.

WESTON FAVELL. Clackmill Close (now Abington Close) in a map of 1840 shows the same mill-name as 'mill called *Clakke*' in Steane (1357 Ipm). Doubtless it was so called from the sound of its working. Wad Cabins were fields in which *woad* was grown in the 18th century. Cf. *supra* 273.

XII. Hamfordshoe Hundred

MEARS ASHBY. Carswell or Corswell, cf. Costwell *supra* 95.

EARLS BARTON. Leasures (1740 *Terrier*) shows a common dialectal form of *leasowe(s)*, 'meadows.'

HOLCOT. Life (*le Lyth* 14th *NthStA*), 'the hill,' *v.* hlið.

SYWELL. Adland (*Headland* 1844 *TA*). Pond Close and Wood Close (*le Pondyard, le Wodeyard* 14th *NthStA*). Middle Well (*Micklewell* 1791 Bridges). Russels (*Rushdales* 1851 *Map*).

WELLINGBOROUGH. Bury More, The Butts Field and Long Marsh (*Berymore, Butt Close, Long mershe* c. 1650 *Finch-Hatton*).

XIII. Wymersley Hundred

CASTLE ASHBY. Cestness (*Cistern House* 1760 *Map*). Pighkels (*Pightle* 1760 *Map*). Sharrag Hill (*Shearhog Hill* 1840 *Map*), *shearhog* being the name for a lamb after the first shearing. Stumpit (*Stonepit* 1760 *Map*).

BRAFIELD. Botlow (*Buttelowehyll* 13th *NthStA*). Crole or Crowhill (*Crowelleslade* 13th *NthStA*).

HARDINGSTONE. Ransel (*Ramsdale* 1879 *Map*). Wot Ground (*Woad Ground* 1752 *Map*, *Wood Ground* 1879 *Map*). Nun Meadow in the Enclosure Award (1768) is *Nonnemede* (1543 LP).

HOUGHTON. Hopwell (*Hopwellemore* 13th *NthStA*), probably descriptive of the spring in the small hop or valley, just to the east of the field.

MILTON. Wood Furlong (1780 *EnclA*) goes back to *Wudefurlong* 12th NRS iv. Humgrum is *Hungerham* (1780 *EnclA*).

QUINTON. The Holt (*Holte* 1317 Ipm).

YARDLEY HASTINGS. Twitchfield (*v.* Twitch Common *supra* 279).

XIV. Corby Hundred

BRIGSTOCK. Band Land (*Banlond* 1480 *Ct*), 'bean land.' Brock Hill (*Brokehill* ib.), probably 'brook hill.' Car Meadow (*le Carre* ib.), 'marsh,' *v.* kiarr. Cockborow (*Cockesbarowe* 1469 *Ct*), 'cock's hill,' *v.* beorg. Cockerhead (*Cok(e)rode* 1469, 1480 *Ct*, *Cockrood* 1805 *EnclA*), 'cock clearing,' *v.* rod. Hungry Hill (*Hungerhill* 1469 *Ct*). Priest Croft (probably *Prattescroft* t. Ed 1 *PeterbB*). Ringwold (*Ringwelle* 1299 *Ct*). Tongue (*Tonge* 1307 Pat). Wallow Lane (*Wallowe, le Walowe* 1399 *Ct*). White Dykes (*Witedich* 1223 *FF*, *Whytedykes* 1469 *Ct*).

COTTINGHAM. Millfield (*Wyndmilnwong* c. 1400 *Rental*), 'windmill-field,' *v.* vangr. Steppings (*le Newestibbynge* c. 1400 *PipewellA*), cf. stybbing *supra* 270.

DEENE and DEENETHORPE. Bufton (*Bovetown Feild* t. Eliz *Terrier*), 'above the village.' There was also a *Neathetown* ib. Grimble White (*Grymbiltweite* 1415 *Brudenell*), '*Grimbold*'s clearing,' *v.* þveit.

DINGLEY. Hassocks (*Hassokes* 1199 FF), *v. supra* 264.

GEDDINGTON. Rising Wood (*boscum q.v. le Rys* 1229 Cl), 'brushwood wood,' *v.* hris.

GRETTON. Standles is probably for *Standelves* from OE *stān-(ge)delf*, 'stone quarry,' for there is an old quarry close at hand. Thrawley (*Thrawle* 1569 AD v).

HARRINGWORTH. Pottingate (*Pottergate* 1773 *EnclA*), 'potters' road,' *v.* gata. Scogate (*Scogate* 1773 *EnclA*) is probably purely Scandinavian, from ON skogr, gata, 'woodland road.' Thrift Close (*Fryth Close* 1619 *Map*) shows a common development of fyrhðe, 'woodland.' Pear Tree Furlong (1773 *EnclA*) is *Peretre near wood of Laxton* (1227 Ch).

MIDDLETON. Middleton Thick (*Myddelton thicke* 1446 Pat).

ROCKINGHAM. On an estate map of 1809 we have Mill furlong (*Milnefurlong* 1203 *FF*) and Pease Leys (*Peseleie* ib.).

WILBARSTON. The Plain (cf. *Wilberstonpleyne* t. Stephen *PipewellA*). Young Wood (1801 *EnclA*) is *Youngwode* c. 1250 *PipewellA*.

XV. Huxloe Hundred

ADDINGTON, GT. The Brooks (cf. *Brocforlange* 1232 WellsR). Ridgeway (*Rigeway* ib.) is an old track running east and west here, across high ground. Slench (*Sleng* ib.) may be the common word *sling*, from some fancied resemblance of the field to a sling.

ADDINGTON, LITTLE. Knolls (*Nolles* 1232 WellsR).

ALDWINKLE. Hubbick (*Hubwick* 1773 *EnclA*). Swilling Holme (*Swyllingholne* (sic) 1513 LP), a low-lying meadow by the Nene.

BARTON SEAGRAVE. Cut Bush (*Cuttbush* 1624 *Clayton*). Dustholme (ib.). Town Field (*Tounefeild* ib.).

DENFORD. The Great Old (*le Wolde* 1325 Ipm). v. **weald.**

FINEDON. Calwell (1808 *EnclA*) is *Caldewell* (1222 *FF*).

GRAFTON UNDERWOOD. Flaxlands (*Flaxeland* 1240 *FF*). Little Hill (*Lutlehull* ib.).

IRTHLINGBOROUGH. Backslade is *Blakeslade* c. 1340 *CartN*. Braitch (*le Breche* ib.), v. **breche** 260 *supra*. Holbush (*Holebusk* c. 1340 *CartN*), 'hollow bush,' v. **buskr.** In the *EnclA* (1813) we have Town Holme (*Tounholm* 1292 *Compotus*, *Towne Hulme* 1630 VCH iii, 208), Wake Meadow (*Wakemede* c. 1400 *Rental*).

ISLIP. Debdale (*Debbedale* 1223 *FF*), 'deep dale.' Copelder is probably for *coppedalder*, 'pollarded alder.'

KETTERING. Broomhill (*Bromhil* c. 1400 *Rental*). Harvest Stile (1587 *Map*) is *Hervestdale*, 'harvest-valley,' c. 1400 (*Rental*).

LOWICK. Allenge, a field-name on the Drayton estate map, lies at the southern extremity of the parish, which almost forms a detached part. It repeats itself in *Allege*, just over the Islip border, and *Alage* just over the Woodford border. This is clearly the word *alange*, *elenge*, 'remote, lonely.'

TWYWELL. Haver Hill (*Havirhul* c. 1250 *Thorney*), 'goat-hill,' v. **hæfer.**

XVI. Higham Ferrers Hundred

BOZEAT. Linghills, Linchills (*Linge Hill* 1799 *EnclA*) is a compound of *linch* and *hill*, v. **hlinc.** Fullwell, Sandwell and Smith Hill are recorded on the All Souls Estate Maps as *Fullewelle*, *Sandewelle* and *Smithill*, the latter for 'smooth hill.'

HARGRAVE. Rowley (*Rowlow* 1591 DuLaMiscBks), 'rough hill,' v. **ruh, hlaw.**

HIGHAM FERRERS. Anker's (*Handcross* 1839 *EnclA*). Mill Holme (*Mylneholme* 1291 Abbr). The Rows (*le Wro* 1313 HistHF, *le Nether-, le Midel-, Over-wro* 1401 *MinAcct, The Wroe* 1839 *EnclA*) are meadows by the Nene, from ON **vra**, 'corner.' Gunsex (1839 *EnclA*) is *Gunnesyke* (1313 HistHF), '*Gunni*'s watercourse,' *v.* **sik** and cf. Gunthorpe *supra* 236.

XVII. Willybrook Hundred

COTTERSTOCK. Stembre (*Stemborough* 1815 *EnclA*), probably 'stone hill,' *v.* **steinn, berg.**

DUDDINGTON. The Margrave is a boundary field, *v.* **(ge)mære.**

EASTON-ON-THE-HILL. Hall Brook Leys (*Hallebrook* 1350 Ipm), 'hall-brook.' The Lawns (*la Lunde* 1230 Ch), 'the wood,' *v.* **lundr.**

FOTHERINGHAY. Stanch Meadow is by a dam in the river. Cf. NED *s.v. stanch.*

GLAPTHORN. Casteepings (cf. *Shortstepinge* 1563 *Brudenell*), cf. **stybbing** *supra* 270. Lynch Hill (*Lynchehill* ib.). Stockwell Sink (*Stockewellesyke* ib.), *v.* **sic.** Thrift (*The Frith* 1815 *EnclA*), 'woodland,' *v.* **fyrhðe.**

NASSINGTON. Rysbeck or Ruth's Bridge Lane (*Rues Bridge* 1773 *EnclA*). Tramples (*Trampole Sale* 1665 *Recov, Trample Sale* 1726 ib.).

TANSOR. Botholme (1778 *EnclA*) is *Batholme* 1381 IpmR.

WOODNEWTON. Boarden Bridge Field has a wooden plank-bridge.

XVIII. Polebrook Hundred

ARMSTON. On a map dated 1716 we have Golden Slade (*Golwynesdale* c. 1280 *Buccleuch*), Inn Croft (*Incroft* c. 1250 ib.), i.e. home-croft, Water Seeks (*le Watersike* c. 1270 ib., *Water Sekes* 1504 ib.), 'water-course,' *v.* **sic.**

HEMINGTON. Langlands (*Langelond* c. 1248 *Buccleuch*).

OUNDLE. Ansdale (*Anisdene* 13th *PeterbB, Annysdale* c. 1400 *Rental*), with interchange of *dene* and *dale*. Blacklands (*Blakeland* 13th *PeterbB*). Blood Hill (*Blodhil(l)* 1250 *Swaffham*, c. 1400 *Rental, Blodehyl* t. Hy 8 *MinAcct*). Cleehill (*Klaihil* 13th *Peterb, Cleyhyll* t. Hy 8 *MinAcct*). Cobthorne (1565 Law). Dodmore (*Dadmore* t. Hy 8 *MinAcct*). Dowell Wong (1565 Law). Goarbroade (*Garebrode* 1261 *FF, Gorbroad* 1565 Law), 'gore-broad,' *v.* **gara.** How Hill (cf. *Howefeld* c. 1400 *Rental*), *v.* hoh. Lark Lane (*Lortlane* (?) c. 1400 *Rental, Lark Lane* 1565 Law). Marsh (*le Mersh* 1287 *Ass*). Mill Holme (*le Holm* 1298 *Woodford*). Mill Yard (*Myln Yerd* t. Hy 8 *MinAcct*). Overflitt (*le Over-, Netherflet* 1292 *Compotus, Fletsyke* c. 1300 *PeterbB*), 'water-course,' *v.* fleot. Pennymeadow (*Penymedouwe* c. 1300 *PeterbB*). Stockwell (*Stokwell* t. Hy 8 *MinAcct*). Stranglyns (*Stranglands* 1565 *Terrier*).

POLEBROOK. Dawthorn (*Dalethorn* c. 1380 *Buccleuch*). Prestall (*Presthull* c. 1370 *Buccleuch, Prestil* 1716 *Map*). In the *EnclA* (1791) we have Dinge Lane (*Denge* c. 1380 *Buccleuch*) from OE *dyncge,* 'manure,' Linch Meadow (*le Lynch* c. 1260 *Buccleuch*), 'hill,' *v.* hlinc.

WARMINGTON. Deadmans Grave (*Dedmansgrove* c. 1400 *Rental*). Goldingdale (*Goldryngdal* ib.). Mill Holme (*le Milneholm* ib.).

XIX. Navisford Hundred

TITCHMARSH. Ham Meadows (*Hamme* 1227 *FF*), *v.* hamm. Mill Holme (1779 *EnclA*) is *Milneholm* 1327 Ipm. Roarem (*Rorholm* 1327 Ipm, *Roar Holme* 1779 *EnclA*).
WADENHOE. Hasland (*Hasleland* 1795 *EnclA*). Locka Wood (1779 *EnclA*) is *Lochawe* 1249 *For*, 'enclosed haw,' *v.* haga.

XX. Nassaburgh Hundred

PETERBOROUGH. We may note the following field-names found in the *EnclA* of 1811: Deadman's Grave (*Dedmanslond* 1380 *Compotus, Dedmanesgrave* 1404 *Fraunc, Deadmans Grave* 1572 *Rental*), Gullymore (*Gulmawebrok* c. 1400 *Rental*), Hammond's Meadow (*Hamondesmedwe* 1380 *Compotus, Hamundesmedew* 1404 *Fraunc*), Common Muckhill (*Mukhyl* 1521 *Compotus*), Steepings (*Ballestibbinges* 1198 *Pytchley, le Stibbynges* 1354 *CartN*), *v.* stybbing *supra* 270, Swanspool (*Swanepol* 1390 *Compotus*), Swine's Meadow (*Swynemede* c. 1400 *Rental*).

WALTON. In the *EnclA* (1805) we have Church Field (*le Kyrk-feld* 1302 *CartN*), Fullbridge (*Fulebrigge* ib.), 'foul bridge.'

PERSONAL NAMES IN FIELD AND OTHER MINOR NAMES

A. OLD ENGLISH.

Abba (*Abbewelle* 1257), Æffa (*Effahaga* 1180, *Affegore* 1305), Ælfhēah (*Alfeyesaker* 1250), Ælflǣd (f) (*Elflededen* 1190, *Alfledhawe* 1250), Ælfrīc (*Alvrichesmad* 1201), Ælfrūn (f) (*Alvrenewong* 1207), Ælfstān (*Alstaneston* 1287), Ælfweald (*Alwoldehul* 1200, *Alvoldesmere* 1270, *Alfwaldesholm* 1329), Ælfwine (*Alwynesfeld* t. Ed 1), Æþelheard (*Athelardeswode* 1250), Æþelmund (*Almondeslowe* 1420), Æþelstān (*Athelstonesmedowe* 1391), Æþelweard (*Aylwardeshalugh* 1262), Æþelwine (*Alwynshale* 1281, *Ailewineswelle* 1404), Bætti (*Battescroft* 1260), Balluc (*Ballokeswelle* 14th), Beaduhild (f) (*Batildacre* 1223), Bealdrīc (*Balderekesbenhil* 1316), Bealdwine (*Baldewineslak* 1219, *Baldewinescroft* 1260, *Baldewynemylnestede* 1270), Beorhtgiefu (f) (*Brihtgeuescroft* 1147), Beorhtsige (*Brixiesdik* 1292, *Brixewelle* 15th, *Bricsysti* c. 1200), Beorngār (*Berngerestibbing* 1330), Beornheard (*Bernardslade* 1227, *Bernardeseng* 1227, *Bernardiswro* 1400, *Bernardyshyll* 14th), Billa (*Byllewelle* 13th), Bōtwulf (*Botolfesbrigge* 1220, *Botolfholm* t. Ed 3, *Botolfesweye* 1400), Brenting (*Brintyngesholm* 1329), Cēolferð (*Celverdescote* 1086), *Ciccel (*Cicceleshame* 1240, *Chichelisholm* 1250), *Cubba (*Cubbewelle* 13th), Cynestān (*Cynestanes heafod* 956), Cynewine (*Kinewinescroft* 1147), Cypping (*Kippingeswell* 1287), Denegȳð (f) (*denegiðegraf* 937), Dēor (*Deresle* t. Ed 1), Dēorman (*Dermanneszerlond* 1312), Dēorulf (*Derolveshill* 1343), Dunn (*Duneswelle* 1260, *Dunnescroft* 1408), Dunnemann (*Dunnemannesmede* t. John), Dūnstān (*Dunstaneswell* 1250), Ēadgifu (f) (*Edthivescroyz* 1250), Ēadrīc (*Edrychesdik* 1302), Ēadwine (*Edwineswell* 1329), Ealdnōð (*Aldnetheshawe* 1250), Ealdrēd (*Aldrediswelle* 13th), Ealdweald (*Eldwoldeshey*), Ealdwine (*Aldewynebuttes* 1403), Ealhfrið (*Ealferðes hlæw* 937), Ealhmund (*Almondeslowe* 1420), Earnweald (*Ernoldesbern* 1345), Earnwulf (*ærnulfes wylle* 944), Folcweard (*Folkwardestaking* 1247), Gōdbeald (*Godboldesmilne* 1275), Gōdgiefu (f) (*Godhiueswong* t. Hy 3), Gōdmund (*Godmundeslee* 1197), Gōdrīc (*Godrikesbuttes* 1229, *Godrikesgore* 1250, *Godricheslade* 1260), Gōdwine (*Godwineswod* 1242, *Godwynsthorn* 1362), Goldwine (*Goldewynespyt* 1250, *Golwynesdale* 1250), Grim (*Grymesputte* 1300, *Grymeswell* 1363), Grimbeald (*Grimbaldtoft* 1246, *Grimboldeshull* 1270, *Grimboldesbrok* 1270, *Grimboldesrode*, *Grimbaldesti* 14th), Hæddi (*Haddesmor* 1287), Heafoc (*Hauekespol* 1287), Heaþubeald

(*Hatheboldesmere* 1235), Helmstān (*Helmstaneslege* 1012), Hereweard (*Herewardwellesike* 1292, *Herewardesmede* 1316), Hild (*Hildescroft* 1253), Hodd (*Hoddesmedewe* 1251), Hucc (*Huckeshawe* 1300), Hūna (*Hunan bricge* 956), Hūnstān (*Hunnestonesmor* 1287), Lēofrīc (*Lefricheshavedlond* 1260, *Lyverychstokkyng* 1279), Lēofmǣr (*Lemereswoda* 1203), Lēofsige (*Lefsiesaker* 13th), Lēofsunu (*Leofsunes heafodæcer* 1022), *Lilling (*Lyllyngeszerde* 1390), Mann (*Mannesfalw* 1338), Ōsgār (*Osgarescroft* 1385), Ōsgȳð (f) (*Ositheswell* 1250), Ōsmund (*Osemundesleg* 1200), Ōsweard (*Oseweardescroft* 1200), *Pinn (*Pynnesdole* 1240), *Pinnoc (*Pinnokeswelle* 1200, *Pynnokesfurlong* 1404), Prætt (*Pratteslound* t. Ed 1, *Pratteslynch* 1330, *Pratteswong* 1345), Rǣdmund (*Radmondeslond* 1346, *Radmundehul* 14th), Seaxwulf (*Sexolleslade* 1347), Sigeflǣd (f) (*Syfletemor* 1250), Sigeweard (*Sewardstan* 13th, *Sywardeshawe* 1250), Snell (*Snellesdalebrok* 1400, *Snelleswelle* 14th), Snot(t) (*Snottescombe* 1430), *Þrawold (*ðrawoldeswelle* 10th), Tott (*Tottesgore* 1280), Weland (*Welandeswong* t. Hy 3), Wibba (*Wybbewelle* 1235), Wīgstān (*Wistanesdale* 1222), Winebeald (*Wymbeldeswode* 1300), Wulfgār (*Wolgerysdale* 13th, *Wlfgoreshei* 14th), Wulfgiefu (f) (*Wolfiveþornhul* 1255), Wulfhere (*Wlfereswelle* 1199, *Wolferesmorhul* 1348), Wulfmǣr (*Wolmeresmede* t. Ed 3), Wulfnōþ (*Wlnotheswong* 1227), Wulfstān (*Wlstonespath* 1377), Wulfweard (*Wolwardesdene* 1245).

B. SCANDINAVIAN.

Arnketill (*Arketyswode* 1300, *Archelwelle* 1355), Ásbjörn (*Osbern Ridyng* 1255, *Osberneswolde* 1404), Ásgautr (*Osgodesfurlang* t. Ed 3), Ásketill (*Asketelescotes* 1250), Aslákr (*Oslokeswong* 1250, *Oselokeswey* 1334), Ásmundr (*Osemundewong* 1253, *Asemondecroft* 1313), Colman (Irish Scand) (*Colmannesholm* 1246, *Colemaneslake* 1336), Fráni (*Franehawe* 1246), Gamall (*Gameleswude* 1205), Grímr (*Grymmeswro* 1302, *Grimeslund* 14th), Gunnhildr (f) (*Gonnildescroft* 1300, *Goneldescroft* 1359, *Gunnildebrige* 14th), Gunni (*Gunnebusc* 1286, *Gunnesyke* 1313), Gunnvǫr (f) (*Gunwarewell* 1404), Guðrún (f) (*Goterhundel* 1245), Hámundr (*Hammundescroft* 1270, *Hamundesplot* 1355, *Hamundesmedew* 1404), Hrafn (*Raveneslund* 1258, *Raunesdale* 14th), Hrólfr (*Roluesmede* 1200), Ingvarr (*Hingvareshey* 1222), Káti (*Katebrig* 1199), Ketill (*Keteleshag* 1224, *Ketelleshull* t. Ed 1), Ormr (*Ormesweyt* (sic) 1246), Siward (ODan) (*Sywardeslund* 1143), Stríkr (*Strikesaker* 1320), Svanhildr (f) (*Swoneldiston* 1270), Sveinn (*Swenesbrigg* 1281, *Sweinesheges* 14th), Þórgautr (OWScand) Thorgot (ODan) (*Torgohtescroft* 1125), Þórgeirr (*Thurgarsholm* t. Hy 8), Þórlákr (*Thurlageswode* 1250, *Thorlokeshegh* 1302), Þórólfr (*Thurulueshill* 1199), Þrúðr (f) (*Trudehawe*

1247), Þúrferð (Anglo-Scandinavian) (*Thurferdislund* 14th), Þúrketill (*Thurkelesdik* 1318), Đurweard (Anglo-Scandinavian) (*Thurwardeshauwe* 1286), Tóki (*pontem Toki* 1227, *Thokyes mulne* 1370), Tosti (*Tostisheuyd* 1251), Úlfr (*Olvesiate* t. Ed 1, *Ulvesdale* 1340), Úlfketill (*Ofketelesdol* 1225).

(B) CELTIC.

Duncan (*Dunkenelond* 13th).

(C) OFR OR CONTINENTAL.

Alexander (*Alisaundresmede* 1412), Archibald (*Archeboldesdyke* 13th), Bertram (*Bertramslogh, -lowe* 14th), Colin (*Colynesholm* 1389), Elliot (*Elyoteshegg* 1300, *Eliotes gappe* 1342), Fulk (*Fulkeshalfehide* 1248), Gilberd (*Gilberdiscroft, Gilbertyspyttes* 14th), Herberd (*Herberdesholm* 13th, *Herberdeswelle* 1330), Huberd (*Huberdesbrigge* 1230, *Huberdiskraft* 1347, *Huberdesmede* 1392), Janekyn (*Janekynesgalle* 1403), Martin (*Martinespit* 1250), Nele, Nigel (*Neleswong* 1404), Nicholas (*Nicholasaker* 1245), Paul (*Pauleswell* 1223), Philip (*Philipeshey* 1245, *Phelipeswode* t. Ed 1), Randolf (*Randolfiscroft* 1349), Reynold (*Reynoldesbrigge* 1330, *Reynaldisrode* 1367), Robelot (*Robeloteswude* 13th), Roberd (*Roberdeswode* 1300), Roger (*Rogeresaker* 1300), Sunegod (*Sunegodescroft* c. 1190), Walter (*Waltereswalles* 1200, *Walteressiche* 1250, *Waltereswong* 1280), Warin (*Warinnesgore* 1143, *Warinstibbing* 13th), William (*Williameswong* 1294).

INDEX

OF SOME OF THE MORE IMPORTANT WORDS USED IN FIELD-NAMES

INDEX

OF PLACE-NAMES IN NORTHAMPTONSHIRE

The primary reference to a place is marked by the use of clarendon type.

INDEX

OF PLACE-NAMES IN COUNTIES OTHER THAN NORTHAMPTONSHIRE

[References to place-names in Bk, Beds, Hu, Wo, NRY, Sx, D are not included, as these have been fully dealt with in the volumes already issued upon the names of those counties.

PRINTED BY W. LEWIS, M.A., AT THE UNIVERSITY PRESS, CAMBRIDGE

H